The Pennsylvania Gardener

All About Gardening in the Keystone State

Derek Fell

Camino Books, Inc.
Philadelphia

Manufactured in the United States of America

1 2 3 4 5   98 97 96 95

Library of Congress Cataloging-in-Publication Data

Fell, Derek
    The Pennsylvania gardener / Derek Fell.
        p. cm.
    Includes index.
    ISBN 0-940159-15-5
    1. Gardening—Pennsylvania. 2. Gardens—Pennsylvania. I. Title
SB451.34.P4F45 1995
635'.09748—dc20   94-33833

Photos by Derek Fell
Line Art: Mary Thompson and Janine Andrew
Development Editor: Joan Bingham
Production Editor: Brad Fisher
Publisher and Editor: E. Jutkowitz

This book is available at a special discount on bulk purchases
for promotional, business and educational use.
For information, write to:

Publisher
Camino Books, Inc.
P.O. Box 59026
Philadelphia, PA 19102

Contents

List of Charts and Diagrams v

Foreword by Jane G. Pepper vii

Acknowledgments ix

CHAPTER 1   Introduction 1

The duPont Dynasty 2
Fordhook Farm 3
The Amish Gardeners 3
The Penn State Flower Trials 6
The Philadelphia Flower Show 7
Pennsylvania's Gardens 7
Pennsylvania's Geology 8
Pennsylvania's Climate 9

CHAPTER 2   Planning and Planting 13

First the Soil 13
Water Drainage, and Irrigation 18
Weeds, Disease, and Pests 21

CHAPTER 3   Annuals 27

Obtaining Plants for the Garden 27
Top-Performing Annuals for Pennsylvania 30

CHAPTER 4   Perennials 51

Designing with Perennials 54
Obtaining Perennial Plants 55
Buying Perennial Plants 58
Perennials for Stunning Borders 60

CHAPTER 5   Bulbs and Water Plants 87

Spring-Flowering Bulbs 87
Summer- and Fall-Flowering Bulbs 94

Top-Performing Spring-Flowering Bulbs 95
Top-Performing Summer- and Fall-Flowering Bulbs 100
Forcing Bulbs 104
Water Plants 106

CHAPTER 6   Wildflowers 111

Popular Pennsylvania Wildflowers 112

CHAPTER 7   Lawn Care 119

Preparing the Seedbed 119
Best Times for Seeding 120
Fertilizing a Lawn 120
Irrigation 120
Weed Control 121
Insect and Disease Control 121
Mowing 121
Timetable for Lawn Care in Pennsylvania 121

CHAPTER 8   Trees and Shrubs 123

Caring for Trees and Shrubs 125
Some Top-Rated Trees and Shrubs 130

CHAPTER 9   Vegetables and Herbs 159

Planning, Planting, and Harvesting 161
Recommended Vegetables for Pennsylvania Gardens 172
Herbs 191

CHAPTER 10   Fruits and Berries 197

Orchard Fruits 199
Berry Fruits 202

Appendix

Places of Interest with Useful Sources and Gardening Advice 205

General Index 227

Plant Index 235

A color section of photographs of the author's farm and notable Pennsylvania gardens appears between pages 118 *and* 119.

Charts and Diagrams

First and Last Frost Dates for Pennsylvania 11

Statewide Precipitation by Month in Inches 12

Pennsylvania State University Soil Test Information Form
  and Sample Soil Test Kit 17

Starting Hard-to-Start Seeds 28

General Characteristics of Selected Annuals 46

Model Cutting Garden for Annuals 48

Courtyard Garden Featuring Annuals in a Formal Design 49

Formal Garden Featuring Annuals 50

Perennial Planting Chart 52

Formal Parterre Garden of Perennials 56

Double Perennial Border 57

Water Garden Featuring Perennials 59

Bulb Planting Charts 89

Garden Pool Planting Diagram 109

Monthly Lawn Care Chart 122

Planting Diagrams for Trees and Shrubs 128

Staking Techniques for Trees 129

Pruning Hybrid Tea Roses 150

Using Hand-Pruners on Rose Canes 150

Principles of Pruning a Floribunda Rose 150

Cutting Garden for Roses 151

Vegetable Garden Plan 162

Vegetable Planting Chart 165

Sixteen Easy Steps to Success in Vegetable Gardening 167

Kitchen Garden Design 169

Decorative Herb Garden 193

Examples of Grafting Fruit Trees 197

Espalier Training of Dwarf Fruit Trees 198

Types of Support for Fruit Trees and Grapevines 200

Four-Arm Training of Grapevines 203

Foreword

The Pennsylvania Gardener has been more than 25 years in the making. During that time, Derek Fell has lived and gardened in Pennsylvania; and though he has traveled all over the world, he says he has found no better place to practice his love of gardening and his profession as a garden writer and garden photographer.

A naturalized American citizen born in England, Derek has visited many Pennsylvania gardens, not only public and private gardens planted for display or food production, but also historical restorations and test gardens, where both old and new plants are evaluated for performance and quality.

This book is not an encyclopedia of every garden-worthy plant grown in the state or every kind of gardening technique successful in Pennsylvania. It is more of an overview that brings into focus plants that Derek has found outstanding. This book also highlights growing techniques Derek has found personally most satisfying.

Derek's first six years in Pennsylvania were with Burpee Seeds, working as their catalog manager at Fordhook Farm, east of Doylestown. He reported directly to David Burpee, "the dean of seedsmen," who was chief executive officer of the company founded by his father.

Derek's experience before his Burpee years was with one of Burpee's most important European customers, Hurst Seeds, headquartered near London. At the time it was Europe's biggest and oldest wholesale seed house, established in 1560. Derek was responsible for their catalog production and the introduction of new flower and vegetable seed varieties. Through Hurst he met David Burpee, who invited him to work for the Burpee company in America.

After David Burpee retired and the company was sold, Derek gained broader experience as executive director of the National Garden Bureau (an information office sponsored by the American garden seed industry) and also All-America Selections (the national seed trials). Establishing an office out of his home near Gardenville, Pennsylvania, Derek acted as a spokesman for the American garden seed industry, meeting seedsmen throughout the world. In addition, he briefly worked as a consultant on gardening to The White House during the Ford Administration.

Derek resigned from seed industry positions to concentrate on writing garden books and building up an extensive horticultural color picture library. He has authored more than 35 successful garden books and garden calendars and contributed numerous garden articles to many national magazines, including *Architectural Digest, The New York Times, Woman's Day, Family Circle, Parade*, and *Organic Gardening*.

Another important influence on Derek's life was a close friendship with the late H. Thomas Hallowell, Jr., owner of Deerfield Garden, near Rydal, Pennsylvania. He met Tom on an assignment to photograph Tom's garden for *Architectural Digest*. After the color feature appeared in their October 1981 issue, he worked with Tom on the production of an award-winning book entitled *Deerfield—An American Garden*

Through Four Seasons. In words and pictures, the book chronicles the history and development of an extraordinarily beautiful 50-acre Pennsylvania garden, with over 100 full-color photographs.

After Burpee's Fordhook Farm test garden and Tom Hallowell's Deerfield Farm display garden figured prominently in his life, Derek was able to purchase historic Cedaridge Farm in Tinicum Township, north of New Hope. Established in 1790, the farm consists of 24 acres where he and his wife, Carolyn, have created numerous cultivated areas for photography. Nothing pleases them more than to walk the property contemplating new planting schemes and images to photograph in every season.

In early spring, sheets of daffodils, Lenten roses, dwarf iris, and aconites bloom along the lawn edges. In summer, a walled vegetable garden and a cutting garden bright with annuals produce bountiful harvests of food crops and flowers. Several perennial beds extend color into autumn when mature stands of sugar maples, American beech, and Japanese maples flaunt brilliant fall foliage colors. In winter, the dried stems of grasses and the decorative lines of a Victorian gazebo are accentuated by snow.

Derek has found his membership in the Pennsylvania Horticultural Society invaluable, and he is a regular contributor to the pages of *Green Scene. The Pennsylvania Gardener* will provide guidance and practical information for today's gardeners in our state and beyond, as well as for the gardeners of future generations.

Jane G. Pepper, President
The Pennsylvania Horticultural Society

Acknowledgments

I need to thank a lot of people who have contributed to my knowledge of gardening over the past 30 years, and during my research for this book, but especially the late David Burpee, who brought me to Pennsylvania and who taught me the most about gardening in the state, and the late H. Thomas Hallowell Jr., owner of Deerfield Garden in Rydal. Thanks also to my wonderful wife, Carolyn, for her encouragement and advice; to Wendy Fields, for supervising the plantings at my home, Cedaridge Farm; and to Kathy Nelson, my administrative assistant, for running the farm office and word processor, and for handling the picture research. Finally, a thanks to Bucks Country Nurseries, Doylestown, for permission to adapt some of their customer service charts and diagrams for use in this book.

Derek Fell

CHAPTER 1

Introduction

Pennsylvania has the richest gardening heritage in North America. The first growers were the peaceful tribe of Lenni-Lenape Indians who cultivated pumpkins, corn, and other North American edible plants in plots fenced to keep out foraging animals. Inspired by reports of a favorable climate and fertile soil, early Quaker settlers from England arrived in 1681 with William Penn, and they established productive farms along the river valleys, especially the Delaware and its tributaries. Penn chose a prime site, several hours by barge up river from Philadelphia, to create a self-sufficient country estate called Pennsbury Manor. It was complete with orchards, herb and flower gardens.

James Logan, overseer to William Penn, established Logan Manor, a farm on a hilly site inland from Philadelphia, at Stenton. It was there he conducted experiments with corn that enabled him to write the first account of the process of pollination in plants, a paper which was published in British scientific circles. Both Pennsbury Manor and Logan Manor are open to the public (see page 210).

For the early colonists, the area around Philadelphia (particularly the counties of Bucks, Chester, and Montgomery) was a verdant paradise with good soil. It was so heavily forested that Penn chose to call the new state Pennsylvania, meaning *Penn's Woods*. When he began laying out the streets for his new city of Philadelphia, Penn named the main cross streets after native trees, such as Walnut, Filbert, Pine, Spruce, and Locust.

The Quakers were interested in exploring the botanical wonders of their new country but first had to establish self-sufficient farms, which generally included a bountiful vegetable garden and an herb garden for the production of useful plants. They grew parsley and thyme to flavor meals, lavender and cloves to disguise household odors, and mints for medicinal value. To do this, the colonists had to clear the land and fence out the wilderness, raise chickens, graze cattle and pigs, and use their waste as manure for fertilizing crops. An authentic restoration of a colonial farmstead can be seen today at the Colonial Plantation in Ridley Creek State Park, Delaware County. A resident family, in period costume, occupies a stone farmhouse and demonstrates life as it was lived in the 1700s, cooking meals, tending farm animals, planting crops and making implements. Authentic zig-zag split-rail fences, stone walls, and structures such as a stone well in a secluded valley, take visitors back in time.

John Bartram, a Quaker with a farm along the banks of the Schuylkill River near what is now Philadelphia International Airport, established one of North America's first botanical gardens. With his son, William—one of nine children—he traveled widely along the East Coast, collecting plants. He corresponded with botanists in England. Bartram introduced the Franklinia tree (*F. alatamaha*) to cultivation, discovering a small grove of them among sand dunes along the banks of the Alatamaha River near Savannah, Georgia—naming this beautiful late-flowering tree after his

1

friend, Benjamin Franklin. The wild species soon became extinct. Its sensitive root system, requiring excellent drainage, is believed to have been attacked by a fungus disease introduced to the South when settlers began planting cotton there. Bartram's Garden is now a national historic monument open to the public (see page 206) and in its day earned such a high reputation that George Washington, Benjamin Franklin, and Thomas Jefferson visited there.

In a spirit of sharing that was important to Quakerism, David Landreth established the first mail order seed business in North America (The David Landreth Seed Company) on Front Street, Philadelphia in 1744, later moving to Bristol. George Washington and Thomas Jefferson were among its distinguished customers. Landreth's success inspired the establishment of other seed houses, making Philadelphia the flower and vegetable seed capital of North America. The company exists to this day as a small seed house in Baltimore.

THE DUPONT DYNASTY

It was a family of Quaker farmers who first cultivated the land near Kennett Square (Chester County) where Longwood Gardens is now located. It is probably the largest, most diverse display garden in the world. Two brothers named Pierce had established a tree nursery there and when the property was in danger of being sold for lumber it attracted the attention of Pierre Samuel duPont, chairman of both the duPont Company and General Motors. He purchased the land and turned the property into a weekend retreat full of spectacular flower and water gardens. On his death, the estate became a public garden containing 500 acres, including five acres under glass. Taking inspiration from European garden styles (especially English, Italian, and French), today it is visited by more than 800,000 people annually. It was the success of the duPont Company and strong family ties to France, where the duPont family had developed a strong appreciation for beautiful gardens, that enabled Pierre S. duPont to afford the time and money for such a splendid sanctuary.

As North America moved from an agrarian society to an industrial society (precipitated by World Wars I and II), profits from trade with other countries produced great wealth for entrepreneurs, particularly the duPont family dynasty. Arriving from France after the French Revolution, the family at first made their fortune from the manufacture of gunpowder along the banks of the Brandywine River, just across the Pennsylvania border near Wilmington, Delaware. Eleuthère Irénée duPont had learned the technique for making a high-grade gunpowder in France. During a visit to the Brandywine Valley, he realized it was a good site for the manufacture of gunpowder. He saw the willow trees as an excellent source of charcoal and the port of Wilmington as a good point of entry for sulphur from Italy and saltpeter from India. Eleuthère duPont saw the Brandywine as a reliable source of water power for driving mills to grind powder and the steep banks as buffers to contain the force of any accidental explosions.

To assure his workers that he held their safety above his own, Eleuthère duPont established his home on a knoll directly above the powder mills, vulnerable to damage. Behind the house he planted a large garden, a restoration of which can be seen today at Eleutherian Mills (see page 208). The garden features the French intensive style of gardening in which maximum use is made of limited space. Apples are trained as cordons (ropes) along low fence rails; and peaches are trained as espaliers, their branches splayed out in a pattern and held in place by a wooden trellis. There is also a magnificent arbor with branches of apple trees trained to create a tunnel.

The influence of the duPont family on the gardens of Pennsylvania and surrounding states was profound. Alfred I. duPont founded Nemours, a mansion near Greenville, Delaware, in the style of Versailles Palace; Henry duPont established Winterthur, a naturalistic woodland paradise near Centerville, Delaware; and Longwood Gardens has such a fine horticultural reputation it has an exchange program with Kew Gardens, the Royal Botanical Garden near London.

FORDHOOK FARM

While the duPont estates were being created as expressions of wealth and artistic appreciation, Burpee's Fordhook Farm was established north of Philadelphia, near Doylestown, for the purpose of testing home garden seeds (both flowers and vegetables) and sharing that knowledge with gardeners throughout North America, through the publication of mail order catalogs. The company Burpee Seeds was founded in 1886 by an 18-year-old boy, W. Atlee Burpee, who borrowed $1,000 from his mother. It quickly became the world's largest mail order seed house. During a visit to the Eastern United States at the turn of the century, Luther Burbank (the California plant wizard) commented that Fordhook Farm was the best of all his Eastern object lessons. He stated that the farm was valuable not only to Burpee's customers but to everyone who cultivates the land.

Fordhook Farm gave its name to the famous Fordhook Lima Bean—the world's first dwarf, large-seeded lima. It is where Golden Bantam Corn—the first tender, yellow-kerneled sweet corn—was discovered. It is also where the famous Big Boy Tomato, Burpee Hybrid Cucumber, Burpee Hybrid Cantaloupe, and other world-renowned vegetable hybrids were developed. At one time, Fordhook was such a popular place to visit during the summer that special trains ran from Philadelphia to Doylestown so crowds could see hundreds of acres of flowers and vegetables grown for evaluation. Fordhook Farm ceased operations as a major breeding facility after the Burpee company was sold in the 1970s, but it exists today as a bed-and-breakfast inn, still owned by Burpee family members.

Visitors to Fordhook can see a great deal of Burpee memorabilia displayed around the walls, especially in David Burpee's old office. There are newspaper clippings describing his famous search for the white marigold, his payment of $10,000 in prize money to an Iowa home gardener who developed the first white marigold; his efforts to get the marigold accepted as the national floral emblem (it finally lost to the rose). Other clippings describe his sumptuous press parties at the Waldorf-Astoria Hotel in New York, where he unveiled his spectacular plant breeding innovations.

THE AMISH GARDENERS

About 50 miles west of Philadelphia is the city of Lancaster, famous for its Amish community—a religious sect that came from Germany. The Amish, who believe in self-sufficiency and scorn modern conveniences, own some of North America's richest farmland. They plow fields using mules, fertilize their fields with cover crops and manure, and drive around the countryside in horse-drawn carriages. The Amish maintain special strains of flowers and vegetable seeds, growing giant watermelons, giant pumpkins, and unusual kinds of squash that make their harvest festivals especially colorful. Perhaps no other group in all of North America has a finer reputation for growing top-quality vegetables and orchard fruits than the Pennsylvania Amish. In summer and fall, tourists flock to the Amish community around Lancaster where Amish farm stands offer delicious melons, apples, sweet potatoes, pumpkins, and other well-grown garden produce.

The history of the Amish began in Europe in the 1600s when a religious group called the Mennonites suffered persecution because they would not conform to the common religious practice of "child baptism." They believed that only an educated adult—willing to choose his faith freely—should be baptized.

Jacob Ammann, a Mennonite minister in the district of Bern, Switzerland, issued strict rules of behavior for his followers aimed at shunning luxuries and frivolous possessions and keeping their lives simple. He declared that all those unwilling to follow his strict code of behavior would be excommunicated.

With about 600 followers, Ammann established the first "Amish" community and chose farming as their means of adopting a self-sufficient lifestyle. They became the best farmers in Europe and had a dedication to improving the soil, making any land they settled better than they found it. The Amish were the first to practice crop rotation and manuring the land between crops so the soil never became impoverished or exhausted. They initiated the practice of growing nitrogen-fixing clover on poor soil to improve its fertility.

In Europe, the Amish never owned their land, but were given the poorest areas to work as tenant farmers. The first Amish in North America arrived in Philadelphia in the early 1700s. Attracted by William Penn's promise of religious freedom and good farmland, they settled in Lancaster which had rich soil and gently contoured topography ideal for farming. It remains the largest Amish settlement in North America. Other Amish soon settled in Ohio, Indiana, Illinois, Iowa, Kansas, and Ontario, Canada. Today, there are over 175 settlements in 23 states and Canada. Averaging seven children per family, the Amish are believed to be the fastest growing ethnic group in America. Their population doubles every 12 years.

The soil is the Amish source of wealth, the horse their source of transportation, and the mule their source of power for plowing and moving heavy loads. The manure from these animals is their principal fertilizer. This reliance on the horse and the mule for power and soil fertility has led to the misconception that the Amish shun all other modern methods of growing and never use chemical fertilizer or hybrid seed. Nothing could be further from the truth.

The Amish keep abreast of all modern farming innovations and are quick to utilize improvements, especially new varieties of seed and sound cultural practices. For example, they were among the first to capitalize on seedless watermelon hybrids. And they were pioneers in growing asparagus from seeds instead of from roots, so they could first weed out the less desirable female plants and transplant only the males for heaviest yields. When all-male asparagus hybrids became available, the Amish instantly started planting them.

Amish growers conduct soil tests to determine precisely when to lime the land. And if the soil test indicates a need for the addition of a particular plant nutrient, they will use a chemical fertilizer to correct the imbalance. However, unlike many other farmers who have developed an almost total reliance on chemical fertilizers, the Amish farmers—with their constant use of manure and nitrogen-fixing cover crops—use far less. So their soil stays in good condition, encouraging healthy populations of earthworms and soil bacteria to continue the natural conditioning cycle.

The problem of pest and weed control is solved in several ways, always seeking an organic control first. For pest control, the Amish gardener uses his family as the first line of defense. Everyone helps to hoe weeds between plant rows and pick off slugs or Japanese beetles before they have a chance to reach plague proportions. If that is insufficient, then a safe insecticide such as BT (*Bacillus thuringensis*) is usually considered. This bacterial control kills only caterpillars, such as the cabbage worm, and is harmless to animals or people. If slugs prove troublesome in spite of hand picking, the Amish grower might use a commercial slug bait. Amish growers are famous for their apples, and for these the preferred pest control is a general purpose home orchard spray combining Captan (a fungicide) and Malathion (a pesticide).

Strawberries and other crops that easily suffer bird damage are protected by muslin or a similar lightweight horticultural fiber. The latter covers crops like a spider's web, blocking entry of pests but admitting adequate sunlight. These horticultural plant coverings are also used by the Amish to exclude frost and extend the harvesting season.

Weeding a flower or vegetable garden is generally a family affair. Weeds are also kept under control by mulching. Many Amish farmers use clean compost as mulch, applying well-decomposed animal manure between rows to a depth of at least 6 inches to suffocate weeds. Of course, the compost ends up feeding the rows of plants.

The Amish specialize in growing crops that store well such as apples, sweet potatoes, Irish potatoes, turnips, and carrots. The women are skilled at canning and making preserves.

The Amish save little of their own seed, preferring to buy top-quality varieties from reputable seedsmen. Some of their main mail-order seed sources are Otis Twilley, Harris Seeds, Stokes, and Burpee (see list of seed sources in the Appendix for addresses).

A popular form of irrigation among Amish growers is drip irrigation hose. This is rolled out along rows of vegetables, covered with straw or black plastic for protection, and connected to a water source. The hose drips moisture from micro-pores. The brand preferred by the Amish is inexpensive enough to be used one season then disposed of (see sources, page 224.)

Of course Amish farmers have individual preferences just like many other growers. They attend university seed trials, such as those conducted by Penn State University at State College and Landisville. They also rely on word-of-mouth recommendations among themselves at their frequent community gatherings. The name of a particularly good new seed variety or a pest control technique soon spreads through their community. The Amish are stewards of the land, and their reputation for being the world's best growers is well deserved.

Close to the Amish country—between Kutztown and Allentown—is an area settled mostly by Mennonite farmers. Here is located the small community of Emmaus, home to Rodale Press, which was founded by a manufacturer of electrical parts, J. I. Rodale. Rodale was inspired to promote the naturalistic style of organic gardening in America after reading the works of an Englishman, Sir Albert Howard. As a result, Rodale started publishing *Organic Gardening & Farming* magazine. During a surge in home gardening activity, following the Arab oil embargo of 1973, the magazine experienced phenomenal growth and today maintains the highest paid circulation of any gardening magazine in America. The original farm J. I. Rodale established as a working model still exists near Emmaus, though visitors are encouraged to see a much larger separate facility, the Rodale Research Farm in nearby Maxatawny.

THE PENN STATE FLOWER TRIALS

Penn State University, located in the center of the state at State College, annually conducts one of the world's most extensive test gardens for the evaluation of home gardening varieties of flowers and vegetables. The Penn State trials are a unique cooperative effort between the academic world and the seed industry. Plant breeders from all over the world pay the university to grow varieties for evaluation during an event called The International Flower Seed Conference, which is held during early August.

Plantings and demonstration plots were first established at Penn State University in 1862 when a botanical garden was laid out in front of the old botany building. The present flower trials were begun in 1932 when W. Ray Hastings, founder and executive director of All-America Seed Selections (the national seed trials), was so impressed with the quality of the flowers being grown in the botanical garden that he persuaded the university to expand it into an official All-America Selections test garden for flower seeds. Later, test gardens for All-America roses and All-America vegetables were added.

Active participants not only include familiar North American companies, such as Burpee Seeds and Park Seeds, but also Sakata Seeds (a leading Japanese breeder), Royal Sluis (a big Dutch breeder), and Ernst Benary (a German seed company).

The flower seed entries are grown in 15-foot rows in rectangular beds featuring all one family, with a heavy emphasis on marigolds, petunias, geraniums, zinnias, salvias, and snapdragons because of their importance for summer bedding. A special shade area features impatiens, begonias, and coleus.

All the plants are grown through plastic mulch to control weeds and retain moisture. The plants are labeled with name and source, except for the All-America entries which are given a coded number so judging can be impartial.

A good showing at the Penn State Flower Trials can propel a new flowering annual into popular demand. When the seedsmen saw the deeper blue coloring of *Salvia farinacea* "VICTORIA" over the established favorite, "CATIMA," it was an instantaneous hit and every major seed house in North America placed substantial orders with Clause, the French breeder. Similarly, when Sakata Seeds exhibited an improvement over the "FOREST FIRE" plumed celosia, calling their Penn State entry "FOREST FIRE IMPROVED," seed houses immediately dropped the old "FOREST FIRE" in favor of the obviously superior newcomer, exhibiting shimmering crimson plumes and bronze foliage.

Conversely, when an established variety shows signs of irregularity at Penn State, seed producers can put pressure on the originator to improve it and threaten to withdraw the variety from their catalogs and seed racks.

The International Seed Conference is always held during a Monday in early August, starting with a tour of the flower trials in the morning and the vegetables in the afternoon. For more information about the facility, see page 217.

THE PHILADELPHIA FLOWER SHOW

Produced by The Pennsylvania Horticultural Society, the Philadelphia Flower Show is another event that draws international acclaim. Held in March at the Civic Center, it is North America's largest and most successful indoor flower show. Comparable to England's great Chelsea Flower Show, the Philadelphia Flower Show draws a week-long attendance of nearly 240,000 visitors from around the world. A smaller event, the Harvest Show, is held in September at the conservatory in Fairmount Park. Gardeners from the area compete for prizes.

PENNSYLVANIA'S GARDENS

The Delaware Valley—especially the area around Philadelphia—has an extraordinary number of gardens open to the general public. A diverse range of garden styles, including English, Italian, and Japanese, reflects the interests of wealthy owners. A list of those open to the general public is featured in the Appendix.

Other properties, established as educational institutions, keep interest in gardening alive and well. The Scott Arboretum at Swarthmore College; the orchards and display gardens at Delaware Valley College of Science and Agriculture in Doylestown, a farm school originally founded by Dr. Joseph Krauskopf to introduce Jewish boys to farming in the new world; the Morris Arboretum of the University of Pennsylvania, Chestnut Hill; and Bowman's Hill Wildflower Preserve near New Hope, all provide training and education in various aspects of horticulture.

In other areas of the state, gardening activity is strong. Pittsburgh, one of the most scenic cities in North America, is a miniature Manhattan surrounded by mountains, rivers, and woodland. It boasts the beautiful Phipps Conservatory. Hershey shares a reputation with Portland, Oregon, as having one of the world's finest rose gardens. It was at Hershey, surrounded by some of the richest dairy farms in North America, where Milton Hershey mixed milk with chocolate to make the popular Hershey candy bar. The profits enabled Hershey to build the fabulous Hershey Hotel, its magnificent formal gardens, and the spacious rose garden—all on a hill overlooking the chocolate factory.

At West Grove (Chester County), Robert Pyle—an enterprising Quaker farmer—established the first mail-order business selling roses. He was responsible for recognizing the unique qualities of the famous Peace rose (developed in France by the Meilland family of rose breeders), introducing it to America, and naming it. Conard-Pyle Company, which markets roses under the "Star Roses" brand, still maintains display gardens and production farms at West Grove.

Another influence on the gardens of Pennsylvania has been the desire for collection. Perhaps the best modern example of this is the Henry Foundation near Gladwyne, where Mrs. Mary Henry Gibson established a garden filled mostly with North American plants she considered of unusual ornamental value. The Henry Foundation is now headed by her daughter, Miss Josephine Henry. Many arboretums throughout the state concentrate on collections of woody plants, especially the Tyler Arboretum at Lima, the Jenkins Arboretum near Wayne, and the Arboretum of the Barnes Foundation in Narberth. These park-like estates all were established by gardening enthusiasts with a passion for collecting. Many of the area's college campuses also have embellished their grounds with collections of beautiful trees and shrubs. Notable among these are Swarthmore College and its superb rhododendron collection; Haverford College with its groves of magnificent trees; Bryn Mawr College where stately trees enhance the environment; and the Ambler campus of Temple University, featuring a superb collection of ornamental trees and several outstanding perennial gardens.

Philadelphia boasts the world's largest city park, Fairmount Park, and possibly the largest number of gardens connected with restoration and historical conservation. In addition to William Penn's country estate, Pennsbury Manor, north of the city, there is Independence National Historical Park in Center City, the Physick Garden at the Pennsylvania Hospital; and the Peter Wentz Farmstead at Worcester, where George Washington stayed during local military campaigns.

Natural conservation abounds in Pennsylvania. Close to Philadelphia are the Bowman's Hill Wildflower Preserve, the Brandywine Conservancy, and the Tinicum National Environmental Center. These wilderness areas that were at one time in danger of urban development are now protected.

In spite of the deer tick (see page 23), gardening is still one of the healthiest and most popular of all pastimes. It provides fresh air, exercise, vitamin-rich produce, and pleasant relaxation from stress. Cool growing conditions in spring and fall; a warm, sunny summer season; and a beautiful dormant winter season in which to plan ahead, provide perfect conditions in Pennsylvania to grow a wide range of plants. The area's rich horticultural history, natural scenic beauty, and spaciousness, help make Pennsylvania a wonderful place to live and also a perfect place to garden.

PENNSYLVANIA'S GEOLOGY

The planet Earth is estimated to be 4.5 billion years old. The Allegheny Plateau around Pittsburgh is approximately three billion years old and is considered one of the Earth's oldest land masses. Though the region is mostly high, flat ground with poor soil, it is heavily forested, has been eroded by streams, and contains pockets of good soil. A second major geological feature, the Craton—approximately defined by the Allegheny Mountain range and its neighboring hills and valleys—is Pennsylvania's second oldest geological feature (perhaps 600 million years old), created when two continental land masses collided. This is sometimes referred to as the Ridge and Valley Region of Pennsylvania. At one time as high as the Himalaya Mountains of Northern India, the Allegheny Mountains have been eroded to less majestic proportions. But some of the Earth's richest farmland exists in the valleys of this region which is characterized by long, straight, low mountain ridges. Though the slopes are rocky, they are heavily wooded, and the valley soils tend to be excellent for farming.

During its geological history, Pennsylvania has been subjected to three continental land mass collisions. The first of these, called the Grenville Collision, occurred 1.1 billion years ago. After the third collision, the continental plates separated, creating what is today the Atlantic Ocean.

A third important Pennsylvania geological feature is the Piedmont Crystalline Belt, composed of two kinds of rock; one, known as Baltimore gneiss, was formed by extremely high temperatures and pressure, such as volcanic activity. The second is called Wissahickon schist, and was formed mostly by sedimentary deposits such as hardened lake mud, often resulting in rocky shale soil that lies close to the surface. Though this area contains some of the state's finest farmland, in some spots the shale is so close to the surface it cannot support cultivated crops unless raised beds are constructed and good topsoil hauled in. Other times the rock or shale forms an impervious substratum, trapping moisture in the topsoil and creating boggy conditions that can only be improved by digging a network of drainage ditches. The Piedmont Crystalline Belt extends in a broad swath from Bucks County through Philadelphia, Lancaster, Harrisburg, and Gettysburg. This area consists of rolling hills and well-drained soils, which are highly fertile. Untouched by glaciers that once scraped away topsoil in the northeast part of the state, the Piedmont Crystalline Belt contains some of North America's finest agricultural soils. This land originally was settled by English Quaker colonists and by Amish and Mennonite farmers from Germany.

Surface soil overlaying the subsurface strata in the Piedmont region has been created mostly by the decomposition of plant waste, especially leaf mold. Over the years, this waste formed a spongy, nutrient-rich, acidic humus. Since almost all of Pennsylvania was forested when colonists began settling the state, Piedmont soil offered a naturally good growing medium the colonists could utilize simply by clearing the land.

Other good soils exist as flood plains along the major rivers, especially the Delaware, the Susquehanna, and the Ohio. Flood plains collect sand, silt, and humus washed down from the forested hillsides. The flood plains can extend many miles wide in certain parts and form an excellent growing medium (or topsoil) that often extends many feet in depth. Colonists referred to this alluvial soil as "bottom land," even carting it to higher ground to improve poor soil. It was the abundance of good topsoil that led some of Europe's most experienced farmers to settle the state. They not only understood the value of good soil for economic survival, but also practiced sound soil management practices, such as manuring the land, liming to reduce acidity, rotating crops, and the planting of nitrogen-fixing cover crops to keep the soil in good condition.

PENNSYLVANIA'S CLIMATE

Pennsylvania encompasses zones 5 and 6 on the United States Department of Agriculture zone map, with a small section of zone 7 roughly south of Philadelphia along the Delaware River to the Delaware state line.

If Pennsylvania's Allegheny Mountain range ran east to west across the top of the state, instead of north to south down its center, Pennsylvania might have a climate like Florida. The Allegheny Mountains run down the center of the state in a broad arc, entering Pennsylvania as the Pocono Mountains at the Delaware Water Gap on the New Jersey border and leaving south of Pittsburgh at the Maryland border.

With the Alleghenies running north and south, the mountains act like a funnel, so Pennsylvania's climate is influenced by two opposing forces—the cold Arctic and the warm Gulf of Mexico. This climatic tug-of-war creates variable winter conditions.

Some years, there is little snow cover and periodic balmy winter days because of the Gulf's influence. Other years, Pennsylvania experiences long periods of bitterly cold weather as the Arctic cold air mass dominates, sweeping down through Canada. That is also why some years the last killing frost in spring occurs in mid April over much of the state, and other years it is delayed until mid May, making it necessary to implement some form of frost protection for tender plants when an unexpected late frost does occur.

Usually Pennsylvania winters include temperatures falling to $-10°F$, and summer temperatures rise to 90°F and more. The average annual rainfall is about 42 inches, some of it falling as snow in winter and much of it as summer thunderstorms. Summer often brings severe dry spells, making some form of irrigation (especially drip irrigation) a wise investment for the Pennsylvania gardener.

A serious detriment to the longevity of some plants (such as snapdragons and lupines, lettuce and spinach) is the high humidity of summer days, with no respite from the heat and humidity at night. Many cool-season plants are governed by *nighttime* temperatures. They will tolerate heat during the day provided there is a rest from heat stress at night in the form of cool temperatures. For many cool-season crops, a mulch of organic material—such as straw, grass clippings, or pine needles—will help keep the roots cool and ensure a longer flowering or cropping season when temperatures and humidity rise dramatically. Conversely, some warm-season plants—such as melons—will experience a detrimental check in growth when night-time temperatures are cool, which is why good growers plant melons through white or black plastic to keep the soil temperature warm when the air temperature drops. A good rule of thumb is to expect hot, humid nights around the Fourth of July, and the return of cool nights after August 15, when it is safe to start replanting peas, lettuce, and cabbage for fall harvests.

Temperature and light have a tremendous influence over plant growth. A 1 degree difference in temperature can mean the difference between plentiful and poor flowering performance in nasturtiums, for example. A 1 percent improvement in light can mean a 100 percent difference in yields of tomatoes, which is why many Pennsylvania greenhouse growers with glass houses can grow tomatoes during winter months when growers with plastic houses (and less light transmission) are unable to do so because of cloudy days and reduction in day length.

The first killing frost in fall usually occurs about mid October. But in high-elevation areas, frost can strike at the end of September. South of Philadelphia killing frosts occur as late as early November. Even so, over most of the state the ground will not actually freeze solid until after Christmas, allowing some super-hardy plants—such as Brussels sprouts, parsley, leeks, kale and Swiss chard—to be grown up to Christmas. The average frost-free growing period is 150 days. But by the use of frost extenders (simple plastic or polypropylene tunnels), the growing season can be extended by at least 21 days at each end, creating a frost-free period of up to 200 days. This allows many cool-season vegetables (such as lettuce, spinach, parsley, and Brussels sprouts) to be grown up to Christmas over most of the state.

Prevailing winds blow across Pennsylvania from the west; therefore, if you have a site that requires shelter from wind it is best to provide extra protection—such as a windbreak—on the west side. Since the mountain ridges are not high enough to form significant climatic barriers (as they are in California and the Pacific Northwest), the entire state experiences similar climatic conditions. The Pocono Mountains and the north central parts do tend to be cooler, but the first and last frost dates between the cooler northern part of the state and the milder southern part vary by little more than 2 weeks (see accompanying frost map).

FIRST AND LAST FROST DATES FOR PENNSYLVANIA

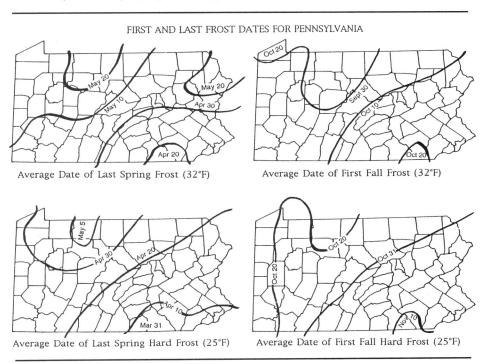

Average Date of Last Spring Frost (32°F)   Average Date of First Fall Frost (32°F)

Average Date of Last Spring Hard Frost (25°F)   Average Date of First Fall Hard Frost (25°F)

Pennsylvania invariably has snow during winter, but the tug-of-war played by the cold northern Arctic air mass and the warm Gulf of Mexico means that alternate thawing and freezing can occur, with snow falling some years as early as October and as late as April. When plants enter winter dormancy and stay frozen until a definite warming trend, they are subject to less danger of winterkill. But if dormancy is interrupted by a January or February thaw, causing tightly wrapped buds to unfold, severe losses will occur. To guard against this, it is always best to provide a layer of organic mulch around plants after the ground has frozen. This will help to keep the ground frozen until spring officially arrives.

One of the prettiest—but potentially deadly—climatic conditions of a Pennsylvania winter is an ice storm, whereby cold rain falls in the night and freezes on branches. If a wind springs up before the sun has a chance to melt the ice, tremendous damage can be done to trees and shrubs—especially those that have not been properly pruned to resist ice damage.

Plentiful rainfall patterns generally provide ample surface distribution over the three major river watersheds—the Ohio, the Susquehanna, and the Delaware. Ground water usually is abundant throughout the state. So despite the few problems, Pennsylvania is a gardener's paradise.

STATEWIDE PRECIPITATION
BY MONTH IN INCHES
Average Total Precipitation = 41.2"

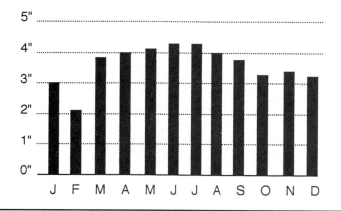

CHAPTER 2

Planning and Planting

FIRST THE SOIL . . .

Perhaps nowhere in North America is the power of good soil more evident than in the state of Pennsylvania. Fly over it from Philadelphia to Pittsburgh, its two largest cities, and whatever is not forested, seems to be farmland. Pennsylvania's forests are a rich assortment of both deciduous trees and evergreens. Over eons of time, the nutrient-rich leaf litter from these trees has helped create a rich, naturally acid soil especially suitable for growing food crops. When early settlers began clearing the land and fencing out the wilderness so they could raise livestock, the waste from these animals provided another valuable source of plant nutrients—manure.

An incredibly diverse range of economic crops is grown on Pennsylvania soil, including orchard fruits such as apples and peaches; berry fruits such as strawberries and grapes; farm stand vegetables such as peas, cabbage, tomatoes, and melons; agricultural crops such as corn and soybeans; and even ornamental plants such as roses, perennials, and ornamental trees.

A soil test in Pennsylvania is not needed so much to determine whether garden soil is alkaline or acidic, but to tell *how acidic* the soil really is. There is virtually no natural alkaline soil in the entire state. The simple question most gardeners need answered is how much and how frequently to lime in order to plant a garden or establish a good lawn from seed. Usually, the amount needed is five pounds per 100 square feet every third year, but only a soil test can tell for sure.

Most cultivated soils in Pennsylvania are rich in earthworms, soil bacteria, beneficial fungus strains, and other organisms that in nature help to manufacture plant nutrients by ingesting soil and expelling it as waste far richer than its original composition.

Good soil is the foundation of good growth. Without it the beneficial effects of sunlight, irrigation, and fertilizer are wasted. Soil not only anchors plants, it provides them with important nutrients which they absorb in soluble form. Pennsylvania soils can be classified as sand, clay, or loam. Clay or a clay-loam blend are the predominant types. Sandy soil is composed of large soil particles that allow water and nutrients to drain away too quickly, and it has poor anchorage. At the other extreme, clay soil is made up of very fine particles. These bind together creating a heavy, impervious mass. Plant roots and moisture cannot easily penetrate clay soil. Loam contains both sand and clay but also lots of humus—a fibrous, spongy material derived from

13

decaying animal and plant parts. Humus is fluffy in texture and has air spaces for plant roots to penetrate the soil freely. It also has good moisture-holding capacity, yet it allows excess moisture to drain away instead of forming puddles, as clay soil does. Adding lots of humus to a soil is the best remedy for improving sandy or clay soil. For heavy clay soils the application of gypsum—a powdery mineral used to make plaster of Paris—is also beneficial. Adding sand to clay soil offers little improvement. Humus is contained in peat moss (available as bales from garden centers); it is also in garden compost, leaf mold, and decayed animal manure.

Garden compost, leaf mold, and decayed animal manure all contain plant nutrients. Their constant use in a garden means that little or no commercial fertilizer should be needed. Horticultural peat, however, is sterile, has little nutrient value, and needs the help of a commercial fertilizer to grow good crops.

Problem Soils

In addition to classifying soil according to its physical properties, soil is classified according to its pH balance, which is an indication of alkalinity, acidity, or neutrality.

Alkaline soils are prevalent in areas with low rainfall, such as deserts. There are virtually no naturally occurring alkaline problem soils in Pennsylvania, though an improper use of chemical fertilizer can produce an alkaline soil through a buildup of salts after the nutrient content has drained away. Alkaline soil is usually lacking in humus and also nutrients. It is often sticky and unpleasant to work with when wet. Plants growing in alkaline soil frequently show signs of chlorosis (yellowing of leaves through lack of nitrogen). Slightly alkaline soils can be improved by adding large amounts of compost or peat moss. These are naturally acidic and also boost the humus content. Sulphur—an organic soil conditioner—can be used to amend heavily alkaline soils.

Acid soils are found throughout Pennsylvania and other places with high rainfall. Highly acid soils retain nutrients so that most plants cannot use them. Acid soils are improved by adding lime at the rate recommended on the bag. However, azaleas, blueberries, hollies, and certain other shrub species thrive in highly acid soil and should not be limed. Only a soil test will give you an accurate rate of application.

Soil pH, lime and sulphur. The scale which measures pH ranges from 0 (highly acid) to 14 (highly alkaline). Seven is neutral. Most cultivated soils range between 4.0 (highly acid) and 8.0 (highly alkaline). Soil pH is important because it directly affects the growth of plants and their ability to flower or yield prolifically, for the following reasons:

1. Beneficial soil bacteria break down humus into soil nutrients most efficiently when soil is in a pH range of 5.5 to 7.0.
2. Plant nutrients leach away from the soil more quickly when pH is below 5.0.
3. Toxic elements may be poisonous to many plants in some soils below pH 5.0.
4. Plants absorb nutrients most efficiently when pH range is between 5.5 and 7.0.
5. Clay soil is easier to work when pH is 5.5 to 7.0.

Most flowering plants prefer a pH range between 6.0 and 7.0. When lime is used on soil to reduce acidity, it also provides calcium, a valuable plant nutrient. Calcium deficiency due to lack of lime is evidenced on flowers by failure of the tip bud and side buds to develop properly and on food crops by rotting of the fruits—especially tomatoes, peppers, peaches, and nectarines. Lime is offered in various forms by garden centers and nurseries. It is usually granular or pulverized into a fine powder. *Granular lime* has a coarse texture and can be applied to soil with a spreader.

Pulverized lime acts more quickly than granular lime because it has a finer texture, like talcum powder. *Dolomitic lime* supplies magnesium, a key secondary element, as well as calcium. Magnesium is often deficient in soils. *Hydrated lime* or *slaked lime* works rapidly but must be used carefully. Overdoses will burn plants and destroy organic material. It is highly caustic. *Quick lime* is unsuitable for gardens. It is far too caustic.

Lime can take up to a year to work its way down to plant roots. Therefore, whenever possible, liming should be done at least several weeks ahead of planting and raked into the upper soil surface.

Fertilizing. There are two popular schools of thought about fertilizing garden soil: (1) *natural* using "organic" fertilizers such as animal manure and growing cover crops such as clover, and (2) *chemical* using an assortment of packaged fertilizers in granular or liquid form. Most gardeners combine the two, using a chemical fertilizer only when a soil test shows a particular deficiency or as a boost at the start of the season. A total reliance on chemical fertilizer without good natural soil conditioners applied in spring and fall can be bad for the soil. It will deplete beneficial soil organisms, such as earthworms and soil bacteria, and encourage a buildup of poisonous alkaline salts. The best soil conditioners to use are leaf mold (made from decomposed leaves), garden compost (made from kitchen and garden wastes), and well-decomposed animal manure (available from dairy or horse farms). Horticultural peat is a popular substitute because it is easy to obtain through garden centers, but it is sterile with no nutrient content, and is commonly used in combination with a chemical fertilizer application.

Mushroom soil. Kennett Square, Pennsylvania, is famous for its mushroom farms. The familiar white button mushroom is grown in special buildings where light is excluded and mushroom spawn is seeded onto special beds filled with a sterile growing medium composed mostly of well-decomposed horse manure, peat moss, lime, straw, and other ingredients. After a mushroom crop has been harvested, the growing medium is dumped outdoors for sale to home gardeners to use as a soil conditioner. It works especially well in flower beds and vegetable gardens.

Spent mushroom soil has a pH of 7.2, which is slightly alkaline, and generally is ideal for mixing with Pennsylvania's high-acid soils. However, it is often exceedingly hot when delivered and should be allowed to cool down before use; also it may need the addition of a high-acid fertilizer—such as Miracid—if it is used around azaleas, blueberries, rhododendrons, and other acid-loving plants. Avoid using spent mushroom soil for containers and greenhouse plantings unless it is mixed at no more than one-third by volume with granular aggregates, such as perlite and vermiculite, to improve drainage.

Nitrogen is the most elusive plant nutrient. Its presence in the soil fluctuates according to thunderstorm activity. Though thunderstorms add nitrogen to the soil through a chemical reaction with the atmosphere, it is quickly leached from the soil by rainfall; and so the policy of Pennsylvania soil test laboratories is not to test for nitrogen, but assume that the soil has none. In addition to thunderstorms, growing clover or other legumes and composting green plant material—such as grass clippings—will increase nitrogen in the soils.

Leguminous plants such as peas and beans have root systems that attract nitrogen-fixing bacteria. These bacteria create nodules on the roots. These nodules are released into the soil when the crop is ploughed under. All fresh, green leafy growth is rich in nitrogen. The addition of nitrogen-rich leaves to a compost pile stimulates soil bacteria to manufacture other nutrients, including trace elements.

Some commerical fertilizers supply the nitrogen in a form that releases it into the soil slowly (called ''slow release''); others supply nitrogen so it is fast-acting. For best results, consider the slow-release kind.

Phosphorus is responsible for healthy roots, flowers, and fruit formation. It moves through the soil slowly and is often deficient in Pennsylvania soils. Phosphorus occurs naturally in bone meal and rock phosphate.

Potash is necessary for vigor and disease resistance. Wood ashes are a natural source of potash (also known as potassium).

The presence of these three major plant nutrients in a bag of fertilizer is shown as percentages of NPK (scientific abbreviations for nitrogen, phosphorus and potash). Therefore, a formula showing 5-10-5 NPK means 5 percent nitrogen, 10 percent phosphorus, and 5 percent potash. The rest is filler—a sterile distributing agent. There are also trace elements such as calcium, iron, and boron, but these are needed in such small amounts they are sometimes not shown.

Commercial fertilizer generally is supplied either in *granular* form—for raking into the upper soil surface, or as a liquid concentrate—for diluting with water. It can be used either as a soil *drench*, watered into the soil surface, or applied as a *spray* on the leaf surfaces (also called foliar feeding).

Soil Test. There are several ways to get your soil tested: through the mail, by sending a sample to the soil testing laboratory at Penn State University; with a do-it-yourself soil test kit available from garden centers; and from certain nurseries or garden centers that conduct soil tests as a customer service.

The soil test laboratory is the best choice because you will receive a detailed analysis that tells you the soil's acidity and nutrient deficiences and gives specific instructions on how to correct any imbalance for particular crop groups.

Reproduced here is a typical kit supplied by Penn State University's soil test laboratory for a soil sample to be sent to them by mail.

Across the top you will see columns with different numbers. The first gives a pH reading. However, because a straight pH reading can be misleading on its own, the lab uses another measurement for acidity, which in this case is 2.7, indicating that some lime is desirable.

Phosphorus content is printed above the letter P and potash content above the letter K. Presence of the trace element magnesium is shown above the letters Mg, and calcium above the letter C. The availability of these nutrients is important. This is shown above the letters CEC, meaning cation exchange capacity. Clay soil with plenty of organic matter usually releases its nutrients freely and has a high value. Sandy soil has a low value. Percent saturation is the concentration of each nutrient, and it helps tell the lab whether the nutrients are properly balanced.

The soil nutrient levels are shown more graphically in a bar that goes from black (low) to white (high) and a striped zone for excessively high.

Nitrogen is not shown because nitrogen levels fluctuate widely. The lab makes a recommendation assuming the nitrogen level is low.

Below the bar, the limestone and fertilizer recommendations for each 100 square

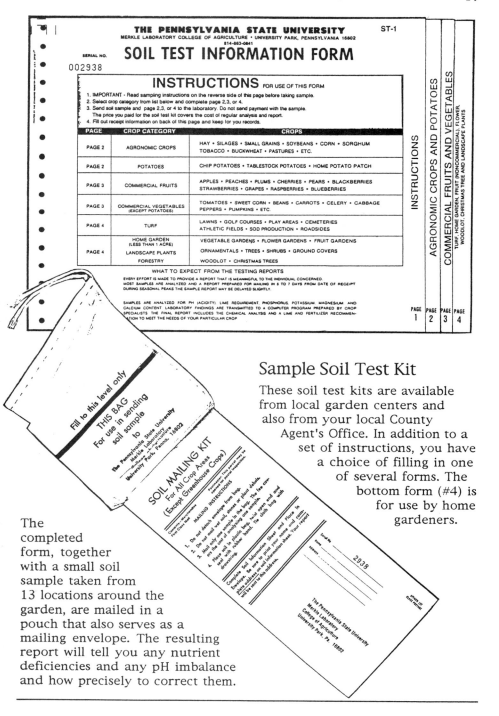

THE PENNSYLVANIA STATE UNIVERSITY   ST-1
MERKLE LABORATORY COLLEGE OF AGRICULTURE • UNIVERSITY PARK, PENNSYLVANIA 16802
814-863-0841

SERIAL NO.   SOIL TEST INFORMATION FORM
002938

INSTRUCTIONS FOR USE OF THIS FORM

1. IMPORTANT - Read sampling instructions on the reverse side of this page before taking sample.
2. Select crop category from list below and complete page 2,3, or 4.
3. Send soil sample and page 2,3, or 4 to the laboratory. Do not send payment with the sample.
   The price you paid for the soil test kit covers the cost of regular analysis and report.
4. Fill out receipt information on back of this page and keep for you records.

PAGE	CROP CATEGORY	CROPS
PAGE 2	AGRONOMIC CROPS	HAY • SILAGES • SMALL GRAINS • SOYBEANS • CORN • SORGHUM TOBACCO • BUCKWHEAT • PASTURES • ETC.
PAGE 2	POTATOES	CHIP POTATOES • TABLESTOCK POTATOES • HOME POTATO PATCH
PAGE 3	COMMERCIAL FRUITS	APPLES • PEACHES • PLUMS • CHERRIES • PEARS • BLACKBERRIES STRAWBERRIES • GRAPES • RASPBERRIES • BLUEBERRIES
PAGE 3	COMMERCIAL VEGETABLES (EXCEPT POTATOES)	TOMATOES • SWEET CORN • BEANS • CARROTS • CELERY • CABBAGE PEPPERS • PUMPKINS • ETC.
PAGE 4	TURF	LAWNS • GOLF COURSES • PLAY AREAS • CEMETERIES ATHLETIC FIELDS • SOD PRODUCTION • ROADSIDES
PAGE 4	HOME GARDEN (LESS THAN 1 ACRE)	VEGETABLE GARDENS • FLOWER GARDENS • FRUIT GARDENS
	LANDSCAPE PLANTS	ORNAMENTALS • TREES • SHRUBS • GROUND COVERS
	FORESTRY	WOODLOT • CHRISTMAS TREES

WHAT TO EXPECT FROM THE TESTING REPORTS

EVERY EFFORT IS MADE TO PROVIDE A REPORT THAT IS MEANINGFUL TO THE INDIVIDUAL CONCERNED.
MOST SAMPLES ARE ANALYZED AND A REPORT PREPARED FOR MAILING IN 6 TO 7 DAYS FROM DATE OF RECEIPT
DURING SEASONAL PEAKS THE SAMPLE REPORT MAY BE DELAYED SLIGHTLY.

SAMPLES ARE ANALYZED FOR PH (ACIDITY). LIME REQUIREMENT. PHOSPHORUS. POTASSIUM. MAGNESIUM AND
CALCIUM CONTENT LABORATORY FINDINGS ARE TRANSMITTED TO A COMPUTER PROGRAM PREPARED BY CROP
SPECIALISTS. THE FINAL REPORT INCLUDES THE CHEMICAL ANALYSIS AND A LIME AND FERTILIZER RECOMMEN-
ATION TO MEET THE NEEDS OF YOUR PARTICULAR CROP.

INSTRUCTIONS

AGRONOMIC CROPS AND POTATOES

COMMERCIAL FRUITS AND VEGETABLES
TURF, HOME GARDEN, FRUIT (NONCOMMERCIAL), FLOWER, WOODLOT, CHRISTMAS TREE AND LANDSCAPE PLANTS

PAGE 1   PAGE 2   PAGE 3   PAGE 4

Fill to this level only

THIS BAG
For use in sending
soil sample
to
The Pennsylvania State University
Merkle Laboratory
College of Agriculture
University Park, Penna. 16802

SOIL MAILING KIT
For All Crop Areas
(Except Greenhouse Crops)

MAILING INSTRUCTIONS

1. Do not detach envelope from bag.
2. Do not mail wet soil, stones or plant debris.
3. Mail only one sample in the bag. The fee cap-
   ers the cost of analyzing one sample, and
4. Place soil in bottle bag, hold open and add
   soil with rubber band. Tie cloth bag with
   drawstring.

Complete Soil Information Sheet and Place in
Envelope. Be sure to print your name and complete address on soil information sheet. Your report
will be sent to this address.

2938

The Pennsylvania State University
Merkle Laboratory
College of Agriculture
University Park, Pa. 16802

Sample Soil Test Kit

These soil test kits are available from local garden centers and also from your local County Agent's Office. In addition to a set of instructions, you have a choice of filling in one of several forms. The bottom form (#4) is for use by home gardeners.

The completed form, together with a small soil sample taken from 13 locations around the garden, are mailed in a pouch that also serves as a mailing envelope. The resulting report will tell you any nutrient deficiencies and any pH imbalance and how precisely to correct them.

feet and for different plant categories are printed. To make things even simpler, the report recommends a specific fertilizer rate to cover all the crop categories.

The first step to getting your soil tested is to obtain a mailing pouch from your local county agent's office. You will find it listed in the telephone book under United States Department of Agriculture or your county's Cooperative Extension Service. For a fee, they will send you a kit containing instructions. This will entail spoonsful of soil from different areas and combining them in the pouch, which is then mailed to the soil test laboratory. Within two weeks, you should receive a report in the form of a computer print-out.

WATER, DRAINAGE, AND IRRIGATION

The term hydrology is used by landscape architects to describe all the water considerations for a property, including patterns of natural rainfall, drainage of excess water, sources of irrigation, and methods for irrigating plants during dry spells. Though the accompanying chart of Pennsylvania's patterns of rainfall shows a fairly even distribution of precipitation during all four seasons of the year, most summer rainfall is produced by torrential downpours during thunderstorms. There can be several weeks with little or no rainfall. Without doubt, one of the best investments a Pennsylvania gardener can make is to consider the installation of an irrigation system so water can be applied where it is needed, whenever it is needed, at the turn of a water faucet. Costs can vary from expensive, overhead sprinkler systems that spray water over plantings to the use of inexpensive, disposable flexible hoses that sweat beads of moisture through micro-pores. These are cost-efficient enough to be used during one growing season and discarded at the end of that season (see section on Irrigation Equipment, page 20).

Water is vital for all healthy plant growth. Not only are nutrients absorbed by plants in soluble form through their roots *only when moisture is present*, but the sugars responsible for good flavor in fruits and vegetables move into the edible parts in soluble form, so lack of moisture can seriously affect flavor as well as yields.

How Much Water?

In a soil that drains well, especially in raised beds, it is difficult to overwater cultivated plants. Tests conducted with drip irrigation systems, which sweat moisture at a steady rate through micro-pores, showed that most edible plants benefit from being watered every day in the absence of natural rainfall. Of course, some plants are able to survive long periods without water—succulents such as stonecrop (*Sedum spectabile*) and desert candle (*Yucca filamentosa*), for example. However, most cultivated plants need moisture on a regular basis.

Vegetables are heavy users of moisture. Radish, beets and many other root crops will stop growing the moment the soil begins to dry out, becoming fibrous. Moisture in steady amounts is important to fruiting vegetables, such as tomatoes and peppers. Irregular watering may cause insufficient absorption of calcium by the plant and result in a physiological disease called "blossom end rot" in which the tips of the fruit turn black and spread until the entire fruit is inedible. Sweet corn demands plenty of moisture at the time of tasseling (when the male flower on top of the plant appears).

This is when the female part of the plant (the silk) is ready to receive pollen for fertilization and to swell the kernels so they are plump and succulent. Insufficient moisture causes many gaps in the rows of kernels, ears that are not filled to the tips, and a significant yield reduction.

Generally speaking, in good loamy topsoil 1 inch of rainfall will penetrate to 12 inches of soil depth. That may not sound like much, but most feeder roots (even of large trees) are located within 12 inches of the soil surface. A rain gauge in the garden allows you to keep track of rainfall and judge whether supplementary amounts of moisture are needed.

Correcting Irrigation Problems

Problem	When to Water	How to Water
Watering newly planted small trees, fruit trees, berry bushes, shrubs, hedges, evergreens with a root ball of 12 inches deep or less (1 gallon capacity or less). Planted in an open, sunny location, lightly mulched.	Immediately after purchase. Water daily until planted and at planting, then weekly spring and fall, twice weekly during summer in the absence of natural rainfall.	Use a watering wand with a soft-spray head, applying the equivalent of 2 gallons of moisture per application.
Large trees, shrubs, evergreens established in a sunny position.	Water once every 2 weeks, April through October, whenever a week goes by without natural rainfall.	Use a root waterer connected to a hose with probe pushed 6 inches into soil and moved around drip line every 6 feet, for at least 30 minutes each station. Or, use lawn sprinkler to surface water.
Annuals, most perennials, vegetables, ground covers planted in an open sunny location, lightly mulched.	Water all plants daily until planted and at planting, then at least twice weekly in absence of natural rainfall, three times weekly where there is no mulch.	Use a lawn sprinkler for large areas, a watering wand for small areas and container plantings. For annuals and vegetables planted in rows, such as a cutting garden, consider drip irrigation hose under black plastic.
Annuals, tender perennials, or vegetables in containers in sun.	Water whenever soil feels dry—usually daily. Hanging baskets in full sun may need watering twice daily.	Use a watering wand with a soft-spray head. Water until droplets spill through drainage holes.
Lawns, newly seeded or newly sodded.	Water daily for 3 weeks.	Use a lawn sprinkler for 1 hour at sunset.

Correcting Irrigation Problems   *(continued)*

Problem	When to Water	How to Water
Lawns, established.	Provide equivalent of 1 inch of water weekly.	Use a lawn sprinkler set to sprinkle for at least 1 hour at sunset.
Vegetables, root crops, leafy crops.	For maximum yields, water daily in absence of natural rainfall.	Use soft-spray watering wand, lawn sprinkler or drip irrigation hose under mulch blanket or black plastic.
Vegetables, fruit crops such as peppers, tomatoes, sweet corn.	Water daily at time of fruit setting, sweet corn at time of tasseling.	Use soft-spray watering wand, lawn sprinkler, or drip irrigation hose covered with mulch blanket or black plastic.

Some plants are extremely sensitive to moisture stress. Pumpkins and other vining vegetable plants will wilt during the heat of the day but perk up at night. Evergreens will lack luster in their leaves. And lawns, usually the first to show stress, will turn brown. Fruit trees may suddenly start to drop their immature fruit. Flowering of annuals and perennials may dwindle. The application of a mulch—particularly shredded leaves, straw, wood chips, or other organic mulches—will help conserve moisture and keep the soil cool. Black plastic is preferred by many vegetable gardeners because it easily rolls out to cover long rows, and it has a warming effect on the soil that benefits certain warm-season crops such as tomatoes, peppers, and melons.

Irrigation Equipment

The most laborious and least efficient method of watering a number of plants is with a watering can. This requires repeated trips to a water source. Even on level ground, a watering can is awkward to lift. But if you have only a small "postage stamp-size" vegetable plot or a few container plants on the patio, then a watering can may suffice. A 2-gallon capacity will cut down on the number of trips you need to make.

A more efficient watering method is to use a garden hose connected to a faucet and fitted with a pistol-grip watering head that adjusts from a fine spray to a powerful jet of water by finger-tip control. However, standing around with a hose can be tedious. A better tool to use is a watering wand with a long handle and a special head that allows you to deliver a soft spray of water directly to the root zone without bending. The watering wand is also efficient for reaching into overhead containers, such as hanging baskets, and through thorny branches, such as raspberry canes and rose brambles, without getting scratched.

Lawn sprinklers are a good way to water large areas effortlessly, such as expanses of turf, vegetable plots and flower beds. Set sprinklers in the evening to water the garden like an overnight rain.

The most efficient way possible to water your garden is with a drip irrigation system, especially the kind that utilizes a soaker hose rather than emitters spaced at preset distances. Though popular in the protected environment of a greenhouse, emitters are prone to clogging outdoors. For outdoor irrigation, soaker hoses are a better choice since they have micro-pores that sweat moisture at a steady rate all along the hose wall. Some of these are made of recycled rubber tires and are long-lasting. Usually they work best for plants spaced out along rows—such as vegetables or annuals in a cutting garden—but free-form beds and borders can be watered by snaking the drip line. These drip lines vary in cost depending on brand. The least expensive is made from a lightweight plastic that costs about $40 to irrigate 500 square feet of garden. It can be discarded at the end of the season or taken up and stored indoors until the next season. Drip hoses work best if covered with a mulch blanket or black plastic since they are easily punctured by stray animals and the hose wall is weakened by exposure to ultraviolet light.

Drainage. Unless the objective is to create a bog garden using plants that tolerate constantly moist soil (see page 106 for recommended water plants), most good gardens should drain excess water away from planting spaces, walks, and buildings.

For complicated drainage problems, the services of a professional landscape architect should be considered; but for simple problems, such as improving a site to plant vegetables or a cutting garden, you can make significant improvements yourself. For example, if the site for a vegetable garden is low-lying, excess water can be eliminated by digging a ditch and laying down a line of drainage pipes to channel the water to a stream, drainage ditch, or pond.

For small spaces, it may be sufficient to simply lay down a bed of crushed stones as a drainage field. You can purchase stone by the ton from a stone quarry. Over the crushed stone, make a raised bed of good topsoil, holding it in place with landscape ties, brick, or stones.

WEEDS, DISEASE, AND PESTS

A garden that becomes choked with weeds, ravaged by disease, or plagued by pests, cannot produce worthwhile yields.

Disease Control

It's sometimes difficult to tell the difference between insect damage and disease damage. In Pennsylvania, mite infestations cause leaves to curl and plants to display disease symptoms, like browning and leaf drop. The action of a borer burrowing into the trunk of a young peach tree or into a zucchini squash vine can cause the sudden wilting typical of wilt diseases. If ever you are in doubt about identification of a pest problem or a disease problem, you can send a sample to the plant pathology laboratory at Penn State University, State College, PA 16802. Experienced scientists will identify the problem, and also recommend a control.

Problem solving for specific diseases can be found in the sections of this book dealing with specific plant categories. Generally speaking, diseases in home gardens are most troublesome on orchard fruits, vegetables, and certain trees and shrubs. Diseases are usually caused by harmful fungus (such as powdery mildew on lilacs), bacteria (such as bacterial wilt on cucumbers), and physiological factors (such as sunscald on tomato fruits).

Prevention, of course, is the best cure; a large number of diseases can be avoided by the following precautions:

1. Winter cleanup and the composting or burning of garden debris. Gather up any old organic mulch (such as straw), any weed stems, dead stalks, or dead branches. Pick up boards, strips of black plastic, and large stones.
2. Select disease-resistant plants. For example, certain crabapples resist fireblight disease which blackens fruit. Some cucumbers are resistant to wilt disease. There are many roses resistant to black spot.
3. Keep plants in good health. High potash content in the soil is especially important since potash builds disease resistance. Irrigate during dry spells, especially in the early stages of establishment. This avoids stress and makes plants less vulnerable to disease. Water by means of a drip irrigation hose or with a long-handled watering wand that puts moisture directly in the root zone. (Excessively wet leaves encourage some diseases such as powdery mildew.)
4. Maintain a high humus content in the soil. This encourages beneficial organisms that can attack potentially destructive fungus organisms. High humus results from the application of organic matter, especially garden compost, leaf mold, well-decomposed animal manure, and peat moss.
5. Keep pests under control. Many harmful diseases are carried by insect pests. (For example, leaf hoppers transmit yellows disease to asters and marigolds; cucumber beetles transmit bacterial wilt disease to cucumbers and melons.)

For some effective pest controls, see the Pest Control section, below.

In the fight against diseases, it's always best to consider using an organic control before a chemical control. The following are some common organic controls that can be found in most garden centers.

Copper. Generally a dust or spray that has a reputation for being a good all-purpose disease control for tomatoes, potatoes, peppers, vine crops, orchard fruits, and ornamentals. It fights early and late blight on vegetables; anthracnose on tomatoes; bacterial spot, leaf spot, rust, downy and powdery mildew, and scab on apples; and black spot on roses. It is available as a rotenone-copper combination so it deals with a wide range of insect pests and diseases in one convenient application.

Sulphur dust is an effective control against cedar/apple rust which defoliates crabapples and orchard apples; black rot on cabbage; brown rot on grapes; and leaf spot, powdery mildew, and scab on apples. Its repellent effect on deer and other foraging animals is a bonus.

Bordeaux Mixture is a spray that controls most fungus diseases on grapes, apples, and peaches.

Though these products are biodegradable, have no long-lasting adverse effects on the soil, and are considered safe to the environment, they should be treated with respect.

Pest Control

Most Pennsylvania pest problems can be classified as *animal pests* (including birds) and *insect pests* (including slugs). You won't know which pests are likely to prove troublesome in your garden until you have been through a growing season and earned some experience. A good idea is to check around among gardening friends in the neighborhood, and find out what problems they have experienced and what remedies have worked for them.

Animal Pests. It used to be that the biggest problem from deer and rodents was the damage they caused by eating both food crops and succulent ornamental plants, but in recent years they have introduced a much more serious hazard to the gardener—Lyme disease. It is caused by the bite of a tiny insect the size of a pinhead—the deer tick (it is also spread by rodents such as mice). The disease is now so widespread that gardening is hazardous without protection. The disease is particularly dangerous to elderly people, since it is a debilitating condition, with flu-like symptoms causing lack of energy, painful joints and other complications—even death if not treated early with antibiotics. To avoid infection, wear light-colored gardening clothes, spray arms and legs with an insect repellent effective against ticks, and keep all grassy areas cut short. Do not stray from paths, especially while walking through woodland or across meadows. A tell-tale symptom is a bull's eye-like rash surrounding the bite, though the rash does not always occur.

The best way to keep foraging animals out of the garden is to fence them out. Vegetable gardens tend to be most vulnerable, and for keeping small animals—like rabbits and woodchucks—out of small plots, a short 3-foot-high chicken-wire fence all around the garden will be sufficient. It provides just enough protection and yet is not an expensive proposition. Deer are a special problem and require higher fences. Usually 5 feet high is sufficient to keep deer out of a small space, but for a large area you may need to go to 10 feet or install a special electrified deer fence, the specifications for which you can obtain through your local county agent's office.

Some gardeners have found it effective to hang bags of human hair (available from a barber shop) from orchard trees to protect them against deer, and also bars of certain toilet soaps. The best protection against deer for ornamental plantings is a deer repellent. Sprayed on leaf surfaces, it makes the entire plant distasteful, and it is effective against other mammals. The spray is odorless, but it cannot be used among edible crops because the repellent flavor can last for several months, depending on the brand.

Newly planted trees are especially vulnerable to attack from rodents and deer. When the bark of a tree is girdled it will invariably die, so be sure to use strong plastic tree-wraps around the trunks of newly planted trees. To protect individual plants from deer damage, cover with bird netting over winter. Though deer can chew through it in dire circumstances, they tend to leave covered plants alone.

Some plants are highly susceptible to bird damage—especially blueberries, cherries and strawberries. Bird-netting can be used to cover an entire tree, and floating row covers will protect smaller plants (see next section). However, many gardeners have found large plastic balloons called ''Scare-Eyes'' effective in scaring birds. The balloons are the size of a beach ball and are hung from high poles—three to an acre. A special bull's eye design is apparently effective in scaring away crows, pigeons, and starlings, yet it does not appear to frighten songbirds such as cardinals and finches.

Floating Row Covers. Though not practical for protecting ornamental plantings such as beds of annuals, foundation plantings, and perennial borders, floating row covers are an extremely good way of protecting rows of vegetables from both animals and insects. Floating row covers are made of polypropylene, a gauze-like fabric that is extremely lightweight, white in color, and has good light transmission. Available in rolls, it is placed over rows of plants, covering them like a spider's web. Insects and many disease organisms cannot penetrate through the fabric, and even foraging animals such as deer and woodchucks will not chew through it.

Insect Pests. It is impossible to guard your plants against every potential pest. For most Pennsylvania home gardeners, a general-purpose insecticide such as a rotenone-pyrethrum combination will be sufficient to guard against the majority of bothersome insect pests. Rotenone (made from the powdered parts of a tropical tree) and pyrethrum (made from the powdered petals of an African daisy) are two of the most effective organic insecticides available. Though toxic if ingested, the compounds are biodegradable and leave no harmful soil residues.

In alphabetical order, the most troublesome insect pests in Pennsylvania include:

Aphids: Small, soft-bodied insects that form colonies around tender plant parts, sucking their juices. Aphids are usually gray, white, or green in color. Caught early, small colonies of aphids can be washed off plants with a strong jet of water.

Bean beetles: Yellow, soft-bodied creatures that skeletonize bean leaves. Rotenone-pyrethrum sprays will deter them.

Borers: The larval stage of beetles or moths. Borers look like caterpillars or worms and burrow into plant stems (especially vine crops and members of the *Prunus* tree family, such as cherries and peaches). Once the worm has entered the stem, it is almost impossible to stop it. Rotenone-pyrethrum organic sprays will deter the adult moth from laying eggs. Dipel—an organic bacterial control—is also effective.

Cabbage worms: The caterpillar stage of the cabbage white butterfly. They are particularly destructive of cabbage, broccoli, and cauliflower. Dipel—the organic bacterial powder—will control them.

Cucumber beetles: Insects that chew cucumber and melon stems, infecting them with wilt disease. A rotenone-pyrethrum organic spray will control them.

Japanese beetles: Destructive as immature grubs when they live in the soil beneath grass roots and mature into even more destructive flying adults that skeletonize leaves, particularly of grapes and many ornamental shrubs. Beetle traps that lure the adults are only partially effective. The preferred organic remedy is Milky Spore—a biological control that kills the grubs while they are in the soil.

Maggots: The worst of these pests are the fruit maggots that burrow into apples, pears, peaches, plums, and nectarines. Organic fruit tree sprays containing a mixture of rotenone, pyrethrum, copper, and sulphur control a wide range of maggot-type pests and also a wide range of diseases.

Mites: Tiny, spider-like insects that colonize tender plant parts, living among fine webs, causing leaves to curl and turn brown. Rotenone-pyrethrum organic sprays are effective controls.

Slugs: Pests that are prevalent after rains and especially destructive of young transplants and salad crops such as lettuce and cabbage. Use slug bait in shallow trays.

Beneficial Insects. There are many insect and animal predators that can be encouraged to live in the garden to help control harmful insect pests. Beneficial insects that can have a significant effect on controlling harmful pests include the following:

Green lacewings: Excellent predators for garden and greenhouse. The larva, called an "aphid lion," constantly eats aphids, mealybugs, scale insects, and whiteflies.

Ladybugs: Control mostly aphids but also the eggs of the Colorado potato beetle.

Praying mantis: Eat a large number of insect pests not preyed on by ladybugs and lacewings, such as grasshoppers. To introduce them to your garden, you may be able to find the brown egg cases attached to brambles and other plant stems during country walks in winter.

Beneficial nematodes: Parasitize many lawn grubs such as armyworms, Japanese beetle grubs, and cutworms as well as carrot weevils and other vegetable pests. Microscopic in size and harmless to people and pets, these beneficial nematodes live in the soil and stand on their tails to enter soft-bodied insect larvae.

Soldier bugs: Shield-shaped insects that in both the adult and larval stage eat cabbage worms and Mexican bean beetles. Use them also to protect broccoli and cauliflower.

Trichogramma wasps: Parasitize over 200 kinds of insect pests by laying eggs which hatch into larvae that feed on the eggs of many harmful moths and butterflies, especially tomato hornworms, cabbage worms, parsley worms, cutworms, and corn borers. The variety *T. pretiosum* is best used to control pests in vegetable gardens. The variety *T. minutum* is best for controlling webworms and other pests.

If not already present in your garden, many of these beneficial insects can be purchased from mail order sources (see sources, page 224).

Weeding

Weed seeds find their way into all cultivated soils, and they can quickly suffocate desirable plants. Annual weeds, such as crabgrass, are particularly troublesome in lawns. Goldenrod and other perennial weeds can completely take over a vegetable garden. Multiflora roses and wild honeysuckle are examples of woody weeds that can kill young trees and shrubs. Weed seeds are transmitted mostly by wind, but animals and birds carry them too.

The best way to keep down the weed population in your garden is to practice cleanliness. Don't allow the garden to be overrun with weeds. Destroy them either by burning or placing them on a compost pile to rot down *before* they have a chance to set seeds.

The most effective means of weed control is mulching, whereby a layer of material is placed over the soil surface around plants. Mulch materials can be organic, composed of shredded leaves, lawn clippings, straw, pine needles, cocoa-bean hulls, and even landscape chips. Artificial mulch materials include mulch blankets made from glass fiber or black plastic. Most artificial mulches are not biodegradable and should be removed from the garden each year, while many organic mulches can be tilled into the soil at the end of the season. Be sure not to use organic mulches that may already contain weed seeds, such as weed-infested straw.

There are three effective ways to control weeds: *hand-pulling* or *hoeing* (taking care not to uproot desirable neighboring plants in the process), *mulching* (covering the soil with a layer of material so that weeds are suffocated), and by *chemical controls* (notably pre-emergence herbicides that are sprayed over soil to kill weed seeds before they germinate, or contact herbicides that are sprayed over plants to kill off all vegetation prior to planting). However, it should be noted that improperly used chemical controls are responsible for devastating effects on wildlife—particularly birds when they eat contaminated insects. Also, applying chemical sprays without a protective face mask can cause cancer.

Mulching is a popular method of weed control for flower beds and vegetable plots, but there are garden purists who don't like to see anything around their plants except bare soil and will spend time at the end of each day pulling weeds or hoeing between rows to keep them weed-free.

The most common contact weedkiller is Roundup. Applied as a spray, Roundup will kill off all vegetation to create a weed-free area that can be dug over and replanted. Roundup can be used selectively by dabbing plants, such as tall thistles, with a sponge attached to a stick, so that only the dabbed plants are killed. Roundup is considered to be an environmentally safe control because it neutralizes on contact with soil.

CHAPTER 3

Annuals

Pennsylvania has a superb climate for growing a vast assortment of flowering annuals, including hardy kinds that generally tolerate mild frosts and bloom best during the cool months of spring and autumn. Also tender kinds that generally are killed by frost, need planting after danger of frost, and bloom best during the warm, sunny months of summer. Pansies, calendulas, and snapdragons are examples of hardy annuals that are especially popular in Pennsylvania gardens; marigolds and zinnias are examples of tender types that will tolerate high heat and humidity during summer.

The lists of annuals in this section do not contain all the annuals that do well in Pennsylvania, but they are generally the most readily available from garden centers or nurseries and produce an unusually colorful display.

There are many public gardens throughout the state where flowering annuals can be seen, including the Pennsylvania Horticultural Society Garden in Center City, Philadelphia; Longwood Gardens, Kennett Square; Hershey Gardens, Hershey; and the Penn State Flower Trials at State College (see page 6).

OBTAINING PLANTS FOR THE GARDEN

Annuals are most often grown from *transplants* and from *seed*. The easiest method is to buy ready-grown transplants from a garden center or nursery. Annuals are mostly offered in ''six-packs'' with each plant grown in a compartment made of plastic or biodegradable fiber. Plants grown in the plastic compartments are easily popped out by pushing up the flexible plastic base. If you buy transplants in six-packs made of fiber, you may be told to simply separate the compartments and plant as is, pot and all, but in reality it is far better to gently tear open the bottom of each fiber compartment to release the roots so they have greater freedom to grow.

Resist the temptation to buy transplants already in bloom. These can suffer severe transplant shock. If instead you ''buy green,'' you will generally find your transplants will grow into stockier plants that quickly overtake the ones in bloom and produce a better, longer-lasting display.

Also avoid long, lanky specimens that appear ''stretched.'' Lack of light, overcrowded roots, and infrequent watering can cause stretched plants, putting them under stress. A short, leafy, compact transplant will produce a better display. If you find yourself with no choice but to accept long, spindly transplants, be sure to pinch out the top to encourage side-branching and a bushy habit.

If the root ball is extremely matted and tangled, gently tease apart the base and ensure good soil contact around the roots by patting down the soil with a hand trowel.

Immediately after transplanting, water your plants thoroughly unless rainfall is predicted.

Biggest failures with transplants are: *dehydration* (lack of moisture following planting), *frost damage* (planting tender kinds too early) and *slug damage* (failure to keep slug infestations under control by using slug bait or hand-picking the pests in the early morning).

STARTING HARD-TO-START SEEDS

1. Pour seeds into teaspoon directly from packet.

2. Pick up seeds individually with end of moist pencil.

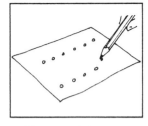

3. Place seeds in rows on moist paper towel.

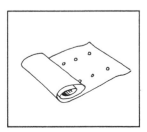

4. Roll towel loosely. Keep warm and moist. Most fine seeds need light to germinate.

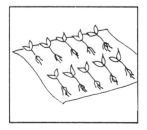

5. Examine towel after required germination period.

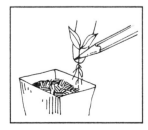

6. Use end of moist pencil and forefinger to pick seedlings off towel. Transfer to individual peat pots.

Annuals from Seed

A much wider selection of annuals is possible by growing them from seed. Also, seed-starting can save money since it is possible to grow hundreds of plants from a single packet. There are two types of seed-starting: *direct seeding,* whereby seeds of easy-to-grow annuals are sown directly into the garden where plants are to bloom, and *indoor seeding,* whereby seeds are first started under glass and transferred to individual pots for transplanting to the garden. Even with seed varieties that can be direct-seeded (such as marigolds and zinnias) it is usually advantageous to consider starting them off indoors because this gives you a head start on the season, often allowing you an extra 5 weeks of bloom.

Direct seeding can begin with hardy annuals in spring, as soon as the soil can be worked. Varieties such as gloriosa daisies, calendulas, cornflowers, Shirley poppies, and wildflower meadow mixtures can be scattered thinly over the soil surface and barely covered with soil—just sufficient to anchor them. They will remain dormant until the soil temperature warms up sufficiently to energize them into germinating. If thinning of some seedlings is necessary to prevent overcrowding, this is best done with a pair of scissors.

Before direct-seeding annuals you must prepare the soil so the surface is raked to a fine, crumbly texture and outline where you want each group of seeds to grow, either with a sharp stick or by scattering a white powder such as flour.

A light covering of straw or similar organic material will help protect the soil from drying out too quickly, otherwise an area that has been direct-seeded must be watered with a lawn sprinkler every day in the absence of natural rainfall until the seeds have germinated and are well established.

Indoor seed starting is easiest if you have a sun room, a greenhouse, or a large window with a wide sill. Seed starting demands bright, *evenly distributed light.* Where you have cramped quarters with small windows that are shaded, you will almost certainly encounter problems from seedlings stretching toward the light, and so you may have to resort to using a ''grow-light'' unit in which seed trays are positioned under special lighting tubes with timers to regulate the amount of daylight.

Generally speaking, indoor seed starting involves a *one-step* or *two-step* approach. The one-step method is used mostly with seeds that are large and easy to handle such as marigolds and zinnias. They are seeded directly into pots filled with a peat-based potting soil, or peat pellets (such as Jiffy-7's). The seeds germinate in the pot, excess seedlings are thinned to leave one to reach transplant size, and the seedling is transferred to the garden as soon as weather conditions allow.

The two-step method is mostly used with small seeds such as begonias, impatiens, and petunias. These seeds are first scattered over the surface of a seed tray and the tray covered with a piece of glass or a plastic bag to maintain a humid micro-climate. As soon as the seeds germinate, the glass or plastic is removed and the seedlings transferred to individual pots to reach transplant size.

It is most important that seedlings receive strong light—but not direct sunlight which will burn their tender leaves or dry out the potting soil too quickly. When watering this must be done with a ''mister'' that produces a fine spray since the flow of water from a watering can generally will disturb the seeds and inhibit germination.

High germination for most annuals is assured if the soil temperature can be maintained at 70°F. To achieve this you may wish to consider using a heating cable laid underneath seed trays.

Some annuals— such as marigolds and zinnias— reach transplant size within 4 to 5 weeks of seeding; others—such as begonias and coleus—may require 10 weeks to reach transplant size.

With all varieties it is essential to use sterile materials such as clean pots and a packaged potting soil since a destructive fungus, called damping-off disease, can destroy entire batches of seedlings, attacking them at the soil line and making them wilt. If you use pots from a previous year, be sure to wash them in a detergent solution to clean out old soil that can harbor the invisible spores, and dip them into bleach.

Before transferring transplants from a protected indoor environment to the changeable outdoors, they should be "hardened-off." This is best done by placing them in a cold frame for about 5 days. In the absence of a cold frame you could place them in an area where they can be covered with clear plastic sheeting at night. This conditions the plants so they do not suffer shock from exposure when placed into garden soil.

TOP-PERFORMING ANNUALS FOR PENNSYLVANIA

The following list includes some biennials and perennials that will bloom the first year. Heights are relative and will vary according to soil fertility, irrigation, and climatic factors.

Ageratum, Floss Flower
(Ageratum houstonianum)

Tender annual, 3 to 12 inches high, blooming from early summer to autumn. Fluffy, floss-like flowers are mostly powder-blue, although white and pink varieties also exist.

Excellent for borders, edgings, window boxes, and other containers. Combines well with marigolds and petunias. New tall varieties are suitable for cutting gardens and as backgrounds.

Recommended varieties: "BLUE DANUBE" hybrid for edging (6 inches); "BAVARIA" for cutting (2 feet tall). All-America white and purple flowering varieties are also available, though they do not do as well as the blues in Pennsylvania.

Best to start seed indoors 6 to 8 weeks before outdoor planting, or purchase young plants to set out after danger of frost.

Alyssum, Sweet
(Lobularia maritima)

Hardy annual, 3 to 8 inches tall, bloom-

ing continuously from early summer to autumn. Dainty, fragrant, four-petalled flowers are freely produced on mound-shaped plants. Prefers full sun. Colors include snow-white, rose, pink and purple.

Possibly the most popular plant for edging a flower border. Excellent as a companion for taller plants in containers; also for planting as drifts in rockeries and as flowering cushions between stepping stones. Especially beautiful when the white kinds are alternated with blue lobelia, another fine edging plant.

"CARPET OF SNOW" (4 inches) forms a dense, low-spreading, white mat. "WONDERLAND" (3 inches), a lovely deep rose-pink, and "ROYAL CARPET" (3 inches), a violet-purple, are both All-America Winners.

Direct-sow seed after frost-danger in spring, or start indoors 4 weeks before outdoor planting.

Amaranthus, Joseph's Coat
(Amaranthus tricolor)

Tender annual, up to 4 feet tall, producing a crown of leaves in iridescent colors—bicolored and tricolored. "PER-

FECTA'' has red and yellow pointed leaves, tipped green; ''ILLUMINA-TION'' has broader orange-red leaves with yellow centers. Both are attractive massed in beds and borders, especially in a sheltered location as they tip easily in high winds.

Direct-sow seeds, or start 6 weeks before outdoor planting after frost-danger.

Aster, China
(Callistephus chinensis)

Half-hardy annual (tolerates mild frost) blooming from midsummer to autumn. One of the ten most popular annuals for Pennsylvania gardens, despite its relatively short bloom season of several weeks in summer. Tall kinds make excellent cut flowers; in fact, entire plants may be uprooted for an instant bouquet. Color range includes light and dark blue (China asters have the largest lavender-blue flowers of any annual). Other colors are white, rose-pink, and crimson.

The following are popular varieties: Burpee's ''TOTEM POLES'' have large, fluffy, informal flower heads, growing 2 feet tall and individual blossoms up to 5 inches across; ''DWARF QUEEN'' and ''DWARF BORDER MIXED'' grow just 10 inches tall, an ideal size for low beds or edgings. Individual blooms are 3 inches across. Aster yellows and wilt are serious problems. To avoid these diseases do not grow China asters in the same place two years in succession.

For earliest bloom, start seed indoors 6 weeks before outdoor planting. Otherwise, direct-sow seed after frost-danger.

Baby's Breath
(Gypsophila elegans)

Hardy annual, 6 inches up to 3 feet tall, forming a cloud of small white or pink flowers. Short bloom season, but flowers are dainty and profuse in a sunny or lightly shaded location, giving a misty effect in the landscape.

Useful in the cutting garden, for it provides an excellent contrast in arrangements with zinnias, marigolds, and other vividly colored flowers. A choice variety is ''COVENT GARDEN WHITE.''

Prefers to be direct-seeded after frost danger. Make several sowings 2 weeks apart for a continuous garden display.

Bachelor's Buttons, Cornflower
(Centaurea cyanus)

Hardy annual, 1 1/2 to 2 1/2 feet tall, blooming for several weeks in early summer and into autumn, with repeat sowings. Best in a sunny location. Thrives in poor soil and prefers cool nights. Blue is the traditional color, but white, pink, and red are also available, separately and in mixtures.

Good for garden display and for cutting. The All-America Winner ''BLUE BOY'' is an especially free-flowering tall variety. ''JUBILEE GEM'' is a compact, blue-flowered All-America Winner that creates a mounded effect, suitable for edging.

Direct-sow seed since plants resent transplanting. Self-sows after flowering to reappear year after year.

Balsam
(Impatiens balsamina)

Erect, spire-like plants grow succulent stems studded with camellia-like, 2-inch-wide flowers in red, pink, white, purple and bicolors. An old-fashioned flower that takes the heat provided it has humus-rich soil. Grows well in full sun or light shade, good for planting in clumps in mixed beds. Combines especially well with calliopsis, sweet peas, and four o'clocks to create an old-fashioned cottage-style garden.

Though many dwarf varieties are available—with flowers on top of the plants—they are not so appealing for low bedding as regular impatiens (see Impatiens). The best tall mixture is "CAMELLIA-FLOWERED MIXED."

Start seed indoors 6 to 8 weeks before outdoor planting after frost-danger. Seeds are highly susceptible to damping-off disease, and only a well-stocked garden center will sell transplants.

Begonia, Tuberous
(Begonia x tuberhybrida)

Noted for spectacular large, double flowers as big as peony blossoms, tuberous begonias were mostly grown from expensive tubers. A fantastic new strain that blooms quickly from seed, the "NONSTOP" hybrids have a much wider color range than wax begonias, including yellow, orange, and apricot, with double and semi-double flowers up to 4 inches across, flowering all summer until fall frost. Sensational in lightly shaded areas, especially in humus-rich soil. Excellent pot plant, too.

Start seed 10 to 12 weeks before outdoor planting. Or purchase transplants from local garden centers.

Begonia, Wax
(Begonia x semperflorens-cultorum)

Treat as a tender annual, 6 to 10 inches tall, blooming from early summer to autumn. Flower color often dazzling: white, pink, scarlet, and red. Leaves may be green or bronze. One of the best annuals for light-to-moderate shade, the hybrid varieties also do well in full sun in humus-rich soil. Excellent for massing in beds, edging borders and containers. Everblooming until fall frost.

Compact hybrids are superior to older sorts. "COCKTAIL" series, in mixed or separate colors, grows to 6 inches and has bronze leaves. "WHISKEY" (white), "GIN" (rosy-pink), and "VODKA" (a rich red) are the best separate colors.

Start seed indoors at least 10 weeks before outdoor planting, or purchase transplants from garden centers since the seedlings need constant misting to become established.

Bells of Ireland
(Moluccella laevis)

Half-hardy annual, 10 to 36 inches tall, blooming from mid- to late summer. Stems are closely set with decorative green, bell-shaped bracts and a dainty white flower at the center. Likes full sun, tolerates heat and drought. Decorative in mixed flower borders, though mostly grown as a cut flower and for dried flower arrangements.

Seed is hard-skinned and sensitive to cold. Direct-sow after frost-danger, first soaking seed overnight in lukewarm water to aid germination. Or start seed 4 weeks before outdoor planting.

Calendula, Pot Marigold
(Calendula officinalis)

Hardy annual, 12 to 24 inches tall, mostly in yellow and orange, and blooming from spring to autumn. Best flowering is during the cool months in full sun. Leaves have a pleasant, spicy odor. Attractive in a border, calendula also makes a good cut flower.

"PACIFIC BEAUTY" (18 inches) resists heat better than most. Lower-growing varieties such as Burpee's "DWARF GEM" (12 inches) are suitable for containers and edging.

Easy to grow from seed direct-sown several weeks before the last frost date, or start indoors 4 weeks before outdoor planting. May reseed itself year after year.

Calliopsis
(Coreopsis tinctoria)

Hardy annual, 9 to 36 inches tall, blooming for several weeks in summer. Plants grow best in a sunny location, tolerate heat, resist drought, and thrive even in poor soils. The bright, daisy-like flowers are yellow, orange, red, and bicolored. Available usually in mixtures.

Dwarf varieties, which are fine for borders, form neat mounds 10 to 12 inches high; tall kinds are excellent for cutting. Easy to grow, and quick to flower when direct-seeded. Repeat sowings every few weeks to ensure a succession of bloom.

Cleome, Spider Flower
(Cleome hasslerana)

Tender annual, 4 feet tall, blooming continuously from midsummer until autumn on slender stems topped with a white, pink, red, or purple crown of flowers. Needs a sunny location. Withstands heat.

Attractive when massed in bold groups in the border and as a background for lower-growing annuals. "HELEN CAMPBELL," a pure white, and "ROSE QUEEN," a deep pink, are the most popular separate colors.

Can be direct-seeded after frost-danger, but starting 6 weeks before outdoor planting assures earliest blooms. Once introduced to the garden, the plants readily self-sow.

Cockscomb
(Celosia cristata, C. c. plumosa)

Tender annual, 6 inches to 3 feet tall, blooming nonstop midsummer to autumn. Two types of cockscomb are popular—the crested and the plumed. Gold, yellow, pink, rose, and red are the basic colors. Both kinds need a warm, sunny location for vivid display. Dwarf celosias are excellent for edging, tall kinds effective for massing in borders. Good for cutting, both fresh and dried.

Breeders have made significant improvements in this old-time garden favorite. Two notable cockscombs are Burpee's "FLORADALE ROSE-PINK," with globe-shaped blooms on compact 16-inch-high plants, and "TOREADOR," having gigantic red combs up to 9 inches across. Among the best plumed kinds are "FOREST FIRE IMPROVED," growing 2 1/2 feet high with dazzling blood-red plumes and bronze leaves, and "APRICOT BRANDY," a more compact (1 1/2 feet) apricot-orange with green leaves, and an All-America Winner. Plant this with another All-America Winner, "RED FOX," for a dazzling red-and-orange color harmony. "FLAMINGO FEATHER" (also known as "PINK TASSLES") has shimmering feather-like plumes that produce a glittering effect, rated one of the best-performing annuals at Longwood Gardens.

Celosia grows quickly, thrives in heat, and resists drought. Seed is best direct-sown. If started indoors, take care not to let the plants grow too tall, since stretching and any check in growth may result in a poor display.

Coleus
(Coleus x hybridus)

Although a perennial in warm climates, coleus is treated as a tender annual in northern gardens. It is planted extensively for its rainbow variegated foliage in combinations of yellow, lime-green, bronze, red, and chocolate for season-long color. The flowers are inconspicuous, pale blue on thin spikes, and should be pruned off to prolong the foliage display. Thrives in sun or shade, in humus-rich soil, generally staying 1 to 2 feet in height.

Useful for mass bedding, edging, and containers. By far the best variety is the "WIZARD" series for it not only has a natural low-branching habit, but it goes to seed only late in the season and stays decorative over a longer period than the inferior "RAINBOW" mixture, which needs constant pruning of the flower heads to keep it compact.

Start seed indoors in soil temperature of 70 to 75°F, 8 to 10 weeks before outdoor planting after frost-danger. Since seed is tiny and susceptible to damping-off disease, young plants should be obtained from garden centers. Desirable forms are easily rooted from cuttings and carried over winter in the house as pot plants.

Coreopsis
(Coreopsis grandiflora)

Hardy perennials with one hardy annual form, the All-America Winner "EARLY SUNRISE" which flowers in 11 weeks, especially if started early indoors 6 to 8 weeks before outdoor planting. Ever-blooming, 2-foot-high plants grow bushy clumps with masses of golden-yellow, semi-double, 1 3/4-inch flowers. Comes back each year as a hardy perennial.

Cosmos
(Cosmos bipinnatus)

Half-hardy annual (tolerates mild frost), 4 feet tall, with feathery foliage and masses of 4-inch summer flowers in white, rose, pink, and magenta-red. A closely related species, C. sulphureus (3 feet), offers yellow, orange, and scarlet in its color range, especially "BRIGHT LIGHTS" with its 2-inch-wide shimmering flowers.

Cosmos thrives even in poor soil, tolerates high heat, and prefers full sun. Tall kinds will need staking unless plants are massed together. Good for massing in beds, as a background highlight, and exquisite for cutting. Direct-sow seed after frost-danger as plants resent transplanting. Readily self-seeds to come back each year.

Dahlia, Bedding Types
(Dahlia x hybrida)

Tender annual, 2 to 5 feet tall, blooming continuously from early summer until autumn in full sun. Requires fertile, humus-rich soil and rigorous dead-heading for best floral display. Both green and bronze-leaf varieties are available, with mostly yellow, orange, red, pink, crimson, and purple flowers up to 3 inches across. Not to be confused with the tall, larger-flowered tuberous dahlias.

Good seed varieties include "RIGO-LETTO" (2 feet) with double and semi-double blooms, and the bronze-foliaged All-America Winner "REDSKIN' (also 2 feet). Both are beautiful massed in borders, as an edging, and mixed as pot plants.

Start seed early indoors 6 to 8 weeks before outdoor planting after frost-danger. Best floral display occurs in autumn.

Dianthus, Pinks
(Dianthus chinensis)

Hardy annual, 8 to 10 inches tall, blooming when nights are still cool during early summer and autumn. In full sun plants form perfect mounds of grass-like gray-green foliage and cheerful, flat, upward-facing flowers—some smooth-petaled, others fringed—in white, pink, and red, plus bicolors. Tolerates poor or sandy soil.

Useful as edgings, also massed in borders and planted as drifts in rock gardens. "MAGIC CHARMS," the first hybrid mixture, is an All-America Winner, as is "SNOWFIRE" hybrid. Its

1 l/4-inch-wide white, serrated petals are splashed with red in the center to produce a distinctive "peppermint" effect, making it a sensational pot plant.

Start seed indoors 8 weeks before outdoor planting. Prune plants after summer flowering to encourage repeat bloom in autumn.

Four O'Clocks
(Mirabilis jalapa)

A tender perennial best treated as a tender annual, 2 feet tall, blooming midsummer to autumn in all colors except blue. Some plants produce several colors on the same plant—such as yellow, pink, and purple-striped with pink. Grow in a sunny location. This old-fashioned favorite takes heat, drought, and poor soil. Bushy plants are covered with tubular flowers which open in the afternoon on sunny days, and stay open all day on cloudy days. Useful as an accent in mixed flower borders.

Start seed indoors 6 weeks before outdoor planting, or direct-seed after frost-danger. Self-sows and sometimes grows back from tuberous roots after a mild winter.

Foxgloves
(Digitalis purpurea)

Hardy biennial with one form grown as a hardy annual. Height averages 2 1/2 feet. Flowers of the All-America Winner "FOXY" appear in midsummer. Trumpet-shaped florets are closely set on tall, tapering spikes. Colors include pink, rose, purple, primrose, and white with beautiful spotted throats. Valuable for lightly shaded locations, but tolerates full sun in humus-rich soil.

"FOXY" blooms in 5 months from seed, each plant producing up to nine side spikes surrounding a main central spike. Good for background accents, massing in bold groups, and for cutting. Plants are not as tall as the common biennial foxgloves, which require two seasons to bloom.

Start seed 8 weeks before outdoor planting. Can be set outdoors several weeks before the last expected frost date.

Gaillardia, Gay Flower
(Gaillardia pulchella)

Hardy annual, 14 to 24 inches tall, blooming in early summer to autumn. Best in full sun. Survives heat, drought, and poor soils. Single and double forms are 2 inches across in yellow, orange, maroon, scarlet, and combinations of these.

Good in mixed flower borders for display and cutting. "GAIETY" (2 feet), with double flowers in mixed colors, includes many bicolors. The All-America Winner "RED PLUME" is an astonishing dark red, the bushy plants covered in flowers for most of summer.

Direct-sow seed or start early indoors 4 to 6 weeks before outdoor planting after frost-danger.

Geranium
(Pelargonium x hortorum)

Tender annual, 1 1/2 feet tall, blooming continuously all summer. Professor Dick Craig, at Penn State University, pioneered the development of seed-grown geraniums. Before his breakthrough breeding lines bedding geraniums were grown mostly from cuttings, to ensure quality and color uniformity. Now, seed-grown strains are popular because they are less expensive to grow than from cuttings, they ensure a longer-lasting display, and they grow true to color. The red, white, pink, and bicolored flowers are borne in clusters on long stems held above bushy plants with rounded leaves and sometimes a decorative brown zone, or "horseshoe," toward the leaf edge.

Popular for beds, borders, and containers. Good varieties for Pennsylvania include the "MULTIBLOOM" hybrids, with masses of flowers continuing until fall frost, and the "ELITE" hybrids, forming larger, more rounded flower heads than the "MULTIBLOOMS."

Start seed indoors 8 to 10 weeks before outdoor planting, or purchase ready-grown plants from garden centers.

Globe Amaranth
(Gomphrena globosa)

Tender annual, growing bushy clumps up to 2 feet high, crowded all season with marble-size, papery, round flower heads. Colors include white, pink, and magenta. Seed mixtures also include a scarlet and orange related species, *G. haageana*.

Heat-tolerant plants prefer full sun, best used sparingly as accents in mixed flower borders and rock gardens. Long rows of mixed colors are popular in cutting gardens, as the flowers make superb dried arrangements.

Direct-seed after frost-danger or start seed indoors 4 to 6 weeks before outdoor planting.

Gloriosa Daisy
(Rudbeckia hirta burpeeii)

Hardy annual, 3 feet tall, blooming mostly in midsummer. The large, 5-inch-wide, daisy-like flowers were developed by Burpee from the familiar wayside perennial rudbeckia, known as "black-eyed Susans." They are mostly yellow, orange, and rusty-red with black or green centers, also bicolored. Good for massing in beds and borders. Especially attractive combined with ornamental grasses, such as variegated eulalia (Miscanthus) and perennial purple coneflowers.

Direct-sow seed several weeks before the last expected frost date in spring, or start seed indoors 6 weeks before outdoor planting. Recommended varieties include "IRISH EYES" (green centers and yellow petals), "DOUBLE GOLD" (dramatic double-flowered) and the "BECKY" series (extra dwarf).

Heliotrope, Sweet
(Heliotrope arborescens)

Tender perennial best grown as a tender annual. Bushy plants grow to 1 1/2 feet, produce dark green, spear-shaped, textured leaves and clusters of small, violet-blue flowers that smell pleasantly of vanilla. The flat flower clusters can measure up to 5 inches across, develop best in full sun, and occur nonstop until fall frost.

Best used as a color harmony with yellow marigolds, the flowers are good for cutting. Popular also as a pot plant, not only during summer to decorate a deck or patio, but also during winter in sun rooms and conservatories. The variety "MARINE" is especially dwarf and compact, growing just 8 to 10 inches high.

Start seed indoors 6 weeks before outdoor planting after frost-danger.

Hibiscus, Hardy
(Hibiscus moscheutos)

Hardy perennial that can be treated as a tender annual, since the hardy roots will overwinter to bloom the next season. Blooms continuously late summer to autumn in full sun on bushy, 3- to 5-foot-tall plants. The flowers—up to 10 inches across—are white, rose, and crimson with contrasting centers.

"SOUTHERN BELLE," an All-America Winner and the tallest, has a striking, tropical appearance. Use it in bold groups in mixed borders and at the edge of a pond or stream since it tolerates moist soil. For a bushier, more compact display choose "DIXIE BELLE" (3 feet). With only slightly smaller flowers it's excellent for planting in tubs as a deck or patio accent.

For flowers the first year sow seed indoors 6 to 8 weeks before outdoor planting, first soaking the rock-hard seeds overnight in lukewarm water to aid germination, and set out plants after frost-danger. Plants will die back to the ground after fall frost, but usually will overwinter to return as a hardy perennial.

Hollyhock
(Alcea rosea)

Hardy annual and hardy perennial, 2 to 6 feet tall, depending on variety, blooming from midsummer to autumn on slender stems surrounded by single or double flowers in white, yellow, pink, and red. Grow it in a sunny location sheltered from wind in deep, fertile soil. Usually requires staking.

Useful as a tall background plant or as a tall accent. Hollyhock is really a perennial, but plant breeders have developed a few annual types of this old favorite. "MAJORETTE" is a dwarf, bushy variety (2 1/2 feet) that will bloom the first year from seed; "SUMMER CARNIVAL" (5 feet), a superb early-flowering strain in mixed colors. Both are double-flowered.

Although seeds can be sown directly in the garden, it is best to start them early indoors, 8 weeks before outdoor planting.

Impatiens, Patience Plant
(Impatiens wallerana)

Tender annual, 6 inches to 2 feet, blooming continuously early summer to autumn. Queen of the shade-tolerant plants, new hybrid varieties are incredibly free-flowering in humus-rich soil. Flowers of All-America Winners "BLITZ" (red) and "TANGO" (a stunning orange) measure 2 inches across—almost as big as some multiflora petunias. The color range includes many shades of purple, orange, pink, rose, and red plus white. There are also bicolor and double forms, though the clear colors are generally more appealing.

Excellent for edgings, massing in borders, and container plantings—including hanging baskets. "SUPER ELFINS" are a popular low-growing (12 inches), large-flowered mixture.

Start seed indoors 8 weeks before outdoor planting, or purchase transplants from garden centers, since the seed is highly susceptible to damping-off disease. In fall, before frost, you might want to take a few cuttings. Rooted in plain water, they can be potted to make beautiful winter-flowering house plants.

Kale, Ornamental
(Brassica oleracea)

Hardy annual, up to 8 inches high, forming a 12-inch-wide rosette of beautiful bicolored leaves in pink-and-green and white-and-green patterns, with ruffled centers. Invaluable for winter gardens since the plants relish cool weather, tolerate heavy frosts that kill other annuals, and remain decorative in the garden until Christmas. Plants are suitable for massing in beds and borders, and also containers—especially window box planters.

Start seed indoors in mid-August to obtain 8-week-old transplants for setting out into the garden. Combines well with displays of cushion chrysanthemums.

Larkspur
(Consolida ambigua)

Hardy annual, 3 to 4 feet tall, blooming

late spring to midsummer in full sun. The spire-like plants produce masses of flower spikes in white, blue, and pink. Staking may be necessary in exposed situations.

Good for backgrounds and massing in borders; also an excellent cut flower. Deep watering in dry weather helps prolong bloom period.

Grows quickly from seed direct-sown several weeks before the last frost date. However, best results are achieved if the seed is direct-sown in late summer to produce stocky, green plants that will survive winter freezes and bloom before the end of spring. Cool weather favors good germination, rapid growth, and profuse flowering. Burpee's "GIANT IMPERIAL MIXED" is a popular strain, selected for dense flower clusters.

Marigold, African
(Tagetes erecta)

Half-hardy annual. Grows 2 to 3 1/2 feet, depending on variety, blooming summer and autumn in full sun. Flowers mostly double, in yellow, orange, and white; leaves indented with a spicy fragrance that is a natural insect repellent. Plants are tolerant of drought and poor soil.

Burpee's "LADY" series—especially the yellow "FIRST LADY"—always produces a magnificent display. The blooms are not so large as the giant-flowered "CLIMAX" series, but the plants are more compact and often display up to 50 flowers fully open at the same time.

Probably Pennsylvania's most popular flowering annual, marigolds seem to outshine everything else in the garden when massed in beds and borders, or grouped in containers. They are also excellent for fresh floral arrangements. No garden flower is less trouble to grow, has a longer period of bloom, or has more decorative value than the marigold.

There are three main types—the dwarf French, tall African (also called American), and Afro-French (also called triploid hybrids and mule marigolds) which are crosses between the other two.

Direct-sow seed after frost-danger, or start early indoors 4 to 6 weeks before outdoor planting.

Marigold, French
(Tagetes patula)

Smaller-flowered and more compact than the African (American) marigold, the French marigold is devoid of white in its color range, but has the addition of rusty-red, plus bicolors. French marigolds are most useful for edging and also for massing in low beds. Heights range from 6 inches ("PETITES") to 12 inches ("QUEEN SOPHIA"). The most popular varieties are double-flowered, but there are single-flowered kinds. The yellow-red bicolor "QUEEN SOPHIA" is a beautiful All-America Winner especially good for growing in containers. Dwarf triploid hybrids—crosses between the tall African (American) and dwarf French—resemble French marigolds more than Africans. They are sterile, do not set viable seed, and place all their energy in flowering. They rush into flower within 5 weeks from starting seed, and continue nonstop until fall frosts, producing tremendous quantities of flowers and also an impressive density of color. Burpee's "NUGGET" series is sensational, as is "RED SEVEN STAR" which has larger flowers (up to 2 1/2 inches across).

Seed of all marigolds, except triploid hybrids, does well when direct-sown, though earlier flowering is possible from starting seed indoors 4 weeks before outdoor planting. Triploid hybrid seed is best started indoors in order to encourage high germination.

Morning Glory
(Ipomoea tricolor)

Tender annual, a fast-growing vine climbing to 10 feet by means of tendrils. Heart-shaped leaves are decorative all season; flared, trumpet-shaped blooms— up to 4 inches across—close in the afternoon. Flowers nonstop from midsummer to fall frost. Useful for covering chain-link fences, growing up trellises, taking color high into the sky.

Best variety for Pennsylvania gardens is "HEAVENLY BLUE," though other beautiful colors are available, including "PEARLY GATES" and "SCARLET O'HARA." They tolerate crowding and can be mixed on an arbor to give an appealing "red-white-and-blue" color harmony. A closely related annual, *Ipomoea alba*—commonly called moonflower—grows flowers up to 5 inches across, flowering in the late afternoon and at night.

Direct-sow seeds of morning glories and moonflowers after frost-danger, or start indoors 4 weeks before outdoor planting. To aid germination, moisten the hard-coated seeds overnight in a damp paper towel.

Nasturtium
(Tropaeolum majus)

Half-hardy annual. Dwarf types (12 inches), semi-tall (3 feet), and vining kinds (up to 6 feet) are available, blooming nonstop from early summer to fall. Needs full sun, and does well in poor soil. Flowers measure up to 2 inches across, with petals arranged in a whorl, and have a sweet nectar-laden spur sought by hummingbirds. Blooms best when nights are cool. Colors include yellow, orange, apricot, white, pink, red and mahogany.

Dwarf varieties are good for borders and containers. Trailing kinds will climb up a trellis, cascade over window boxes and cover banks. The flowers make lovely arrangements. The whole plant is edible, the stems, flowers, and leaves having spicy flavor similar to garden cress. They are delicious in salads. Seeds may be pickled in vinegar.

"WHIRLIBIRD" has a mounded, compact habit and its flowers are "spurless," causing them to face up on top of the plants. Direct-sow or start early indoors 4 weeks before outdoor planting. Germination is hastened by soaking the hard seeds overnight in a moist paper towel.

Nicotiana, Flowering Tobacco
(Nicotiana alata)

Half-hardy annual, 1 to 3 feet tall, depending on variety, blooming dramatically for several weeks in midsummer and then sporadically into fall. Thrives in sun, but will tolerate part shade. Resists heat and drought, tolerates poor soil. The fragrant, star-shaped flowers grow at the ends of long stems on bushy plants. Colors include crimson, pink, yellow, lime green, and white.

The "NICKI" hybrids (12 to 18 inches high) are far superior to taller strains, suitable for massing in borders, and planters.

Start seed indoors 6 weeks before outdoor planting after frost-danger. If plants are cut back after the first spurt of flowering, they will make new growth and another flush of flowers in the fall.

Pansy
(Viola x wittrockiana)

Hardy annual, 6 inches high, blooming best during cool weather of spring and fall.

Pansies used to be considered biennials, requiring seed to be sown in late summer so plants could be overwintered in cold frames for transplanting into the garden in early spring, even before the last spring frosts, but new hybrids—such as the Swiss "ROGGLI" hybrids and "MAJESTIC GIANTS"—can be started indoors 10 weeks before outdoor planting. Perhaps the favorite pansy color is blue, and the best of these for Pennsylvania is "IMPERIAL BLUE." It is so vigorous and heat-resistant that plants will bloom continuously from early spring until Christmas.

Exquisite for massing in beds, borders and containers, including hanging baskets. Garden centers in spring offer a wide selection of ready-grown pansies in bloom or bud.

Petunia
(Petunia x hybrida)

Half-hardy annual, growing 1 to 2 feet, and flowering from midsummer to fall in an extensive color range, including red, white, blue, pink, and yellow, plus bicolors. Useful for massing in sunny borders, edging, cascading from containers—especially hanging baskets and window boxes. The four most popular classes of petunia are the grandiflora single-flowered (giant, ruffled flowers), the multiflora single-flowered (smaller-flowered, but more of them and providing a greater density of color), the grandiflora doubles, and the multiflora doubles.

Though the single grandiflora types—such as the "DADDY" series—tend to be more popular because they look good in market packets, sold in garden centers, they do not produce such a dramatic or long-lasting display as the multiflora types. At Longwood Gardens and the Penn State Flower Trials, visitors are thrilled by the "PEARLS" series in pastel shades of red, pink, and white, and the "MADNESS" series, which combines the size of the grandifloras with the garden performance and wet weather tolerance of the multifloras.

Petunias like a humus-rich soil and regular watering, but avoid drenching the delicate petals.

Seed is tiny and should be started indoors 8 weeks before outdoor planting after frost-danger. A good way to start petunia seeds is to sprinkle them on a wad of tissue paper and make it into a roll, keeping it moist and warm. After the tiny seedlings have sprouted, transfer them with care to individual peat pots for later transplanting. Or purchase transplants from a nursery, choosing compact plants with just one or two flowers formed, in order to minimize transplant shock.

Phlox, Annual
(Phlox drummondii)

Half-hardy annual, growing 7 to 15 inches high, flowering mostly in early summer and fall while nights are still cool. Star-shaped, l-inch flowers include red, white, and blue, some with contrasting "eyes."

"DWARF BEAUTY" is a low-growing mixture ideal for edging beds, borders and containers—especially window box planters and shallow terracotta dishes.

Direct-seed several weeks before the last frost date, or start seed 6 weeks before outdoor planting.

Poppy, California
(Eschscholzia californica)

Hardy annual, 10 to 12 inches tall, blooming spring to early summer in full sun. Sensational during cool weather of early spring. Tolerates even poor, sandy soil. Plants have a spreading habit and poppy-like petals that shine with a satin texture. Golden-yellow flowers are the most common, though mixtures contain cream, yellow-orange, pink, rose, and scarlet. The flowers remain closed on cloudy days and at night. Burpee's "BALLERINA" mixture has distinctive fluted petals and semi-double flowers that seem to glimmer in the sun.

Direct-sow several weeks before the last expected spring frost date as the plants resent transplanting. In sheltered locations seed can be sown in September so plants form bushy, mature clumps that will survive winter and bloom extra-early in spring.

Poppy, Iceland
(Papaver nudicaule)

Hardy perennial best treated as a hardy annual, growing to 18 inches high. Plants produce rosettes of leaves and cup-shaped, 5-inch flowers on long stems. The petals have an appearance and texture of crepe paper. Flowers in June, mostly in white, red, orange, and yellow. Best grown in informal drifts among mixed perennials. Also suitable as a cut flower, if the flower stems are scorched to seal the ends before immersing in water. Otherwise they collapse when cut.

Likes a sunny location in fertile loam or sandy soil with good drainage. Start seed indoors 6 to 8 weeks before outdoor planting. Plants tolerate mild frosts and can be set into the garden several weeks before the last spring frost date. Or sow seeds directly into the garden in early spring. If started indoors, use peat pots, since they do not transplant well if the roots are disturbed. "CHAMPAGNE BUBBLES" is a vigorous hybrid mixture with large, long-lasting flowers.

Poppy, Shirley
(Papaver rhoeas)

Hardy annual, 1 1/2 feet tall, blooming from early summer to autumn. The del-

icate, brightly colored flowers are mostly red and pink, but also white and bicolored. The large, golden-yellow anthers create a lovely contrast. Beautiful planted in bold masses in mixed borders, and naturalizing on a sunny bank.

Direct-sow seed several weeks before the last frost date as they resent transplanting. Mix with blue cornflowers for a beautiful color harmony. For a really stunning effect plant a "poppy garden," mixing Shirley poppies with Iceland poppies and California poppies.

Portulaca, Moss Rose
(Portulaca grandiflora)

Tender annual. The low, spreading, 6-inch-high plants are good to brighten up hot, dry, sunny parts of the garden. Shimmering 2-inch single and semi-double flowers resemble miniature rose blossoms that close up on cloudy days and in the late afternoon. Creates a spectacular flush of color for several weeks in summer, then flowers sporadically through autumn.

Color range includes white, yellow, pink, red, and lavender, available in a mixture and as separate colors.

Direct-sow after frost-danger, or start seed 6 weeks before outdoor planting. For best results choose hybrid varieties such as "SUNDIAL," since hybrids spread wider and grow larger flowers than older varieties.

Scarlet Sage
(Salvia splendens)

Tender annual, 7 to 24 inches tall, blooming continuously from early summer to autumn. Mostly grown for its bold flower spikes, studded with blazing red, pink, white, and purple tubular flowers. Prefers full sun, tolerates light shade and high heat. Good for massing in beds and borders. At Leaming's Run Garden,

Swainton, New Jersey, a "serpentine" bed is planted entirely with scarlet sage, leading to a Victorian gazebo.

"CARIB"—also called "CARIBI-NIERE"—has especially bold flower spikes. "RAMBO" and "BONFIRE" are tall varieties good to use at the back of a flower border and with blue salvia (*S. farinacea*) for a dramatic color harmony.

Start seed indoors 6 weeks before outdoor planting, or purchase transplants to set outside after frost-danger.

Small Gourds, Large Gourds
(Cucurbita pepo, Lagenaria vulgaris)

Tender annuals, vining 12 feet and producing decorative fruits in late summer or early autumn. Both kinds prefer full sun and rich soil. Can be trained to grow up a trellis.

Small kinds are the most widely grown, since the ripened fruits can be quickly dried and varnished to make beautiful ornaments. Colors include yellow, orange, lime green, dark green, and white, plus bicolors; shapes can resemble apples, pears, pumpkins, miniature bottles, and eggs. Direct-sow in a sunny position after all danger of frost.

Snapdragon
(Antirrhinum majus)

Treat as hardy annual, 6 inches to 3 feet tall, blooming best in the cool spring and autumn months. The flowers, in spikes, come in practically every color except blue. A good border plant and excellent for flower arrangements.

Hybridization has produced spectacular kinds. "ROCKET" strain, in mixed colors, is the tallest; plants are vigorous and produce 3-foot spikes with up to 100 flowers and buds on a stem. "BUTTER-FLY" strains are novel. Their flowers have flared, wide-open throats instead of the tight-lipped sort more common among snapdragons. "MADAME BUT-TERFLY" has unique double blooms resembling double azaleas, especially good for arrangements. "FLORAL CARPET" strain, in mixed or separate colors, grows to 6 to 7 inches and is fine for a low-growing carpet. Each plant has up to 25 tiny, 3-inch spikes.

For a magnificent early summer display start seed indoors 6 to 8 weeks before outdoor planting. Young plants can also be purchased in spring from a garden center or nursery. Snapdragons may stop flowering during midsummer heat, but if old spikes are cut back, they will make new growth to provide a repeat display well into autumn. Plants will tolerate mild frosts.

Snow-in-Summer
(Euphorbia marginata)

Tender annual grown mostly for its dazzling, bright, variegated foliage—blue-green leaves with white margins. The plants grow to 2 feet tall, coloring up in midsummer. Inconspicuous white flowers are nestled among the topmost whorl of ornamental leaves, called "bracts." An old-fashioned favorite for sunny beds and borders. It creates a spectacular color harmony with blue flowers—especially asters and ageratum.

Direct-sow seeds after frost-danger, or start seed indoors 6 weeks before outdoor planting. Take care handling transplants. If the stems and leaves are cut, they ooze a milky sap that can cause a skin rash.

Statice
(Limonium sinuatum)

Half-hardy annual flowering from midsummer to fall frost on bushy plants 2 to 3 feet high. Stiff, branching stems support clusters of small, papery flowers in mostly purple, blue, red, and pink with white. Mostly grown in cutting gardens. Valued by flower arrangers for "everlasting" arrangements. Prefers sandy or loam soil in full sun. Direct-sow seed after frost-danger, or start seed indoors 6 weeks before outdoor planting.

Stock
(Matthiola incana)

Hardy annual, 1 to 2 feet tall, blooming from late spring to early summer. The fragrant flowers are borne on heavy spikes. Colors include wine red, royal purple, white, and pink, usually available in a mixture. Best in full sun, but satisfactory in part shade.

Stocks are not common in Pennsylvania gardens because the plants will stop blooming when days turn hot. However, Burpee's "GIANT IMPERIAL" mixture is well worth space in the cutting garden. Start seed 6 to 8 weeks before outdoor planting, and transplant several weeks before the last frost date.

Strawflower
(Helichrysum bracteatum)

There are numerous annuals which can be included under the group name of strawflowers, but helichrysum is the most widely seen in gardens. A tender annual, it grows 2 1/2 to 4 feet tall depending on variety.

Tall double mixtures produce the largest flowers—up to 2 1/2 inches across—in a glistening range of colors that includes white, yellow, orange, pink, rosy red, and crimson—many with yellow "button" centers. The orange-flowered "MONSTROSA"—adored by dried flower arrangers—grows 3-inch flowers on stalks that can top 6 feet by the end of the season. "BRIGHT BIKINIS" is a low, compact-growing mixture less than 2 feet high.

Helichrysum colors are retained over a long period in dried arrangements if the flowers are removed from their stems and mounted on metal wires. To dry helichrysum, cut long stems, strip away the leaves, and tie the stems in bunches of separate colors. Wrap the bunches in a newspaper cone and hang upside down in a dark, dry place.

Direct-sow seed or start 4 to 6 weeks before outdoor planting after frost-danger.

Sunflower
(Helianthus annuus)

Tender annual, growing 3 to 7 feet, blooming midsummer to fall in yellow, orange, and rusty red. Takes heat, drought, and poor soil; prefers full sun.

The tall, large-flowered kinds, such as "MAMMOTH RUSSIAN," make bold background flowers, and their meaty kernels can be saved to feed the birds in winter. This is the variety that wins in giant sunflower growing contests, with some heads reaching 24 inches or more across. "SUNGOLD" has double flower heads up to 6 inches wide on 6-foot-tall plants. It has a dwarf version, "TEDDY BEAR," just 2 feet tall with 5-inch flower heads resembling those of a Van Gogh painting.

Direct-sow the large, easy-to-handle seeds after frost-danger. For largest flower heads, plant in deep, fertile loam soil.

Sweet Pea
(Lathyrus odoratus)

Hardy annual vines, up to 6 feet tall, flowering in late spring and early summer. Mostly pastel colors in shades of red and blue, plus white. Many sweet peas are delightfully scented. Older climbing varieties need support, but new "bush-types"—such as the "ROYALTY" series—are self-supporting.

Tall sweet peas—such as Burpee's "GALAXY" series—are popular for growing up trellises and chain-link fencing. They make superb cut flowers.

Unfortunately, Pennsylvania's summers are a little too hot for exhibition-quality sweet peas, and a root rot often kills off the vines before they have a chance to flower. Their most important requirement is bright light and a cool, deep, humus-rich soil. Either direct-sow seeds in early spring several weeks before the last expected frost date, or start seeds 4 weeks before outdoor planting in Jiffy-7 peat pellets so they can be transplanted without root disturbance. To aid germination, soak the bullet-hard seeds overnight in water. Also, rolling the seeds in legume "inoculant" (used for improving yields of peas and beans) will improve sweet pea displays.

Sweet Scabious, Pincushion Flower
(Scabiosa atropurpurea)

Hardy annual growing to 2 1/2 feet high, with 3-inch, dome-shaped blooms in blue, white, pink, red, and black. The center of each flower is raised to form a crown or "pincushion." Plants prefer full sun, deserve to be much more widely grown, and are best for massing in mixed borders and cutting gardens.

"GIANT IMPERIAL MIXED" is a popular color blend. Some keen Pennsylvania gardeners like to save their own seed of the blue and the black varieties, since these are especially appealing colors that are rarely offered separately by seed companies.

Direct-sow seed several weeks before the last frost date in spring, or start seed indoors 4 weeks before outdoor planting.

Verbena
(Verbena x hybrida)

Half-hardy annual. Grows 6 to 12 inches high, blooms from midsummer to autumn in a wide range of colors, including white, lavender-blue, red, pink and salmon, some with contrasting "eyes." Flowers resemble primulas, arranged in tight clusters on tough, spreading plants which form a dense mass withstanding heat and poor soil. Best in sun.

Verbena is useful for edging, as a ground cover, and in the rock garden. Although mixtures such as "IDEAL FLORIST" are popular, some individual colors have won All-America awards: "AMETHYST" for its lovely lavender-blue flowers and "BLAZE" for its dazzling bright scarlet color.

Direct-sow seed after danger of frost, or start indoors 6 weeks before outdoor planting.

Vinca, Madagascar Periwinkle
(Catharanthus roseus)

Tender annual, 4 to 15 inches tall, blooming midsummer to autumn. Best in sun, but thrives in light shade. Flowers are white, shades of rose, and pink, some with a contrasting "eye." Leaves are dark glossy green, stems fleshy. Some varieties grow upright, but the most popular ones are spreaders.

Good for edging, massing as a ground cover, and in containers as well. The "PRETTY" series (white, pink, and rose) are All-America Winners with to 1 1/2-inch blooms on 10-inch-high plants. Another All-America Winner—"VINCA PARASOL"—has fine white flowers with a red eye, which creates an appealing "peppermint" effect most gardeners seem to prefer in vincas. This variety also has the largest flower size in vincas—up to 2 inches across.

Start seeds indoors 6 to 8 weeks before outdoor planting, or purchase young plants from garden centers as the seed is tiny and germination can be erratic.

Zinnia
(*Zinnia elegans*)

Tender annual, up to 3 1/2 feet tall, blooming from midsummer to autumn frost. Brightly colored flowers in single- and double-flowered types. Color range includes white, yellow, orange, pink, red, purple, and green, plus bicolors. Best in full sun.

The dwarf types—such as the "DASHER" hybrids—are excellent for massing in low beds and borders, and also for edging. Taller kinds— such as the "BORDER BEAUTY" hybrids— have large flowers resembling a dahlia on tall stems excellent for cutting. The largest-flowered of any zinnia are the "ZENITH" hybrids, with individual blooms up to 6 inches across and quilled, ruffled petals referred to as "cactus flowers." Next in popularity among the giants are dahlia-flowered types, with wide, flat petals forming a rounded flower head up to 5 inches across. Giant tetraploid varieties, of which "STATE FAIR MIXTURE" is a good example, have even larger blooms than the dahlia-flowered type. They also are more disease-resistant.

A serious disease problem in Pennsylvania is mildew, which starts off as a powdery white coating on the leaves, soon turning the entire plant brown and brittle. The most mildew-resistant zinnias are the "RUFFLES" series, a cutting type that flowers within 5 weeks from seed. Also highly mildew-resistant is the "PINWHEEL" series of single-flowered zinnias. The flowers resemble daisies, and are excellent for cutting and for garden display. This and most of the other zinnia varieties mentioned here were developed by a Doylestown, Pennsylvania, resident—Ms. Jeannette Lowe—while employed as a plant breeder by Burpee Seeds.

Zinnias are easy and dependable when grown from seed sown directly in the garden. They are sensitive to transplanting unless the transplants are young, stocky, and planted with minimum root disturbance.

General Characteristics of Selected Annuals

Name	Annual	Biennial	Sun	Partial Shade	Shade	Spring	Summer	Fall	Cut Flowers	Tall Backgrounds	Bedding & Borders	Edging	Rock Gardens	Climbers	Pots & Containers	Easy to Grow
			Shade			Bloom Time			Uses							
African Daisy	•		•				•	•	•							
Ageratum	•		•	•			•	•			•	•	•		•	
Alyssum	•		•	•			•	•			•	•	•		•	•
Amaranthus	•		•				•		•	•						•
Asters	•		•	•			•	•	•		•	•			•	•
Balsam	•		•				•	•	•						•	
Begonia, Fibrous	•			•			•	•			•	•	•		•	
Begonia, Tuberous	•			•			•	•	•						•	
Bells of Ireland	•			•	•		•		•		•					
Browallia	•			•			•		•						•	
Calendula	•		•			•	•	•	•						•	•
California Poppy	•		•			•	•	•	•				•			•
Candytuft	•		•			•	•	•	•		•	•				•
Canterbury Bells	•	•	•	•		•	•					•	•			
Cardinal Climber	•		•				•	•						•		
Carnation	•	•	•			•	•	•	•						•	
Celosia	•		•				•	•	•						•	•
Chrysanthemum	•		•	•			•	•	•		•	•			•	•
Cleome	•		•				•	•	•	•						•
Cornflower	•		•				•	•	•							•
Cosmos	•		•				•	•	•							•
Dahlia	•		•				•	•	•	•	•					
Dianthus	•		•				•	•			•	•			•	
Dusty Miller	•		•				•				•	•	•		•	
Euphorbia	•		•	•			•	•	•							
Forget-Me-Not	•	•	•	•		•			•		•	•	•			
Four O'Clock	•		•				•	•	•						•	
Foxglove		•	•	•			•		•	•						
Gaillardia	•		•				•	•	•							•
Gazania	•		•				•	•			•	•	•			
Geranium	•		•	•			•				•				•	•
Gloriosa Daisy	•		•				•	•	•							•
Gypsophila	•		•			•	•		•				•			•

	Annual	Biennial	Sun	Partial Shade	Shade	Spring	Summer	Fall	Cut Flowers	Tall Backgrounds	Bedding & Borders	Edging	Rock Gardens	Climbers	Pots & Containers	Easy to Grow
Shade / Bloom Time / Uses																
Heliotrope	•		•	•			•	•		•					•	
Hollyhock	•		•				•		•	•						•
Honesty		•	•				•		•		•					•
Impatiens	•			•	•	•	•	•		•	•				•	•
Job's Tears	•		•				•		•							•
Kochia	•		•				•		•	•						•
Larkspur	•		•			•			•	•						•
Lobelia	•		•	•		•	•	•		•	•	•	•			
Marigold	•		•				•	•	•	•	•	•	•		•	•
Moonflower	•		•				•	•						•		
Morning Glory	•		•				•	•						•		
Nicotiana	•		•				•		•		•	•	•	•	•	•
Nasturtium	•		•	•			•	•		•	•					•
Pansy	•	•		•		•	•			•	•	•	•	•		•
Petunia	•		•				•	•		•	•	•			•	•
Phlox	•		•				•	•	•	•	•					•
Portulaca	•		•				•	•		•	•	•			•	•
Salvia	•		•				•	•		•	•				•	•
Scabiosa	•		•				•	•	•	•						•
Snapdragon	•		•	•			•	•	•	•	•	•			•	
Statice	•		•				•		•		•					
Stock	•		•			•	•		•		•					•
Sunflower	•		•				•	•	•	•	•					•
Sweet Pea	•		•			•		•		•	•	•			•	•
Sweet William		•	•				•		•		•	•				•
Thunbergia	•		•				•							•	•	•
Venidium	•		•				•	•	•		•					
Verbena	•		•				•	•	•		•	•			•	
Vinca	•		•	•			•	•			•	•				•
Viola	•	•		•			•	•			•	•	•			
Xeranthemum	•		•				•		•							•
Zinnia	•		•				•	•	•	•	•	•	•			•

MODEL CUTTING GARDEN FOR ANNUALS

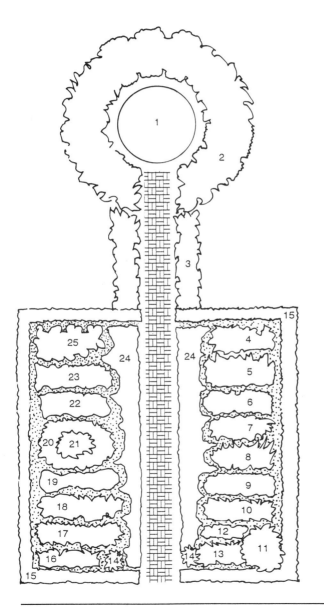

The Cedaridge Farm Cutting Garden, depicted here, was winner of the 1991 Homestyle Garden Design Contest for a successful interpretation of an Impressionist garden and received an award from the Pennsylvania Horticultural Society for Best Flower Garden in their 1993 Garden Contest. Here it is seen in midsummer.

1-Gazebo
2-Shade garden
3-Tuberous Begonia "Nonstop"
4-Cosmos "Sensation"
5-Antirrhinum majus
6-Centaurea cyanus
7-Calendula officinalis
   "Pacific Mixed"
8-Salvia farinacea "Victoria"
9-Consolida ambigua
   "Imperial Blue"
10-Papaver rhoeas
11-Syringa vulgaris
12-Pompon Dahlias
13-Gladiolus
14-Datura (in pots)
15-Box hedging
16-Heliotrope "Marine"
17-Scabiosa atropurpurea
18-Gomphrena globosa
19-Coreopsis tinctoria
20-Gypsophila elegans
21-Callistephus
22-Celosia "Apricot Beauty"
23-Zinnia "Cherry Ruffles"
24-Tagetes patula
25-Helianthus annuus

COURTYARD GARDEN

FEATURING ANNUALS IN A FORMAL DESIGN

Based on a design at the Pennsylvania Horticultural Society Headquarters

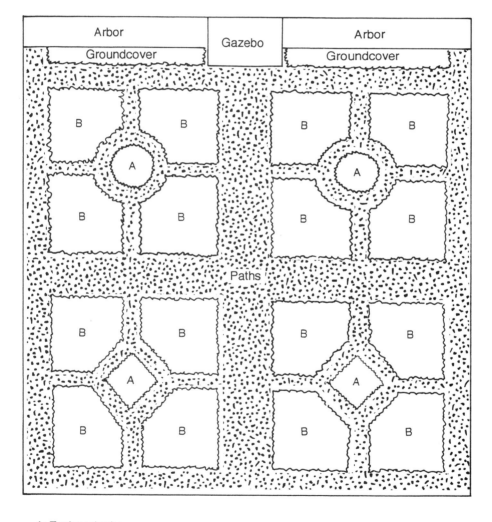

A: Topiary shrubs

B: Annuals in summer; tulips in spring; chrysanthemums in fall; flowering kale in winter

FORMAL GARDEN

FEATURING ANNUALS

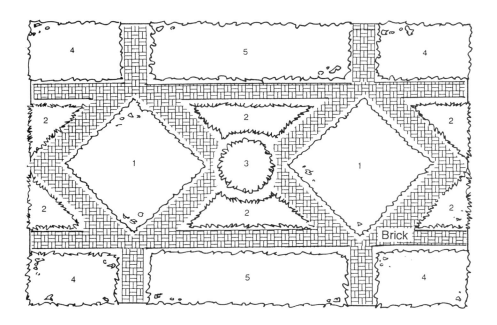

1-Marigold "Discovery Yellow"
2-French Marigold "Queen Sophia"
3-Scarlet Sage
4-Salvia farinacea "Victoria"
5-Petunia "Pearls Mixed Colors"

CHAPTER 4

Perennials

Pennsylvania's cold winters and warm summers are perfect for growing a wide range of flowering perennials, particularly the "Top Ten" selection based on state-wide sales—daylilies, bearded iris, Siberian iris, Oriental poppies, hostas, New England asters, Shasta daisies, summer phlox, peonies, and rudbeckia. Ferns and ornamental grasses—grown mostly for foliage effect—are also highly popular. Indeed, Pennsylvania is such a good state for growing perennials that many specialist perennial nurseries have sprung up, some supplying a local market through local sales; others supplying a national market through mail-order sales.

Perennials are characterized as plants that live indefinitely from year to year, growing a healthy crown of foliage the first year and flowering the second and succeeding years. This sounds like they are totally carefree, but they do need some common-sense care and maintenance, such as staking tall kinds to avoid wind damage, fertilizing to maintain healthy vigor, and weeding to stop aggressive weeds from suffocating their roots. Also, most perennials are attractive to deer, and many have succulent roots that are relished by mice and shrews.

Some plants classified as perennials are "biennials," forming leaves the first year, flowering the second, and dying out soon after flowering. Sweet William, money plant, and foxgloves are representative of this group. To complicate things even more, plant breeders have been able to make some herbaceous perennials behave like annuals. For example, they have coaxed the black-eyed Susan (*Rudbeckia hirta*) and the swamp mallow (*Hibiscus moscheutos*) to flower the first year from seed, giving birth to a new classification—the *Per-Annual* (a perennial that blooms the first year like an annual).

Normally, the most successful perennial plantings are combined with annuals, since few perennials maintain color for more than 2 or 3 weeks, while certain annuals will bloom throughout the summer, providing continuous color while the perennials come in and out of bloom. After the third season many perennials will need dividing to keep them within bounds. But this is not an unpleasant chore. In fact, few activities in the world of gardening can match the excitement and sense of satisfaction experienced when you dig up a clump of healthy perennials, such as Siberian iris or Shasta daisies, and divide them, using a hand fork, into smaller divisions. It's an easy, inexpensive way to obtain plenty of perennial plants to create masses of color in your garden. For best results—particularly if you are interested in developing a small cottage industry supplying perennial plants locally—construct an inexpensive "hoop house"—an unheated plastic tunnel that shelters young plants from severe temperature drops, and ensures a high success rate from dividing perennials.

In good soil, many perennials have a tendency to grow tall. Stems of summer phlox, beebalm, and Shasta daisies, for example, can be damaged in high winds unless they are staked (which is a chore), or unless you choose special "dwarf" varieties

Perennial Planting Chart

Name	Sun, Shade	Bloom Time	Color Range	Space Plants	Average Height
Achillea	○	June-July	White, red	1-1.5' apart	18-24"
Alyssum (Basket of Gold)	○	April-May	Yellow	1-2' apart	12"
Anthemis	○	June-August	Yellow	1.5' apart	24"
Aster (Michaelmas Daisy)	○	May-June	Many colors	1.5' apart	8-24"
Astilbe	○◐	June-July	White, pink, red	1' apart	12"
Aubrieta	◐	April-May	Pink to purple	6-12" apart	6"
Bleeding Heart	○◐	May-June	Pink, red	1-1.5' apart	24"
Campanula (C. carpatica)	○◐	July-September	Blue	1' apart	10"
Candytuft	○	May-June	White	1' apart	10-12"
Carpet Bugle (Ajuga)	○◐●	May-June	Blue, purple flowers; green or bronze foliage	8-10" apart	4-8"
Cerastium (Snow in Summer)	○	July-August	White	1' apart	6"
Chinese Lanterns	○	October-November	Bright orange	1.5-2' apart	12-24"
Chrysanthemum	○	Summer-frost	Many colors	2-3' apart	8-36"
Columbine (Aquilegia)	○◐	June-July	Many colors and bicolors	1.5' apart	18-30"
Coneflower, Purple (Echinacea purpurea)	○	July-October	Reddish-purple	1.5-2' apart	36"
Coral Bells	◐	June-September	Red, pink	1-1.5' apart	12-18"
Coreopsis	○	May-frost	Yellow	1.5' apart	24"
Daisy, Gloriosa	○	July-August	Yellow, mahogany	1-2' apart	18-36"
Daisy, Painted	○◐	May-June	White, pink, red	1.5' apart	24"
Daisy, Shasta	○◐	June-August	White	1.5' apart	12-42"
Daylily	○◐	June-August	Many colors	2' apart	26-38"
Delphinium	○◐	June-July	Many colors	1.5-3' apart	27-60"
Dianthus (Pinks)	○	May-June	White, pink, red	6-12" apart	8-18"
Ferns	◐●		Green foliage	1-3' apart	12-48"
Festuca (F. ovina glauca)	○◐		Silvery blue foliage	1' apart	10"
Gaillardia	○	June-September	Yellow, red and bicolors	1-1.5' apart	12-30"
Geranium, Wild (G. sanguineum, Cranesbill)	○◐	May-August	Rose-red, pink	1-1.5' apart	18"
Gerbera	○◐	June-July	Many colors	1-1.5' apart	12-24"
Geum	○	June-September	Red, yellow	1' apart	20"
Gypsophila	○	June-July	White, pink	2-3' apart	18-36"
Helianthemum	○	May-June	White, yellow, pink, rose	1' apart	12"
Heliopsis	○	August-September	Yellow	2-3' apart	24-36"
Hibiscus	○	August-September	White, pink, rose, red	2-3' apart	36-72"

P e r e n n i a l   P l a n t i n g   C h a r t

Name	Sun, Shade	Bloom Time	Color Range	Space Plants	Average Height
Hollyhock	○	July-August	Yellow, white, red, pink	1.5-2' apart	60"
Hosta	○◐●	July	Flowers lavender, white; foliage shades of green and blue-green	1-1.5' apart	18"
Iris, Bearded (I. germanica)	○	May-June	Many colors	1-1.5' apart	36"
Lathyrus (Perennial Sweet Pea)	○	June-September	Pink, red	1.5' apart	60"
Lavender	○	July-August	Lavender-blue flowers; gray-green foliage	1-1.5' apart	12-24"
Leadwort	○◐	August-frost	Deep blue flowers; dark foliage	8-10" apart	10-12"
Lily, Hardy Garden	○◐	June-August	Many colors	6-8" apart	24-72"
Lupine	◐	May-June	Many colors and bicolors	1.5-2.5' apart	24-36"
Lychnis (Maltese Cross)	○	June-July	Scarlet	1.5' apart	36"
Nepeta (Catmint)	○◐●	May-September	Lavender-blue	1.5-2' apart	12"
Penstemon (Bearded Tongue)	○	June-July	Red, pink and blue shades	1-1.5' apart	18-24"
Peony	○	May-June	White, pink, crimson, red, other shades	3' apart	36"
Phlox, Creeping (Mountain Pinks)	○◐	April-May	Red, white, pink, violet	1' apart	4-6"
Phlox, Hardy Garden	○◐	June-September	Red, white, pink, violet	1.5-2' apart	24-30"
Poppy, Iceland	○	June	Many colors	1-1.5' apart	15-16"
Poppy, Oriental	○	May-June	White, pink and red shades	1.5' apart	36"
Primula	◐●	May	Many colors and bicolors	1' apart	6-8"
Rudbeckia	○	July-August	Golden yellow	1.5' apart	18"
Salvia Superba	○◐	June-August	Violet-purple	1.5-2' apart	24-36"
Sedum	○	Varies	Yellow, red, pink flowers; attractive foliage	6-12" apart	2-9"
Statice (Caspia, Dumosa, Latifolia)	○	August-September	White, lavender	6-12" apart	12-36"
Tritoma	○	July-August	Red/yellow	1.5' apart	36-48"
Veronica (Speedwell)	○	June-August	Red, pink, blue	1-1.5' apart	15-30"
Viola tricolor	◐	June-frost	Purple/lavender/yellow	6-12" apart	6-12"
Yarrow, Fern Leaf	○	July-September	Golden yellow	2.5-3.5' apart	36-48"
Yucca	○	July	Creamy white	3' apart	60-72"

that keep a low, mounded growth habit. There are dwarf kinds of Oriental poppies ("ALLEGRO"), dwarf Shasta daisies ("MISS MUFFET"), and a semi-dwarf obedient plant ("VIVID"), for example. These compact plants are especially important for small-space gardens.

Pennsylvania abounds with many good places to observe perennials, which generally are classified as early, mid-season, and late-blooming. Longwood Gardens, in Chester County, features perennials through all seasons; Conestoga House, in Lancaster, has some particularly good late perennial borders featuring boltonias, Japanese anemones, "AUTUMN JOY" sedum, and New England asters. The rock garden at Longwood is particularly rich in early perennials, such as creeping phlox, blue bugle, forget-me-nots, and candytuft.

DESIGNING WITH PERENNIALS

At Doe Run Farm, near Unionville, Pennsylvania, Sir John Thouron, a native of Scotland, has created a magnificent perennial garden featuring many ways to display perennials. A tour of the farm usually begins at the formal border—parallel rectangular beds divided by a broad flagstone path, each border backed by a dense, evergreen hemlock hedge. The straight path leads from a parking lot to the front entrance of the house. In the formal borders perennials are grouped informally in "drifts" or masses of all one color, with tall plants at the back of the border and short plants as an edging, their billowing shapes spilling over onto the path.

From the formal border a path leads to the informal border and island beds that edge a broad sweep of lawn. The informal border is a free-form shape, its edges curving in and out, creating a broad planting area at the top and a narrow curling sweep at the bottom. Perennials are planted within the border in groups of all one color, the planting scheme orchestrated so peak color occurs in early summer, but something is always coming into bloom, from March (with Christmas and Lenten roses) to October (with chrysanthemums).

The island beds are mostly kidney-shaped or oval, and are surrounded by lawn. Tall plants are positioned in the middle, shorter ones around the edges, so a pleasing visual effect is seen no matter from what direction the bed is approached.

Behind the informal border is a meadow garden, where the preponderance of color is produced from flowering annuals, such as Shirley poppies and blue cornflowers. The meadow is ploughed and seeded each year to maintain the density of color, with seed saved from the seed pods. In other Pennsylvania meadow gardens, however, perennial varieties are mixed in among annuals, particularly perennial white Shasta daisies, yellow coreopsis and helianthus, orange butterfly weed, red gaillardia, and tawny daylilies.

At the back of Doe Run house are two dry gardens—one is a flight of stone steps with stone terraces containing beds where dwarf drought-tolerant perennials flower in clumps. This dry garden is especially beautiful in spring when yellow perennial alyssum, white candytuft, yellow dwarf bearded iris, pink thrift and alpine columbines bloom.

Beyond the stone steps is an informal rock garden featuring a stream that tumbles downhill in a series of waterfalls and pools. Along the edges of the stream, among boulders and rock ledges, is a vast assortment of mostly ground-hugging and cushion-shaped perennials (particularly veronica and helianthemum), plus some moisture-loving perennials (such as astilbe and bergenias) planted close to the water in moist soil. A different type of dry rock garden can be seen at Longwood Gardens (Kennett Square, Pennsylvania) where an entire hillside is formed by rock ledges and flagstone planted extensively with dwarf conifers, dwarf rhododendrons and perennials in broad sweeps of color, especially *Phlox subulata* (creeping phlox), *Arabis* (rock cress), *Sedum acre* (gold carpet sedum) and *Ajuga reptans* (bugle weed). An outstanding example of a dry wall borders the rose garden on two sides at the Morris Arboretum, Chestnut Hill. Planted into crevices, the wall is most colorful in early spring when white perennial candytuft (*Iberis sempervirens*), blue Dalmatian bellflower (*Campanula portenschlagiana*) and yellow perennial alyssum (*Aurinia saxatilis*) spill down the walls in billowing clouds, contrasting with feathery clumps of ferns and mantles of Kenilworth ivy.

The lower reaches of the rock garden at Doe Run turn into a bog garden, where more moisture-loving plants thrive, especially Siberian iris, rose mallow and Joe-pye weed. The Pennsylvania Horticultural Society frequently arranges tours of Doe Run Farm for its membership.

Some of the finest bog gardens can be found at Winterthur, just south of the Pennsylvania state line, in Delaware. The most successful perennials used there are yellow flag irises (*Iris pseudacorus*), Siberian irises (*Iris sibirica*), Japanese iris (*Iris kaempferi*) and candelabra primulas (*Primula japonica*). The mass planting of *Primula japonica* in the Quarry Garden is especially beautiful in early May. At one time an even more impressive planting occupied parts of Clenny Run, a stream that meanders through the property, but following the death of Henry duPont, founder of the garden, the staff were unable to keep up with the task of keeping the boggy soil free of weeds, and so these lavish plantings gradually petered out.

Temple University's horticulture department, at the Ambler campus, maintains a well-designed perennial garden in two pairs of parallel borders, separated by a wide lawn walk and backed by hedges of hemlock. It is full of good ideas.

When looking for perennial planting ideas in books, take care to determine ahead of time whether the book is by a reputable American author or by a British author. Books by Pamela Harper and Frederick McGourty, for example, tend to be good references. Too many books of British origin favor many plants that cannot tolerate the extremes of hot summers and cold winters experienced in Pennsylvania. For example, the blue poppy (*Mecanopsis grandis*) burns up in the heat, while pampas plum (*Cortaderia sellouana*) succumbs to the cold. Conversely, they tend to overlook heat-tolerant plants such as butterfly weed (*Asclepias tuberosa*) and hardy hibiscus (*Hibiscus moscheutos*), both of which perform poorly in Britain's cool climate, but which should be in *every* Pennsylvania perennial garden.

OBTAINING PERENNIAL PLANTS

Though the majority of ornamental perennials are easy to raise from seed, the practice of seed starting is not nearly so popular as buying ready-grown plants from a specialist perennial nursery. Most perennials grown from seed take two seasons to bloom (sometimes more) and the results may be inferior to the parent plant since many good, cultivated perennials are the result of hybridizing or special selections. In these cases

FORMAL PARTERRE GARDEN
OF PERENNIALS

This design also works well planted exclusively with
roses, flowering bulbs, or annuals.

1-Achillea "Moonbeam"
2-Alchemilla vulgaris
3-Anthemis tinctoria
4-Lavandula angustifolia
5-Astilbe x arendsii
6-Dicentra spectabilis
7-Hosta "Honey Bells"
8-Aster nova-angliae "Harrington's Pink"
9-Aquilegia vulgaris
10-Chrysanthemum maximum
11-Gaillardia grandiflora
12-Heliopsis helianthoides
13-Heuchera sanguinea

14-Lilium Asiatic hybrids
15-Centranthus ruber
16-Aster x frikartii "Monch"
17-Iris germanica
18-Miscanthus sinensis "Zebrinus"
19-Campanula glomerata
20-Monarda didyma
21-Doronicum caudatum
22-Hemerocallis "Stella d'Oro"
23-Sweet Violets
24-Ajuga reptans
25-Dianthus deltoides
26-Armeria maritima

DOUBLE PERENNIAL BORDER

Based on designs at Doe Run Farm and Meadowbrook Farm

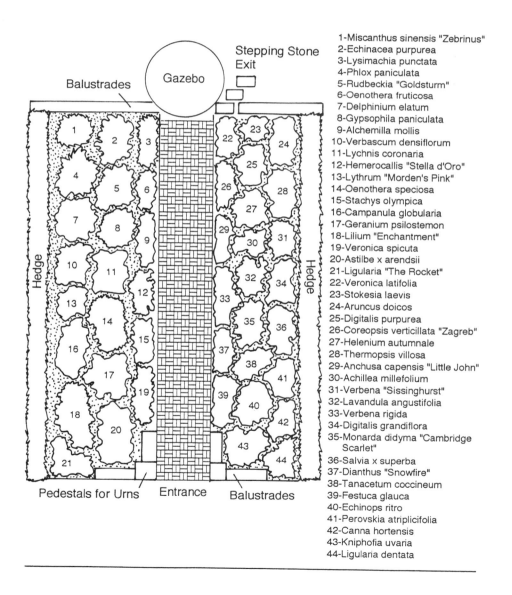

1-Miscanthus sinensis "Zebrinus"
2-Echinacea purpurea
3-Lysimachia punctata
4-Phlox paniculata
5-Rudbeckia "Goldsturm"
6-Oenothera fruticosa
7-Delphinium elatum
8-Gypsophila paniculata
9-Alchemilla mollis
10-Verbascum densiflorum
11-Lychnis coronaria
12-Hemerocallis "Stella d'Oro"
13-Lythrum "Morden's Pink"
14-Oenothera speciosa
15-Stachys olympica
16-Campanula globularia
17-Geranium psilostemon
18-Lilium "Enchantment"
19-Veronica spicuta
20-Astilbe x arendsii
21-Ligularia "The Rocket"
22-Veronica latifolia
23-Stokesia laevis
24-Aruncus doicos
25-Digitalis purpurea
26-Coreopsis verticillata "Zagreb"
27-Helenium autumnale
28-Thermopsis villosa
29-Anchusa capensis "Little John"
30-Achillea millefolium
31-Verbena "Sissinghurst"
32-Lavandula angustifolia
33-Verbena rigida
34-Digitalis grandiflora
35-Monarda didyma "Cambridge Scarlet"
36-Salvia x superba
37-Dianthus "Snowfire"
38-Tanacetum coccineum
39-Festuca glauca
40-Echinops ritro
41-Perovskia atriplicifolia
42-Canna hortensis
43-Kniphofia uvaria
44-Ligularia dentata

the progeny is kept pure by cuttings, root division, meristem culture or other asexual (non-seed) methods of reproduction. Nevertheless, many mail-order seedsmen do offer seed of popular perennial varieties and it is possible to raise hundreds of plants at a cost of pennies per plant.

One way to grow perennials from seed is to start them indoors by the two-step method of using seed trays to first gain germination of as many seeds as possible, then transferring them to individual pots when large enough to handle. This system is described in more detail on page 29 in the Annuals section.

Another way to grow lots of perennials from seed is to make a special seed bed in a lightly shaded area of the garden. The seed bed should be raised slightly above the surrounding soil surface to ensure good drainage, and it should have a level, crumbly, weed-free surface into which seeds can be sown, in shallow furrows, and lightly covered over—just sufficient to anchor the seeds. A shaded site will not only prevent the young seedling from suffering sunburn, but also help retain soil moisture, since seed beds must never be allowed to dry out.

A good time to start many perennials from seed is mid-spring to midsummer. This allows the plants to grow sufficiently large to withstand winter freezes and to be moved to their permanent flowering positions in early spring. Alternatively, they can be transferred to individual pots in autumn, held over winter in a cold frame, and sold as pot plants in spring.

BUYING PERENNIAL PLANTS

Perennial plants can be purchased by mail from specialist perennial plant growers or locally from a nursery or garden center. When you buy plants through the mail you generally receive a smaller plant than you might purchase locally, and sometimes the plant will be "bare-root" rather than potted, but the selection will be much wider from the mail-order specialist. Indeed, many perennial plant growers will ship dormant roots that first need to be potted or grown in protected areas before being set into permanent positions.

Pennsylvania has many "cottage industry" perennial plant growers. Some deal in a wide assortment of a particular plant group, such as daylilies, iris, peonies or ornamental grasses (see Appendix). Normally, these perennial plant specialists will offer perennial plants in half-gallon or gallon containers, ready to flower, and sometimes will allow you to dig clumps in full bloom directly from the field so you can pick exactly the color combinations you desire.

In addition to spring, autumn is a good time to plant many perennials. Cool conditions and reliable rainfall help newly planted perennials establish strong root systems and healthy clumps by the following spring.

Root division is one of the easiest ways to propagate perennials. With each successive year perennial plants grow thicker clumps. These well-established clumps can be dug up with a spade or garden fork and divided into smaller pieces. Oriental poppies, Shasta daisies, Siberian iris and peonies are all examples of popular perennials that can be easily divided, in spring or fall, and which will quickly form healthy clumps if watered regularly. Plants grown by root division can be arranged in straight rows in a special holding area ("nursery bed") or transferred directly into the garden.

WATER GARDEN

FEATURING PERENNIALS

This design can also be planted
with a combination of perennials and annuals.

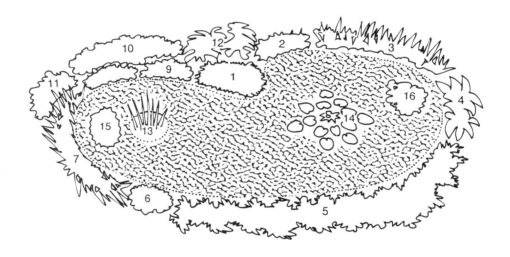

1-Lobelia cardinalis
2-Lythrum "Morden's Pink"
3-Iris sibirica
4-Hostas
5-Astilbe x arendsii (mixed colors)
6-Hibiscus moscheutos
7-Iris pseudacorus
8-Primula japonica

9-Miscanthus sinensis "Zebinus"
10-Exbury Azaleas
11-Lilium lanceolatum
12-Rhododendron "Nova Zembla"
13-Cat-tails in submerged pot
14-Water Lily in submerged pot
15-Water Canna in submerged pot
16-Hardy Lotus in submerged pot

Normally root cuttings demand a protected environment under glass to be successful. Carnations and chrysanthemums are examples of popular perennials which are easily propagated by taking a 5-inch-long section of stem, removing the lower leaves, dipping the cut end in a rooting hormone and inserting the cutting into a peat-based potting soil such as a peat-and-perlite mix. Usually, a seed flat is used to start a large batch of cuttings at one time, or a clay pot can be used to start a smaller batch. The cuttings need to be kept out of direct sunlight, watered regularly so the soil does not dry out, and once a root system has been established they should be transferred to individual pots to reach transplant size. Alternatively, they can be planted in temporary nursery beds to "size up" before planting out into their flowering positions.

Watering. Newly planted perennials need to be watered regularly. Some moisture-loving perennials such as candelabra primulas and flag iris demand constantly wet feet and certain Alpine plants—such as perennial alyssum—demand excellent drainage, but most perennials like a loam soil that drains well, and need to be watered deeply during dry periods and mulched to maintain a cool temperature.

Fertilizing. Most perennials prefer high phosphorus, granular, or liquid fertilizers applied to the upper soil surface each spring. Though they can be heavy feeders, if the original planting site is properly prepared (with plenty of organic matter worked in and at least 12 inches of fine, crumbly loam soil), only light applications of fertilizer are needed in subsequent years.

Mulching. A layer of organic material over the soil surface—especially something decorative like wood chips, pine bark, or pine needles—is highly beneficial in many ways. It helps keep the soil cool during hot spells, deters weeds, and conserves soil moisture. In winter, newly planted perennials especially will benefit from a light layer of mulch covering the crowns—particularly shredded leaves or pine needles which will not introduce weed seeds into the soil.

Apply mulches for winter protection after the first killing frost and after pruning away browned stems to within 4 inches of the soil surface, unless the plants have interesting seed heads or foliage color that can add winter interest, such as ornamental grasses and the dried flower heads of *Sedum spectabile.*

PERENNIALS FOR STUNNING BORDERS

The following listing features the most useful and readily available kinds of perennials for Pennsylvania. Recommendations for each type of propagation are given, as well as information about whether the perennial has a particularly desirable variety or strain.

Some biennials are included in the list, and these are identified.

Acanthus, Bear's Breech
(Acanthus spinosus)

Hardy perennial, marginally hardy for southeastern Pennsylvania in a sheltered location. Valued for its glossy, dark green, thistle-like leaves and tall, pale blue flower spikes composed of tubular flowers. Plants grow to 4 feet high and are more dependable in Pennsylvania than *Acanthus mollis* which has broader, larger, more interesting leaves. Good for growing in terracotta urns and as tall background accents in mixed perennial borders.

Achillea, Yarrow
(Achillea fillipendulina)

Hardy perennial, 2 feet high, blooming from June to September, producing flat panicles of tight yellow flower clusters, the panicles measuring up to 4 inches across. Makes a good display flower for a sunny perennial border. Also good as a long-lasting cut flower.

New annual kinds are easily grown from seed. Plants of named varieties— such as ''GOLD PLATE''—are also readily available from nurseries and by propagation from cuttings or root division in spring or fall.

When plants have ceased flowering, cut the stems back. Since well-established plants grow vigorously, it is best to lift roots, divide, and replant every third year, spacing 36 inches apart.

Other good species and varieties are ''FIRE KING'' (*Achillea millefolium*), a rosy red with cream centers, and ''THE PEARL'' (*Achillea ptarmica*), growing clusters of small, white, pompom-like flowers. All are best used sparingly as an accent in borders.

A sensational recent introduction in achilleas is a series of hybrid mixtures resulting from crosses with *Achillea taygetea,* native to Greece. ''SUMMER PASTELS'' won an All-America Award because it will bloom the first year from seed started 6 weeks before outdoor planting. Colors include not only the common yellow and rosy-red, but also white, purple, orange, crimson, and pink. Plants rebloom after cutting, and will flower from year to year.

Alyssum, Yellow
(Aurinia saxatile)

Hardy perennial, 9 to 12 inches high, creating a dense mound of golden-yellow flowers in early spring. Excellent for rock gardens and crevices in dry-walls and as an edging to borders of spring-flowering bulbs. Thrives in a sunny location, even in dry soil, but does best in slightly sandy soil.

Easily grown from seed direct-sown in spring or summer. This is the most valuable rock garden plant for Pennsylvania gardens, since no other rock garden subject can match it for sheer brilliance. Combines especially well with red tulips, blue forget-me-nots, pink creeping phlox, and white candytuft.

Anchusa, Italian Bugloss
(Anchusa italica)

Upright, branching plants grow 4 to 5 feet tall, producing long flower stems covered with hundreds of 3/4-inch blue flowers resembling large forget-me-nots, in late spring and early summer. Useful in perennial borders, especially as a background highlight, and as a cut flower.

Easily grown from seed direct-sown outdoors anytime from May to September in a sunny position. Space plants at least 24 inches apart. Seed germinates in 20 days, aided by chilling in a refrigerator for 7 days.

There is an attractive dwarf form, ''LITTLE JOHN,'' effective for edging. There are also annual forms of anchusa, but generally these prefer cooler conditions than Pennsylvania summers can provide.

Anemone, Japanese
(Anemone x hybrida)

There are many kinds of anemones, some hardy and others—such as *Anemone coronaria* (French anemones)—a little too tender for Pennsylvania. The Japanese anemone is a late-summer/early-fall flowering plant, producing masses of mostly white or pink flowers on tall stems to 4 feet. It is reliably hardy throughout Pennsylvania, increasing vigorously by root division. "WHIRL-WIND," a semi-double white, is particularly striking. A single-flowered, pink-flowering non-hybrid, "SEPTEMBER CHARM," is a good companion. Both tolerate light shade and prefer a humus-rich loam soil.

Also popular among the hardy anemones are *Anemone pulsatilla* (pasque-flower), producing large, purple flowers in early spring, and *Anemone blanda* (Grecian windflower). Grown from bulbs, it is a spectacular sight on lightly shaded slopes at Winterthur, Delaware, creating a carpet of starry, deep blue flowers with yellow centers.

Arabis, Rock Cress
(*Arabis alpina*)

Superb edging plant, 8 to 12 inches high, growing masses of tiny pink or white flowers in such profusion that they create a low, spreading plant excellent for rock gardens and crevices in dry walls. Reaches peak bloom in early spring, preferring a slightly shaded location.

Start plants from seed anytime from May to September, to flower the following season; or purchase nursery-grown plants, spacing 12 inches apart. Seeds germinate in 5 days.

Artemesia, Silver Mound
(*Artemesia schmidtiana*)

Averages 12 inches high and grows as a mound of silver-blue foliage suitable for borders and rock gardens. Although it does produce panicles of yellow and white flowers, its silky, finely divided foliage is the reason to grow it. An excellent edging plant, it creates a spectacular color harmony with most daylilies and ornamental grasses, and also the sedum "AUTUMN JOY."

"POWIS CASTLE"—a hybrid—is a valuable tall, billowing version of "SILVER MOUND," growing to 3 feet high, and exquisite when used as a background highlight close to white flowers, such as "ICEBERG" roses, and other silver-leafed perennials, such as lamb's ears and sage. Prefers a warm, sunny location. Best propagated by division.

Aster, Hardy
(*Aster* species)

Hardy perennials, 1 to 2 feet high, in white, pink and shades of blue, with golden-yellow centers. Valuable for rock gardens and massing in perennial borders, blooming in June through September, depending on variety. The compact, low-growing Alpine aster (*A. alpinus*) is spring-flowering and easily grown from seed direct-sown in spring in a sunny location.

Michaelmas daisies, a common name used to describe a number of fall-blooming perennial asters (mostly hybrids of *A. novae-anglae* and *A.belgii*), make a much bolder display. The daisy-like flowers almost smother the plants and provide a density of color few other plants can match at that time of year. Full sun and moist soil are their chief requirements, although they will tolerate a wide range of soil conditions. Variety "MONCH" (*A. x frikartii*) is a beautiful powder-blue blooming all summer; "ALMA POTSCKE" is a vivid pink flowering for up to 6 weeks, beginning in September.

Aster, Stokes
(*Stokesia laevis*)

Hardy perennial, 15 inches high, flowering from July to August with masses of blue flowers resembling giant cornflowers on plants with a spreading, bushy habit. There is a good white form, "ALBA." Excellent massed at the front of mixed perennial borders and as drifts in a rock garden.

Needs a sunny location and a well-drained, humus-rich soil. Propagate by root divisions or from seed direct-sown in summer for bloom the following summer. Combines well with coreopsis, dwarf goldenrods, evening primroses, and dwarf yellow daylilies.

Astilbe, Spirea
(Astilbe x arendsii)

Hardy perennial, 2 1/2 to 3 feet high, creating bushy clumps of elegant, feathery flower spikes in white, pink, and red during midsummer. Plants flower in sun or light shade, do best in fertile, humus-rich soil, especially if it contains leaf mold or well-decomposed animal manure. Popular for growing along the margins of streams and ponds. Combines well with ornamental grasses and makes a good cut flower. Propagate favorite varieties from root divisions after flowering.

Superb varieties for Pennsylvania gardens are "RHEINLAND" (deep pink), "PEACH BLOSSOM" (light pink), "DEUTSCHLAND" (white), and "FANAL" (dark red). Sensational when all four colors are massed.

Aubretia, False Rock Cress
(Aubretia deltoidea)

Hardy perennial, 6 inches high, used extensively in rock gardens and dry walls. Superb for edging beds and borders. A dwarf spreading plant, its cheerful purple flowers last from late April until late June.

Direct-sow outdoors anytime from spring to late August in light shade. Well-established plants can be divided in late summer and then planted 12 inches apart.

Baby's Breath
(Gypsophila paniculata)

Hardy perennial, 2 to 4 feet high, with billowing, airy sprays of double white and pink flowers, blooming for several weeks in early summer. The dainty flowers appear in such profusion that they create the appearance of mist when viewed from a distance. Thrives in a well-drained soil and full sun or partial shade. Sensational planted as a highlight in rock gardens and to spill over dry retaining walls. Valuable as a cut flower and for dried arrangements. "BRISTOL FAIRY"—a vigorous bushy white—grows to 4 feet in height. "PINK FAIRY" grows half as high.

Easily grown from seed direct-sown from spring to September. Propagation by division and cuttings is difficult.

Balloon Flower
(Platycodon grandiflorus)

Hardy perennial, 20 inches high, flowering from June until frost with lovely, bell-shaped blue, pink, or white flowers resembling giant harebells. Especially valued as a good blue accent ideal for the front of mixed flower borders. Needs full sun and a sandy or well-drained loam soil. Several plants each of the white and blue together create a beautiful color harmony, especially close to yellow coreopsis and yellow evening primrose. Plants make exquisite cut flowers.

There is an annual form, "SENTIMENTAL BLUE," which will bloom the first year from seed started indoors 10 weeks before outdoor planting. A modest floral display occurs the first season, followed by a much more extravagant display in successive years. Established plants can be divided in spring or fall. Mulch to protect plants over winter.

Bee Balm, Bergamot, Monarda
(Monarda didyma)

Hardy perennial, growing to 3 feet high, flowering in July and August, creating a dense cluster of tubular flowers that form a crown on long stems excellent for cutting. Colors include pink, red, white, orange, and burgundy. Thrives even in impoverished soil in sun or light shade. Use sparingly in the mixed perennial border. One plant makes a striking display.

Color selections—such as "CAMBRIDGE SCARLET" and "CROFTWAY'S PINK"—should be propagated by dividing established plants and replanting in spring or fall. Good near streams and at the edge of woods. The variety "MONARCH MIXED" is easily grown from seeds direct-sown in spring or summer.

Begonia, Hardy
(Begonia grandis)

Hardy perennial, surviving Pennsylvania winters in a sheltered location. Plants grow 2 to 3 feet high, creating a beautiful mound of handsome, heart-shaped, pointed leaves typical of "angel wing" begonias, and masses of nodding pink flowers from late August to fall frost. Plants are superb for shaded areas, especially planted along paths and next to ponds in humus-rich soil. Propagate by "offsets" that develop along the succulent stems and that fall to the ground when ready for rooting.

Bellflowers
(Campanula species)

Unfortunately, many bellflowers popular in European gardens are weak-flowering and short-lived in Pennsylvania. Two notable exceptions are *Campanula percisifolia* (willow-leaf bellflower), growing erect stalks studded with nodding cup-shaped blooms in white and blue (both tolerate light shade); and *C. glomerata* (globe bellflower), growing erect stems topped with clusters of upward-facing cup-shaped flowers that form a ball.

The globe bellflower makes a beautiful color harmony with yellow loosestrife (*Lysimachia punctata*). The willow-leaf bellflower makes a sensational cut flower and looks best when both the blue and the white are massed together in a generous clump. Both of these grow up to 3 feet high, and bear masses of violet-blue flowers in June. These generally produce a more satisfactory display in Pennsylvania than Canterbury bells (*C. media*), a biennial that can perform well only if raised under glass and bedded-out early in bud.

Black-eyed Susans
(Rudbeckia hirta)

Few other hardy perennials provide such a brilliant display of long-lasting color as rudbeckias. They tolerate fierce summer heat and poor soil and the bright golden-yellow, 4-inch, daisy-like flowers with black centers can be seen for miles. Though plants are easily raised from seeds direct-sown, the best perennial rudbeckia, "GOLDSTURM," is sterile and is usually propagated by division. (For annual forms of black-eyed Susans grown from seed to flower the first year, see gloriosa daisies under Annuals.)

Growing 3 feet high, rudbeckias produce their flowers in midsummer to early fall on long stems that are excellent for cutting. Massed in a mixed perennial border, they outshine everything else in the garden. They are also spectacular planted to form a "hedge" effect. Related to the wild black-eyed Susans found growing along waysides throughout Pennsylvania, these carefree plants are probably the most rewarding perennial grown in the home garden.

A glorious pink and yellow color harmony combines black-eyed Susans with purple coneflower (*Echinacea purpurea*), especially at the edge of a swimming pool, and along stream banks and pond margins.

Bleeding Heart, Old-fashioned
(Dicentra spectabilis)

Hardy perennial flowering in April and May. Bushy plants grow to 3 feet, and have blue-green, heavily indented leaves that give the plant an airy appearance. Beautiful arching flower stems are hung with heart-shaped pink or white flowers.

Plants tolerate light shade and make an interesting centerpiece to beds of tulips and pansies. A related species, *D. eximia*—native to the Pennsylvania woodlands—was used to produce a hybrid bleeding heart, "LUXURI-ANT." Though a little later-flowering, it has a much more compact habit than the old-fashioned bleeding heart, and its arching sprays of deep, reddish-pink flowers are produced nonstop from May until fall frost, especially planted in light shade. A fertile, humus-rich soil suits both types best.

Blue Bugle, Ajuga
(Ajuga reptans)

Hardy perennial, 6 inches high, useful as a fast-spreading ground cover in sun or shade. Tolerates a wide range of soil conditions, including poor, dry soil. Grows colorful rosettes of leaves in green or bronze with masses of deep blue flower spikes, studded with small tubular flowers in early spring.

Spreads by runners. Best planted in spring or fall from root divisions spaced 6 inches apart. Stays evergreen all year.

Butterfly Weed
(Asclepias tuberosa)

Hardy perennial, 2 to 3 feet high, native to Pennsylvania, forming clusters of mostly bright orange star-shaped flowers. These appear in July and August, attracting flocks of butterflies. The bushy plants prefer full sun and a sandy or well-drained soil. They are good to use as highlights in mixed perennial borders and as components in wildflower meadow mixtures.

Propagated mostly by seed (divisions are hardy to transplant), butterfly weed is good for cutting. Though the most popular color is bright orange, there are yellow, pink and red forms in the seed mixture called "GAY BUTTER-FLIES."

Candytuft
(Iberis sempervirens)

Hardy perennial, 10 inches high, with dark-green, needle-like, evergreen foliage. Plants flower in late May and early June in white, creating what seems like a mound of snow. Does well in dry places, such as rock gardens, and as an edging or ground cover in beds and borders. A popular companion to perennial alyssum. Annual varieties with pink and red in their color range are also available (see section on annuals). To grow the perennial kind, sow seeds in spring or fall in a lightly shaded location and transplant into a sunny spot. Shear faded flower stems to promote branching, low-spreading plants.

Cardinal Flower
(Lobelia cardinalis)

Hardy perennial native to Pennsylvania swamps and stream banks, plants grow 5-foot spires of dark red florets that are highly attractive to hummingbirds.

Flowering in August, they are best planted in bold groups as highlights in a perennial border, and along pond margins and stream banks. Plants are so tolerant of moist, boggy soil that their roots can be permanently immersed in running water. Propagated by seed and division.

There is also a blue-flowered species, *L. siphylitica*, that tends to be more compact (3 to 4 feet). It, too, is native to Pennsylvania swampy areas and makes an appealing pond accent.

Chinese Lanterns
(Physalis alkegengi)

Hardy perennial, 2 feet high, grown for its decorative orange-red, lantern-shaped seed pods, which mature in the fall of the second year. They are easily dried for long-lasting dried flower arrangements, and look sensational combined with the silvery dried seed pods of money plant. "GIGANTEA" is a special selection that produces the largest and deepest red coloration.

Plants thrive in a wide range of garden soils in a sunny location. The simplest method of propagation is to divide plants into rooted sections and replant in early spring. Also easily grown from seed direct-sown in spring or summer. Spreads aggressively and can become a nuisance unless confined to a special section of the garden away from main beds and borders.

Chrysanthemum, Cushion Mum
(Chrysanthemum x morifolium)

Hardy chrysanthemums are star performers for late summer and fall color. Nothing among flowering perennials will provide the color range equal to cushion mums from early September until hard frosts.

Sensational plantings of cushion mums can be seen each year at Ott's Greenhouses on Schwenksville Pike near Collegeville. Each year the owners plant a huge mound containing 10,000 plants in rainbow colors. Paths lead up to the top and across the summit to a gazebo, providing a spectacular view along all four sides of the miniature "mountain." The path descends through more dazzling flowers to a tunnel that leads back to the parking lot. Yellow is a particularly popular color in Ott's display, and the variety "YELLOW JACKET" covers itself in so many flowers that the foliage is completely hidden.

The official classification of outdoor mums is rather complex, but basically there are the *decoratives*, growing the largest flowers and some with bold incurving petals; *pompoms*, forming compact ball-shaped blooms; *spoons*, with curled petals; and *spiders*, having long, narrow petals.

Ott's chrysanthemums are grown from rooted cuttings, raised in fields, and transplanted in bud. However, it is possible to raise some varieties of cushion mums from seed. "AUTUMN GLORY" is a mixture of cushion mums developed in Japan, suitable for bedding. Plants are hardy enough to overwinter in Pennsylvania. Seed is started indoors in March and 8-week-old transplants are placed outdoors after frost-danger, for flowering in fall. If the lead shoots are kept pinched, plants cover themselves in 2 1/2-inch flowers in all the popular chrysanthemum colors, including red, pink, bronze, yellow, orange, purple, and white.

Cushion mums like a sunny position, fertile soil, and watering during dry spells. They are readily increased by root division made in spring or fall and by cuttings started in February or March.

To get a full cushion effect, it is most important to pinch off the lead shoot when the plants are 4 inches high. This will encourage side shoots and a fuller plant. Plants may need pinching back a total of three times during the growing season to keep them mound-shaped and compact enough to form a "cushion."

Not all cushion mums bought at garden centers are hardy enough to survive the winter. Yoder Bros., a leading Ohio breeder located just across the Pennsylvania border north of Pittsburgh, recommends their "ELITE" series for fall display and wintering over.

Columbine, Granny's Bonnets
(Aquilegia x hybrida)

These hardy perennials have one of the most endearing flower forms of all perennials. The vigorous, bushy plants can produce dozens of stems topped by graceful flowers made up of three distinct portions—a group of tubular petals at the middle, surrounded by five wide, flat petals, all ending in an elegant, long arching spur.

The largest-flowered variety of all is *"McKANA GIANTS,"* bred by an amateur gardener. They were the first perennial ever to win an All-America Award, and although entered by Burpee Seeds, they were the first All-America Winner ever to be bred as a new flower by an amateur. Growing 2 to 3 feet high, individual flowers measure up to 2 inches across, in a range of pastel colors including white, cream, yellow, pink, red, and blue, plus bicolors. The blue-green foliage is finely divided and creates a billowing, airy effect in the garden.

Plants tolerate light shade, and combine well with foxgloves and delphiniums in the perennial border. An outstanding blue hybrid variety, "HENSOL HAREBELL," was produced by crossing the wild American species, *A. alpina,* with the wild European species, *A. vulgaris.* Inheriting the best qualities of both parents—large flowers (up to 3 inches across) on strong, 3-foot

stems—it blooms continuously from late April until early July.

Most columbines are easily raised from seed ("McKANA GIANTS" need starting 6 to 8 weeks before outdoor planting), to flower the first season. *A. vulgaris* reseeds itself readily, creating large, colorful colonies; "HENSOL HAREBELL" requires propagating by division.

Individual stems of the tall varieties are long enough to be cut to make appealing flower arrangements.

Cone Flower, Purple
(Echinacea purpurea)

Hardy perennial, 3 feet tall, native to open meadows of Pennsylvania. Looks like a rudbeckia (black-eyed Susan), but with pink, purple, and white flowers. The daisy-like, 3-inch blooms have a conspicuous coppery or maroon dome in the middle, surrounded by swept-back petals. Drought-tolerant plants begin flowering in early July and continue until fall frost. Use them as accents in sunny, mixed borders, and mass along stream banks and pond margins. Sensational combined with yellow rudbeckias, blue Russian sage, and ornamental grasses for a "wild prairie" effect.

Two exceptional color selections, "BRIGHT STAR" (dark purple) and "WHITE SWAN," make excellent cut flowers, and tolerate partial shade.

Coral Bells
(Heuchera sanguinea)

Hardy perennial, growing 2 feet high, forming a neat mound of ruffled, leathery, heart-shaped leaves bearing long, slender flower spikes with dainty red, white, or pink flowers. Blooming in May and June, coral bells are good for rock gardens, wild gardens, and perennial borders in sun or light shade. The long flower stems make them useful as a cut flower. The pink makes a superb color harmony with blue perennial flax.

Plants prefer a humus-rich soil, and may need dividing every third year. Mixtures are easily grown from seed direct-sown in spring or fall for blooms the following season.

Coral bells have been crossed with the beautiful native Pennsylvania foam flower to create a new plant family called *Heucherella*. The best of these is "BRIDGET BLOOM," with beautiful coral-pink flowers on plants that are more compact than regular coral bells.

Coreopsis
(*Coreopsis grandiflora*)

Hardy perennial, 2 to 3 feet high, growing clear yellow single and double flowers from May until fall. Showy in the garden as a display plant and excellent for cutting, it likes a sunny location and will resist drought. Thrives on neglect, and doesn't mind crowding.

Plants are easily propagated from root divisions made in early spring or fall. There is one variety, an All-America Winner developed by Burpee, that will flower the first year from seed started early indoors 6 weeks before outdoor planting. Called "EARLY SUNRISE," it will start to flower within 11 weeks and continue nonstop until fall frost. These plants are excellent companions to perennial gaillardia.

Daisy, English
(*Bellis perennis*)

Hardy biennial, 6 inches high, used for edging beds and borders, also for mass plantings, especially in a rock garden and shallow dish planters. Plants flower best during cool weather of early spring and fall. Likes humus-rich, well-drained soil. The compact plants form tight ro-

settes of leaves, with double 1-inch flowers in white, crimson, and pink.

Easily grown from seed sown in late summer, held in cold frames over winter, and bedded-out in spring at the same time as pansies.

Daisy, Painted
(*Pyrethrum roseum*)

Hardy perennial, growing to 30 inches high, flowering throughout June with 3-inch, daisy-like flowers in white, pink, and red. Thrives in most well-drained soils exposed to full sun. Makes an eye-catching border perennial and valuable cut flower. Direct-sow seeds in spring or summer for blooms the following year. Three-year-old clumps are also easily divided.

Daisy, Shasta
(*Chrysanthemum x superbum*)

Hardy perennial, 2 to 3 feet high. Famous for its large, white daisy flowers with yellow button centers, each flower is up to 6 inches across. Used extensively in sunny and semi-shaded perennial borders where it makes a magnificent display and provides a source of lovely cut flowers for dazzling indoor arrangements.

Plants bloom in late June and early July. Both single- and double-flowered kinds are available. Propagation is mostly by division of three-year-old plants, but several varieties grow easily from seed, flowering the first year. Notable is the All-America Winner, "SNOW LADY," a dwarf variety growing just 10 inches high, with 2 1/2-inch-wide flowers. Start seed indoors 6 weeks before outdoor planting after frost-danger. "STARBURST" hybrid was developed by Burpee. Extra-large blooms—up to 6 inches across—cover the 3 1/2-foot-high plants.

An earlier-flowering type of daisy—the "ox-eye daisy" (*C. leucanthemum*)—is often confused with the Shasta daisy. It is much smaller-flowered, but earlier-flowering (mid-June), and it has naturalized over many parts of Pennsylvania. It makes a good companion to the blue Siberian iris and red Oriental poppies.

Daylilies
(Hemerocallis hybrids)

Hardy perennials, daylilies are carefree and free-flowering in Pennsylvania's climate. The state has several leading daylily breeders and many specialist nurseries offering large selections. Arthur M. Kroll, owner of Stover Mill Gardens, Carversville, supplies daylilies to the famous Klehm Nurseries, a Chicago mail-order house, and Dr. Darrell Apps, former director of education at Longwood Gardens, is an active daylily breeder. Plants thrive in sun or partial shade, in a wide range of soils. About the only conditions they dislike are boggy soil and dense shade.

Some varieties of daylilies (such as "MARY TODD") have flowers almost as big as amaryllis, and if breeding continues at its present pace the amaryllis-size daylily is not far away. Although the trumpet-shaped flowers last only a day, there are sufficient numbers on each stem to ensure a succession of bloom a month or more during July and August. The orange wayside daylily (*Hemerocallis fulga*), from Japan, grows wild along hedgerows throughout Pennsylvania and makes a good slope cover, though its peak flowering display lasts only a few weeks. Hybrids offer a much longer flowering season and a wider color range, including cream, red, yellow, blue, green, maroon and bicolors.

Plants usually grow a mound of foliage up to 2 feet high, with the flowers adding another 2 feet of height. The slender, arching, sword-shaped leaves remain ornamental all through the growing season.

The trumpet-shaped flowers open at dawn and close at dusk, and they are edible. In the Orient they are considered a delicacy—eaten raw or served as appetizers dipped in batter and fried.

Planting of daylily roots can be done anytime, although spring and fall are especially favorable, setting the fleshy roots 1 inch below the soil line. For stunning, all-around display of daylilies nothing quite beats the yellow, fragrant "HYPERION." A dwarf orange-yellow, "STELLA D'ORO," will flower nonstop from late May until October if dead-headed. Also worth space in every perennial border is the fragrant, early-flowering, lemon-yellow daylily known as *Hemerocallis citrina*, seen in late May and early June.

Though daylily mixtures can be grown from seed, flowering in 16 months, the easiest form of propagation is division of mature clumps.

A very good book, entitled *Daylilies—The Perfect Perennial* by Lewis and Nancy Hill, is available from Storey Communications.

Delphiniums
(Delphinium elatum)

Delphiniums grow up to 6 feet tall, make stunning background accents in the mixed perennial border, and their immense flower spikes create spectacular floral arrangements. They are one of the most popular hardy perennials grown from seed, second only to rudbeckias or gloriosa daisies. Though only marginally hardy over most of Pennsylvania (usually a 50-60% survival rate), it is worth mulching around the plants to try to bring them back each year. Single and double 2-inch, star-shaped florets encircle the flowering stems. Colors include light blue, deep blue, purple, pink, and white. Many have a contrasting white or black center called a "bee." Black bees are especially appealing.

Generally the best flowering displays are from the tall varieties. "GIANT PACIFIC MIXED" is one of the best for Pennsylvania's climate. Though they can be treated as annuals, starting seed 10 weeks before outdoor planting, most good growers start seed in the fall, pot the plants individually and hold them over winter the first year in cold frames, so that extra-large, vigorous plants can be transferred to their permanent locations after danger of killing frost.

Breeders have developed some dwarf strains that resist wind damage, such as the "MAGIC FOUNTAINS" series (resembling "PACIFIC GIANTS," only shorter), and "CONNECTICUT YANKEES" (low-growing, bushy, mounded plants that grow just 2 feet high). Delphiniums bloom from late spring through early summer when nights are cool. They demand a fertile, humus-rich loam soil and full sun. If cut back when flowering dwindles in midsummer and fed a booster fertilizer, this will stimulate a new flush of flower spikes during the cooler days of fall.

Good companion plants with delphiniums are foxgloves, lilies, and climbing roses. They bloom at the same time in early summer, and have a similar tall, tapering habit.

Eulalia Grass
(Miscanthus sinensis)

Hardy perennial ornamental grass, up to 5 feet tall, admired for its fountain of slender leaves and decorative flower plumes that appear in September on long, strong stems, persisting on the plant in dried form into winter. There are many distinct varieties: "VARIEGA-

TUS" has white and green variegation running the length of each leaf blade, creating a silvery effect; "ZEBRINUS" has yellow bands running across the leaf blades, creating a glittering effect.

Plants grow best in full sun, tolerate drought, prefer loam soil. They make beautiful foliage accents in mixed perennial borders, and at the edge of ponds, with the bonus of decorative plumes in fall. Propagation is by division.

Miscanthus is just one of some 250 hardy ornamental grass varieties and grass-like plants that are useful in the home landscape. Limerock Ornamental Grasses of Port Matilda, Pennsylvania, and Kurt Bluemel of Baldwin, Maryland, are specialist growers supplying home gardeners, landscape architects, and retail nurseries. By careful selection, an ornamental garden planted entirely with ornamental grasses can be an appealing feature, especially around swimming pools. Grasses are not only green, but also yellow, pink, blue, and red—many of them turning beautiful russet colors in fall. Both Longwood Gardens and Hershey Gardens have large display areas featuring ornamental grasses.

Foam Flower
(Tiarella cordifolia)

See Wildflowers.

Gaillardia, Blanket Flower
(Gaillardia x grandiflora)

Hardy perennial, 30 inches high, covering itself with 3-inch, daisy-like blooms which are generally yellow with maroon centers, flowering from early summer to fall frost. Plants like sun and tolerate dry soil. The "MONARCH" strain is easily grown from seed sown directly into the garden from April to the end of August. These make superb cut flowers and look sensational massed as a mixture. Annual forms are also popular grown from seed (see section on annuals). For edging and containers consider the hybrid variety "GOBLIN." A compact, bushy bicolor, growing just 12 inches high, it must be increased by root division, as must the taller "BURGUNDY," displaying unusual maroon flowers.

Geranium, Blue
(Geranium x grandiflorum)

Hardy perennial, up to 2 feet tall. The variety "JOHNSON'S BLUE" creates a mound of deeply serrated leaves covered with 2-inch, cup-shaped blue flowers that almost completely hide the foliage in June and continue sporadically until fall frost. Plants prefer a humus-rich loam soil and light shade but bloom well in full sun. They are especially good for edging mixed perennial beds and massing along paths. Propagate by division.

There are many other species and hybrids of geranium suitable for Pennsylvania gardens, though they tend to be shy-flowering. A notable exception is the Armenian geranium *(G. psilostemon)*. This is late-June-flowering and taller-growing (to 3 feet), with 1 1/2-inch magenta flowers accented in the middle with a black "eye." Give it full sun and a well-drained loam soil.

Geum
(Geum chiloense)

Hardy perennial, 2 feet high, blooming continuously from spring to fall with a strong flush of color in May. Plants resemble strawberries, though the flowers are usually semi-double and more colorful, predominating in scarlet, orange and golden yellow. One of the earliest perennials to flower in spring, geums look good planted among forget-me-nots. "MRS. BRADSHAW" (orange-scarlet) and "LADY STRATHEDEN" (yellow) are good varieties for Pennsylvania, both valued for cutting.

Plants grow best in full sun or light shade and humus-rich soil. Easily grown from seed sown outdoors in spring or summer. Mulch heavily for complete winter protection.

Globe Thistle
(Echinops ritro)

Hardy perennial, 4 feet high, growing globular, blue flower heads on long, slender stems bearing prickly foliage. The flower heads change to metallic blue, rounded seed heads valued by flower arrangers for adding dramatic effect to indoor arrangements, especially dried flower centerpieces.

Flowers in midsummer but stays ornamental into fall, enjoying a wide range of soils. Combines well with summer-flowering phlox and Russian sage.

Easily grown from seeds sown outdoors in April or May, by root divisions made in fall or early spring, or by root cuttings taken in fall or winter and raised in a cold frame.

Goatsbeard
(Aruncus dioicus)

Hardy perennial, 4 to 5 feet tall, resembles astilbe, but larger-flowered and more billowing. Plants produce handsome, white flower plumes in June, and make good accents in mixed perennial borders, especially in front of tall delphiniums and foxgloves. Prefers humus-rich soil, tolerates moist soil, in sun or light shade. Beautiful massed along stream banks and pond margins, contrasting effectively with hardy bamboo and Japanese butterbur. Propagate by division after flowering.

Golden Marguerite
(Anthemis tinctoria)

Cushion-like perennial, 2 feet high, with 3-inch, yellow, daisy-like flowers appearing in late spring. The finely cut foliage is highly ornamental and slightly aromatic. Thrives in a wide range of soil conditions, but does especially well in dry, sandy soil and rock gardens.

Makes an excellent cut flower and grows easily from seed direct-sown. However, the truly beautiful "E.C. BUXTON" (lemon-yellow with golden yellow button center) is propagated by division.

Helleborus, Lenten Rose
(Helleborus orientalis)

Hardy perennial sometimes confused with the Christmas rose (*Helleborus niger*), which it resembles. Though the true Christmas rose will grow in Pennsylvania, it is more demanding of a shady, humus-rich soil. Also, it is a misnomer, blooming no earlier than Lenten roses, which bloom continuously from early March until early May. Plants of the Lenten rose grow to 1 1/2 feet, producing lovely, cup-shaped flowers up to 2 1/2 inches across. Colors include dark purple, pink, and white, mostly with contrasting freckles and a dome of powdery yellow stamens in the center. The flowers fade to a lime green and persist into June when they finally shrivel and disappear. They are good to use in lightly shaded parts of rock gardens, woodland gardens and as edging to bulb borders. Use them prolifically as a ground cover around azaleas and rhododendrons.

Mature plants resent transplanting and are not easily divided. Also, seed purchased from seed houses can be locked into a state of dormancy that sometimes takes two winters to break. To establish a colony of Lenten roses, either purchase young plants from a nursery, or seek out an established colony, part the leaves and see if any seedlings have sprouted around the mother plant. These young "volunteer" seedlings are easily dug up and transferred to pots to make reliable transplants after a season's growth.

Honesty, Money Plant
(Lunaria biennis)

Hardy biennial, up to 3 feet high, grown principally for its silvery, oval seed pods, which are useful alone as a dried flower arrangement or mixed with other everlasting flowers. The mostly purple flowers appear in early May the second season after sowing seed, followed by the decorative seed pods in the fall. Dark-colored outer membranes sometimes have to be peeled off to reveal the more desirable silvery inner membrane.

Easily grown from seeds direct-sown from spring to midsummer. Tolerates semi-shade and reseeds so readily it gives the impression of being a perennial.

Hosta, Plantain Lily
(Hosta seiboldiana)

Hardy perennial forming an attractive rosette of broad, textured leaves 2 to 3 feet high, topped in summer by fragrant white or pale blue flower spikes. Good to create a decorative ground cover for shady places.

Prefers moist, humus-rich soil, and looks especially good in woodland gardens and along the margins of streams or ponds. A line of hostas can quickly dress up a house foundation, and most have lovely flowers the size of foxgloves excellent for cutting. They are good for lining driveways and encircling trees. The variety "FRANCES WILLIAMS," a particularly attractive hosta, has bicolored leaves, blue-green in the middle and creamy yellow along the margins. The flowers are pale blue, bell-shaped, arranged on long spikes, and occur in summer.

The leading hosta hybridizer, Paul Aden, lives on Long Island. Author of *The Hosta Book* (Timber Press), he looks a lot like the movie actor Sean Connery. One of his finest introductions is "BLUE ANGEL," which grows large blue leaves and lovely white flowers. Some hostas are delightfully fragrant—particularly "ROYAL STANDARD," producing huge, white, honey-scented tubular flowers that create a fine color harmony with the rudbeckia "GOLD-STURM." The leaves of "ROYAL STANDARD" are a large, lustrous light green with prominent veining.

Because hostas lose their leaves after frost and don't start to sprout new growth until spring they are excellent companions to bulbs, covering over dead bulb foliage after the bulb display has finished. About their only problem is slugs that may chew holes in their leaves. Control these pests with slug bait or by hand-picking populations when they are active in the early morning.

Iris, Bearded
(Iris x germanica)

Hardy perennials in a color range that is richer than any other flowering perennial. Colors include all shades of blue, yellow, red, orange, pink, and purple, plus white and bicolors. There is even a pale green and a black. Easy to grow from swollen root segments called rhizomes, the plants first produce shiny, blue-green, sword-like leaves that stay decorative for most of the year. Some of the flowers measure 5 inches across, composed of a group of three ruffled, upward-facing petals called "standards," and three broad, downward-fac-

ing petals called "falls." Though many public gardens feature extensive plantings of bearded iris, including Longwood Gardens and Hershey Gardens, Pennsylvania gardeners interested in seeing a vast assortment of varieties, including old-fashioned varieties and modern hybrids, should pay a visit to the Presby Memorial Iris Gardens in Montclair, New Jersey, where every known variety is arranged in beds in chronological order, showing year of introduction.

Although bearded iris thrive in a wide range of soils, they respond better to a humus-rich loam soil, well drained and fed with a fertilizer low in nitrogen and high in phosphorus. An application of bone meal (high in phosphorus) every spring and fall will produce the best flowers. Create a special iris border with all colors of the rainbow, mass them on sunny slopes, and spot them among mixed flower borders for a splash of color that usually peaks by Memorial Day weekend. Also good for cutting, they impart a pleasant, spicy fragrance when taken indoors.

As iris clumps spread and multiply, you should break up the rhizomes with a garden fork and replant, adding fresh humus—such as garden compost—and fertilizer. The rhizomes can be lifted and replanted at any time of year—even in full bloom.

When planting a new bed or border, choose a sunny location. At least half a day of sunshine is necessary for good flowers. Plant the fleshy rhizomes 1 inch deep and 2 feet apart; divide again every 3 to 4 years.

"BLUE SAPPHIRE" is one of the finest light blues, with graceful, arching petals and a heavy, golden-yellow beard that contrasts beautifully with the cool petal colors. "ROCOCO" is a magnificent white, richly edged with bright blue. The beard is deep yellow and the flowers can reach an enormous size. "BLACK

SWAN'' may satisfy those looking for the ultimate in dark iris. The almost black petals are velvety smooth and very wide. ''CLOUD CAP'' is a large-flowered pink with a bright tangerine beard.

There are many mail-order specialists offering hundreds of varieties, and Pennsylvania is full of small specialist iris nurseries, many of which will sell a healthy clump of rhizomes in a supermarket bag for a few dollars apiece.

Iris, Japanese
(Iris ensata)

Hardy perennials, these large-flowered plants are the last members of the iris family to bloom, usually reaching their peak around the Fourth of July. They have large, flat flower heads on erect, 4- to 5-foot-high plants, in many shades of blue, plus purple and white. Plant them in clumps between shrubs in a sunny border, as accents in a mixed perennial border, and also along stream banks and pond margins. Japanese iris have broad, arching, sword-shaped leaves, and the roots can be permanently immersed in water. Propagate by division every 3 years.

Iris, Siberian
(Iris siberica)

Hardy perennial blooming in late May and early June, soon after the main bearded iris displays. Principal colors are shades of blue, plus white. They form upright grass-like clumps and tolerate a wide range of soil conditions, including boggy soil—which bearded iris detest. Siberian iris are good companions to ox-eye daisies. Though they are striking plants for mixed perennial borders, they are best seen massed along stream banks and pond margins. About their only problem is rodents that can burrow into the roots and eat them. Moth flakes, an old-fashioned rodent repellent sprinkled among the roots in fall, is a good deterrent. Propagate by division every 3 years.

Joe-pye Weed
(Eupatorium purpureum)

Hardy perennial native to boggy Pennsylvania meadows, 4- to 5-foot-high plants grow erect flower stalks topped with billowing clusters of pink florets in August. Prefers full sun and moist soil. Suitable as a tall background highlight in mixed perennial borders, especially in company with ornamental grasses such as *Miscanthus*. Plants are most easily propagated by division.

Johnny Jump-Ups
(Viola tricolor)

Hardy perennial, 6 inches high, blooming continuously from early spring until fall frost. The flowers resemble miniature pansies in shades of red, white, blue, and yellow, plus bicolors. Fine in rock gardens, container plantings, and as an edging to beds or borders. Plants prefer a cool, fertile, humus-rich soil, slightly shaded. They will bloom the first year from seed started 10 weeks before outdoor planting, but second-year growth is bushier and more free-flowering.

A related species, *V. cornuta* (tufted pansies), is slightly larger-flowered and available in a wider range of clear colors, including yellow, blue, orange, red, and white. Though they normally sulk during Pennsylvania's high summer heat, ''BLUE GEM'' will flower continuously from early spring until fall frost in light shade.

Lady's Mantle
(Alchemilla mollis)

Hardy perennial, 12 inches high, growing an attractive mound of ivy-shaped, scalloped, blue-green leaves and loose clusters of small, lime-green flowers that create a misty appearance when observed from a distance. Invaluable for edging and massing as a ground cover for sunny and lightly shaded places, especially along stream banks and pond margins. Blooms begin in May and continue all summer.

Lavender, English
(Lavendula angustifolia)

Hardy perennial, 2 feet high, flowering June to September. Creates a dense, bushy plant with long, slender stems topped by clusters of tiny, blue, purple or white flowers which impart the famous lavender fragrance, especially when cut and dried in a cool, ventilated place. The deepest blue variety is "HIDCOTE," though it is not quite so hardy as "MUNSTEAD," a lighter blue.

"LAVENDER LADY" is a special selection developed by Burpee, flowering the first year from seed. Otherwise, plants are best propagated from cuttings. Does well in a wide range of fertile, well-drained soils, producing a minty accent for rock gardens and herb gardens. Lavender is especially beautiful when planted around roses.

Liatris, Blazing Star
(Liatris pycnostachya)

Hardy perennial, 4 to 6 feet high, used mostly as an accent in mixed borders and desirable as a cut flower. Especially effective planted among ornamental grasses. Slender flower spikes—up to 10 inches long—resemble a bottle brush, and bloom in white or purple. Grows well in most garden soils, in sun or partial shade.

Liatris are native American plants, and the species *spicata* can be found growing in moist, open fields in parts of

Pennsylvania. A variety of *L. spicata,* "KOBOLD," is more compact than most, staying under 3 feet. Liatris bloom mostly in midsummer; best propagated by root divisions. Perhaps the finest collection of wild liatris can be found at the Henry Foundation in Gladwyne.

Lilies, Garden
(Lilium species and hybrids)

The true family of lilies is one of the most confusing in all the flower world. Among many imposters are lily-of-the-valley, calla lilies, daylilies, plantain lilies, and spider lilies. Lilium—the true lilies—used to have a reputation for being temperamental and difficult to grow, until an Oregon hybridizer, the late Jan de Graaff, began introducing easy-to-grow, disease-resistant varieties. Many of these new hybrids are so exotic in their beauty it's difficult to believe they are hardy and easy to grow over most of Pennsylvania. The Asiatic hybrids—such as the "MID-CENTURY" mixture "ENCHANTMENT" (a deep orange) and "CONNECTICUT KING" (a bright yellow)—are especially recommended. "ENCHANTMENT" and "CONNECTICUT KING" make beautiful companions. Both are June-July flowering. They have upward-facing, chalice-shaped blooms, with pointed petals and they look beautiful just about anywhere—massed in beds, planted singly between shrubs, and grouped in a mixed perennial border, grouped in containers. The "MID-CENTURY" hybrids make particularly fine cut flowers. The full color range includes white, yellow, orange, red, pink, and purple. Though they will take full sun, they prefer light shade, and about their only demand is a humus-rich, fertile soil. Indeed, they are almost as easy to grow as daffodils, coming back year after year, and even multiplying freely.

Most regal of all lilies are the Oriental hybrids—mostly developed from the enormous, fragrant *L. autatum* lily of Japan. They have enchanting names like "IMPERIAL SILVER" (a sumptuous white with yellow highlights), "CRIMSON IMPERIAL," and "PLATYPHYLLUM," all with huge, spotted, nodding flowers up to 10 inches across. These will grow to 5 feet tall, and bloom in August.

The Aurelian hybrids are another distinctive class, mainly July-blooming, and predominating in trumpet-shaped flowers. "BLACK DRAGON" is a superlative variety. The inside of the flower is pure white, while the outside is dark brown, margined white. Its vigor is remarkable, producing plants that will stand 5 feet tall, so heavily clustered with flowers that the stems will need staking.

Plant lily bulbs in spring or fall to a depth about three times the depth of the bulb. An application of well-decomposed manure, leaf-mold, or peat moss several times during the growing season will keep them robust. Propagate dividing up clusters of bulbs, by removing individual bulb scales for planting, and by bulbils that form on many varieties in the leaf axils. A particularly prolific producer of bulbils is the popular tiger lily (*L. lanceolatum*). This flowers in late July, growing 5-foot stems topped with nodding orange flowers up to 4 inches wide.

Lily flowers make beautiful indoor flower arrangements, but take care not to cut too much stem length or foliage since these are needed to build next year's growth. If mice or shrews are a menace in your garden, plant rodent repellent flakes with the bulbs.

Loosestrife, Purple
(*Lythrum salicaria*)

Hardy perennial, up to 5 feet tall, blooming in July and August with masses of purple-pink flower spikes. Does best when planted in a moist, fertile soil in a sunny location, such as close to a pond or stream. Use sparingly in flower borders, since it can be overpowering unless massed among ornamental grasses and misty-blue Russian sage.

Best grown from root divisions made in spring or fall. The variety "MORDEN'S PINK" does extremely well in Pennsylvania. "HAPPY" is a compact variety, flowering at 2 feet.

Lupines
(*Lupinus polyphyllus*)

Hardy perennial, 3 feet tall, used as accents in borders, massed in beds, and valued as a cut flower. The flower spikes are packed with closely set, pea-shaped florets in mostly red, white, blue, pink, yellow, plus many bicolors. Plants bloom in late May, June, and early July when cool night-time temperatures favor flowering.

Lupines like a humus-rich, well-drained soil in a sunny location. Easily grown from seed which is bullet-hard and needs soaking in water overnight before planting to ensure reliable germination. Seed can be direct-sown in spring and summer for blooms the following season. After blooming, cut off dead flower spikes to prevent weakening the plants. Maintain an organic mulch around the plants to keep soil cool and moist. Although classed as perennials, lupines tend to exhaust themselves after several years and may need replenishing with new plants. "RUSSELL HYBRIDS" are a tall strain; "MINARETTE" is a dwarf strain growing a foot shorter at 2 feet tall.

Maltese Cross
(*Lychnis chalcedonica*)

Hardy perennial, 2 to 3 feet high, growing clusters of bright scarlet flowers on long, slender stems in June and July. Does well as a tall background highlight in sunny borders with good drainage.

Propagate by divisions at any time after flowering.

Marsh Marigold
(Caltha palustris)

Hardy perennial forming clumps 12 inches high. Plants grow wild in boggy areas throughout Pennsylvania, even tolerate their roots submerged in shallow water. One of the earliest flowers to bloom in spring, first flowers opening in March and continuing until early May. Handsome dark green, lustrous leaves are a bold contrast to the bright yellow 2-inch flowers that resemble large buttercups. There is a double-flowered form, but it is a little less shy-blooming than the single. Superb planted along streams, at the edge of ponds and moist soil in sun or light shade. Easily propagated by division.

Meadowfoam
(Filipendulina rubra)

Hardy perennial native to Pennsylvania swampy meadows, growing up to 5 feet high, striking the sky with slender flower stems topped with pink flowers that resemble cotton candy. The deep rosy-pink garden variety "VENUSTA" is especially desirable as a tall background highlight for mixed perennial borders, and for massing along stream banks and pond margins, flowering in early June. Plants tolerate light shade, can be propagated by division, and may need staking.

Mountain Bluet
(Centaurea montana)

Hardy perennial, 2 feet high, blooming from June to September. The clear blue flowers resemble cornflowers, but they are much larger—up to 3 inches across.

Useful in borders and as a cut flower, they are easy to grow from seed direct-sown in midsummer. Combines well with evening primrose, particularly *Oenothera fruticosa*.

Mullein, Giant
(Verbascum olympicum)

Hardy biennial growing 6 feet tall, first producing a rosette of silvery, gray-green leaves that feel like velvet. The rosette then elongates into a slender flower spike that opens out into a candelabra of yellow, star-shaped flowers in late June and early July. Plants make good tall background highlights for mixed perennial borders, especially in bold clumps behind blue veronicas and violet-blue *Salvia x superba*. Plants may need staking. Give them full sun and a loam soil. Direct-sow seed in spring or summer for flowering the second season. After flowering, plants usually self-seed. A related species, *V. bombyciferum*, grows wild along the waysides all over Pennsylvania. It can be introduced into perennial gardens as a tall background highlight by planting from seed. The woolly, silvery flower spike is studded with yellow florets that do not get top-heavy, so they require no staking to keep them erect.

Obedient Plant
(Physostegia virginiana)

Hardy perennial native to Pennsylvania, growing 3 to 5 feet high depending on variety, valued for its attractive spires of pink, snapdragon-like flowers that bloom in late summer or early fall. Plants form dense clumps, tolerate moist soil, and prefer full sun.

There is a white-flowered variety,

"ALBA" and an appealing, compact, 3-foot-high, deep-pink dwarf selection, "VIVID." Called obedient plant because the rows of florets can be twisted into different positions and remain in place. An excellent companion to species of *Helianthus* (perennial sunflowers) and *Boltonia* (white fall-flowering asters). Easily propagated by seed direct-sown and by division.

Peony, Herbaceous
(Paeonia officinalis)

Two kinds of hardy peonies have won the hearts of Pennsylvania gardeners—the familiar herbaceous peony in double and single forms, and the much more spectacular tree peonies (*P. suffruticosa*).

Herbaceous peonies are the most widely cultivated because they are easiest to grow, generally flowering in June. Colors include white, red, and pink—many enhanced by a dome of golden yellow stamens and delightfully fragrant. Some of the best for Pennsylvania conditions have been developed by Klehm Nurseries, near Chicago, especially a strain of extra-large-flowered hybrids collectively known as "ESTATE" peonies (some have flowers up to 10 inches across). One of the most free-flowering—with up to 50 large flowers open all at one time—is "BARRINGTON BELLE," a deep pink with a dome of red stamens flecked with orange. Other outstanding varieties include "PINK PARFAIT," a fragrant double pink; "BOWL OF CREAM," a large, sweetly scented double white; "RASPBERRY SUNDAE," a massive double white with raspberry petals clustered in the center; and "JAYCEE," a patented, large double red with petals tipped silver.

Herbaceous peonies need a fertile, humus-rich soil, in sun or light shade, and prefer to be planted in fall from root divisions, although plants in gallon containers will take spring planting. Feed around the plants early in spring before new growth is far advanced. Plant roots of herbaceous peonies no more than 2 inches below ground level. Any piece of root with an "eye" is capable of growing a new plant, although 3 to 5 eye divisions are preferable.

Peony, Tree
(Paeonia suffruticosa)

Hardy perennials sometimes classified as shrubs because they develop woody stems, but listed here as perennials because they are most often planted in mixed perennial borders. The flowers of both kinds tend to be damaged by heavy rains, and benefit from a sheltered location.

The flowers of tree peonies tend to be larger than those of herbaceous peonies, with blooms up to 12 inches across and petals that appear to be made of crepe paper. They have a more sophisticated presence in the garden, with layers of heavily indented, gray-green leaves that create mounded plants. One well-grown tree peony will outshine an entire border of herbaceous peonies. The color range is more extensive than that of herbaceous peonies, extending to yellow and orange. Though many bear Oriental names, the most desirable of tree peonies is undoubtedly "ROCK'S VARIETY," named for an American plant explorer, Joseph Rock, who discovered the plant in a Chinese monastery garden during an expedition sponsored by the National Geographic Society. Plants will grow to 5 feet and produce huge single, cream-colored flowers with handsome maroon markings at the base of each petal, rather like a gigantic Oriental poppy. A single root regularly sells for $100. A special group of tree peonies are called "LUTEA" hybrids. Developed by American peony hybridizer Professor A.P. Saunders, they excel in fragrant yellow hues. Perhaps the best for Pennsylvania gardens is "CANARY"—try it with a yellow-flowering golden chain tree (*Laburnum x vossii*) in the background to create a stunning all-yellow color scheme.

Tree peonies generally are not so hardy as herbaceous peonies, and like to be planted against a stone wall so the roots and new shoots are sheltered from cold winds. They grow in sun or light shade, and demand a humus-rich, fertile loam soil. Unlike the herbaceous peonies, tree peony roots should be set comparatively deep—up to 6 inches—in planting holes that have been deeply dug—at least 1 1/2 feet—and well fertilized with garden compost to encourage healthy root development. Feed with a granular commercial fertilizer low in nitrogen, but high in phosphorus and potash. They are gross feeders and will benefit from subsequent applications of garden compost and bone meal after flowers have ceased to bloom. April and October are ideal planting times.

Phlox, Blue
(*Phlox divaricata*)

Hardy perennial, 8 to 10 inches high, flowering in April and May with fragrant blue, purple, or white 1-inch blooms, held erect in clusters. Selected from the pale blue wild species native to Pennsylvania woodlands, plants tolerate light shade. Highly desirable for massing in woodland, edging rustic paths, and planting as bold drifts among clumps of tulips and daffodils, or in a rockery where it can create a dense carpet of bloom. Plants are best propagated from seed direct-sown in summer. Self-seeds easily. A hybrid of *Phlox divaricata*, "CHATTAHOOCHIE" is a vigorous-flowering, pale blue variety with deep pink "eyes." It flowers for most of May

and June, and looks sensational planted near yellow lily-flowered tulips and yellow loosestrife.

Phlox, Creeping
(*Phlox subulata*)

Hardy perennial, 4 inches high, creating a dense, flowering carpet of 1/2-inch, star-shaped flowers in April and early May. Colors include white and shades of red, blue, and purple. Peak flowering lasts about 2 weeks. Used extensively in rock gardens and dry slopes. Tolerates light shade, but enjoys full sun. Moss-like, gray-green foliage stays evergreen during winter.

Creeping phlox is superb for edging beds and borders, and also for creating a "flowering lawn," especially on a sunny slope. Many varieties have been selected. The best colors have "MILL-STREAM" in their name—selections made by the late Link Foster, rock garden expert, at his beautiful home and backyard nursery in the Berkshire Mountains.

Phlox, Creeping Blue
(*Phlox stolonifera*)

Hardy perennial, 10 inches high, native to Pennsylvania woods. Plants are mostly blue and purple, and create a dense weave of ground-hugging stems that can spread rapidly to create a dramatic carpet of blue in early May. Resembles blue phlox in appearance, but slightly larger-flowered and a little more appealing. Both white ("BRUCE'S WHITE") and rose-pink ("HOMEFIRES") are good color selections, though the deep blue is unsurpassable and a good companion to yellow primroses, white foam flowers, and red columbines in shady beds. Easily propagated by dividing large clumps.

Phlox, Early Border
(Phlox maculata)

Hardy perennnial, growing 2 to 3 feet high, producing strong, erect stems topped with large, cone-shaped, pleasantly fragrant flower clusters up to 12 inches long and 6 inches wide. Flowering in late June and early July, colors include white, light pink and rose-pink, many with contrasting "eyes." They are superb massed in mixed perennial borders, and are excellent for cutting.

In appearance, early border phlox resemble the later-flowering summer phlox (*P. paniculata*), but they are distinctly different in satisfaction. Whereas summer phlox are highly susceptible to deer damage, wind damage and powdery mildew disease, early border phlox are not. Plants prefer full sun and a fertile, humus-rich loam soil. Propagate by division of 3-year-old plants after flowering.

Phlox, Summer
(Phlox paniculata)

Hardy perennial, growing to 4 feet, flowering in mid-July and August, with immense, cone-shaped clusters of flowers in white, red, orange, and purple, usually with a contrasting "eye." Though taller-growing than *P. maculata*, and better for planting between foundation shrubs, summer phlox suffer badly from powdery mildew unless sprayed with a fungicide. Otherwise culture and propagation are the same as for early border phlox.

Pincushion Flower
(Scabiosa caucasica)

Hardy perennial, 3 feet high, flowering all summer, and far superior to the annual type (*S. atropurpurea*), though the color range is not so extensive, being limited to shades of blue, plus white. Prefers full sun and good drainage. Exceptionally fine for cutting.

Direct-sow seed in summer, or increase by dividing color selections, such as lavender-blue "CLIVE GREAVES" and deep blue "FAMA." Plants start to flower in June, and combine well with yellow coreopsis and yellow yarrow.

Pinks, Carnations
(Dianthus species)

Hardy perennials invaluable for rock gardens, dry walls and sunny borders. Growing to 12 inches high and blooming mostly in May and June, they have grass-like leaves and do best in soils with excellent drainage. They tolerate stony soils and many are fragrant, making excellent cut flowers.

The cottage pinks (or *Dianthus plumarius*) have fragrant flowers in both double and single forms in shades of red, white, and pink. The maiden pinks (*Dianthus deltoides*) are characterized by red or pink blooms with a contrasting eye of deeper color, forming a dense mass of low-growing leaves and flowers effective as a ground cover or trailing plant. Smaller-flowered Chedder pinks (*Dianthus gratianopolitanus*) are exquisite planted as an edging to perennial borders, among stepping stones, or forming clumps of color on dry walls. *Dianthus caryopteris* (carnations) are not reliably hardy in Pennsylvania, but a hybrid between the carnation and cottage pinks has resulted in plants with the hardiness of the cottage pink and double or semi-double flowers resembling carnations. Called "ALLWOOD" hybrids, the color range includes red, pink, white, cream and yellow, plus bicolors. Plants flower nonstop from June until fall frost.

Start seed at any time from spring to September. Plants are also easily propagated by root division and by stem cuttings since they are capable of rooting at every leaf node.

Poppy, Oriental
(Papaver orientale)

Hardy perennial, 2 1/2 feet high, with the largest blooms and richest colors of any poppy, some measuring up to 10 inches across, and many handsomely marked with black patches at the base of each petal. Colors include white, pale pink, orange and red, plus bicolors. Use in bold color groups on fertile, humus-rich well-drained loam soil in a sunny but sheltered position, since they are susceptible to wind damage in exposed locations.

Propagate color selections by root division after flowering, or direct-sow seed mixtures in summer. Since poppies do not transplant well, sowings started indoors should be made into peat pots, ensuring no root disturbance on planting. Though flowers do not last long—especially after heavy rains—poppies are good companions to bearded iris, ox-eye daisies and foxgloves, flowering in May. "ALLEGRO" is a dwarf strain, growing 1 1/2 to 2 feet high; "HELEN ELIZABETH" is a beautiful, tall-flowered, cool pink; and "BEAUTY OF LIVERMORE" is the largest-flowering tall crimson.

Prickly Pear, Hardy
(Opuntia humifusa)

Incredible though it may sound, this true member of the cactus family grows wild in Pennsylvania, especially along ledges of south-facing cliffs. There is a particularly large wild colony of prickly pears along the Delaware River, facing Upper Black Eddy, Pennsylvania, on the New Jersey side of the river. They fall limp and flat to the ground in winter, but revive in spring and make spreading clumps, 12 inches high, of oval, prickly pads. Beautiful bright yellow, iridescent, cup-shaped flowers, up to 4 inches across, form on the ends of the pads and after flowering produce dull red, pear-shaped fruits. Cut open, the interior is dark purple with a juicy, blackberry-flavored pulp filled with seeds. Filtered through a cheesecloth, the juice is tasty to drink.

The hardy prickly pear is good for edging mixed perennial beds, and allowing to cascade over dry walls. It does well in containers, and looks especially interesting planted as a colony in a rock garden. Propagate by breaking off one of the pads and rooting the broken end in moist sand.

Red Hot Poker
(Kniphofia uvaria)

Hardy perennial, 4 feet tall, flowering in late June. Plants grow in thick, fleshy, spiky clumps. From the center of each clump emerge up to 50 stout flower stems topped with mostly red, orange, and yellow bicolored "pokers," formed by scores of tubular florets.

Good used sparingly as highlights in the perennial border and for dramatic cut-flower arrangements. Needs a sunny location, and thrives even in poor, dry soil, tolerating drought. Propagate color selections from root division, mixtures from seed started indoors, or direct-sown, in spring and summer. Mulch plants with straw to protect from severe winters.

Rock Rose
(Helianthemum nummularium)

Hardy perennial, growing 1 foot high, dwarf evergreen plants covered with hundreds of orange-scarlet, rose, pink, yellow, or white flowers in May. Thrives in dry, sunny locations, especially rock gardens and along dry walls. Also suitable for edging mixed borders. The yellow "WISLEY'S PRIMROSE" and scarlet-red "FIREDRAGON" are sensational color selections.

Easily grown from seed direct-sown from spring to September. Named varieties need propagating by division.

Sage, Russian
(Perovskia atriplicifolia)

Hardy perennial, up to 4 feet high, creating a billowing mound of gray-green, spear-shaped leaves and large, loose clusters of small, powder-blue flowers that look like clouds of mist from a distance. Flowering in July, August, and September, plants make good accents for mixed perennial borders, especially in combination with ornamental grasses and purple loosestrife. The flower stems are good for cutting, and the plants are easily divided. Give them a well-drained loam soil and full sun.

Sage, Violet
(Salvia x superba)

Hardy perennial growing to 3 feet high, blooming in June and early July with slender, graceful spires of deep violet-blue flowers on long stems useful for cutting. Prefers a sunny or partly shaded location and a well-drained, humus-rich loam soil.

"VIOLET QUEEN" is a vigorous-spreading variety densely packed with strikingly bold flower stems. Combines well with pink veronica and yellow foxgloves (Digitalis grandiflora). Plants are best propagated from root divisions.

Sea Pinks, Thrift
(Armeria maritima)

Carefree, cushion-like plants, 6 to 8 inches high, blooming in spring and summer. Useful in rock gardens, also as a ground cover on dry, sunny slopes, and planted between flagstones. The evergreen plants form gray-green, grass-like tufts, while the globular flowers—in shades of pink, plus white—grow on stems long enough for cutting and dense enough to create a carpet of color.

Direct-sow seed mixtures in spring or summer in sandy soil. Special color selections, such as "PRIDE OF DUSSELDORF"—a deep rosy pink—can be divided in spring or fall.

Snakeroot
(Cimicifuga racemosa)

Hardy perennial native to Pennsylvania woodlands, plants grow to 6 feet tall, producing towering pointed flower spikes set with small, creamy-white florets.

Suitable for tall background accents in mixed perennial beds, in sun or light shade. Plants may need staking to remain erect, and demand humus-rich soil, flowering in July and August.

A related species, C. simplex, also good for shade, has an excellent garden variety, "THE PEARL." September-flowering, the 3- to 4-foot plants are more compact than common snakeroot, and more free-flowering. The white flower spikes resemble candles.

Sneezeweed
(Helenium autumnale)

Hardy perennial native to Pennsylvania open meadows, growing stout, 5-foot stems crowned with a mass of yellow or orange, daisy-like flowers with round, "button" centers and slightly swept-back petals. Plants invariably need staking to keep them erect, but they are good to use as background highlights, flowering in late August and September. The tall *heleniums* combine well with ornamental grasses. Some compact garden varieties include "BUTTERPAT" (yellow flowers, 3 feet tall) and "GYPSY" (bronze and gold flowers, 3 feet tall). These blend well with fall-flowering New England asters.

Snow-in-Summer
(Cerastium tomentosum)

Hardy perennial, 6 inches high, forming a dense low-growing mass of brilliant white flowers. Used extensively in rock gardens, dry walls and as a ground cover. Blooms in May and June, thriving in dry, sunny locations.

The silvery-white, woolly foliage is equally decorative when the plants are not in bloom. Easy to grow from seeds sown outdoors in spring and summer and by division of clumps.

Soapwort
(Saponaria ocymoides)

Hardy perennial, 6 inches high, forming a low, spreading mass of small rose-pink flowers that look sensational planted as bold drifts at the edge of perennial borders, along dry walls and among boulders in a rock garden. Combines well with other low-spreading rock garden plants, such as candytuft, yellow alyssum, and pinks. May-flowering. Propagate by division.

Stonecrop
(Sedum spectabile)

Hardy perennial, 2 feet high, forming mounds of oval, succulent blue-green leaves. The flower stems are held erect, looking like heads of broccoli in bud, and opening out into brilliant, flat pink flower clusters that are highly attractive to butterflies in late August and early September. A hybrid of *S. spectabile*, "AUTUMN JOY," is an especially

beautiful variety. Its mounded flower clusters start off deep pink in the bud stage, turn a deep rusty-red when mature and dry to a beautiful bronze, the dried flower cluster staying decorative for a month or more after its flowering peak.

Plants prefer full sun and good drainage. They can be increased by division, but also by snapping off the leaves and rooting the base in a moist, sandy soil mixture. They are especially attractive planted among ornamental grasses and to complement fall-blooming asters.

Sunflower, False
(Heliopsis helianthoides scabra)

Hardy perennial, growing 4 feet high, native to open meadows of Pennsylvania. The erect stems are topped with golden yellow daisy-like flowers, resembling small sunflowers. They are suitable for tall background highlights in mixed perennial borders, and excellent for cutting. The flowers bloom during July, and last up to 10 days as a cut flower. A particularly fine garden variety, "KARAT," has flowers fully 5 inches across. Heliopsis love the sun, a fertile loam soil, and they are drought-resistant. Propagate by division of 3-year-old plants.

Sunflower, Perennial
(Helianthus x multiflorus)

Although the name helianthus is commonly used to describe the tall, giant-flowered annual sunflower widely grown for its edible seeds, a large group of perennial sunflowers are useful in the perennial border, the best of which is probably the hybrid, *Helianthus x multiflorus*. The variety "FLORE PLENO" is double-flowered, growing 4 to 5 feet high, and producing quantities of bright yellow, 3-inch-wide flowers on long stems useful for cutting. Plants generally are so top-heavy with blooms that they will need staking—or grow them against a picket fence so the plants can lean forward and spill over the railing and between them.

Tolerates a wide range of soils (including poor, dry soil), resists heat, and blooms in midsummer. Easily grown from seed direct-sown in spring or summer, and from root divisions in spring or fall.

Sweet Pea, Perennial
(Lathyrus latifolius)

Hardy perennial, covering the ground with dense vines spreading 5 to 6 feet. Can be trained up a trellis. Flowers resemble sweet peas, but not fragrant and limited in color range to rose-pink and white. Flowers mostly in July.

Succeeds in poor soil, tolerates drought, creating excellent ground cover for dry slopes and requiring little or no care once established. Also excellent for erosion control. Direct-sow seed mixtures in spring or summer. Propagate color selections from root division.

Sweet William
(Dianthus barbatus)

Hardy biennial, available in dwarf and tall varieties up to 18 inches high, flowering mostly in June and July, with clusters of bright, bicolored florets. Some annual forms are available, such as "WEE WILLIE" and "SUMMER BEAUTY." Plants produce a good display in fertile, well-drained soils in a sunny position. Self-seeding is common.

Biennial sweet Williams can be sown outdoors until mid-August for blooms the following spring. Annual sweet Williams can be sown indoors in mid-February for July flowering or outdoors in May for September flowers. Seed germinates in 5 days.

Tickseed
(Coreopsis verticillata)

Hardy perennial, growing 1 to 2 feet depending on variety. Mounded plants have brittle stems and narrow leaves, covered in July and August with masses of star-shaped, 1-inch yellow or lemon-colored flowers. Prefers full sun and humus-rich loam soil, and is most effective as an edging to mixed perennial beds, but also good for massing in generous drifts in rock gardens.

"ZAGREB" is a golden yellow, and "MOONBEAM" a lovely lemon-yellow, though not so profuse-flowering. Both are sensational planted with English lavender to create a yellow-blue color harmony.

Veronica, Speedwell
(Veronica spicata)

Hardy perennial, growing 18 inches high, flowering in June and July. Mound-shaped plants produce numerous flower spikes tightly packed with blue, pink, and white flowers excellent for rock gardens. Dense colonies of plants are effective in perennial borders or rock gardens—especially when the rose pink ("RED FOX") and the blue ("BLUE PETER") are together. "GOODNESS GROWS" is an extremely free-flowering violet-blue that will bloom continually until fall frost. Plants prefer full sun, but tolerate light shade. Though easily propagated from seed direct-sown, special color selections are best increased by division in spring or fall.

Wallflower, Siberian
(Cheiranthus allionii)

Hardy biennial, 15 inches high, blooming in May and June with sprays of golden-orange or lemon-yellow flowers that resemble wallflowers. True English wallflowers (with pink, mahogany, and white in their color range) do not do well in Pennsylvania, but the Siberian wallflower produces a satisfying, long-lasting display. Good for massed beds and borders during cool weather. Tolerates poor soils in a sunny position. Useful in rock gardens and as a cut flower. Start seed outdoors in June where the plants are to bloom, for flowers the following season.

Good companions to blue pansies, pink tulips, and blue forget-me-nots.

Yucca, Spanish Dagger
(Yucca filamentosa)

Hardy annual forming evergreen clumps of stiff, pointed leaves with sharp spines up to 2 feet high. From the center of each emerges a tall flower spike, at first resembling a gigantic asparagus spear. This opens out into a beautiful loose cluster of nodding cream-colored, bell-shaped flowers that are edible and taste like lettuce. The flower stem can exceed 5 feet in height. The plants make attractive tall accents for the back of perennial borders, especially among other drought-tolerant plants such as opuntia and sedums, as seen in the Thomas Church Mediterranean garden at Longwood Gardens in Chester County. Yuccas are also good for massing to control soil erosion on dry slopes.

CHAPTER 5

Bulbs and Water Plants

A vast number of flowering bulbs do well in Pennsylvania, including spring-flowering bulbs (which need planting in fall), summer-flowering bulbs (which need planting in spring), and autumn-flowering bulbs (which need planting in spring or early summer). Of all plants classified as flowering bulbs, by far the most admired are daffodils and tulips. Daffodils bloom dependably from year to year with minimum care, and tulips possess the most diverse color range in all the plant kingdom.

SPRING-FLOWERING BULBS

Mass plantings of daffodils can be seen in many fine gardens in early spring, but the most sensational are at Winterthur—just south of the Pennsylvania border—in Delaware. The late Henry F. duPont, owner and creator of its vast woodland and meadow gardens, had a special area where he would first grow daffodil varieties to test. He not only noted which kinds multiplied freely, but also which kinds held their heads up high to make an especially big splash in the landscape. He planted them in bold drifts so that in mid-April the daffodils seem to flow like a glacier down slopes surrounding several large ponds.

One of the most famous plantings at Winterthur is the "March Walk" which relies heavily on early-flowering, naturalized plantings of spring-flowering bulbs for its color. The parade of color begins in February when nodding white snowdrops (*Galanthus nivalis*) and shimmering yellow aconites (*Eranthis hyemalis*)—with cup-shaped, buttercup-like flowers—bloom together. The iridescent yellow *Adonis amurensis*—which resembles a giant aconite—is also among the earliest to flower. Color continues with pale purple snow crocuses (*Crocus tomasinianus*), dwarf blue iris (*Iris reticulata*), and cheerful blue and white Grecian windflowers (*Anemone blanda*). One of the most delightful sights along the March Walk occurs when a late snowfall blankets the garden in the night, and starts to melt as the sun gathers strength at daybreak. The combination of flowers and melting snow is spectacular. This special early show is enhanced by large beds of Christmas and Lenten roses (*Helleborus* species), and early-flowering shrubs—especially witch hazels (*Hamaemelis* species), with their spidery yellow and orange-red blossoms, and winter hazels (*Corylopsis spicata*), with yellow pendant flower clusters. Star magnolias (*Magnolia stellata*) erupt with gleaming white, waterlily-like flowers, creating a beautiful color harmony close to the lovely shocking pink *Rhododendron mucronulatum*, variety "CORNEL PINK." All this occurs even before the daffodils bloom.

Winterthur is famous for its magnificent collection of azaleas, planted under the high canopy of tulip poplar trees. But the azaleas would not be so beautiful without a carpet of Spanish bluebells (*Endymion hispanica*), which are showier and much more reliable for Pennsylvania gardens than the English bluebell (*Endymion non-scriptus*). At Winterthur in summer large displays of garden lilies (*Lilium* species) thrive in the rich leaf mold at the edge of the woods, and in September sheets of pink autumn crocus (*Colchicum autumnale*) light up the sunny side of grassy slopes with huge pink blossoms on leafless stems, each flower four times larger than the largest spring-flowering crocus.

The Winterthur garden does not use many tulips, but nearby at Longwood Gardens (Kennett Square, Chester County) there are always sensational tulip displays looking their best around the first week of May. These are displayed in large, formal beds like the famous Keukenhof Gardens, near Amsterdam, Holland. However, nothing quite compares with the unusual bulb garden called Lenteboden (meaning "Herald of Spring"), situated north of New Hope (Bucks County), on the River Road.

A Bulb Expert's Spring Garden

Comprising several acres overlooking the Delaware River, Lenteboden was created by the late Charles H. Mueller as a "living bulb catalog." The company Mr. Mueller founded puts its main selling effort into growing hundreds of varieties of tulips, daffodils, and other spring-flowering bulbs in demonstration plots surrounding an old stone farmhouse. Customers are invited to tour the gardens in spring and make selections from the flowering displays for shipment of the bulbs in fall at the proper planting time.

Over 50,000 bulbs are planted on three levels of a sunny slope, each level a distinct blooming period—early, mid-season, and late. The whole display begins around April 15 with daffodils planted throughout a shady woodland area and across a sunny sloping lawn. Early-flowering species tulips—such as *T. kaufmannia* (with blossoms that open out flat like a waterlily), *T. fosteriana* (with the most intense iridescent red coloring and largest flowers among tulips), and *T. greigii* (with striped leaves)—are displayed in a large, sunny rockery overlooking a pond. A long, curving border of spectacular Darwin hybrid tulips marks the peak blooming period (usually around May 1), while lily-flowered tulips (with reflexed, pointed petals), fringed tulips (with lace-edged petals), parrot tulips (with feathery petals), and peony-flowered tulips (with huge double flowers) carry the display through mid-May.

The most often-asked question of customers is how to keep daffodils coming back every year, and multiplying freely. The staff recommends bone meal because it is high in phosphorus, a plant nutrient needed for strong bulb development. For large plantings, however, bone meal can be prohibitively expensive, so super-phosphate is used as an economical alternative. Where large drifts of daffodils need to be fertilized, it is best to add the super-phosphate twice a year—in spring before the bulbs bloom and again in fall after the first frost. Daffodils will even come back through sod if fertilized on this schedule.

Tulips are not as good for naturalizing as daffodils, though some species tulips (especially the *T. kaufmannia* types) will naturalize on a sunny slope, provided the soil is kept weed-free. Most other tulips will come back one more year, but after that the bulbs tend to diminish.

BULB PLANTING CHART

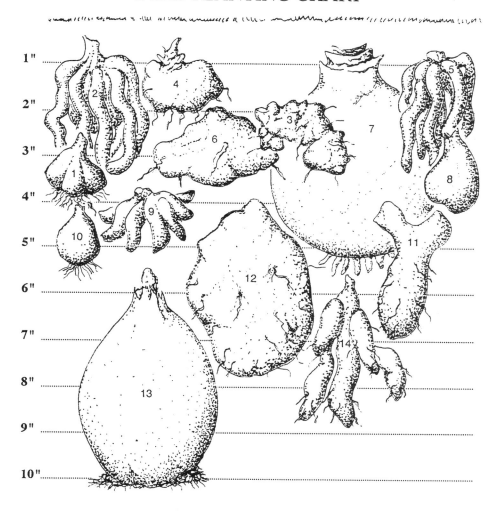

1-Acidanthera
2-Agapanthus
3-Anemone
4-Begonia
5-Belamcanda
6-Caladium
7-Cardiocrinum

8-Colchicum
9-Bletilla
10-Camassia
11-Canna
12-Colocasia
13-Allium giganteum
14-Alstroemeria

BULB PLANTING CHART

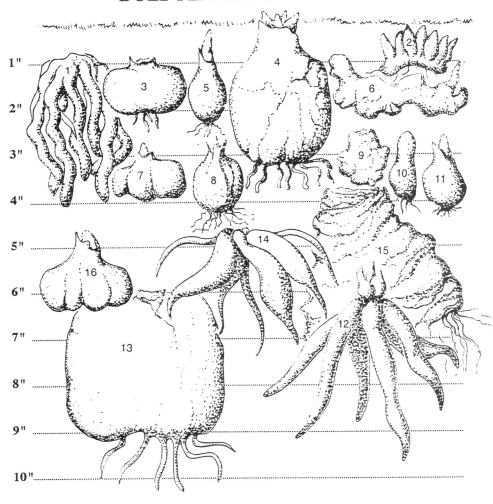

1-Clivia
2-Convallaria
3-Cyclamen
4-Eucharis
5-Freesia
6-Gloriosa

7-Crocus
8-Crocosmia
9-Eranthis
10-Erythronium
11-Galanthus
12-Eremurus

13-Fritallaria imperialis
14-Dahlia
15-Eucomis
16-Gladiolus

BULB PLANTING CHART

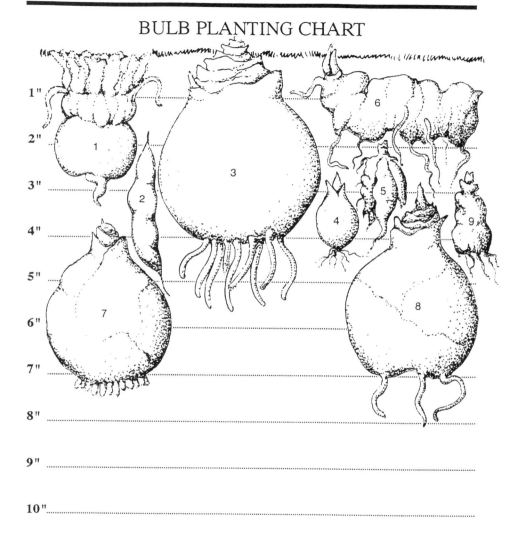

1-Haemanthus
2-Hemerocallis
3-Hippeastrum
4-Hyacinthoides
5-Incarvillea

6-Iris germanica
7-Hyacinthus
8-Hymenocallis
9-Ipheion

BULB PLANTING CHART

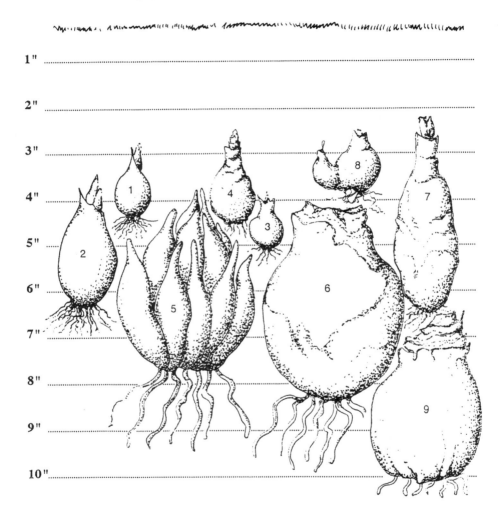

1-Iris reticulata
2-Iris hollandicus
3-Ixia
4-Leucojum
5-Lilium

6-Ismene
7-Lycoris
8-Muscari
9-Narcissus

BULB PLANTING CHART

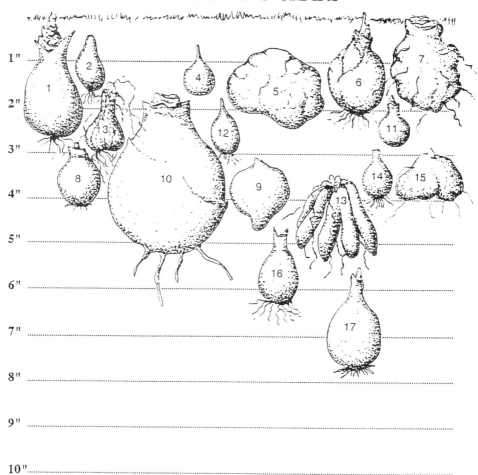

1-Nerine	7-Veltheima	13-Ranunculus
2-Ornithogalum	8-Scilla sibirica	14-Sparaxis
3-Oxalis	9-Zantedeschia	15-Watsonia
4-Pleione	10-Polianthes	16-Sternbergia
5-Sinningia	11-Zephyranthus	17-Tulipa
6-Sprekelia	12-Puschkinia	

Daffodils and hyacinths are naturally repellent to rodents and deer, but tulips and crocus can suffer heavy losses unless controlled by scattering rodent-repellent flakes in the soil at planting time, and drenching the new foliage with a distasteful, but odorless, deer-repellent spray.

For more information about visiting Lenteboden, see page 221.

Some of the most beautiful spring-flowering bulbs are a little too tender for growing outdoors in Pennsylvania, though it is possible to grow them successfully with the protection of cold frames. These include ranunculus, florist anemones, and calla lilies.

SUMMER- AND FALL-FLOWERING BULBS

Many of the popular summer-flowering bulbs are too tender to survive Pennsylvania winters, and need replanting each year. These include tuberous dahlias, gladiolus, tuberous begonias, and cannas. The most popular of hardy summer-flowering bulbs is the garden lily, especially the carefree Asiatic hybrids, such as the "MID-CEN-TURY MIXTURE," "ENCHANTMENT" (an orange), and "CONNECTICUT KING" (a clear yellow). These are not so temperamental as the species and will come back reliably each year, especially when planted in a semi-shaded location in a humus-rich soil with good drainage.

One of the best locations to see summer-flowering bulbs used creatively is the New Jersey display garden, Leaming's Run, in the village of Swainton, near Cape May. Here you will find immense tender elephant's ears (*Caladium esculentum)* with many leaves up to 5 feet long. Though tender, they tolerate boggy soil, and the giant bulbs are easily lifted in fall for storage indoors during winter months.

Most popular among the fall-flowering bulbs are hardy sternbergias (resembling a large yellow crocus) and hardy colchicums (resembling a giant purple crocus). These are especially beautiful planted at the edge of shrub borders and perennial beds.

Cultivation

A big appeal of flowering bulbs is their ease of planting (compared to seeds) and their dependability. Although some of the smaller bulbs are no larger than a pea, many are the size of a golf ball. Whatever their size, they are easy to handle and not so perishable as seeds or bare-root plants. Bulbs will survive long periods of drought or cold because they have built-in reserves that see them through long periods of stress. Hardy bulbs (such as tulips and daffodils) will lay dormant in the soil until a warming trend triggers them to sprout and bloom. Tender bulbs (such as dahlias and gladiolus) need to be lifted after frost has killed the top growth, the bulbs cleaned of soil and dried, for storage in a cool, frost-free place with good ventilation. If that sounds like a chore, then purchase new bulbs each season.

When planting bulbs it's good to know which end is up (usually the pointed end), though planting upside-down will not normally cause a problem. A good rule of thumb is to plant bulbs to a depth three times their height, measuring from the top of the bulb. Most bulbs demand good drainage, a sunny location (though many tolerate light shade), and a fertile, humus-rich soil. In soils that drain poorly, consider a few bog-lovers like tender callas and elephant's ears which will grow with their roots permanently covered with water.

The best soil for most bulbs is one loaded with leaf mold; to keep beds in good condition it is useful to have several large wire bins of shredded leaves in different stages of decomposition. The black, fluffy organic matter should be added to beds every year in fall. Failing access to leaf mold, a good alternative is garden compost, well-decomposed animal manure (particularly cow manure), spent mushroom soil, or peat moss (though the latter is generally expensive and lacking in nutrients).

Listed below are some of the top-performing bulbs for Pennsylvania, divided into spring-flowering and summer/fall-flowering varieties.

TOP-PERFORMING SPRING-FLOWERING BULBS

The following varieties and species are hardy unless otherwise stated. They should be planted in fall between September 1 and Christmas. Flowering times are for bulbs planted early. If planting is delayed flowering times will be later, by up to 4 weeks.

Aconite, Winter
(Eranthis hyemalis)

Iridescent, yellow, buttercup-like flowers—up to 1 inch across with a green "collar"—bloom in February at the same time as snowdrops. Just 2 inches high, the flowers appear before the main leaves, which are deeply indented. Plants grow to just 4 inches high, forming colonies if planted in a sunny or lightly shaded location in humus-rich soil kept free of weeds. Excellent for naturalizing in deciduous woodland, along rustic paths, especially in combination with snowdrops. Plant bulb-like tubers 3 to 4 inches deep, almost touching, in clumps.

Allium, Ornamental Onion
(Allium species)

Relatives of the onion, plants produce mostly globular flower heads and strap-like leaves. *Allium christophii* (star of Persia) grows to 2 feet, crowned with immense, 14-inch-diameter balls of star-shaped purple flowers, suitable for mass-ing in mixed perennial borders to bloom in May. Also valued for cutting and dried flower arrangements.

Allium giganteum (giant allium) grows to 5 feet, with erect stems and deep purple, globular flowers up to 6 inches across. Plant in groups of 5 or more in mixed perennial borders. Late-spring-flowering, suitable for sun or light shade. Plant bulbs 5 inches deep, at least 12 inches apart (smaller-flowered alliums can be spaced closer apart and planted less deep).

Allium moly (lily leek) is yellow-flowered and low-growing, suitable for edging paths. *Allium schoenoprasum* (chives), though commonly used in herb gardens, is sufficiently ornamental for planting in mixed perennial borders because of its masses of bright pink flowers.

Amaryllis
(Hippeastrum hybrids)

See Forcing Bulbs, page 104.

Anemone, French
(Anemone coronaria)

Not reliably hardy in Pennsylvania, though plants will overwinter south of Washington, D.C. Worth growing in pots under glass, or massing in a cold frame to give them the slight extra frost protection they need. The poppy-like flowers are mostly red, pink, white, blue, and purple, with black powdery centers. They are valued for cutting. A special strain—"MONA LISA" hybrids—always a big hit in the Philadelphia Flower Show trade section because of its extra-large flowers, is grown from seed. Other varieties must be planted from tubers planted 4 inches deep.

Anemone, Windflower
(Anemone blanda)

Plants grow just 4 inches high, spreading to form dense colonies with deeply indented, fern-like leaves and 2-inch, anemone-like flowers in mostly white, pink, and blue. Often used for naturalizing in lightly shaded areas—especially in rock gardens and as an edging to paths. Plant bulbs 2 inches deep, 4 inches apart.

Bluebell, Spanish
(Hyacinthoides hispanicus)

Nodding, bell-shaped flowers hang from arching, erect flower stems up to 8 inches high. Similar to English bluebells, but with more flowers to a stem. Though not as fragrant as English bluebells (H. non-scriptus), Spanish bluebells come in white and pink as well as blue, and they are easier to grow. Plants combine well with ferns, tolerate sun or light shade, and in a humus-rich soil they will multiply freely. Vast acres of Spanish bluebells carpet woodland at Winterthur in Delaware, flowering among azaleas.

Plant bulbs 3 inches deep, 4 to 6 inches apart.

Camassia, Wild Hyacinth
(Camassia scilloides)

Native to the Pacific Northwest, plants grow spiky, grass-like leaves and beautiful, spire-like flower heads, up to 12 inches long, in deep blue, light blue, and white. Beautiful massed in full sun among mixed perennials. Flowers in May. Plant bulbs 4 inches deep, 6 inches apart.

Checkered Lily
(Fritillaria meleagris)

Nodding, bell-shaped, 2-inch-wide flowers are mostly bicolored with a checkerboard or honeycomb pattern on the outer petals. Colors include combinations of white, cream, pink and purple. Plants grow erect stems and slender, grass-like leaves. Grows in sun or light shade. Best planted as informal drifts in rock gardens, stream banks, and clearings in deciduous woodland. Plant bulbs 4 inches deep, 3 inches apart.

Crocus
(Crocus species)

The large-flowered Dutch crocus, C. vernus, flowers in April in an assortment of colors, including white, blue, purple and yellow. The 2-inch-wide flowers form an urn shape on cloudy days, open out flat like a waterlily on sunny days. Thrives in sun or light shade. Good for edging beds and borders, and planted in colonies along woodland paths. C. chrysanthus (yellow) and C. tomasinianus (lavender-blue) are commonly called snow crocus because they bloom up to 3 weeks earlier, in March. Plant corms 4 inches deep, almost touching, in clumps.

Crown Imperial
(Fritillaria imperialis)

Plants produce erect flower stems up to 3 feet high, topped with clusters of beautiful, nodding, bell-shaped flowers in orange and yellow. The flower clusters—which appear in late April—can be 6 inches wide, with a handsome, pineapple-like crown of spiky leaves above them. The slender, pointed, bright green leaves and the brownish flower stem have an odor that smells of skunk when cut or bruised. Plants are effective planted in groups at the edge of woodland, and as an accent in mixed beds of tulips and daffodils. Though hardy, the bulbs are not normally long-lived, as they are susceptible to rot in all but the best-draining soil. Plant bulbs on their sides, 6 inches deep above the bulb nose, since the top of the bulb has a hollow depression that can collect water and rot. Space 12 inches apart.

Daffodils
(Narcissus hybrids)

There are numerous classifications for daffodils—too numerous to describe in a book of this scope—but for Pennsylvania, some superb varieties to grow include: trumpet-flowered kinds, such as the giant "FORTISSIMO" (yellow outer petals and orange trumpet); "ASCOT" (a highly fragrant double-flowered yellow with orange flecks); and "ACTAEA" (white poet's daffodil with red-rimmed "eye," sensational for naturalizing).

To evaluate the best varieties, visit Lenteboden Bulb Garden, New Hope, after April 15. Hundreds of varieties are displayed in a woodland setting for viewing and purchase. Plant bulbs 6 inches deep, 4 inches apart. Use them massed in beds and borders, naturalized along stream banks, and in deciduous woodland and open meadows. Leave the leaves for at least 6 weeks after the flowers have faded so the bulbs regenerate to flower again.

Dogtooth Violet
(Erythronium hybrids)

Though a wildflower species, E. americanum is native to Pennsylvania, prolific in moist deciduous woods, hybrids such as "PAGODA" are better for naturalizing in woodlands and rock gardens because the nodding, lemon-yellow, lily-like flowers are twice the size of the wild species, up to 3 inches wide. Plant tubers 4 inches deep, 6 inches apart.

Dutch Hyacinth
(Hyacinthus orientalis)

Star-shaped, fragrant florets cluster around a thick, succulent stem, creating a floral "column" up to 6 inches high and 4 inches wide, in white, yellow, blue, pink, red, and maroon. Suitable for massing in beds and borders, and also containers—especially shallow, dish-shaped planters. Pre-chilled bulbs are offered by many dealers for forcing indoors to have winter blooms, but outdoor flowering normally occurs in late April.

Freesia
(Freesia x hybrida)

Not hardy in Pennsylvania, but popular as a spring-flowering pot plant. Arching flower stems are topped with fragrant, trumpet-shaped flowers in yellow, orange, blue, red, pink, purple, white, and bicolors. Leaves are narrow and sword-shaped, forming clumps 1 to 2 feet high. Plant corms 1 inch deep.

Glory-of-the-Snow
(Chionodoxa luciliae)

Low, clump-forming, 4-inch plants produce masses of blue, 1/2-inch, star-shaped flowers. Most effective natural-ized in light shade, under deciduous trees to form a carpet-like ground cover. Also suitable for edging bulb borders and forming drifts in rock gardens. April-flowering. Plant bulbs 4 inches deep, 4 inches apart.

Grape Hyacinth
(Muscari armeniaca)

There is a wild species native to Penn-sylvania (*M. botryoides*), but it is not so showy. Nodding, bell-shaped, blue flow-ers cluster around short, erect stems above clumps of narrow, grass-like leaves. Self-seeds freely and increases by division, flowering in April. Plant bulbs 4 inches deep, almost touching, to create colonies in rock gardens, and at the edge of early tulip and daffodil beds.

Iris, Dutch
(Iris x hollandica)

Beautiful, elegant hybrids cherished by floral arrangers. Erect, slender stems are crowned with 4-inch iris flowers in blue, yellow, cream, ginger, and white. Though bulbs generally will survive the first winter to bloom spectacularly, in subsequent years the plants may be blind (fail to flower) or fail to appear. Plant bulbs 6 inches deep, 4 to 6 inches apart, in sun or light shade.

Iris, Snow
(Iris reticulata)

Plants form colonies when planted in hu-mus-rich soil in full sun, perfect minia-tures of Dutch iris (*I. x hollandica*), which often do not survive Pennsylvania winters. Colors include blue and purple, the flowers appearing before the spiky, grass-like leaves. Excellent for planting as drifts in rock gardens, and forcing in

containers. Good companions to snow crocus which bloom at the same time. Plant bulbs 4 inches deep, 3 inches apart.

Lily-of-the-Valley
(Convallaria majalis)

Aggressive, low-growing plants with broad, spear-shaped leaves. Will thrive even in impoverished soil, in sun or light shade. Fragrant, nodding, bell-shaped flowers are borne in arching clusters above the leaves in May. Suitable for edging borders and paths, and as a ground cover in hard-to-plant places. Plant rhizomes (called "pips") 1 inch deep, 4 inches apart.

Ranunculus, Persian Buttercup
(Ranunculus asiaticus)

Not hardy in Pennsylvania, but popular as a spring-flowering pot plant, raised under glass. Plants resemble poppies, and grow to 2 feet high. The erect stems are topped with 4-inch-wide double flowers with black centers. Colors in-clude yellow, orange, peach, red, pink, and bicolors. A particularly good large-flowered strain is the "TECALOTE" hybrids, available in separate colors and two mixtures—a rainbow mixture and picotee mixture that predominates in peach and pink tones. Plant bulbs 3 inches deep, grouping three to a 6-inch pot.

Snowdrop
(Galanthus elwesii)

Nodding white flowers, shaped like tear drops, strike through the soil in Febru-ary. Plants form 4- to 6-inch-high, grass-like clumps, increase by division, and self-seed—especially in lightly shaded locations, such as under deciduous trees. The flowers will even tolerate being cov-ered with snow.

Plant bulbs 4 inches deep, almost touching, in clusters. Good companions with winter aconites that bloom at the same time.

Snowflake, Spring
(Leucojum vernum)

Resembles snowdrops, with its nodding, white, bell-shaped flowers and clump-forming habit. Plants are a little later-flowered (usually March and April), and prefer a lightly shaded location along paths in woodland gardens. Plant bulbs 3 inches deep, almost touching.

Closely related but taller-growing and later-flowering, *L. aestivum* (summer snowflake) produces larger flowers on 2-foot-high plants in May. The variety "GRAVEYTE GIANT" grows to 3 feet, and makes the best floral display. Use as an accent in mixed perennial borders, and grouped in a rock garden.

Sparaxis, Harlequin Flower
(Sparaxis tricolor)

Not reliably hardy in Pennsylvania, though plants will overwinter outdoors south of Washington, D.C. Worth trying in a sheltered location or massing in a cold frame to provide the extra frost protection needed. Plants form clumps of sword-shaped leaves, 12 inches high, and erect flower stems crowned with clusters of star-shaped, tricolored flowers in mostly red, orange, maroon, and white—all with yellow centers, and some with a black zone. They make wonderful cut flowers, and beautiful pot plants. Plant corms 4 inches deep, 6 inches apart.

Squill, Siberian
(Scilla sibirica)

Nodding, blue, 1-inch, star-shaped flowers look like snowdrops tinted blue.

Plants grow to 5 inches high, and form colonies, especially in humus-rich soil in light shade. Mostly April-flowering, "SPRING BEAUTY" is a sterile selection with extra-large flowers. Plant bulbs 4 inches deep, 4 inches apart. Frequently blooms before the last snowfalls of winter. Combines well with tete-a-tete miniature daffodils.

Star Flower
(Tritelia uniflora)

One-inch, star-shaped flowers bloom in early May. Plants form clumps of grass-like leaves with an onion odor, multiplying freely from bulb division and self-seeding. Most attractive planted as drifts in rock gardens and as an edging to paths and borders. Plant bulbs 4 inches deep, 3 inches apart.

Star-of-Bethlehem
(Ornithogalum ubellatum)

Plants grow wild throughout meadows and at the edge of woodlands throughout Pennsylvania, forming fountain-like clumps of grass-like leaves, 6 inches high, covered in May with 1/4-inch, star-like, white flowers. Plant bulbs 4 inches deep, almost touching, in groups. Use them as drifts in rock gardens and for edging beds and borders.

Tulips
(Tulipa species)

For an appreciation of the many kinds of tulips suitable for Pennsylvania, visit the Lenteboden Bulb Garden in New Hope from April 15—when the early-flowered species bloom, through May 15—when lily-flowered (such as yellow "WEST POINT") and late double tulips (such as rose-pink "MAYTIME") finish up the parade of color.

The earliest-flowering tulips are varieties of *T. kaufmannia* (called waterlily tulips)—particularly the yellow and red bicolor "STRESA" and the *T. fosteriana* hybrids—especially the large-flowered "RED EMPEROR" and even larger-flowered "PINKEEN," which is sometimes called "PINK EMPEROR" because it looks like "RED EMPEROR," but with a pink sheen on the petal undersides. "DARWIN HYBRIDS" have traditional cup-shaped flowers on 3-foot stems. The flowers are not long-lasting (usually giving 5 days of spectacular color), and the petal colors are iridescent in a bold color range that includes yellow, red, pink, white, orange, and bicolors, peaking by May 1.

Though not so large, the old-fashioned "COTTAGE" and "TRIUMPH" tulips are generally longer-lasting, by as much as a week.

Plant bulbs 4 inches deep, 4 inches apart. After flowers are faded, let the leaves persist until they turn brown, and if a seed head starts to develop, snap it off. This helps the bulb conserve energy for flowering another year. Most tulips will give a satisfying repeat performance the second season, but only the species tulips—such as *T. kaufmannia* and *T. fosteriana*—will keep going. These are suitable for naturalizing in rock gardens and sunny or lightly shaded terraced beds.

TOP-PERFORMING SUMMER- AND FALL-FLOWERING BULBS

The following list includes both hardy and tender varieties commonly grown in Pennsylvania. All prefer planting in spring—usually after the last expected frost date. Tender kinds can be left in the soil until a fall frost kills the top growth. The bulbs can then be lifted and stored for replanting the following spring.

Agapanthus, Lily-of-the-Nile
(Agapanthus africanus)

Not reliably hardy for Pennsylvania, though "HEADBORNE HYBRIDS"— a special British strain—will survive outdoors south of Washington, D.C., flowering in early summer. Worth growing in tubs so the bulbs can be moved indoors over winter. Plants grow mound-shaped clusters of trumpet-shaped, blue or white flowers on 3-foot-long stems above strap-like leaves. Plant bulbs 2 inches deep.

Begonia, Tuberous
(Begonia x tuberhybrida)

Plants grow dark green, "angel-wing" leaves and double, camellia-like blooms up to 8 inches across in red, pink, orange, yellow, and white, plus bicolors. Plants grow to 8 inches high, prefer a lightly shaded, humus-rich soil. Popular for massing in shady beds and containers— especially windowboxes and hanging baskets. Since the introduction of the "NONSTOP" series of tuberous begonias, grown inexpensively to transplant size from seed and offered by many nurseries in ready-bloom stage, growing begonias from tubers has become less appealing. Plant the tubers (actually "corms") 1 inch deep in seed trays filled with a peat-based potting soil, and when the tubers have sprouted a set of four leaves, transfer to the garden after frost-danger. Ever-blooming until fall frost.

Blackberry Lily
(Belamcanda chinensis)

Star-shaped, 3-inch flowers are clustered on erect stems above hardy clumps of daylily-like foliage, 3 to 4 feet high. The flowers are orange and spotted red, bloom in July, and after fading develop unusual seed pods filled with glossy, blue-black, pea-size seeds. Both the fresh flowers and the dried pods are valued by flower arrangers. A hybrid variety, "CANDY LILIES" has a more extensive color range that includes yellow, pink, and white. Plant rhizomes 2 inches deep, at least 2 feet apart.

Caladium, Rainbow Plant
(Caladium x hortulanum)

Grown for its decorative, heart-shaped, heavily veined leaves which can be white and bicolored in shades of red, pink, and green. Plants grow to 3 feet high, and though tender, the bulbs can be lifted and stored during winter. Plants are especially valued for their tolerance to shade, and also their appeal in containers—especially planter boxes and tubs. Highly heat-tolerant, remaining decorative until fall frost.

Calla Lily
(Zantedeschia aethiopica)

Not reliably hardy for Pennsylvania, plants are popular for growing in tubs because the handsome, spear-shaped, ruffled green leaves and elegant, chalice-shaped white flower spathes make a beautiful accent in tubs to decorate decks and patios. The knobbly rhizomes tolerate boggy conditions, and look especially beautiful positioned close to streams and ponds. It is well worth creating a special cold frame to provide the plants the slight frost protection they demand, since the plants are hardy south of Washington, D.C., where they survive with their roots permanently submerged in shallow water.

Plant the rhizomes 4 inches deep, spaced 6 inches apart. Plants grow to 3 feet high, and form vigorous clumps. Other colors—including yellow and pink—are available by planting hybrids and related species.

Canna
(Canna x generalis)

Erect stems, up to 5 feet high, have banana-like green or bronze leaves and a dramatic cluster of gladiolus-like flowers forming a spike. Color range includes red, pink, orange, and yellow, plus bicolors. Popular as an accent in mixed beds and borders. Tender plants are popular planted in groups as an accent in mixed flower beds, and between shrubs along a house foundation. Plant bulbs 4 to 6 inches deep, spaced 12 inches apart. Blooms mostly from midsummer to fall frost.

There is a tender perennial canna that can be grown from seed to flower the first year. Called the "Tropicals," seed should be started indoors 6 to 8 weeks before outdoor planting. There is also a family of tender hybrid "water cannas" developed at Longwood Gardens, called the "Longwood Cannas." These are best grown in containers submerged under 6 to 12 inches of water, sheltered indoors during winter.

Clivia, Kafir Lily
(Clivia miniata)

Trumpet-shaped, orange or yellow flowers are arranged in a domed cluster, held erect above strap-like leaves. The plants are tender and are mostly grown as pot plants to flower indoors in March through May. The bulbs (actually fleshy roots) like to be pot-bound, and should be planted initially in gallon-capacity pots, 3 inches deep.

Colchicum, Autumn Crocus
(Colchicum autumnale)

Mostly late-summer-flowering (first week of September), plants grow slender, green leaves in early summer, and after fading send up pink flowers, resembling waterlilies, on naked stems that can reach 8 inches high. Individual flowers measure up to 5 inches across, sometimes double. Plants are hardy, good for edging paths, growing between shrubs along a house foundation, and naturalizing on sunny slopes.

Cyclamen, Hardy
(Cyclamen neopolitanum)

Hardy, fall-blooming plants grow clumps of ruffled, ivy-shaped leaves and nodding, pink, 1-inch flowers with swept-back petals. They are miniature replicas of the familiar florist's cyclamen (C. persicum) and can only be grown in Pennsylvania as a pot plant, under glass. Plant them in light shade, especially grouped along woodland paths and between shrubs along the shady side of a house foundation. Plant corms 2 inches deep, spaced at least 3 inches apart.

Dahlia, Tuberous
(Dahlia hybrids)

Tender tubers produce glossy green, heavily indented leaves and succulent, erect flower stems up to 5 feet high. Beautiful, colorful flowers grow up to 14 inches across, with rounded or pointed petals, double- and single-flowered, depending on variety. Plant tubers in full sun, 1 inch deep after frost-danger, into fertile loam soil. Tall kinds generally need staking. Color range includes yellow, orange, white, red, pink, maroon, purple, and bicolors.

Tuberous dahlias are best purchased from the mail-order specialists (see Sources). "CROYDON ACE" (yellow) and "MARGARET DUROSS" (golden orange) are two "show-quality" dinnerplate varieties that grow well in Pennsylvania. Also search out "JAPANESE BISHOP" (also known as "THE BISHOP"), growing scarlet red, daisy-like flowers on long stems against dark bronze—almost black—foliage. It grows 3 to 4 feet high and creates a stunning hedge effect behind beds of bright annuals or low-growing perennials.

Though tubers will occasionally survive Pennsylvania winters, they are best taken up after foliage has died in the fall and stored in a dry, well-ventilated, frost-free place for replanting the following spring.

Elephant's Ear
(Colocasia esculenta)

Tender corms produce massive, heart-shaped leaves—often 5 feet long. A relative of taro—the Polynesian food staple—plants grow to 8 feet high, especially in humus-rich, moist soil. Adds a tropical appearance to mixed flower borders and pond margins. Plant the large corms 4 inches deep, 6 feet apart, or grow in containers. Lift corms from soil after frost and store over winter in a dry, frost-free place. Most bulb suppliers sell small corms, which will grow progressively bigger each season. To grow the largest leaves and enjoy the longest display, start the corms indoors in March, and transplant after frost-danger. Good companions to cannas.

Gladiolus
(Gladiolus x hortulanus)

Tender, erect, spire-like plants have sword-shaped leaves and tapering flower clusters that can reach 5 feet, with 2 feet of flowering stem. The ruffled, 5-inch-wide flowers come in a wide range of rainbow colors, including yellow, orange, white, red, pink, purple, lavender blue, peach, and even green, plus bicolors. Many of the best gladiolus available today originated at the Walker Gladiolus Farm in New Hope, a specialist breeder that has now ceased operations.

The most tedious part of growing gladiolus is keeping them erect, for they tend to fall over easily. Use bamboo stakes and twist-ties to hold stems straight—or plant a dense hedge of dwarf marigolds around the plants. By the time the gladiolus have become top-heavy with blooms (usually late July and August), the marigolds reach a third of the way up the stems to give them support.

Though the corms will survive mild Pennsylvania winters, especially planted extra-deep (4 to 5 inches instead of the recommended 3 inches), it is safer to lift them and store indoors over winter. Plant the corms at least 6 inches apart. The long stems are excellent for cutting, and the plants are good companions to tuberous dahlias.

Iris Bearded
(Iris, x germanica

See Perennials.

Lily, Garden
(Lilium hybrids)

See Perennials.

Montbretia
(Crocosmia x crocosmiiflora)

Not reliably hardy in Pennsylvania, though they are a popular feature of gardens south of Washington, D.C. The orange-red, freesia-like flowers appear in summer, and grow from corms that should be planted 3 inches deep, 6 to 12 inches apart. Worth growing in a special cold frame to provide the extra amount of frost protection they need. The hybrid "LUCIFER" (scarlet-red flowers) is the hardiest. Plants grow to 3 feet high.

Naked Ladies
(Lycoris squamigera)

Beautiful, peachy-pink, 10-inch-long, trumpet-shaped blooms appear in clusters atop naked brown stems in August, after the long, arching, strap-like leaves have appeared in spring. Plants grow 2 to 3 feet high, form colonies, and are sufficiently hardy to survive winter over most areas of Pennsylvania. Grow them grouped as accents in mixed perennial borders and beds of annuals. Plant bulbs 4 inches deep into a sandy or well-drained soil, ensuring full sun.

Peacock Flower
(Acidanthera bicolor)

Resembles gladiolus, usually too tender to survive winter, but valued as a cut flower. White, outward-facing flowers have a maroon "eye." Plants grow to 4 feet high, and produce iris-like leaves. Best grown in groups as an accent in mixed flower borders to flower in August. Plant bulbs 3 inches deep, 4 to 6 inches apart. Lift plants in fall and store indoors for replanting in spring.

Sternbergia, Autumn Daffodil
(Sternbergia lutea)

Hardy, crocus-like, yellow flowers appear in September. After the flowers have faded, slender green leaves appear and persist through winter. They are good to use for edging mixed flower borders, and also for adding color in front of shrubs along the house foundation—particularly the blue mist shrub, which flowers at the same time.

Tuberose
(Polianthus x tuberosa)

Erect stems are topped with clusters of highly fragrant, white flowers forming a spike. Flowers occur in August and September, and can be double or single, with the singles pervading the air with the strongest fragrance, reminiscent of gar-denias. Plants grow to 3 feet high, have broad, sword-shaped leaves, and are excellent for cutting. Plant them as accents near decks and patios. Though the rhizomes will survive mild winters, second-year plants are usually weak and fail to flower. Better to buy new rhizomes each spring. Plant 2 inches deep, spaced 6 inches apart.

FORCING BULBS

Many winter-hardy flowering bulbs can be forced indoors to bloom during winter months. The most important requirement is a "cooling period" of 8 to 15 weeks, depending on variety (see chart). For the "cooling period," bulbs must be held in darkness at a temperature of 35 to 50° F, then moved to bright light at 60° F or higher. Paperwhite narcissus, amaryllis, and other "tender" bulbs do not need a cooling period. Some bulb suppliers sell hyacinths pre-cooled.

Selection

The best hardy bulbs for forcing include special varieties of tulips (especially "CHRISTMAS MARVEL" and "APRICOT BEAUTY"), daffodils (especially the "TETE-A-TETE" miniature daffodil and "FLOWER RECORD"—white with an orange cup), plus crocus, hyacinths, grape hyacinths, and snow iris (Iris reticulata). Use only "top-size" bulbs.

Planting

Generally speaking, plant in October using 6-inch pots for best results. Bulbs will bloom within 3 to 4 weeks after the following cooling period:

Variety	Number of Bulbs/6" Pot	Cooling Period in Weeks
Crocus	12–15	8
Iris	10–12	8
Grape Hyacinth	10–12	8
Daffodils	6	12–14
Tulip	6–8	13–15
Hyacinth	1–3	8

Potting Soil

Peat-based commercial potting soils are best, with broken clay pieces of pot over the drainage hole to provide good drainage. A good do-it-yourself soil mix comprises equal parts of garden topsoil (loam), peat moss, and sand. When using clay pots, soak pots overnight in water so the clay does not draw moisture from the soil and cause rapid drying. This procedure is not necessary with plastic pots.

Fill pot with potting soil, ensuring that top of bulb is level with the rim and soil surface is 1/2 inch below the rim. If soil settles after watering, add more potting soil, label with name of bulb and date planted. Place pots in a cool, dark, frost-free place, such as a basement, attic, or cold frame, and check pots weekly for dryness indicating a need for water. If bulbs are cooled outdoors in a cold frame, they must be protected with mulch such as a 4- to 6-inch layer of shredded leaves, so they do not freeze. In the absence of a cold frame, bulbs can be cooled outdoors in a trench 6 inches wider and 3 inches deeper than the pots. Line bottom of trench with a 1-inch layer of gravel. Fill between pots to top of trench with loose soil and cover with 3 to 4 inches of straw. Protect from mice by encasing pots in a roll of fine wire mesh, or sprinkle surface liberally with mice-repellent flakes or mothballs.

Forcing Period

Mark your calendar with the termination dates for each cooling period, and when the cooling period is over, move pots indoors for forcing. Indoor temperature must be 60° F or higher (70° F is optimum). Bright sunlight is needed to initiate strong stem and leaf growth prior to flowering. If light is directional, rotate pots regularly and keep soil moist. Bulbs should start to bloom in 3 to 4 weeks after moving indoors.

After forcing, discard bulbs or plant outdoors into fertile soil where they have a chance to rejuvenate themselves. Forced bulbs generally are drained of too much energy to be forced again, but by keeping the leaves green until after the last frost date and planting outdoors into fertile, well-drained soil, they may continue to flower in subsequent years.

Forcing Paperwhites

The highly fragrant paperwhite narcissus is a tender daffodil that will not overwinter outdoors in Pennsylvania. It can be forced into flower about 6 weeks after planting in early October, or until Christmas. Paperwhites do not need soil to flower. A popular way to grow them is to fill a container half-full with gravel and add water to just below the surface of the gravel. Then place the bulbs on the gravel and anchor with more gravel. Keep cool (50 to 60° F) and in low light until green shoots appear (usually 2 to 3 weeks), then move to bright light. Keep the water level to just below the bulbs so the roots are always in moisture, but the bulbs themselves remain dry. Discard the bulbs after flowering.

Forcing Amaryllis

There are two kinds of amaryllis suitable for forcing—African hybrid amaryllis and Dutch hybrid amaryllis. They are both tender varieties of *Hippeastrum* and will not survive Pennsylvania winters planted outdoors into the garden. The African hybrids—such as ''CHRISTMAS RED''—have been grown in Africa (usually below the equator) where the seasons are the reverse of North America. The bulbs become available about Thanksgiving and will start to sprout immediately after being watered, normally flowering within 4 weeks—and usually in time for Christmas. The Dutch hybrids—

such as "SCARLET BABY" (an extraordinarily free-flowering miniature variety)—may take up to 10 weeks to bloom, flowering about the middle of January to the middle of March. Both kinds are sold as bare bulbs, to be placed into 6-inch pots filled with a peat-based potting soil; and also pre-potted, so all you add is water.

Some amaryllis bulbs will produce two—and even three—flower spikes, each lasting about 6 to 8 days. After the flowers die, the stems can be trimmed away, leaving a cluster of fleshy, arching, strap-like leaves. To rejuvenate an amaryllis so it blooms again the following year, keep the leaves green by continuing to water with a weak-strength liquid fertilizer added to the water once every 2 weeks. After all danger of frost, remove the root ball from its pot and transfer to a fertile, humus-rich, lightly shaded location in the garden. Keep watered and rake a high-phosphorus fertilizer, such as bone meal, into the upper soil surface. After the leaves die down in fall, lift the bulb, clean away the soil, and move to a dark, cool, frost-free location for 8 to 10 weeks. Then repot, bring into the light, water, and a new shoot should appear, flowering within 4 weeks.

WATER PLANTS

Most water plants grow from bulbs or bulb-like roots, and so it seems appropriate to feature them at the conclusion of a chapter on bulbs. Pennsylvania has many farm ponds that beg to be decorated with water plants, and of course many suburban homes are enhanced with a waterlily pool or pond. But even if you don't have a pond, and don't care for the expense of creating even a small pool, it's possible to enjoy a beautiful, diverse water garden, planted entirely in a fair-sized, wooden half-barrel, to use as a decorative patio accent during summer. Dwarf varieties of water plants can be chosen (even dwarf kinds of lotus and waterlilies), and they can be arranged into pleasing foliage and color harmonies, by planting in pots and submerging at different heights within the barrel. Rigid plastic liners can be purchased from commercial water gardens that will fit snuggly inside a half-barrel.

One of the most interesting wetland preserves in Pennsylvania is the Tinicum National Environmental Center, consisting of 900 acres bordering Philadelphia Airport. Dry trails encircle a tidewater marsh and lead through habitats where herons, egrets, and ducks find refuge among beautiful, bog-loving, native wildflowers, such as swamp mallow (*Hibiscus moscheutos*), purple loosestrife (*Lythrum salicaria*), pickerel rush (*Pontederia cordata*), and native waterlily (*Nymphaea odorata*). A good time of year to see the largest number of plants in bloom is July.

Following is a description of the most useful water plants for Pennsylvania, with cultural instructions.

Waterlilies and Lotus

Nymphaea hybrids (Waterlilies). There are two types—the hardies, which are day-bloomers, and the tender tropicals, many of which are night-blooming. Tropical waterlilies grow to 10 inches across—twice the size of the hardies. Many of the tropicals have magnificent mottled leaves, and a strong yet pleasant fragrance, but they will not survive Pennsylvania's winters and must be moved into a protected, frost-free space. Also, if your pond or pool is spring-fed, it's unlikely they will succeed, since they need a higher water temperature (preferably above 70° F), and the water temperature must be stable. Contrary to popular belief, the tropicals can bloom longer than the hardies. The hardies flower predominantly in July and August, dwindling by the middle of September, while the tropicals can continue another 4 weeks—until frost.

Modern hardy waterlilies are mostly hybrids between wild species from North America, Central America, and Europe. Most are descended from an aggressive breeding program begun by a Frenchman, Latour Marliac, including "MARLIAC ALBIDA" (fragrant white), "CHROMATELLA" (yellow), "ESCARBOUCLE" (deep rosy pink), and "COMANCHE" (orange). The plants grow horizontally across the surface of water, forming "islands" of rounded leaves. It is best to confine the roots to large containers—a 32-quart (1-bushel) tub is ideal. Other acceptable containers are wooden boxes made from untreated lumber. Do not use redwood which is toxic underwater. Also good to use are half-barrels and metal tubs that have been painted with a good coating of underwater-type nontoxic paint.

Use good garden soil including topsoil, and mix in some well-rotted manure. Avoid packaged potting soil and dried manures. Fill tub or box half full with garden soil and well-rotted manure mixed at a ratio of four parts soil to one part manure. Add 1/2 cup (4 oz.) of granular 10-10-10 fertilizer and mix thoroughly. Fill container up to approximately 2 inches from the top. Firm the soil around the rhizome, leaving the crown exposed. Add 1 inch of gravel over the top of the soil to anchor it, and wherever muskrats are a problem, create a dome of chicken-wire over the container to prevent these pests from eating the waterlily shoots. Carefully lower the completed planting into the pool approximately 6 inches below the water surface. After good growth is established, the container can be lowered so its top is submerged 12 to 18 inches. If the pool depth is greater than this, put containers on cinder blocks or bricks to bring them up to the proper depth.

It's also possible to buy waterlilies ready-planted in plastic tubs, with leaves and flower buds already formed. One of the largest waterlily growers in North America, Lilypons Water Gardens, is located just below the Pennsylvania-Maryland border, near Frederickstown, and there are many other water garden specialists serving smaller localities. Visit water gardens in early summer and choose the colors you like for an instant floral effect. However, be sure to place damp newspaper over the leaves when transporting them from the nursery to their new home, since any drying out of the leaf will kill it. To maintain soil fertility push fertilizer tablets specially formulated for waterlilies into the upper soil surface at least every 2 weeks during their flowering period.

Nelumbo hybrids (Hardy lotus). Individual flowers can measure more than 12 inches across on long, tall stems that will grow to 5 feet high, surrounded by large leaves shaped like a parasol. When lotus blooms fade they produce saucer-size seed pods that rattle with pea-size seeds. These dried seed pods are valued by floral arrangers. Since lotus are extremely aggressive and can crowd out all other plant life in a pond, it is best to confine them to sunken containers. The larger the container the better; one plant will generally need at least a 3-gallon plastic tub. Submerged "kiddy pools" filled with a fertile clay loam are ideal if a small grouping of plants is desired.

Colors are mostly pink and white, though there is a smaller-flowered, wild yellow lotus native to Pennsylvania (*N. lutea*) with a globular flower head the size of a golf ball.

Other Beautiful Water Plants

In the world of water gardening there are three major categories: bog plants that will grow with their roots permanently immersed in water, floating plants that rest their leaves on the surface of water, and margin plants that will tolerate moist soil. Following is a description of hardy plants that help to beautify Pennsylvania ponds, pools, and streams. Asterisked varieties will grow with roots submerged in water.

*Arrow Head Plant
(Sagitarria latifolia)

Erect stems up to 2 feet tall have decorative, arrow-shaped leaves and attractive, loose spikes of 2-inch, four-petalled white flowers.

Astilbe
(Astilbe x arendsi)

See Perennials.

*Cardinal Flower
(Lobelia cardinalis)

See Perennials.

*Cat-tail, Narrow-leaf
(Typha latifolia)

More graceful than its relative, broadleaf cat-tail (*T. angustifolia*), both of which are native to Pennsylvania. Plants grow to 6 feet high, forming clumps of narrow, needle-like leaves and erect, cigar-shaped, dark brown flower clusters atop long stems. Plants are best confined to sunken tubs as they can become invasive.

*Forget-me-not, Water
(Myosotis palustris)

Identical to regular garden forget-me-nots, but plants will grow with roots submerged. Sensational planted along small, spring-fed streams.

Hardy Hibiscus, Swamp Mallow
(Hibiscus moscheutos)

See Perennials.

*Iris, Blue Flag
(Iris versicolor)

Similar to yellow flag iris, but with lovely blue flowers in June, and not so tall.

*Iris, Japanese
(Iris ensata)

See Perennials.

*Iris, Yellow Flag
(Iris pseudacorus)

Naturalized throughout Pennsylvania. Plants grow to 4 feet high, produce clumps of sword-shaped leaves and masses of 4- to 5-inch yellow flowers in June and July.

Loosestrife, Purple
(Lythrum salicaria)

See Perennials.

Loosestrife, Yellow
(Lisymachia punctata)

See Perennials.

*Parrot's Feather
(Myriophylum aquaticum)

Feathery, light green foliage trails over the water surface. Especially beautiful contrasted with water clover, the two together making excellent spawning places for fish. Like water clover, it should be planted in submerged pots since it can spread rapidly.

*Pickerel Rush
(Pontederia cordata)

Native to Pennsylvania tidal marshes, plants grow clumps of spear-shaped leaves up to 3 feet high, and erect flower stems with blue or white, poker-like flower spikes in summer. Can be invasive if not confined to a submerged tub.

*Sweet Flag, Variegated
(Acorus calamus variegatus)

Though the flowers are insignificant, the bold, white and green striped, iris-like leaves make sensational accents, especially contrasted with cat-tails, water cannas and waterlilies.

*Water Clover
(Marsilia mutica)

Beautiful floating leaves resemble four-leaf clovers. Best planted in a submerged container as it tends to spread rapidly in pools and ponds with earth bottoms.

GARDEN POOL PLANTING DIAGRAM

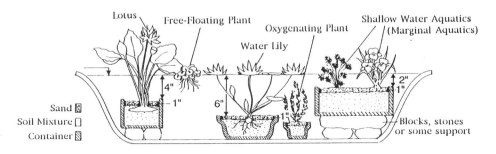

CHAPTER 6

Wildflowers

The welcome sight of wildflowers and appealing wild foliage plants—such as ferns—is found everywhere in the woods and meadows of Pennsylvania from February, when skunk cabbage pushes its purple and green mottled flower spathe through swampy soil, to October's final fling of wild blue asters and yellow goldenrod.

When spring is warming to its task and the strengthening power of the sun touches the forest floor, dormant wildflowers receive the energy they need to burst into bloom. A walk in the woods during late April or early May can be especially delightful because Pennsylvania's wildflowers are more prolific during spring than at any other time of year. Many will grow, flower, store food, and make next year's seeds before the trees are in full leaf. Later in the season wild colonies of shrubby, evergreen mountain laurel (*Kalmia latifolia*), the state flower, and evergreen *Rhododendron maximum* bloom throughout the state.

For observing the wildflower extravaganza at close range there's Bowman's Hill Wildflower Preserve south of New Hope in Bucks County; Winterthur Gardens near Wilmington, Delaware; the Brandywine Conservancy, Chadds Ford; Longwood Gardens, Chester County; and Valley Forge State Park, Montgomery County. In the center of the state, Bear Meadows, near State College, is a wildflower paradise, as are many other state parks.

An extremely unusual wildflower garden can be seen at the Henry Foundation, near Gladwyne, where on 50 sloping acres you will find a collection of hardy plants collected from all over North America, including Pennsylvania. The garden not only has a wooded area where shade-loving plants—like three-petalled trilliums—thrive, but it also has a natural rock garden with mass plantings of *Liatris spicata* (bottlebrush), *Yucca filamentosa* (Spanish dagger), *Baptisia australis* (false indigo), and many other fine specimens of perennial wildflowers. Native trees and shrubs abound. The garden is at its best during the month of May—when spring wildflowers are at their peak—and again in July when lilies and liatris present an impressive display (see page 209 for opening times).

Perhaps the most remarkable flower in the woods is Jack-in-the-pulpit. All young Jack-in-the-pulpits begin life as males, but after 3 or 4 years they become females. In the fall, fertilized females produce clusters of brilliant red berries containing seed to propagate the species. The sex change is possible only when the plant has built up enough energy in its underground bulb. If the plant is in a poor location and cannot find sufficient nourishment, it stays male all its life and never sets seed. If, after becoming female, its reserves of energy are depleted, it changes back into a male. Look for Jack-in-the-pulpit in misty, shady places near streams and ponds during the first week of April.

For sunny sites, a wildflower meadow garden may be the answer. Two private gardens in Pennsylvania featuring extensive wildflower meadow gardens are Doe

Run, near Unionville, Chester County; and Chanticleer, near Wayne, Delaware County. However, in both cases, the wildflowers are not native perennial wildflowers, but annual mixtures featuring mostly Shirley poppies (*Papaver rhoeas*) and bachelor's buttons (*Centaurea cyanus*). They are seeded onto bare soil in early spring for blooming in early June.

Bowman's Hill Wildflower Preserve is a rich source of wildflowers, where potted plants are offered for sale. The picturesque commercial nursery of Jacob's Ladder Wild Gardens (formerly Vick's Wildgardens) on Conshohocken State Road, near Gladwyne, also sells potted wildflowers.

Albert Vick is a true conservationist. He is considered the only nurseryman in America who attempts to propagate wildflowers, no mean achievement when you consider that trout lilies, for example, may take 7 years to germinate from seed, trilliums up to 5 years, and Jack-in-the-pulpits up to 3. You can't just go out into the countryside and dig up wildflower plants for your home garden. Most are fully protected by Pennsylvania conservation laws. At Al Vick's wildflower nursery, that trout lily that took 7 years to grow will cost you just a few dollars per potted plant.

Mr. Vick also designs, builds, and maintains wild gardens all over the eastern United States. He knows the mysteries and peculiarities of every wildflower, their soil requirements, their ecological relationship to other organisms, and the kinds of settings that best show off their foliage and blossoms. He's the man to see if your idea of a garden is a shady nook bordered with hardy azalea and cinnamon fern; or a natural dam with pools, waterfalls, and rustic bridges; or even a naturalistic Japanese-style garden with boulders, stepping stones, and miniature Bonsai trees. Maybe you would prefer a small, wild corner by the back fence. One of Al Vick's very best wild gardens was for the late H. Thomas Hallowell, Jr. at Deerfield Farm in Rydal, Montgomery County. There Mr. Vick helped to create a magnificent valley garden along the steep sides of a stream. The sides of the wooded valley are planted extensively with azaleas, rhododendrons, dogwoods, ostrich ferns, lilies, hostas, and primulas. Seven springs, bubbling up from the soil at one end of the property, merge to create the stream. Vick outlined each of the springs with stone and made rustic paths around them, crossing each flow of water with either stepping stones or bridges, and creating a series of waterfalls. In another area of the property, he planted a fern garden under the shade of some tall pines, making it a pleasant place to sit and cool off during the heat of summer.

Al Vick comes from a long line of horticulturists. His great-grandfather founded James Vick's, Inc. of Rochester, New York, one of the oldest mail-order seed businesses in America. His father founded the present wildflower nursery in 1929. A garden planted with wildflowers and ferns, featuring outcroppings of rock and delicately landscaped with mountain laurel around an informal lily pond fed by a sparkling stream, is the kind of idyllic spot that can be a reality.

POPULAR PENNSYLVANIA WILDFLOWERS

Following are some descriptions of the most desirable and most beautiful wildflowers to grace the Pennsylvania countryside. Some are natives; others (such as the wild multiflora rose from China) are escapees into the wild from foreign lands. Many prefer humus-rich, shaded soil; others thrive in open, sunny positions such as meadows. The vast majority are easily raised from seed, and will self-seed readily. A raised bed of humus-rich soil under light shade can create ideal conditions for growing many wildflowers from seed direct-sown.

Arrowhead
(Sagittaria latifolia)

See Water Plants.

Beebalm
(Monarda didyma)

See Perennials.

Black-eyed Susan
(Rudbeckia hirta)

A stunning wildflower that can literally cover an acre field from end to end. The orange, daisy-like flowers are up to 4 inches across, with dark brown, button-like centers. Plants grow to 3 feet high, prefer full sun, and bloom mostly in July. Easily grown from seeds, direct-sown, and by division. See also Perennials for cultivated varieties.

Bleeding Heart, Fernleaf
(Dicentra eximia)

See Perennials.

Bloodroot
(Sanguinaria canadensis)

Beautiful, pure white, anemone-like flowers grow in low, spreading clumps in light shade, and bloom in early spring. Plant the tuberous roots (which bleed red when cut) in humus-rich soil along woodland walks. There is also an unusual double-flowered variety. Plants grow to just 10 inches in height. Easily propagated by dividing rhizomes. Plants self-seed easily.

Blue-eyed Grass
(Sisyrinchium angustifolium)

Relatives of the iris family, plants grow grass-like clumps in moist, sunny meadows. Masses of blue, 1/2-inch-wide flax-like flowers appear in late May and early June. Easily propagated by seed and by division. Plants grow to 18 inches high.

Bluets or Quaker Ladies
(Hedyotis caerulea)

Tiny, four-petalled flowers, pale blue in color and delicate. They will carpet the ground in spring, either in open, sunny positions or in clearings among woodland. They are especially fond of growing through cushions of moss. Plants grow just 4 inches high. Propagate by division of healthy clumps.

Butterfly Weed
(Asclepias tuberosa)

See Perennials.

Canada Lily
(Lilium canadense)

Gorgeous, pendant lily flowers are yellow with handsome brown spots. Slender, lance-like leaves grow along the wiry, strong stems that can reach up to 5 feet high. Plants will grow in sun or light shade, flower in early summer, and prefer open fields, meadows, and swampy soil. Easily propagated from seed.

Cardinal Flower
(Lobelia cardinalis)

See Perennials.

Cat-tail
(Typha latifolia)

See Water Plants.

Columbine, Wild
(Aquilegia canadensis)

Grows abundantly in rocky woodland, especially beside streams. The pendant, scarlet flowers are shaped like miniature fuchsias, borne in dense clusters above fern-like foliage in early spring. Easily propagated by seed.

Creeping Jenny
(Lysimachia nummularia)

A spreading plant with small, yellow, cup-shaped flowers in summer. A hardy perennial introduced from Europe. Easily divided.

Dames Rocket
(Hesperis matronalis)

Perennial, phlox-like plants grow erect stems with lance-like leaves, up to 3 feet high, topped with clusters of pink, white, or purple, four-petalled flowers. Blooms mostly in late May and early June in meadows and lightly shaded woodland. Easily propagated by seed, direct-sown.

Dogtooth Violet
(Erythronium americanum)

Likes moist woodland. The yellow flowers resemble a miniature Turk's cap lily and appear in early spring. The leaves are slender, pointed, and mottled, in pairs emanating from a fleshy root. Plants grow to 6 inches high. A hybrid developed from this species, called "PAGODA," is taller and has flowers twice the size. Propagate by dividing root offsets from the parent corm. Plants may take several years to flower from seed.

Dutchman's Breeches
(Dicentra cucullaria)

Slender, arching flower stems are strung with up to seven white, yellow-tipped flowers resembling a Dutchman's pantaloons hung upside down. The feathery, gray-green foliage is decorative, creating a good ground cover for shady slopes with humus-rich or gravelly soil. Plants bloom in early spring, and grow just 9 inches high. Divide bulb clusters after flowering.

Ferns

For Pennsylvania gardens, favorites are the native ostrich fern (*Matteuccia pennsylvanica*) and the native maidenhair fern (*Adiantum pedatum*). The ostrich fern grows tallest, up to 5 feet high. The fronds stand upright, arching gracefully as the season progresses. It likes moist soil—even boggy ground. It is especially beautiful planted along stream banks or pond margins. The maidenhair fern has delicate-looking, lacy fronds that spread out in lovely layers. Plants grow to 2 feet high and demand a shaded, moist position. They are exquisite planted among rocks and close to clumps of moss near a waterfall.

Foam Flower
(Tiarella cordifolia)

Creates a compact mound of decorative, ivy-shaped leaves from which sprout dense clusters of white, frothy flower spikes. Plants grow just 12 inches high, and look good alone or planted in bold drifts along woodland walks. A wonderful ground cover, flowering in spring. Easily propagated by division.

Honeysuckle, Scarlet
(Lonicera sempervirens)

See Trees and Shrubs.

Iris, Blue Flag
(Iris versicolor)

See Water Plants.

Iris, Crested Dwarf
(Iris cristata)

Perfect miniatures of the tall bearded iris, the blue or white flowers appear in spring on low, spreading plants with sword-shaped leaves. They quickly form large colonies, especially in woodland and shady slopes, in humus-rich soil. Plants grow to just 4 inches high. Propagate by dividing rhizomes.

Joe-pye Weed
(Eupatorium fistulosum)

See Perennials.

Lady-slipper, Pink
(Cypripedium acaule)

Hard to establish since this plant has a symbiotic relationship with soil bacteria indigenous mostly to oak trees and pines. Where the bacteria are present the plants form attractive colonies in light shade. The pink, slipper-like flower blooms on an 8-inch stalk in early May. Some private wildflower preserves in New England supply mail-order nurseries with blooming-size transplants, but losses are high. Plants demand a moist, humus-rich, acid soil, mulched with oak leaves or pine needles in a lightly shaded location.

Lady-slipper, Yellow
(Cypripedium calceolus parviflorum)

Gorgeous yellow, slipper-like blossoms appear in spring on erect stems that often form dense clumps with broad, arching, spear-shaped leaves. Prefers the shade of oak trees or high, widely planted pines. Plants grow to 18 inches high, and look especially good planted beside streams, pools, and in the shady section of rock gardens. Much easier to establish than the pink lady-slipper. Obtain transplants from plant sales at wildflower preserves.

Lobelia, Blue
(Lobelia siphilitica)

See Perennials.

Loosestrife, Purple
(Lythrum salicaria)

See Perennials.

Marsh Marigold
(Caltha palustris)

See Perennials.

May Apple
(Podophyllum peltatum)

Covers the woodland floor in colonies, each plant displaying a pair of umbrella-like leaves resembling giant-size pachysandra leaves. Almost hidden by the foliage is a waxy white flower, up to 2 1/2 inches across, which bears a yellow, oblong fruit. All parts of the May apple are poisonous, but the fruit is edible as jelly or jam. Drifts of May apples make a good ground cover along woodland paths. Direct-sow seeds or divide rhizomes in fall.

Multiflora Rose
(Rosa multiflora)

See Roses.

New England Aster
(Aster novae anglae)

See Perennials.

Obedient Plant
(Physostegia virginica)

See Perennials.

Ox-eye Daisy
(Chrysanthemum leucanthemum)

See Perennials.

Pasture Rose
(Rosa carolina)

See Roses.

Pickerel Weed
(Pontederia cordata)

See Water Plants.

Phlox, Blue
(Phlox divaricata)

See Perennials.

Phlox, Creeping Blue
(Phlox stolonifera)

See Perennials.

Prickly Pear, Hardy
(Opuntia humifusa)

See Perennials.

Queen-of-the-Prairie
(Filipendulina rubra)

Floss-like flower clusters are borne on 4-foot stems in summer. Tolerates moist soil.

Snakeroot
(Cimicifuga racemosa)

See Perennials.

Star-of-Bethlehem
(Ornithogalum umbellatum)

See Bulbs.

Sundrops
(Oenothera fruticosa)

Summer-flowering perennial with yellow, cup-shaped flowers. Forms dense clumps. Easily divided.

Swamp Sunflower
(Helianthus angustifolius)

Widespread in moist and boggy soils, especially moist, sunny meadows and waysides. The daisy-like, yellow flowers grow up to 6 feet in height. Propagate by division of healthy clumps, and by direct-seeding.

Sweet Autumn Clematis
(Clematis maximowicziana)

See Trees and Shrubs.

Trillium, Large-flowered
(Trillium grandiflorum)

Four-inch, three-petalled, white or pink-tinged flowers are borne in profusion on low, bushy plants, 8 to 15 inches high. Plants prefer a humus-rich acid soil. Best propagated by division though plants self-seed readily. Flowers in early May.

Trumpet Creeper
(Campsis radicans)

See Trees and Shrubs.

Violet, Common
(Viola papilionacea)

Small, blue, pansy-like flowers appear in early spring above cushion-like plants with rounded, heart-shaped leaves. Grows in full sun or light shade; especially likes humus-rich, moist soil. Plants grow just 6 inches high, are easily propagated by division, and self-seed readily.

The yellow violet (*V. pennsylvanica*) is beautiful when established in tight colonies, while the sweet white violet (*V. blanda*) creates a lovely ground cover and edging.

Virginia Bluebell
(Mertensia virginica)

Delicate clusters of blue, bell-shaped flowers crown the tips of arching stems in spring. Plants transplant easily, and self-seed reliably in moist, humus-rich shaded sites, especially along woodland walks. Plants grow to 2 feet high. There is a rare white-flowering variety. Propagate by seed, direct-sown, and by root division.

Waterlily, White
(Nymphaea odorata)

In midsummer the sight of acres of these lovely water plants blooming on ponds and lakes through the New Jersey Pine Barrens, east of Philadelphia, is an uplifting sight. The snow white, star-shaped, 5-inch blooms have golden yellow stamens. The flowers usually are held a few inches above the floating, rounded leaves. Easily grown from root tubers. See also Water Plants.

Wild Geranium or Cranesbill
(Geranium maculatum)

Prolific in deciduous woods and waysides, bearing pink, 1-inch flowers in clusters. Plants grow to just 2 feet high, and prefer a loam or humus-rich, moist soil, creating an open, bushy habit. Plants blend beautifully with Spanish bluebells. Propagate by division of healthy clumps.

Wood Lily
(Lilium philadelphicum)

The chalice-like, upward-facing orange flowers are 2 1/4 inches wide, have spotted throats, and grow in lightly shaded woodlands and clearings throughout the state, flowering mainly in July. Plants grow to 3 feet high, and prefer a humus-rich soil. Mostly propagated from seed.

Bowman's Hill Wildflower Preserve has produced an excellent book describing dozens of other wildflowers, and also explaining a variety of propagation techniques. Entitled *Ways with Wildflowers,* copies can be obtained by contacting Bowman's Hill Wildflower Preserve, Washingtons Crossing, PA 18977. Incidentally, Bowman's Hill has two popular plant sales—in spring and fall—when many unusual wildflowers and native trees can be purchased at reasonable prices.

Cedaridge Farm
A Pennsylvania Garden Through Four Seasons

Historic Cedaridge Farm, in Bucks County, Pennsylvania, is where the author gardens year-round. Featuring award-winning theme gardens—including a cutting garden, cottage garden, vegetable garden, orchard, woodland garden, stream garden, pond, and several perennial beds—color is maintained through all the seasons.

Above: Perennial beds newly dug in the early spring are ready for planting on a sunny slope at Cedaridge Farm.

Below: The same beds by midsummer, overflowing with perennials (such as rudbeckia), summer-flowering bulbs (such as gladiolus), and annuals (especially petunias).

Spring Fruits and Vegetables

Above: Vegetable garden at Cedaridge Farm is mulched with straw for weed control. Stone wall and sheep hurdles help to keep deer and other animal pests out of the garden.

Below: Early crop of salad greens, including Chinese cabbage and loose leaf lettuce, thrive in raised beds.

Above: Aerial view of the vegetable garden shows blocks of lettuce, spinach, and cabbage, creating a decorative quilt design.

Below: Strawberries are the first berry crop to mature at Cedaridge Farm. Both large-fruited June-bearers and medium-size day-neutral everbearers are grown.

Summer Fruits and Vegetables

Above: Vegetable garden at Cedaridge Farm in high summer produces a bountiful crop of tomatoes and peppers. Block of bush beans (right) has replaced a lettuce crop.

Below: Harvest of tomatoes includes Supersteak large-fruited red, Big Early large-fruited red, Jubilee orange-fruited, red and yellow cherry and yellow pear.

Above: Harvest of
peaches, yellow
plums, apricots, blue-
berries, and black and
red raspberries.
Though apricots are a
risky crop, they fruit
heavily when flowers
are protected from
frosts.

Below: Crop of luscious
melons includes Early
Hybrid Crenshaw (top),
Burpee Hybrid Canta-
loupe (bottom), Honey-
dew (left), and Sugar
Baby Watermelon
(right).

Spring Flowers

Above: The author's wife, Carolyn, harvests daffodils in April at Cedaridge Farm. Daffodils, hyacinths, and hellebores are some of the early spring flowers untroubled by deer.

Below: Pansies in a mixed display provide early color. This space is later planted with annuals for cutting.

Above: Small meadow garden planted with Shirley poppies and blue bachelor's buttons.

Below: Many of the flowers in this small informal border reseed themselves to come back each year, particularly the larkspur and yellow coreopsis.

Summer Flowers

Above: Cutting garden at Cedaridge Farm is vibrant with orange cosmos, blue salvia, yellow marigolds, and mixed zinnias.

Below: Here the author is dead-heading (removing spent blossoms) in the cottage garden to keep the flowers blooming.

Above: Entrance gate to cottage garden festooned with nasturtiums and morning glories. Spider flowers shimmer in the background.

Below: Pond-side planting features hardy hybrid hibiscus, cardinal flowers and spider flowers.

Autumn Color

Above: Tender orange angel's trumpets bloom in
pots at the entrance to the
cutting garden at Cedaridge
Farm.

Below: Chrysanthemums are
late-blooming flowers, even
surviving light frosts.

Below: Ornamental grass garden planted on both sides of a stream produces flowers and russet colors in autumn.

Above: Red footbridge complements the colors of autumn leaves. Grove of Heritage river birch at left displays honey- colored bark.

Above: Old sleigh on the front lawn at Cedaridge Farm makes an interesting garden accent decorated with pine branches.

Below: Many dried seed cases, such as Chinese lanterns and silvery money plant, are harvested in winter to make indoor arrangements.

Above: Pyracantha (firethorn) berries remain decorative until Christmas, and tolerate even heavy burdens of snow.

Below: Cheerful display of forced hyacinths, daffodils and other spring bulbs decorates a sun-room at Cedaridge Farm while snow still covers the garden outdoors.

Pennsylvania Gardens to Visit

Above: Lenteboden Bulb Garden, near New Hope, features thousands of tulips and daffodils during late April and early May.

For information on where to find the public gardens featured here, see the Appendix under Places of Interest.

Center: Part of a formal Colonial-style garden at the headquarters of the Pennsylvania Horticultural Society, Philadelphia. Plants are changed with the season.

Below: Greatest show under glass—the conservatory at Longwood Gardens, Kennett Square—features cymbidium orchid displays in February.

Above: Perhaps the world's most beautiful landscape design surrounds Frank Lloyd Wright's "Falling-water," a residence and country retreat designed for a Pittsburgh family.

Center: Conestoga House, Lancaster, is the former home of a newspaper magnate, with many beautiful formal areas, including a perennial garden and herb gardens.

Below: Historic Peter Wentz farmhouse, Worcester, features a kitchen herb garden in a quadrant design. George Washington slept here.

Above: The internationally famous flower test garden at Penn State University, State College, displays summer annuals to perfection.

Center: Hershey Rose Gardens overlook the famous chocolate factory. On a hill above the gardens is the beautiful Hershey Hotel.

Below: A magnificent chrysanthemum display is featured every autumn at Ott's Greenhouses on Schwenksville Pike near Collegeville.

Printed in Hong Kong

CHAPTER 7

Lawn Care

Generally speaking, lawns in Pennsylvania can be established by *seeding, sodding,* or *plugging.* Bluegrass, perennial ryegrass, and similar turf grasses commonly established by seeding are the most highly recommended lawn grasses for Pennsylvania when a lawn is in full sun. In light shade, a fine fescue is most desirable. As an alternative to seeding, these grasses can be sodded by purchasing squares of ready-grown turf from a turf farm. However, the cost of buying turf, transporting it to the site, and laying it in place is high compared to seeding. At Penn State University, turf experts have developed improved perennial ryegrasses that germinate in 3 days and show green within 5 days, making the establishment of a new lawn almost as fast as laying sod.

Plug-type lawns are mostly composed of zoysia. The plugs are planted 12 inches apart and spread by runners, eventually knitting together to create a weed-suffocating turf. However, zoysia, though root-hardy in Pennsylvania, is not recommended. The top growth turns brown at the first sign of frost and stays an ugly brown color until the beginning of May. Moreover, the plugs can take upwards of 2 years to make a thick turf cover.

For an attractive, hard-wearing lawn, Kentucky bluegrass used to be the preferred lawn grass for Pennsylvania. But in recent years groundskeepers have been switching to improved perennial ryegrasses. They are indistinguishable from Kentucky bluegrass, have better heat tolerance, and better winter hardiness. There are years when an improved perennial ryegrass lawn will stay green all winter.

For optimum results, a lawn should be seeded as a mixture. The best all-purpose lawn mixture is a formula containing 20% improved perennial ryegrass, 70% Kentucky bluegrass, and 10% fine fescue. Under normal circumstances, the improved perennial ryegrass will germinate first—within 3 days under favorable conditions—and in 10 days, the Kentucky bluegrass will germinate to fill in any bare spots. If there are any shady areas that inhibit germination of the ryegrass and bluegrass, the fine fescue will establish itself.

In deep shade, it may be best not to try a turf lawn, but to use a shade-tolerant ground cover such as *Vinca minor*, *Pachysandra terminalis*, or *Hedera helix* (English ivy).

PREPARING THE SEEDBED

Since most Pennsylvania soils are highly acid, a soil test is desirable to determine how much lime may be needed to reduce the acidity for a luxuriant lawn (see page 16 for more information on soil tests). The soil test also will advise whether any humus-rich soil conditioner is needed and what fertilizer formula to apply. Normally,

Pennsylvania soils require the addition of some lime (see page 15 for more information on liming) and the addition of a soil conditioner such as peat moss. Lime is generally recommended for use on a lawn every 3 years. It is applied in the form of granular limestone which will not burn grass. The most important nutrient needed to establish a beautiful lawn will be nitrogen.

The site for a new lawn must first be rough-graded. This means turning over the top 4 to 6 inches with a tiller or spade and filling in any holes. Soil conditioner, lime, and fertilizer should be raked into this upper soil surface prior to seeding, and the surface raked to a fine, granular texture, called "fine grading." Sprinkle seed at the rate recommended on the package, and to ensure good soil contact, roll the seeded surface with a dry, heavy roller or firm by pressing boards onto the soil.

To prevent the soil surface from drying out and killing the seed embryos, it is advisable to spread a layer of straw over the seeded area and water the site for an hour each day until the green grass shoots appear. Muslin or a lightweight horticultural fabric such as polypropylene also can be used as a mulch to conserve soil moisture. Remove the fabric as soon as the green grass shoots poke through it.

BEST TIMES FOR SEEDING

Over most of Pennsylvania the very best time to seed a new lawn is the middle of August when nights start to turn cool. Conditions during late summer and early fall are most favorable for germinating grass seed. Also, at that time of year, most weed seeds are dormant and will not compete with germinating grass seed. Seeding for good turf grass establishment can be done until mid-September.

The next best time of year to establish a new lawn is in spring, from early April through mid-May, when cool conditions and reliable natural rainfall generally prevail.

FERTILIZING A LAWN

If you are going to feed your lawn only once, do it in the fall. Feeding then helps to establish a vigorous root system and a good, green, spring color. However, twice-yearly feeding is better—one application in spring before the last frost date and another in fall after Labor Day. The spring feeding can be a combination fertilizer and weed killer (called "Weed 'n Feed") so that noxious weeds, such as dandelions and chickweed, can be controlled (see also Weed Control). For organic enthusiasts there are organic lawn fertilizers available, but none that include an organic weed killer.

IRRIGATION

For most small lawns, an oscillating lawn sprinkler can provide moisture during dry spells. However, there are many years when dry spells cause turf grasses to turn brown, even with the aid of a lawn sprinkler. For a picture-perfect lawn all summer, you need to install an underground lawn sprinkler system, turned on for an hour late in each afternoon.

WEED CONTROL

The most noxious weed in Pennsylvania lawns is crabgrass. An annual, it does not germinate until after frost-danger in spring and dies down at the first frost in fall, turning brown and leaving ugly patches. The best control is a pre-emergence crabgrass weed killer which prevents the seeds from germinating. Different types are needed for new lawns and established lawns (check the label). Both are granular, can be applied with a lawn spreader, and should be watered-in if natural rainfall does not occur within 3 days.

An alternative to pre-emergence control is post-emergence control, for applying in June *after* the crabgrass has germinated and established itself. This kills the crabgrass outright, leaving brown patches which should be raked with a leaf rake to remove the dead parts and then seeded over to establish turf grass.

Other weeds are known as broadleaf weeds. These include dandelion, plantain, chickweed, and mock strawberry. The best control for an established lawn is a Weed 'n Feed, applied when the grass is damp and when there is no prediction of rain for another 48 hours. Weed 'n Feed products kill the noxious weeds, at the same time feeding grass.

INSECT AND DISEASE CONTROL

Lawn grass diseases are generally caused by fungus and are difficult to diagnose. To prevent fungus diseases taking hold, keep the lawn mowed at 3 to 4 inches; fertilize in spring and fall to maintain vigor and natural disease resistance; water frequently during dry spells; and de-thatch with a lawn rake in the fall before fertilizing.

The most serious insect pests are grubs, especially white, crescent-shaped grubs which are the larva stage of Japanese beetles. You can see them by lifting up a section of sod with about 2 inches of soil attached. They not only chew grass roots, causing the grass to wither and die, they attract voles and moles which cause ugly piles of soil and undesirable raised tunnels that tear apart when touched by mower blades. A good natural control is Milky Spore Disease, a powdery product that releases spores into the soil, killing the grubs.

MOWING

It is not important to cut your lawn close to the ground for a luxuriant appearance. What is more important is a *uniform* cut, not the height of the cut. In fact, a lawn cut with the blades set at 3 to 4 inches puts less stress on the grass, especially during summer dry spells.

TIMETABLE FOR LAWN CARE IN PENNSYLVANIA

For a picture-perfect lawn in Pennsylvania you may use one of several reputable professional lawn care services, such as Lawn Doctor and ChemLawn, or you can do it yourself using the following timetable. Because of the concerns among homeowners over chemicals that might harm the environment and the danger of poisoning young children and animals, these lawn care services now offer the option of organic lawn care, or a combination of chemical and organic treatments.

For quick-reference here's a recommended lawn care chart for Pennsylvania:

Monthly Lawn Care

	Jan	Feb	Mar	Apr	May	Jun	Jul	Aug	Sept	Oct	Nov	Dec
Aeration/ De-thatching				←→			←——→					
Fertilization				←→			←—→					
Irrigation				←— As Needed —→								
Liming				←——→					←Best Time→			
Mowing				←— As Needed —→								
Seeding			←—— Best Time ——→									
Weed Control			(Broad Leaf) ←→					←→				
			(Crabgrass) ←→					←→				
			(Pre-emergent)				(Post-emergent)					

CHAPTER 8

Trees and Shrubs

When William Penn landed in Pennsylvania he was delighted to find so many beautiful native trees, and founded Philadelphia as a "greene country towne" in 1682. The early colonists not only discovered many majestic deciduous trees—such as tulip poplars, hickories, osage oranges, black walnuts, and white oaks—but also towering evergreens, particularly the spire-like junipers (commonly called red cedar) that forested dry ground, and durable bald cypresses that forested swampy places.

The colonists discovered many new ornamental shrubs—notably the early-flowering amelanchiers (producing a blizzard of hawthorn-like blossoms in early spring), new species of rhododendron (such as lovely pink- and yellow-flowered azaleas), and the winterberry (a deciduous holly that bears masses of bright red berries in fall). They discovered the curious paw-paw (a tropical survivor of the Ice Age, bearing oval green fruits with a custard-like, banana-flavored interior), and the delicious butternut (a close relative of the black walnut, yielding the tastiest meat of any nut tree). The colonists also discovered that European orchard trees produced abundantly in Pennsylvania—not only apples and pears, but also stone fruits such as plums, cherries, and peaches.

Perhaps no one expressed the value of trees more dramatically than Henry F. duPont, owner of the Winterthur estate in Delaware. In spite of the fact that his house contained a priceless collection of antiques, he instructed his staff that in case of a fire they were to hose down the trees and forget about the house, for he could always rebuild it, while the magnificent tulip trees surrounding it could never be replaced.

The natural verdant beauty of Pennsylvania inspired the establishment of many beautiful tree collections, called arboretums, and also public parks. The English style of landscape design advocated by Capability Brown—meandering driveways leading to a mansion surrounded by park-like vistas, lakes, bridges, and groves of trees—was ideal for Pennsylvania's tree-rich environment, and with the acquisition of wealth, many beautiful mansions were built emulating the British "gardenesque" concept of landscape design. Though Pennsylvania has many surviving examples (including the Morris Arboretum in Chestnut Hill and The Highlands in Fort Washington), the most impressive estate garden in the gardenesque style is Rockwood, located in Wilmington, just across the Pennsylvania border in Delaware.

Joseph Shipley, the creator of Rockwood, started his successful career as a cotton merchant in Philadelphia. After living a number of years in England, in 1851 he returned to his roots, using his former English residence near Liverpool as a model for a new estate. This involved a Gothic mansion with a magnificent Victorian conservatory and romantic gardens that contrasted smooth contours and curving outlines of the land with sharply defined patterns of tree plantings. Thus, the low, graceful, flowing outline of a Japanese maple is contrasted with the bizarre, erect, angular profile of a monkey puzzle tree and the billowing, cloud-like bulk of an evergreen rhododendron. The trees are grouped into a pleasing harmony of leaf shapes, bark coloration, canopy profile and flowering effect. Particular attention is paid to their color harmonies in autumn when the tree canopy blazes with the molten red brilliance of a towering black tupelo and the buttercup yellow of a massive Chinese ginkgo. The concept holds up especially well in winter as the shapes and textures are accentuated by snowfall. The cascading branches of a Sargent's weeping hemlock resemble a frozen waterfall, while nearby the coils of a massive wisteria vine—as thick as an elephant's foot—resemble frozen stalagmites when coated with snow.

In Joseph Shipley's time over 100 ornamental trees and shrubs were introduced to the property, many of them purchased across the border in Pennsylvania from the Pierce Tree Nursery in Kennett Square—a property that was later acquired by Pierre S. duPont for the creation of Longwood Gardens, the most ambitious display garden in the world.

By the time Shipley moved into Rockwood he was seriously crippled with gout, and needed a wheelchair to get around. The slow pace of the life he was forced to lead after retiring from business gave him the time to study the landscape carefully and wait patiently for young tree plantings to mature. Today, the Rockwood estate is remarkably well preserved, inviting a leisurely stroll across its spacious lawns, along its picturesque vistas, and into its magnificent woodland.

Though John Bartram (1699-1777) and his son, William, are credited with introducing into cultivation the largest number of North American plant species—another Pennsylvania farmer, Humphrey Marshall, helped foster an early understanding of the value of trees in the home landscape. A first cousin to John Bartram, Marshall founded a botanical garden at West Bradford, Chester County, close to the Pierce Brothers tree nursery (which later became the nucleus for Longwood Gardens), and also close to the Painter brothers who developed what was to become the beautiful Tyler Arboretum at Lima. In 1785 Marshall published the first book on native trees and shrubs, entitled *Arbustum Americanum.*

Today, Martin Brooks, owner of Brooks Rare Plant Nursery near Doylestown, Pennsylvania, carries on the tradition of collecting beautiful tree specimens. He has made a specialty of growing and selling mature specimens of rare and unusual trees— both deciduous and evergreen—but with emphasis on conifers.

A graduate of Delaware Valley College of Science and Agriculture, Brooks started his tree nursery in 1955 on 45 acres that had been used to grow tomatoes for Campbell Soup. He was greatly influenced by the now-defunct Bergmann "Rariflora" Nursery near Feasterville, Bucks County, which contained one of the finest collections of dwarf conifers in North America, until it was auctioned off in 1970 following the owner's death. Martin Brooks had befriended the owner and with his permission began building up his own collection of rare trees from cuttings.

The Rariflora auction attracted some of the country's wealthiest private garden owners and many prestigious public botanical gardens. Brooks helped catalog and evaluate the collection of more than 5000 specimens, and took payment in the form of plants. The Arnold Arboretum, near Boston; the National Arboretum, in Washington, D.C.; and New York's Central Park were among the discriminating bidders. A cultivar of Japanese white pine (*Pinus parviflora* "BERGMAN") sold for $35,000— setting a record price for a single plant specimen (though Martin Brooks himself has since beaten that record, selling specimen trees from his own collection for twice that figure).

Martin Brooks acquired many of the plants in his collection by tracking down large estates that were in the process of being sold for development, and also by visiting family-owned businesses that were changing ownership, often picking up bargains because the old owners wanted a good home for certain treasured plants. Brooks especially likes to collect trees with cascading or weeping forms, notably the Alaskan weeping cedar (*Chamaecyparis nootkatensis* "PENDULA") and the weeping blue spruce (*Picea pungens glauca* "PENDULA").

Among the unusual aspects of the Brooks Rare Plant Nursery is not only the enthusiastic and dynamic personality of the owner (usually sporting a tee-shirt and chomping a fat cigar), but the artistic way that much of the collection is displayed— free-form island beds with leaf color, texture, and form carefully taken into consideration to create a spectacular treescape that is so visually beautiful and inspiring that it is easy for visitors to understand why an individual specimen might sell for $100,000 or more. Though plants are often sold with no guarantee of survival after the tree is transplanted, Brooks digs extra-large root balls and makes site inspections to ensure a high rate of success.

Another important promoter of garden-worthy trees and shrubs in Pennsylvania is Dr. J. Franklin Styer, plant breeder and nurseryman, who established an award given by The Pennsylvania Horticultural Society—The Styer Award of Garden Merit (later changed to the Gold Medal Plant Award)—for the purpose of recognizing outstanding new woody ornamental plants.

Following the next section devoted to general tree and shrub culture is a sampling of woody plants that grow well over most of Pennsylvania, with Gold Medal Awards identified. The list includes both deciduous woody plants (which lose their leaves in winter) and evergreens (which keep their leaves over winter). Also, trees and shrubs are noted for their flowering effect, fall coloring, or for functional reasons (hedging, screening, cooling shade).

CARING FOR TREES AND SHRUBS

Pennsylvania's soils and climate favor the healthy growth of many handsome trees and ornamental shrubs. An extremely large number of garden-worthy woody plants are native to the state, and at Bowman's Hill Wildflower Preserve, New Hope—in and around an area known as Penn's Woods—it's possible to see a collection of almost all the most important trees and shrubs present in the Pennsylvania landscape when William Penn arrived.

Abundant moisture in spring to produce healthy new growth, warm summers with frequent rainstorms to maintain fast sustained growth, and sharp winters to induce a restful "dormancy" period combine to create a lush, verdant landscape. However, these very conditions that promote luxurious tree growth can also hinder it. When the ground is soft from too much moisture, trees can be uprooted by high winds that accompany frequent thunderstorms, especially during the hurricane season of August and September. When the leaf canopy is too dense, the foliage growth of healthy trees can catch the wind like a sail, causing them to blow over. The best insurance against damage to valuable trees is regular pruning. A tree canopy that is properly thinned can often withstand high winds that tumble unpruned trees like nine-pins. However, do not attempt pruning of tall trees yourself. The accident rate among homeowners trying to prune tall trees is high. Call in a tree service for a free consultation and estimate.

In winter, occasional ice storms can cause severe damage—particularly when rain falls in the night and freezes on tree branches. When the air stays still and the sun comes out to melt the ice, little damage is evident, but if a wind should blow as the skies clear, then huge limbs can come crashing down, and trunks split apart from the weight of the ice.

When shrubs—especially boxwoods and azaleas—are planted close to the house, and are susceptible to damage from snow sliding off the roof, take the precaution of covering the plants with temporary wooden shelters. Many plants—such as boxwoods—though hardy in Pennsylvania, cannot stand to have their leaves covered with frozen snow. After a snowfall take a broom and sweep off the snow from branches of valuable small trees and shrubs.

Dehydration is probably the most common cause of death among woody plants, especially during winter. Newly planted trees are especially susceptible. If a tree has not had a chance to extend its roots into the surrounding soil and take in sufficient moisture, then drying winter winds can quickly starve the plant of moisture, turning it brown and lifeless. A good precaution is to stake newly planted trees so there is no movement of the root ball, and not to fertilize newly planted trees the first year, which generally causes too much top growth for the root system to accommodate. Also, the use of a tree-wrap around the trunk will help avoid dehydration, as well as providing some protection from damage by deer and rodents.

Another extremely common cause of tree losses is injury from a carelessly handled lawn mower—particularly from hand mowers scraping away bark for disease organisms to enter. Be sure valued trees and shrubs have a circle of mulched soil extending out some distance from the trunk so mowers don't need to cut close to the bark.

Selecting Trees and Shrubs

Plants purchased from mail-order sources often are "bare-root" cuttings or year-old seedlings that have been pulled from the nursery fields and the roots cleaned of any soil for economical shipment. The success rate of bare-root plants is not as high as for plants that are "containered" (usually grown in a 1- or 3-gallon plastic pot)—or "balled" (the root ball is wrapped in burlap sacking). You are most likely to obtain containered or balled trees from nurseries and garden centers. Specialist tree farms are also good places to buy woody plants—for example, you may have a small grower in your area who grows only azaleas and rhododendrons, another who offers only selections of Japanese maple; specialists in evergreens are common.

Usually, a higher success rate is assured with bare-root woody plants if the plant is potted-up and held in a lightly shaded area until a healthy mass of roots fills the pot. Then it will take transplanting to a permanent position without shock. Sometimes bare-root stock arrives with a few superficial roots or branches broken. These can be trimmed away. However, if the leader or the main taproot is broken, return the shipment for a replacement or refund.

With containered plants it's an easy matter to slide the root ball out of the pot and plant into a permanent position with little root disturbance. A new growing technique pioneered by Forrest-Keeling tree nurseries in Missouri, increases the success rate of transplanting trees with large taproots. Called "milk carton" transplants, they are raised from seed in deep pots that are open at the bottom. As the taproot pokes through the bottom it is "air-pruned" (it automatically shrivels up and dies, except for the portion of the root covered with soil). This air-pruning of the tap-root forces more feeder roots to sprout and to fill the pot space. When transplanted the extra feeder roots help the plant to overcome transplant shock, ensuring a high survival rate.

With "balled" plants, it's important to loosen the top of the burlap sacking, since plastic string is often tightly tied around the trunk, and this can strangle the tree if not removed. Also, nails are sometimes used to hold burlap around a root ball, and these should be removed.

Examine the trunk for any signs of rodent damage—mice will gnaw the base of trees, girdling the bark. While the tree may look healthy for a while, it will invariably perish after transplanting.

Also look for signs of borer damage (holes in the trunk oozing sap or a gummy resin), and look at the leaf undersides for any signs of insect colonies—such as aphids and mite infestations.

Stroke the leaves and branches, particularly of evergreens. If the leaves feel brittle and easily fall off the branch, the plant may be on the verge of dehydration.

Planting Stock

Determine if the stock you are buying is seedling stock (transplants grown from seed), grafted stock (whereby a special cold-hardy or dwarfing root stock has been used), or vegetative stock (such as rooted cuttings). Seedling stock is usually the least expensive and it can produce variable results. For example, seedlings of sugar maple trees will have variable forms of fall coloration—some may even be rather drab.

Grafted stock is usually the most expensive because it involves carefully connecting a desirable "top" to a more desirable "bottom." Where the two meet is usually just above the soil line, recognizable as a swollen area. It is extremely important to keep this swollen section above the soil line, and to prune away any side-shoots (suckers) that emerge from the root portion, as these will be inferior.

Woody plants grown from rooted cuttings will generally show the same characteristics of the mother plant. Usually they are not much more expensive than seedling-grown stock, but of better quality.

When to Plant

Spring planting is generally the best time of year to transplant trees and shrubs, especially after a spring thaw, when the ground has started to warm up. Fall is another good planting time for hardy woody plants, but generally not for bare-root stock. Care should be taken in fall planting that the soil is mulched, and the plants do not dry out. High success rates from fall planting are possible using "milk-carton" transplants, because these have a large portion of roots compared to top growth.

Christmas is a favorite time to buy balled evergreen trees to serve as a decorated tree over the holiday season, and then go into the garden. It is important that the balled tree be watered while indoors, and transferred to the outdoors in stages after serving as a Christmas tree. If it goes straight from a warm, comfortable room environment to a cold winter landscape, chances are the tree will perish from shock. However, if the tree is first moved to an unheated garage for 7 to 10 days before moving outside, that is usually sufficient to acclimatize it. Because the ground may be frozen when you want to make the transfer, have your planting hole already dug, and keep the soil on a tarp or in a wheelbarrow—in a place where it will not freeze solid. Then, when you place your precious Christmas tree outdoors, you will have loose soil with which to fill in around the root ball.

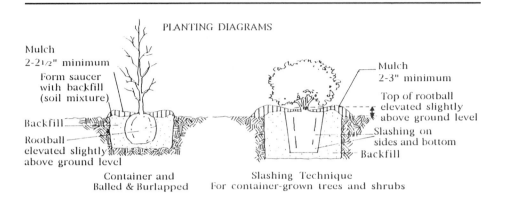

PLANTING DIAGRAMS

Mulch
2-2½" minimum
Form saucer
with backfill
(soil mixture)
Backfill
Rootball
elevated slightly
above ground level

Mulch
2-3" minimum
Top of rootball
elevated slightly
above ground level
Slashing on
sides and bottom
Backfill

Container and
Balled & Burlapped

Slashing Technique
For container-grown trees and shrubs

The Planting Hole

Tests by the U.S. Forest Service have shown that if the soil is reasonably good—a sandy or clay loam—then trees do not need "backfill"—a term to describe improved soil that is used under and around a root ball. The sooner a newly planted tree can knit its roots into the indigenous soil, the faster it will grow. However, if the soil is poor—particularly if it is stony or impervious clay—then "backfilling" is advisable. Simply dig a hole at least twice the width of the root ball and twice as deep, filling half the depth with a soil mix of 50% topsoil and 50% humus, such as peat moss. Water, let the soil settle, and backfill some more. Place the tree in the hole so the top of the root ball is slightly above ground level. Fill around the sides with your soil mix and tamp the soil firmly with your foot to ensure good soil contact with the side of the root ball. Water thoroughly and leave a saucer-shaped rim around the trunk to the edges of the hole as a "catchment" for natural rainfall. Over the depression place a loose covering of organic mulch, such as shredded pine bark, for moisture conservation and weed control.

Wrap the trunk with tree wrap to help prevent sun-scald and pest intrusions such as deer and borer damage. In addition, it is advisable to stake the tree to prevent rocking of the root ball during wind. Plants must receive a thorough soaking at the time of planting, and if a week goes by without a good, soaking, overnight rain, water thoroughly again.

Fertilizing

Tests by the U.S. Forest Service have shown that on level surfaces, surface feeding of trees is preferred to root feeding. Surface feeding is achieved simply by scattering a dry, granular fertilizer around the drip line and raking it gently into the upper soil surface. Or, the soil can be drenched with a liquid feed. Rain carries the nutrients to the tree's feeder roots which are located mostly in the top 12 inches of soil.

Root feeding is the practice of drilling holes around the drip line of a tree and pouring fertilizer into the holes, on the theory that it reaches roots more quickly than a surface application. This is advisable only where trees are on a slope, and where turf grows up to the trunk, making an even surface penetration difficult.

Also, it is advisable not to feed a newly planted tree the first year because the feeding tends to stimulate more top-growth than the roots can handle. Better to wait a year for the roots to be well established before feeding.

Pruning

Various types of pruning help to keep trees and shrubs healthy. For most shrubs pruning is done to maintain a pleasing, compact shape, to cut out any dead or diseased branches, and to thin out dense growth from the interior so there is better air circulation for improved vigor. With flowering shrubs—such as azaleas—pruning should be done after flowering, giving the plants time to develop new flower buds. With other shrubs autumn is a preferred time for pruning, especially after frost.

Trees need pruning for many other reasons—such as to remove a broken limb. Tree experts used to recommend wrapping any large pruning wounds with a tree-wound dressing, but studies have shown that trees are generally more efficient at healing themselves if a tree-wound dressing is not used, and fresh air can circulate around the wound.

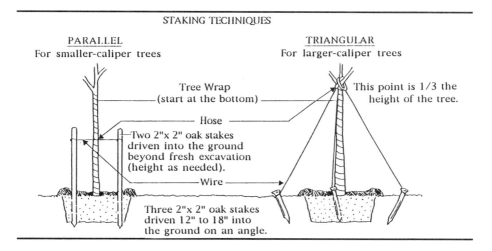

STAKING TECHNIQUES

PARALLEL
For smaller-caliper trees

TRIANGULAR
For larger-caliper trees

Tree Wrap
(start at the bottom)

This point is 1/3 the height of the tree.

Hose

Two 2"x 2" oak stakes driven into the ground beyond fresh excavation (height as needed).

Wire

Three 2"x 2" oak stakes driven 12" to 18" into the ground on an angle.

It is important to remove "constrictors"—branches that cross and rub against each other, causing an open wound into which disease organisms can enter.

Useful pruning tools include hand saws to cut through large limbs, long-handled lopping pruners to cut through limbs no thicker than a person's wrist, and hand pruners to cut through pencil-thick branches. Electric hedge trimmers are suitable for shaping shrubs with dense foliage cover.

Insect and Disease Control

Mites, aphids, chewing caterpillars such as gypsy moths, borers, and beetles are some of the most prevalent insect pests that attack trees. Some cause defoliation, while others cause cankers and root rot, sometimes resulting in the death of a valuable tree. Similarly, there are many diseases caused by fungus and bacteria. One of the most disheartening in Pennsylvania is known as "dogwood decline" or "lower branch dieback"—a fungus disease that attacks weakened dogwood trees, causing wholesale death. Most tree diseases are avoidable by planting disease-resistant strains (the "HERITAGE" river birch, for example, is resistant to many of the problems affecting white birch; the Chinese chestnut is resistant to blight disease that has killed off almost all the native stands of American chestnut), and by a proper diagnosis and control. Though Penn State University has entymologists who will diagnose problems by inspecting an infected branch or leaf, usually it's better to call in a professional arborist. Better still—if your property has a lot of trees—contract with a professional tree service to visit at least once a year.

SOME TOP-RATED TREES AND SHRUBS

Andromeda, Japanese
(*Pieris japonica*)

Slightly fragrant, urn-shaped white or pinkish flowers are borne in cascading clusters in early April and May. A broad-leaved evergreen, plants grow 9 to 12 feet high, prefer light shade, and are good companions to azaleas. Many varieties are available, such as "DOROTHY WYCOFF," a 6-foot-tall plant with red flower buds that open pink. The new foliage of "MOUNTAIN FIRE" is bright red, the flowers are white. "PYGMAEA" has small leaves and a mature height of only 3 feet, good for a ground cover effect. Plants prefer a humus-rich, moist, acid soil, and will tolerate light shade.

Arborvitae, American
(*Thuja occidentalis*)

The dense, light green evergreen foliage of this native conifer can be pruned into geometric shapes to make tall formal hedges resembling walls. Dwarf varieties such as "HETZ MIDGET" form 5-to 6-foot mounds, while "PYRAMIDALIS" is an upright columnar form. The variety "TECHNY" has deep green winter coloring. Unnamed varieties are usually broad and pyramidal in shape, growing up to 3 feet a year to 60 feet high. Plants are kept compact by annual pruning. Newly planted specimens need protection from deer who find it a favorite food.

Ash, Green
(*Fraxinus pennsylvanica*)

Native Pennsylvania deciduous tree, growing to 60 feet high. Selected forms have a beautiful, mounded growth habit and striking, yellow fall foliage. Widely used for creating wooded lots because of its tolerance of poor soil.

Ash, Mountain
(*Sorbus aucuparia*)

Prolific fall fruiting makes this a sensational ornamental tree for Pennsylvania. Growing to 30 or 40 feet with a spread of 20 to 30 feet, its leaves are composed of 9 to 15 spear-shaped leaflets. Beautiful white flowers in flat clusters appear in June. Berry-like, orange-red fruits start to show color in September. Good varieties include "APRICOT QUEEN" (apricot-colored fruit), "BRILLIANT PINK" (pink fruit), "CARPET OF GOLD" (yellowish-orange fruit), and "XANTHOCARPA" (yellow fruit). Transplant balled and burlapped plants into well-drained soils. Excellent as a lawn highlight, but susceptible to fireblight disease, a fungus disease that blackens the fruit.

Aucuba, Japanese
(Aucuba japonica)

A slow-growing evergreen plant that forms a mounded shape. The common species has glossy, dark green, lance-shaped leaves, but it is the variegated forms, in yellow and green, which are more popular. Eventually, plants grow to 8 feet high, and are either male or female. When a male is present the female plants set clusters of small, scarlet fruit. Plants prefer well-drained, moist, acid soil in light shade. "VARIEGATA" is a yellow-flecked female variety, known as the "Gold Dust Plant." All plants need a sheltered location to prevent damage to the leaves from chilling winds and ice.

Azaleas and Rhododendrons
(Rhododendron species)

Many species of azalea and rhododendron are native to Pennsylvania. Rhododendrons with large, oval, evergreen leaves and large, rounded flower trusses are not so widely adaptable as the so-called azaleas, with small leaves and small flowers. The large rhododendrons generally do best in a lightly shaded location, cooled by the presence of water. They thrive in moist locations, such as along shaded stream banks and at the base of rocky cliffs. The most successful for Pennsylvania conditions are the "iron-clad hybrids," such as "AMERICA" (red) and "ROSEUM ELEGANS" (pink), with characteristics from Himalayan and North American species. Colors among rhododendrons include white, pink, red, purple, creamy-yellow, and bicolors. Azaleas have bright yellow and orange in their color range. Among the most heat-tolerant rhododendrons for Pennsylvania is "SCINTILLATION." Its slightly fragrant, pale pink flowers are flushed a deeper pink and handsomely blotched in the throat with chocolate-colored freckles on a yellow background. Up to 15 bell-shaped flowers make up the huge flower trusses.

Three Pennsylvania men are immortalized in the annals of the American Rhododendron Society—the late Dr. John C. Wister, director of the Scott Arboretum at Swarthmore College; the late Joseph B. Gable (1886-1972), a farmer from Stewartstown, Pennsylvania; and G. Guy Nearing (1890-), born in Morris Run, Pennsylvania. It was Dr. Wister who organized a systematic search for the "lost" hybrids of a New England hybridizer, Charles Owen Dexter (1862-1943). Prior to his death, Dexter had sent out hundreds of hybrids for evaluation at botanical gardens and estate gardens throughout North America, and they were in danger of being lost except for the determination of Dr. Wister to locate as many as possible, evaluate them as garden-worthy plants, and propagate them for public introduction. "SCINTILLATION" was one of the discoveries, made in a remote part of the New York Botanical Garden.

Joseph Gable was made famous by an article in the *Saturday Evening Post* headlined, "The Flowering Forest of Joe Gable." With spectacular pictures of his nursery near York, and an account of his tireless hybridizing work on both rhododendrons and azaleas, Joseph Gable became an overnight celebrity and his Pennsylvania hybrids highly sought after. One of his most famous rhododendrons is "CADIS" (with large pink flowers), while his most famous azalea is "STEWARTSTONIAN" (a striking red evergreen azalea with bronze winter foliage).

After graduating from the University of Pennsylvania, Guy Nearing opened a rhododendron nursery, first in Arden, Delaware, and then in Ridgewood, New Jersey. He was good friends with Joe Gable, and the two of them shared their knowledge of rhododendron breeding. Most of Nearing's best-known introductions do well in Pennsylvania—especially "WINDBEAM" (a compact, mounded plant growing to 6 feet, with masses of small apricot-yellow blooms that appear in early May). An excellent border or edging plant is Nearing's "RAMAPO" (a hardy dwarf with small, early light purple flowers). Both are ideal for planting in rock gardens and as decorative accents in tulip borders.

"EXBURY" azaleas—developed in England by the late Lionel de Rothschild—are extremely popular in Pennsylvania gardens. They predominate in yellow and orange, are highly fragrant, and lose their leaves in winter. "MOLLIS" hybrids are similar in appearance to the "EXBURY" types—and also highly fragrant—but they are generally more adaptable to dry conditions. The "EXBURY" hybrids need cool, moist, humus-rich soil, while the "MOLLIS" hybrids will tolerate full sun.

Barberry, Japanese
(Berberis thunbergii var. atropurpurea)

At Hershey, Pennsylvania, the words "Hershey Chocolate" are spelled out in hedges of this remarkably hardy shrub. Deep purple foliage is distinctive, a fine contrast to the green lawns and green shrubs. Unpruned plants grow to 6 feet high and 7 feet wide. Thorny branches help make the plants impenetrable once established. Yellow flowers are followed by red fruits, but neither are conspicuous. In a shady location the purple coloration changes to green. "CRIMSON PYGMY"—a dwarf compact variety—can be used to create a miniature hedge for edging garden spaces.

Beauty Berry
(Callicarpa dichotoma)

Though several callicarpas are good to grow in Pennsylvania for their beautiful purple berry clusters (including C. americana, native to Pennsylvania), C. dichotoma produces the best berry display, winning a Gold Medal Award from the Pennsylvania Horticultural Society. Plants grow to 6 feet high, with an equal spread, in sun or light shade.

Beautybush
(Kolkwitzia amabilis)

A dramatic late-spring-flowering shrub that needs room to spread. Plants grow to 15 feet high and nearly as wide. Pink, funnel-shaped flowers 5/8 of an inch long almost smother the plant in late spring, afterward fading to white. Leaves are dark green and spear-shaped, on cascading branches. Best transplanted from containers. Though tolerant of poor soil, plants need good drainage. Prune to thin out crowded stems every other year. Prefers full sun.

Beech, European
(Fagus sylvatica)

A stately, slow-growing tree that can attain a height of 50 to 60 feet or more, with a spread even greater. Trees are rounded or dome-shaped when mature. The smooth, gray bark resembles an elephant's hide. Serrated, pointed leaves are a lustrous dark green in summer, turning golden and russet-brown in fall. "ATROPUNICEA" and "RIVERSII" are deep bronze-black leaves. "TRICOLOR" has purple leaves that are margined in creamy white and pink. "PENDULA" is a handsome weeping form. Plants prefer acid loam soil and full sun, but will grow in partial shade. A superb lawn specimen where it has room to spread. Generally more desirable than the native American beech (*Fagus grandiflora*).

Birch, White Birch
(*Betula papyrifera*)

Gleaming white bark and buttercup-yellow fall foliage are good reasons to grow this species as a lawn highlight, and as a grove. Trees grow to 50 feet and spread about 30 feet. The bark on older specimens turns a chalky-white and peels for a decorative effect. Plants have an upright, round-headed habit. Prefers acid, well-drained, sandy or loam soils. Hardy throughout Pennsylvania, though plantings south of Philadelphia may suffer heat stress in exposed locations. Beautiful when contrasted with the blue green foliage of junipers and hollies.

Because of insect and disease problems, a special clone of the native river birch (*B. nigra*) is being used to replace the paper birch. Called "HERITAGE" birch, it is extremely fast-growing (up to 5 feet a year). Unlike the wild river birches that grow along stream banks throughout Pennsylvania, "HERITAGE" has blond, peeling bark with an ornamental effect similar to the white birch. The leaves turn a beautiful buttery yellow in fall. Because of its value as a landscape tree, "HERITAGE" won a

Gold Medal Award for excellence from the Pennsylvania Horticultural Society.

Black Locust
(*Robinia pseudoacacia*)

White, fragrant flowers that hang in chains like wisteria decorate this strong, upright tree for 7 to 10 days in late May and early June. Even young trees flower. They are fast-growing to 50 feet in height with a spread of 20 to 30 feet. Leaves are compound, up to 14 inches long, consisting of 6 to 19 slender, pointed leaflets. Occasional root suckers need to be removed. Transplants easily and tolerates a wide range of soils, provided drainage is good. Beautiful textured bark has a pronounced "basket weave" pattern. Makes a splendid grove, the light, airy tree canopy allowing grass to grow up to the trunk.

Blue Mist Shrub
(*Caryopteris incarna*)

A compact shrub with a cascading, mounded habit. Though top growth is usually killed back to the ground over most of Pennsylvania, the roots are winter-hardy, sending up aggressive new growth in spring. Plants are valued for blue flowers, clustered all along the stems, producing a misty effect when seen from a distance. Flowering in August and September, plants prefer full sun, and are useful for growing as a highlight in mixed perennial borders. A hybrid, *C. x clandonensis* "DARK KNIGHT," has the deepest blue coloring, but the variety "LONGWOOD"— with sky-blue flowers—won a Gold Medal Award from the Pennsylvania Horticultural Society.

Boxwood
(*Buxus sempervirens*)

The slow growth and dense evergreen

foliage make boxwood one of the most desirable garden shrubs for hedging. Plants are rounded if left unpruned and generally grow just 1 inch each year. Many varieties are available including the favorite for edging, "SUFFRUTI-COSA," which eventually reaches 4 to 5 feet, and the upright dwarf "INGLIS," which will reach little more than 10 inches. "NORTHERN FIND" and "VARDER VALLEY" are examples of extra-hardy plants especially suitable for Pennsylvania. Plants like moist, fertile loam soils that are neutral or slightly acid. Plants tolerate heavy pruning and can be sheared to make mazes. Sweeping snow off the leaves in winter will prevent freezing and leaf burn. Deerfield Garden in Rydal, Montgomery County, has some of the finest boxwood plantings in North America, including a half-size replica of the maze at Hampton Court Palace, England.

Broom, Scotch
(Cytisus scoparius)

Feathery, fine-textured evergreen stems are covered with pea-like yellow flowers in early May. Plants grow 5 to 6 feet high in a mounded, spreading shape. The hybrid C. x praecox, commonly called Warminster broom, creates a billowing mass of pale yellow flowers. Newer varieties include garnet-red, rose-pink, lilac, white, and bicolors. Brooms thrive on sandy, well-drained, infertile soil in full sun. Since broom is difficult to transplant, buy container-grown plants and plant with the root ball intact. Especially good to grow on sunny, steep slopes where other shrubs will not grow.

Burning Bush
(Euonymus alatus)

Though native to China, plants have naturalized in deciduous woodland through-

out Pennsylvania. Outstanding brilliant-red fall color, especially when planted against a background of evergreens. In winter its corky-winged branches catch snow and accentuate the intricate branch pattern. Left unpruned, plants will grow to 20 feet high and equally wide, but it can be sheared to almost any desired height. Tolerant of a wide range of soils, provided drainage is good.

Butterfly Bush, Summer Lilac
(Buddlea davidii)

Frequently used as a highlight in perennial borders, its lilac-like, fragrant flowers bloom continuously all summer long. Colors include white, pink, lavender and deep purple. Butterflies find the arching flower spikes irresistible. The gray-green foliage is a good contrast to the darker green hues of other shrubs. Plants prefer well-drained, fertile loam or sandy soil and full sun. Can be pruned 6 to 12 inches from the ground each spring to maintain a compact habit. Heavy pruning encourages vigorous new shoots and largest flowers excellent for cutting. Good varieties include "BLACK KNIGHT" (dark purple), "WHITE PROFUSION" (pure white), and "CHARMING" (pink).

Buttonwood, American Sycamore
(Platanus occidentalis)

Growing to 100 feet tall with an equal spread, this native Pennsylvania tree is prolific along river banks and creeks. Besides its massive bulk, an impressive decorative feature is its mottled bark—a mixture of silver, gray, and green patches. The leaves are large, resembling maples, but the fall foliage display is not so spectacular—a parchment brown. Plants tolerate moist soil and are good for creating an avenue over a driveway. The "LONDON PLANE TREE"—valued for its pollution tolerance—is a hybrid of the buttonwood, popular for city streets, and widely planted in Philadelphia's Fairmount Park.

Callery Pear
(Pyrus calleryana)

These small trees were brought to Pennsylvania from northern China as an understock for the common pear to help make it resistant to fire blight disease. The common species is ornamental in its own right with beautiful white flowers in early spring and crimson fall foliage. However, several thornless varieties have been selected for use as street trees and lawn specimens. "BRADFORD" is a 30-foot-tall, wide-branching selection that tends to be short-lived because of susceptibility to splitting. It flowers profusely in March and April, and has good late-season, orange-red foliage color. "CHANTICLEER" is a fine, upright pyramidal form less prone to damage and slightly hardier than "BRADFORD." The small, brown, crabapple-like fruits that may form are not edible. Plants prefer full sun and tolerate poor soils, provided drainage is good.

Camellia, Japanese
(Camellia japonica)

Between 1840 and 1850, at the height of their popularity, Philadelphia was a center for camellia growing. It was considered stylish to have a special "camellia house"—a type of sun room or orangerie—where frost was excluded so camellias could be grown to perfection. Though they are not reliably hardy north of Philadelphia, they have pliable branches that can be espaliered against a sheltered wall to escape frost damage. Though the plants are reasonably hardy, the buds often open during a brief warming spell, only to be blasted to an ugly brown mess on fully opening. The lustrous, dark-green, evergreen foliage is attractive, while the beautiful, rounded, single or double flowers can be up to 5 inches across in white, pink, red, and bicolors. They are ideal for growing in containers, kept in a sun room room during inclement weather, and moved to a porch or patio after severe frosts. A superb collection of camellias can be seen in the conservatory at Longwood Gardens, Chester County, Pennsylvania.

Catalpa, Northern
(Catalpa speciosa)

Sensational deciduous shade tree native to Pennsylvania, valued for its tropical-looking, heart-shaped leaves up to a foot long, and domed clusters of white, rhododendron-like flowers that cover the tree in June. The leaves turn golden yellow in fall. Fast-growing to 50 feet high. Almost a trade-mark of Pennsylvania farms, where specimens are grown to shade barnyards, patios, and ponds. Prefers full sun and tolerates a wide range of soils.

Cedar, Atlas
(Cedrus atlantica)

Related to cedar of Lebanon, plants have wide, spreading branches that bend like rubber and shed snow, and handsome blue-green foliage. In its juvenile stage the tree is an erect and pyramidal shape. Height at maturity is 40 to 60 feet, with a spread 40 to 50 feet. Some forms are silver-blue, while others are shades of dark green. Attractive as a lawn highlight, there is an especially beautiful pendulous variety that can be espaliered along a wall to create a curtain of attractive, weeping branches. Purchase only container plants as it is difficult to transplant. Plants prefer fertile, well-drained loam soil and a sheltered position.

Though hardy in Pennsylvania, the related cedar of Lebanon (*Cedrus libani*) grows too big and too wide for most Pennsylvania gardens. A particularly fine specimen can be seen at the Tyler Arboretum in Delaware County.

The deodar cedar (*Cedrus deodara*), though one of nature's most attractive evergreens with pendulous, layered foliage sweeping to the ground, is not sufficiently hardy for Pennsylvania gardens.

Cherry, Japanese
(*Prunus* species and hybrids)

Most flowering cherry varieties reach 20 to 25 feet and almost smother themselves with pink or white flowers in mid-spring. Flowers are greatly variable, ranging from singles to doubles and from 1/2 to 2 1/2 inches in diameter. "KWAN-ZAN" is the most popular variety and one of the hardiest with large double pink flowers. Some varieties are pink when they first open and fade to almost white when they mature. This is particularly true of the popular weeping cherry, *P. serrulata* "PENDULA."

Prunus "OKAME"—a hybrid of *P. incisa* and *P. campanulata* introduced into Pennsylvania from England by the Morris Arboretum in Chestnut Hill—is an attractive, oval-shaped tree with small, clear-pink flowers, winning a Gold Medal Award from the Pennsylvania Horticultural Society for its early-flowering display, which is longer-lasting than other cherries because of the bright red coloring of the flower bud and calyx. Cherries tolerate a wide range of soil types, though they like good drainage and full sun. Use them as a lawn highlight and for lining driveways. Plants may need a sheltered position in northern sections of the state. Young plantings are highly susceptible to borer infestations, and generally need protection with tree wrap for several years.

Chestnut, European
(*Aesculus hippocastanum*)

Though native to Greece and Albania, this species thrives in Pennsylvania, making a 60-foot-tall, stately, billowing deciduous tree covered in conspicuous, cone-shaped white or pink flower clusters in spring. Groups of large oval, serrated green leaves are arranged in a fan shape. Good to use as a lawn highlight and an "avenue."

There is a beautiful, red-flowered hybrid horse chestnut, *A. x carnea*, that is a cross between the European horse-chestnut and the Southern red buckeye (*A. pavia*). Plants grow to 40 feet high, with a rounded habit and masses of large, red flower clusters in May.

Clematis
(*Clematis* species and hybrids)

Mostly flowering vines, one of the most beautiful is a fall-blooming Pennsylvania native—*C. maximowitziana* (also known as *C. paniculata*). Its highly fragrant, starry-white flowers can grow to 10 feet or more. It is especially beautiful when trained up trellises and along fences. Another extremely free-flowering species, originally from the Himalayas—*C. montana*—almost suffocates itself with 3-inch, four-petalled, pale-pink flowers that are the earliest to appear, in late May. For summer flowering choose two old-fashioned favorites—"NELLY MOSER" (a deep pink and white bicolor bred by a Frenchman, flowering in June) and "JACKMANI" (a large-flowered violet-blue developed by an Englishman, flowering in July). Both date back to the 1800s. A more recent introduction, *C. viticella* "BETTY CORNING," received a Gold Medal Award from the Pennsylvania Horticultural Society.

Clematis generally prefer a humus-rich, fertile loam soil. Though they tolerate light shade, they bloom best in full sun—provided their roots are shaded.

Crabapple, Japanese
(*Malus floribunda*)

Mostly broad-spreading, rounded trees, 20 to 25 feet tall at maturity. Flower buds are at first pink or red, opening to white. The avalanche of fragrant flowers is followed by ornamental fruits that ripen to yellow or red in the fall, depending on variety. The fruits are half an inch across and persist after the leaves have fallen. Crabapples tolerate poor soils, provided drainage is good, but prefer acid loam soil in full sun. Plants are susceptible to scab disease and powdery mildew, but hybrid varieties offer good disease resistance. The hybrid "DONALD WYMAN" (a rounded form with single white flowers and abundant, bright red fruits) received a Gold Medal Award from the Pennsylvania Horticultural Society for its excellent disease resistance—especially to scab, fireblight, cedar-apple rust, as well as mildew. "JEWELBERRY" is also a Gold Medal Award recipient, similar in habit and disease resistance to "DONALD WYMAN," but with pink-edged flowers and larger, bright red fruits. Plants are best used as a lawn specimen and in groves of mixed colors.

Crape Myrtle
(*Lagerstroemia indica*)

Few trees can rival the beauty of the bark of this 20- to 30-foot small tree. Smooth and gray, it peels to form patches with variable coloring like a painted pony. Spectacular lilac-like flower clusters are produced from midsummer to fall. Flower colors range from white, lavender, pink, and rose to dark red. Though normally not hardy north of Philadelphia, new hybrids named after Indian tribes have been released by the National Arboretum and these are proving to be hardy farther north in sheltered positions. The tops of these new hybrids will invariably winterkill after a hard frost, but roots will remain dormant through winter and sprout new flowering branches in spring. Plants prefer a moist, humus-rich soil in full sun.

Cryptomeria, Japanese Cedar
(*Cryptomeria japonica*)

The cultivar "LOBBII" has a beautiful, spire-like form, good for Pennsylvania landscapes to create a pleasant grove or background for other plants. The strong, straight trunk features an attractive, reddish-brown, shredding bark. The branches sweep down from the trunk and end in a flourish of soft, slender leaves that turn bronze in autumn. Plants grow 60 to 80 feet high, and prefer a fertile, acid soil and a sheltered site.

Cypress, Bald
(*Taxodium distichum*)

A stately, narrow, pyramidal tree common to wetlands in the South. Though native to Delaware south to Louisiana, it is hardy in most of Pennsylvania, especially planted along stream banks and pond margins in moist soil. Bald cypress is a deciduous tree taking on golden amber shades prior to fall needle drop. Trees grow 50 to 70 feet tall and 20 feet wide. In summer the 1/2-inch-long needles are a bright green. Leaves are slow to appear in spring. Transplants easily balled and burlapped. Trees appear chlorotic in high-pH soils. Mature trees develop "knees" (wooded protrusions from underground roots). These occur on land and also in shallow water. Some fine examples of cypress knees can be seen at the Tyler Arboretum in Lima, and at Longwood Gardens in Kennett Square.

Cypress, False
(Chamaecyparis pisifera)

A pyramid-shaped tree with feathery, green, flattened foliage. Plants grow to 60 feet high and up to 20 feet wide. Several varieties are superb foundation plants. "FILIFERA AUREA," or "GOLD LACE," is an easily sheared form with yellow foliage that stays neat and compact. "SQUARROSA" has soft, gray-green foliage. "BOULE-VARD" creates a handsome, blue-green pyramid. Plants prefer full sun and a humus-rich loam soil. The bright range of foliage colors is especially good for creating winter color in Pennsylvania gardens.

Dogwood, Flowering
(Cornus florida)

Pennsylvania's most beautiful native tree, with four seasons of landscape interest. Masses of white or pink flower bracts enhance the green flowers in spring, opening out in a blizzard of color before its leaves unfold. Summer foliage is a glossy dark green. Red berries and purple foliage highlight the plant in fall, and the distinct pyramidal silhouette features a delicate tracery of branches in winter. Mature trees have horizontal branching, grow to 20 feet tall and spread 20 to 30 feet, though some trees reach 30 to 40 feet. Many distinct varieties are available. "APPLE BLOS-SOM" has light pink flower bracts, while "CHEROKEE CHIEF" is a rich ruby-red. "PLURIBRACTEATA" has unusual double-flower bracts. "RAIN-BOW" is a variegated yellow and green foliage form, while "WELCHII" is a tricolor—green, cream, and pink all in the same leaf. Dogwoods prefer, moist, well-drained, humus-rich acid soil. Excellent as a lawn specimen or silhouetted against a background of evergreen trees.

To combat a disease known as "dogwood decline" or "lower branch dieback," keep plants fertilized and prune away any branches that die from the base of the plant. A type of fungus disease, the ailment is lethal to weak trees.

Rutgers University has created some sensational disease-resistant hybrids between the Korean and the American dogwood. Two have won gold medals from the Pennsylvania Horticultural Society. They are "AURORA" and "RUTH EL-LEN." Plant them both as they have distinct blooming times, "RUTH ELLEN" blooming in early May about the same time as native dogwoods.

Dogwood, Kousa
(Cornus kousa)

Masses of pointed, four-petalled white flower bracts open about 3 weeks after the native flowering dogwood. Introduced from Korea, trees reach 30 feet in height and spread to 30 feet or more when older. Sometimes the flowering display is so spectacular that the bright green pointed leaves are almost completely hidden. The best specimen trees have limbs to the ground. In late summer mature trees produce edible, 1-inch, strawberry-like fruits. Fall color is a brilliant red. "MILKY WAY" is an especially attractive variety with heavy flowering and fruiting. Plants prefer humus-rich, well-drained acid soils. May need a protected location in northern parts of the state. Plants are resistant to the troublesome dogwood disease known as "dogwood decline."

Dogwood, Red-twig
(Cornus alba)

A shrubby deciduous plant valued for its bright red, juvenile stems that stand out in a wintry landscape. Plants grow to 15 feet high, but are kept below 5 feet by annual pruning in summer to force new growth. Strongest stem coloration occurs in winter. Mostly used as an accent along house foundations and in mixed borders. Inconspicuous white flowers occur in spring, followed by inconspicuous blue berries. Plants tolerate poor soil, even moist locations, if planted in full sun.

Douglas Fir
(Pseudotsuga menziesii)

One of the most popular Christmas trees because of its ability to retain needles when cut or dug. An excellent plant for backgrounds and massing in groves. Trees reach 10 to 15 feet in a 10-year period, with the potential to reach more than 100 feet and live several hundred years. Plants produce 3- to 4-inch-long, light brown cones that are pendulous and have distinct, three-prong bracts. Leaves vary depending on the seed strain provenience. Rocky Mountain types are bluish-green and hardy over almost all of Pennsylvania, while Pacific types are dark green and only reliably hardy in the southeastern section. Prefers neutral or slightly acid, well-drained, moist soils. Not recommended for sandy soils or exposed sites.

Fir, White or Concolor
(Abies concolor)

An attractive pyramidal-needle evergreen tree with 2- to 3-inch-long, blue-green needles that curve upward on the branches. Plants grow 30 to 50 feet tall, but may reach 100 feet under optimum conditions. The stalked cones stand out like candles on the branches, are 3 to 6 inches long, and are green with a purple tint. The variety "VIOLACEA" has attractive, silvery-blue needles. It prefers fertile, moist, sandy loam soil that is well-drained and in full sun. Native to Colorado.

Firethorn
(Pyracantha coccinea)

A broad-leaf evergreen shrub with sharp thorns and red, orange, or yellow berries, depending on variety. The lustrous, dark green, pointed leaves are a good contrast to the generous clusters of fruit. Good for exposed and dry sites such as the south side of a house foundation. Small, white, fragrant, hawthorn-like flowers cover plants in June. Though tolerant of poor soils, firethorn is difficult to transplant unless purchased as a container plant. Along the south wall of Gates Hall, administrative office of the Morris Arboretum in Chestnut Hill, there is a fine, espaliered specimen of the variety "MOHAVE," with masses of orange-red berries.

Forsythia
(Forsythia species)

Several different forsythias are of value to residential landscapes. Forsythia viridissima "BRONXENSIS" grows just 12 inches high, spreading up to 3 feet and useful as a slope cover. "ARNOLD DWARF" grows to 5 feet tall and 7 feet wide, preferred for mass plantings to control soil erosion on slopes. Forsythia x intermedia "LYNWOOD GOLD" is the most widely planted, growing arching canes to 10 feet high and 10 feet wide, covered with bright yellow flowers in early spring. Forsythia suspensa has a weeping habit, suitable for planting along retaining walls so its branches form a curtain. Forsythia does well on many different soils and sites, so long as it receives full sun. When plants become too tall and sparse-flowering, they can be cut back to within 12 inches of the ground and the soil fertilized to promote renewed growth and improved flowering. Combines well with weeping cherries.

Fringe Tree
(Chionanthus virginicus)

Native to Pennsylvania, this beautiful deciduous tree resembles an erect form of willow, producing a dazzling display of fragrant white blossoms that hang in generous clusters. There are two forms—male and female—with the male producing the best floral display. Grows to 30 feet high, sometimes multi-stemmed. Prefers fertile, well-drained soil in full sun. Magnificent planted between tall evergreens.

Ginkgo
(Ginkgo biloba)

At one time these tall deciduous trees covered Pennsylvania, helping to form the state's vast coal deposits during pre-historic times, but they became extinct everywhere on earth, except for parts of China. The ginkgo is sometimes referred to as a living fossil since it has been in existence for more than 150 million years. Mostly upright-growing to 80 feet, trees are either male or female. Fruiting female trees are undesirable because of the malodorous smell of the rotting plum-like yellow fruits. Leaves are clustered on spurs and are fan-shaped. Fall coloring is a brilliant buttercup yellow. Trees grow very slowly and usually mature to a pyramid shape. They transplant easily and grow on all but marshy soils. Most desirable as a lawn highlight and as street trees, though only grafted male plants should be used.

Golden Rain Tree
(Koelreuteria paniculata)

Large clusters of small yellow flowers (12 to 15 inches long) decorate this dome-shaped deciduous tree in early July after most other trees have flowered. The spectacular flower clusters immedi-ately develop into lime-green capsules that eventually turn parchment-brown. These capsules are highly ornamental at all stages. Plants grow to 30 feet tall with an equal—or greater—spread. Tolerant of drought, air pollution, wind, and poor soil. Prefers full sun.

Hawthorn, Washington
(Crataegus phaenopyrum)

This and the variety of hawthorn identified as *C. viridis* "WINTER KING" are the best hawthorns among hundreds available for Pennsylvania landscapes. *C. phaenopyrum* and *C. viridis* are native to the southeastern United States, but "WINTER KING" was discovered in an Indiana nursery, and won a Gold Medal Award from the Pennsylvania Horticultural Society. Both grow to 30 feet high, with a mounded crown and masses of white flowers in May, resembling tiny multiflora roses. These are followed by beautiful red berry clusters in fall, though the berry display of "WINTER KING" is better and brighter. Plants prefer a sunny location in fertile, well-drained soil.

Hemlock, Canadian
(Tsuga canadensis)

This handsome native evergreen has sweeping branches and fine-textured needles that tolerate shade. Unpruned the plants will become gigantic. A particularly fine stand of mature trees can be seen at Bowman's Hill Wildflower Preserve along the banks of Pidcock Creek. Prefers moist, well-drained acid soils, but will grow in full sun, provided drainage is good and plants are not exposed to high winds. With annual pruning they make an excellent, impenetrable hedge. Many of the tall hedges of Maryland's famous Ladew Topiary Garden, in Monkton, are of hemlock. A weeping form, "SARGENTS," resembles a living green waterfall. It is prized for creating beautiful lawn highlights and for planting at the edge of ponds.

Unfortunately, Pennsylvania's hemlocks have become infected with an aphid-like insect pest that is causing serious decline of this handsome evergreen.

Hickory, Shagbark
(*Carya ovata*)

A stately native Pennsylvania tree growing to 80 feet or more, with a spread that can exceed 35 feet, valued for its beautiful, golden yellow, early fall coloring. Also productive of tasty, edible nuts, though the meat is small and the nut case difficult to open. The shaggy bark is ornamental—especially contrasting with other hardwood deciduous trees in a grove.

Holly, American
(*Ilex opaca*)

Long-lived evergreen trees, native to Pennsylvania, growing to 50 feet in height and spreading to 20 feet. Plants are pyramid-shaped when young, becoming more irregular and tree-like when mature. Not as glossy-leaved as English holly (*Ilex aquifolium*), but more winter-hardy for Pennsylvania gardens. Both male and female plants are needed for fruiting. Plants prefer acid, well-drained soils and a sheltered location. Best planted in spring from containers. "JERSEY PRINCESS" is a newer selection with dark, lustrous green leaves and a heavy cropping potential of dark red berries. Good to use as a lawn highlight, for foundation plantings, and mass planting. A particularly fine collection of holly varieties can be seen in the arboretum at Rutgers University, New Brunswick, New Jersey.

Holly, Blue
(*Ilex x meserveae*)

Introduced by nurserymen from the Conard-Pyle Company of Chester County, this group of hybrid hollies was made by crossing various hardy species with the very hardy *Ilex rugosa*. The crossing of *I. aquifolia* with *I. rugosa*, for example, produced "BLUE BOY," "BLUE GIRL," "BLUE PRINCE," and "BLUE PRINCESS." They all display thick, blue-green, prickly foliage and become broadly pyramidal, but require shearing to maintain a neat plant. Only the female plants bear shiny red fruits that persist all winter. For a prolific crop of berries in fall, plant one male to six females.

A cross of *Ilex rugosa* with *Ilex cornuta* produced "CHINA BOY" and "CHINA GIRL," which resemble the Chinese holly. These are exceptionally fine hardy plants for decorative hedges.

Holly, Japanese
(*Ilex crenata*)

A good evergreen for hedging and ground cover—especially the dwarf compact varieties. Plants produce a dense cover of lustrous, dark green, oval-shaped leaves, similar to boxwood. Prefers moist, well-drained, slightly acid loam soils in sun or light shade. Withstands heavy pruning and can be sheared to formal shapes. Over 60 varieties are available commercially, ranging from 2 feet to 15 feet high. Some are upright but most are dense and wide-spreading. Varieties good for hedging include "COMPACTA," "GREEN LUSTER," and "HELLERI."

Honey Locust, Thornless
(*Gleditsia triacanthos var. inermis*)

Valued for its light, filtered shade, allowing grass to grow up to the trunk. Foliage is feathery, with each leaf composed of 20 to 30 slender, lance-like leaflets. Only the thornless varieties should be used since children can be hurt on the vicious thorns extending all along the trunk on wild thorny varieties, which are prevalent in Pennsylvania woodland. Some of the various thorn-free varieties include "IMPERIAL," "MAJESTIC," and "SHADEMASTER" (valued for its golden-yellow juvenile foliage). Tolerant of pollution and poor soils, the plants grow best in full sun.

Honeysuckle, Scarlet
(*Lonicera sempervirens*)

A beautiful flowering vine native to Pennsylvania. Plants grow to 10 feet high, bear clusters of red tubular flowers on twining stems in May. Tolerates poor soil, and is good for training along fence rails and over arbors. Not so invasive as the yellow-flowered Japanese honeysuckle (*L. japonica*), a weedy, rampant vine that has naturalized throughout the waysides of Pennsylvania, suffocating small trees. Two good varieties of the scarlet honeysuckle are "MAGNIFICA" (bright red flowers) and "SULPHUREA" (bright yellow).

Hornbeam, American
(*Carpinus caroliniana*)

The American hornbeam is generally a better plant than the European hornbeams, popular for hedging in formal gardens such as Versailles in France. Heart-shaped leaves are up to 5 inches long and 2 inches wide. Fall color is generally yellow green. Unpruned trees grow to 20 feet high. Branches are an attractive charcoal gray, strong and shiny after rain. Transplant container plants in spring since bare-root plants generally suffer transplant shock. Grows best in fertile, moist, acid soil. Tolerates heavy shade.

Hydrangea
(*Hydrangea* species and hybrids)

Though the French hydrangeas (*H. hortensis*) are generally the most popular for Pennsylvania gardens (especially the compact, 2- to 3-feet-high, summer-flowering variety "FOREVER PINK"), two white-flowered varieties are worth garden space for the sheer size and volume of their blooms. These are *H. arborescens* "ANNABELLE" (growing 12-inch globular blooms on 4-foot-high plants) and *H. quercifolia* "SNOW QUEEN" (winner of a Gold Medal Award from the Pennsylvania Horticultural Society for its spectacular cone-shaped flowers up to 14 inches long on 5-foot-high plants).

Among blue-flowering hydrangeas, *H. macrophyla* "OTAKSA" produces huge blue flowers in acid soil, pink in alkaline soil. "BLUE BILLOW" won a Styer Award from the Pennsylvania Horticultural Society for its lovely, old-fashioned, summer-flowering "lace-cap" blooms.

For fall color, nothing can outshine *Hydrangea paniculata* "PEE GEE." Flowering young, plants grow to 10 feet tall, erect stems bending with the sheer weight of huge white flower clusters that turn pink and then bronze with age.

Hydrangeas prefer a humus-rich sandy or loam soil in sun or light shade. Their flowers are valued for fresh and dried floral arrangements.

Juniper, Chinese
(*Juniperus chinensis*)

Many varieties have been developed from this species, ranging in habit from prostrate forms to upright trees. It is best to avoid the common species and select only varieties that have been introduced for their value as landscape plants. Some of the most popular upright forms are: "AMES," forming a broad pyramid with steel-blue foliage and maturing at 10 feet, and "MOUNTBATTEN," a narrow, upright, dense pyramid shape growing up to 12 feet high with grayish-green foliage. "KAIZUKA"—also known as "TORTULOSA" and "The Hollywood Juniper," is a deep green female clone with curious twisted branches growing to 20 feet, popular for planting along house foundations.

Juniper, Spreading
(Juniperus horizontalis)

The variety "BLUE RUG" is a low, spreading, evergreen blue-green juniper that covers the ground with a dense weed-suffocating mass of needle-like foliage. A substitute for grass on steep banks and other hard-to-mow places. Prefers full sun and well-drained soils.

Kerria, Japanese
(Kerria japonica)

The original species is a single, yellow-flowered, broadly spreading shrub with delicate, green arching stems. Leaves are bright green or variegated (depending on variety) and are 2 to 4 inches long. Flowering is prolific, occurring in early May. "PLENIFLORA" is a double-flowering clone with ball-shaped flowers 1 to 2 inches in diameter. Plants prefer a humus-rich fertile soil in light shade. Needs annual pruning after flowering to remove dead branches.

Laburnum, Golden Chain Tree
(Laburnum x watereri)

Prized for its 6- to 10-inch-long chains of wisteria-like yellow flowers that cover the tree in late May and early June.

Plants grow a strong, straight trunk and a branching canopy to form a round-headed or column-like specimen. Branches and twigs are olive-green in color; leaves are trifoliate and about 2 inches long. Plants prefer light shade during the hottest part of the day, and a sheltered location when grown in the northern part of the state. Not a long-lived tree, but beautiful along a house foundation. In Europe trees are trained over walks to provide beautiful yellow floral tunnels. The Ladew Topiary Gardens in Monkton, Maryland, has a small laburnum walk.

Lilac, Common
(Syringa vulgaris)

There is an especially large collection of lilacs at Swarthmore College (Delaware County) and also at the Tyler Arboretum (Lima, PA). Though the common purple-flowered fragrant lilac is widely planted throughout the state, French hybrid varieties have much larger flower trusses. The heart-shaped leaves are light green, becoming covered in mildew as summer advances. Plants grow to 15 feet high and up to 12 feet wide. Flowers are either single or double and range from shades of white, blue, and lilac to deep purple. There are over 400 named cultivars. Some of the more popular single forms suitable for Pennsylvania gardens are "MONT BLANC" (white); "CAVOUR" (violet); "PRESIDENT LINCOLN" (blue); "LUCIE BALLET" (pink); "CONGO" (magenta); and "LUDWIG SPAETH" (purple). Plants prefer fertile, well-drained loam soil. Flowering is stimulated if plants are not allowed to set seed by removing faded blooms. When a lilac becomes overgrown and persistently weak-flowering, it can be cut to within 12 inches of the ground. This will stimulate new juvenile growth that will flower profusely, especially if the plant is fertilized.

Linden, Viburnum
(*Viburnum dilatatum*)

This is one of the best shrubs for autumn berry color. The bright red fruits are borne in heavy clusters persisting from September to December. Flowers are white, lasting 7 to 10 days in late spring. The leaves are lustrous dark green, sharply indented, changing to ruby-red colors in the fall. Plants prefer moist, humus-rich acid soil in full sun. "IROQUOIS" is an especially good variety developed by the U.S. National Arboretum, and selected both for its handsome dark green leaves and abundance of flowers and berry clusters. Plants grow to 8 feet tall and 10 feet wide.

Magnolia, Saucer
(*Magnolia x soulangiana*)

Few flowering trees can rival the magnolias when in full bloom, though in Pennsylvania plants often bloom during a brief warming spell, only to have the spectacular floral display browned by frost in the night, unless located in a sheltered position. The 20- to 30-foot-tall trees cover themselves with cup-shaped pinkish or white blossoms measuring 5 to 10 inches in diameter. The habit is usually a wide-spreading, low-branched shrub when young, and an upright mounded tree when mature. An especially fine collection of magnolias can be seen on the campus of Swarthmore College, in Delaware County. "LENNEI" has dark purple or magenta petals and is white inside. New hybrids released by the U.S. National Arboretum in Washington, D.C., are especially free-flowering—all with girls' names. There is a spectacular yellow among the group named "ELIZABETH," the recipient of

a Gold Medal Award from the Pennsylvania Horticultural Society.

Two smaller-size magnolias for home landscapes are *M. stellata* (star magnolia), smaller-flowered and earlier-flowering than the saucer magnolia, and the native *M. virginiana* (sweetbay magnolia), flowering in June with fragrant, cream-colored, 4-inch cupped flowers. Both grow to 30 feet with an equal spread.

Magnolia, Southern
(*Magnolia grandiflora*)

Though not reliably hardy north of Philadelphia, this handsome, broad-leaf evergreen is well worth trying to establish in a sheltered position. Valued for its large, oval, lustrous dark green leaves (up to 10 inches long), and huge white perfumed flowers (up to 12 inches wide) that appear in early summer. Mature trees grow to 80 feet in height and spread to 40 feet. The variety "EDITH BOGUE" won a Gold Medal Award from the Pennsylvania Horticultural Society for its extra-hardiness; it was propagated from a parent tree discovered in Montclair, New Jersey. Transplant balled and burlapped trees in early spring. Prefers fertile, well-drained soils and partial shade. Best sites are in slightly shaded locations not exposed to too much bright winter sun or cold winds.

Mahonia, Leatherleaf
(*Mahonia bealei*)

An unusual broad-leaf evergreen shrub, 10 to 12 feet high, with glossy, leathery, holly-like leaves. Named for a Pennsylvania nurseryman, Bernard McMahon (1775-1816), who nurtured seeds of this Pacific Northwest native following the Lewis and Clark Expedition. From his premises in Germantown, he also produced America's first practical gardening book, entitled *The American Gardener's Calendar*, which went through eleven editions in 50 years.

The leatherleaf mahonia is best used sparingly as a companion to azaleas and rhododendrons. It withstands summer heat better than its relative, *Mahonia aquifolium*. Fragrant, bright yellow flower clusters appear in early spring followed by beautiful, grape-like clusters of dusky, blue-black berries that persist from late summer into fall. Prefers moist, humus-rich, well-drained acid soil in partial shade. Exposed plants are subject to leaf-browning from chilling winds.

Maple, Amur
(*Acer ginnala*)

Prized for its beautiful fall coloration—ranging from light yellow to crimson. Can be pruned to form a large hedge 12 to 15 feet high, or left unpruned to form a billowing hedge up to 8 feet high. Leaves are three-lobed, medium green, and 2 to 3 inches long. The winged seeds are also ornamental and are brightly colored in late summer. Native to China.

Maple, Japanese
(*Acer palmatum*)

Handsome small, deciduous trees with attractive, indented, 2- to 5-inch-long, green- or bronze-colored leaves, though there is considerable leaf color and size variation among varieties. "BLOODGOOD" is an especially good variety for holding its bronze leaf color all season. "DISSECTUM ATROPURPUREUM" has deep bronze, finely dissected, lace-like foliage. It is slow-growing and can be kept compact. "SENKAKI," the coral-bark maple, has beautiful, coral-red young twigs that stand out in the winter landscape. Its foliage is an appealing lime green. All Japanese maples like humus-rich loam soil

and adequate moisture. They make excellent lawn specimens and foundation plants. Use them in perennial borders as accents, and in large containers. Needs a sheltered location in the northern parts of Pennsylvania. Native to Japan.

Maple, Red
(*Acer rubrum*)

Native throughout Pennsylvania—especially along stream banks—its beautiful rounded shape and intense red fall coloring make it a popular tree for planting in groves and as a lawn highlight. Tolerates moist soil. Grows to 80 feet in height. Since the fall coloring can be variable (orange in some specimens), choose trees in autumn from tree nurseries.

Maple, Silver
(*Acer saccharinum*)

Upright, tall, fast-growing deciduous tree featuring green leaves with silvery undersides. The slightest breeze produces a shimmering, glittering effect. Leaves turn yellow and orange in fall. Popular lawn highlight. Other popular native Pennsylvania maples include the sugar maple (*A. saccharum*) and the black maple (*A. nigra*)—much better in the landscape than the immigrant Norway maple (*Acer platanoides*), since their fall coloring is more intense. All these trees can grow to 60 feet tall (and sometimes more) with a spread of 40 feet.

Mountain Laurel, Kalmia
(*Kalmia latifolia*)

The state flower of Pennsylvania, this long-lived broad-leaf evergreen shrub is native to Pennsylvania. Exquisite in mass displays at the edges of woods or in light shade. Plants are slow-growing to 15 feet high. Flowers are white, pink, red, or banded with purple, blooming in late spring or early summer depending on the variety. Flowers are especially attractive in bud just prior to opening. Prefers cool, humus-rich, well-drained acid soils. Dr. Richard Jaynes of New Haven, Connecticut has bred several outstanding new varieties including "OTSBO RED" (a red-budded variety) and "ALBA" (a pure white). Plants combine well with azaleas and rhododendrons, since they enjoy similar conditions.

Oak, Willow
(*Quercus phellos*)

One of the handsomest native shade trees for Pennsylvania, though not reliably hardy in northern regions. Its common name reflects the foliage resemblance to willow. Good pyramidal shape when young, maturing to an oval crown. Leaves change from green to yellow to russet-brown before dropping in the fall. Compared to other oaks it is easy to transplant. Prefers moist, fertile, well-drained acid soils. Tolerant of city conditions and a good choice for lining streets.

Other good native oaks for the home landscape include the pin oak (*Quercus palustris*) and the scarlet oak (*Quercus coccinea*). Both are deciduous shade trees tolerant of moist soil. They have a similar pyramidal growth habit, and are hard to tell apart except in fall when the pin oak's leaves change to a parchment-brown color and the scarlet oak's change to brilliant red. They are especially popular for forming avenues along driveways.

The most dominant native oak in the Pennsylvania landscape is the white oak (*Q.alba*). Resembling an old English oak in its wide spread and the massive girth of its trunk on old specimens, white oaks grow to 90 feet high, with a spread of 100 feet or more.

Unfortunately, oaks are a favorite food of the gypsy moth—an immigrant caterpillar with a voracious appetite that can defoliate oak trees, eventually killing them. Fortunately, the gypsy moth has fallen victim to its own predators, and it is not the serious pest it once was.

Because of their long taproots, oaks—and many other large native Pennsylvania trees (such as the tulip poplar and buttonwood)—are difficult to transplant unless grown as "milk carton" transplants (see Plant Care, page 126).

Olive, Russian
(*Eleagnus angustifolia*)

A small tree valued for its attractive, silvery-gray foliage. Can grow to 30 feet, but is usually in the 15- to 20-foot range, and equally as wide. Resembles a small willow, sometimes multi-stemmed. Valued for its silvery leaves and wind resistance. Fragrant, silvery flowers are inconspicuous, appearing in late spring. These are followed in early fall by small, round, yellow fruits. Prefers full sun and good drainage. Especially beautiful when contrasted with purple-leaf ornamental plum, blue spruce, and yellow thread-leaf false cypress. Plants can be sheared to form a dense hedge and windbreak screen.

Orange, Hardy
(*Poncirus trifoliata*)

Especially beautiful specimens of this mounded shrub are planted around the Japanese garden in Philadelphia's Fairmount Park, and also in the drought-tolerant Mediterranean garden at Longwood Gardens. Usually 8 to 10 feet tall but sometimes reaching 20 feet if trained against a wall. In early May, plants display beautiful, waxy white "orange-blossom" flowers against lustrous, dark green oval leaves. Golfball-sized, fuzzy yellow astringent oranges are prominent in the fall, remaining on the tree after the leaves have dropped. The fruits have a delightful fragrance, similar to lemon soap. Plants prefer a sunny location and a well-drained acid soil.

Pachysandra, Japanese Spurge
(Pachysandra terminalis)

A superb evergreen ground cover for deep shade and acid soils, especially around trees and acid-loving shrubs such as azaleas and rhododendrons. Planted 12 inches apart, the spreading plants knit together quickly. Whorled, umbrella-like glossy green foliage turns light green in sunny spots and stays a lustrous dark green in shade. Fragrant white flower spikes appear in early spring.

Periwinkle
(Vinca minor)

Dark, glossy, evergreen leaves knit together to form a dense ground-hugging, weed-suffocating mat. Blue star-like flowers occur in early spring about the same time as crocus, and persist intermittently until the end of June. Thrives in sun or shade. Space plants 12 inches apart in humus-rich soil to create an effective ground cover. There is also a white form.

Pine, Eastern White
(Pinus strobus)

A fast-growing native Pennsylvania pine displaying blue-tinted evergreen needles. Forest trees will reach 80 feet with a spread of 20 to 40 feet. Young trees are perfect pyramids. Trees are easily transplanted because of wide-spreading roots. Tolerates a wide range of soils,

provided drainage is good. Susceptible to air pollutants (ozone, sulfur dioxide), white pine tip weevils, and white pine blister rust. Trees exhibit preference to provenience—those raised in the south do best there, while those raised in a northern nursery are better in northern landscapes.

Pine, Japanese Black
(Pinus thunbergiana)

Displays an irregular growth pattern which makes it useful for informal landscapes, such as rock gardens and Japanese bonsai plantings. Cultivated trees reach 20 to 40 feet and are usually broadly pyramidal when young. Young twigs are light brown, turning charcoal gray with age. Tolerates many different soil types, but will grow best on fertile, well-drained soils. "OCULUS-DRACONIS" is an unusual variety displaying needles striped with yellow bands.

Pine, Mugo
(Pinus mugo)

The variety "MUGO" is a low, slow-growing, mounded form of the tall-growing species. Plants of "MUGO" can be kept low and compact—in the 2- to 3-foot range—by removal of two-thirds of the new upright growth each year once plants have reached the desired landscape size. Foliage color is a medium green in winter and light green in summer. Prefers full sun and well-drained soils. Spaced 3 to 5 feet apart, the overall effect can be a soothing, cushion-like quality.

Poplar Hybrids
(Populus hybrids)

Crosses between European and American poplars (particularly the eastern cottonwood—native to Pennsylvania) were developed as a means of quickly restoring vegetation to dry, stony sites denuded by Pennsylvania strip mines. Miles Fry, a tree farmer from Ephrata, Pennsylvania, pioneered their use as landscape trees after finding that certain varieties—such as "ANDROSCROGGIN"—are capable of growing to 8 feet in a single season. Plants have an erect growth habit, reach 40 feet high, and tolerate poor soil in full sun. Mostly used to establish a quick screen along property boundaries and avenues or to create a windbreak.

Privet, Japanese
(Ligustrum japonica)

Dense evergreen with lustrous dark green foliage, composed of 2 1/2- to 4-inch-long, slender, pointed leaves. Fragrant, creamy white flowers are produced in clusters in early summer. Small black fruits last well into winter. Plants grow to 6 feet tall and up to 8 feet wide. They can be sheared into formal shapes, and are most often used for formal hedges in a sunny position.

Quince, Flowering
(Chaenomeles speciosa)

Valued for its showy red, pink, or white flowers in early spring. The broad, spreading plant is a deciduous shrub that can form a dense hedge. The dark, lustrous green leaves grow up to 3 inches long. At the base of the leaves are thorns. Plants tolerate a wide range of soil types, but need full sun for heavy flowering. Shearing after flowering encourages new branches and heavier flowering the following spring. In some seasons leaf spot diseases may cause some premature leaf drop.

Redbud
(Cercis canadensis)

In spring this handsome, small tree—native to Pennsylvania—covers its branches and sometimes the trunk with pea-like pink or white flowers, depending on variety. The pink form combines well with dogwoods and azaleas. Grows to 30 feet and spreads as wide. Leaves are heart-shaped and up to 5 inches long. "FOREST PANSY" displays dramatic purple leaves when planted in a sunny location. Transplant only young trees that are container-grown into well-drained, fertile soil in sun or light shade. Prune by removing only dead branches.

Rhododendrons

See Azaleas and Rhododendrons.

Rose of Sharon
(Hibiscus syriacus)

Bushy plants grow 8 to 12 feet high and up to 10 feet wide, producing 4- to 6-inch, hibiscus-like flowers in white, pink, blue and bicolors, depending on variety. Plants tolerate a wide range of poor soils, provided drainage is good. Plant in full sun for best flowering. Pruning back to two or three buds on each branch in spring keeps plants compact and encourages larger flowers. Most rose of Sharons close their flowers at night.

"BLUE BIRD" (blue with a purple eye) and "RED HEART" (white with a red eye) are good companions. Both are 4 inches across, though new varieties of triploid hybrids bred at the United States National Arboretum are twice the size. "DIANE" (recipient of a Gold Medal Award from the Pennsylvania Horticultural Society) has pure white flowers that remain open at night from midsummer into fall. "HELENE' is pink with a red eye. There are several double-flowered varieties, but these tend to look sickly in the landscape, as though eaten by insects.

Roses
(*Rosa* species and hybrids)

The months of June and early July are best to appreciate the dramatic beauty of roses in Pennsylvania. Some of the most beautiful rose gardens are at the Morris Arboretum, in Chestnut Hill; Swarthmore College, in Delaware County; Longwood Gardens, in Kennett Square; and at Hershey Gardens, in Hershey, Pennsylvania, where one of the world's largest collections of old and modern roses is spread out over a vast hillside overlooking the Hershey chocolate factory.

Though many modern roses—particularly hybrid teas, grandifloras and floribundas—bloom continuously from June until fall frost, many others give just one spectacular burst of color during early summer while nights are still cool. Even the so-called everbloomers tend to lack vigor in hot, humid weather, reviving for a final flourish in fall.

One of the world's most progressive rose growers is located at West Grove, Pennsylvania. Established as the Conard-Pyle Company, the firm also trades under the name Star Roses. The company has a long-established trading relationship with Meilland, the celebrated French rose breeders, who developed the most famous rose of all—"PEACE" (a large yellow hybrid tea, flushed carmine-pink at the petal tips).

Dick Hutton, chairman of Conard-Pyle Company—which has to make payment of one red rose each year to a descendant of William Penn, as part of a land deed—is a judge for All-America Rose Selections, which makes awards annually to the best new roses. He attributes the popularity of roses to the fact that "they have only one purpose in life—to flower." If a rose fails to flower he looks first at the possibility of insufficient light, since their most important requirement is bright light. Though roses will tolerate impoverished soil, they bloom spectacularly in fertile loam soil, especially one that is enriched with compost or well-decomposed animal manure. Their most serious insect pest is Japanese beetles, which first attack the petals and then the leaves, and black-spot, which can rapidly defoliate a plant soon after it has started to flower. Some roses are resistant to black-spot and Japanese beetles (*R. rugosa*, for example).

The best flowering displays are possible when the soil is heavily mulched with either an organic mulch—such as cocoa beans, shredded leaves, or straw—or stone landscape chips, which will keep the soil even cooler than an organic mulch. Regular watering to keep the soil cool also ensures the longest-lasting floral display.

One of the finest old rose collections can be seen at historic Wyck House, in Germantown. There has been a tremendous surge of interest in old-fashioned roses because they are often heavily fragrant, and many have a "swirling" petal composition that is most attractive in fresh floral arrangements. A progressive British breeder, David Austin, anticipated the public's demand for old-fashioned roses and developed a special strain of hybrids with the benefits of the old varieties (fragrance and intense doubling), but incorporating other benefits—such as continuous bloom, vigor and disease resistance. The everblooming, highly fragrant "CONSTANCE SPRY" performs especially well in Pennsylvania, its long, arching canes often reaching to heights of 10 feet (though it can be pruned to a more compact shrub shape). Following are some examples of roses suitable for Pennsylvania gardens.

The most popular kinds of roses for

home gardens fit into four major categories, although the official classifications for roses carry many others.

Hybrid Tea. These are the most popular modern roses for flower beds and display gardens, since they are hardy and generally grow the largest flowers. The classic urn-shaped blooms are a common feature of this class. They are the best for cutting, since each flower grows on a single stem. Heaviest bloom occurs in June and September. Plants grow from 3 to 6 feet, depending on soil fertility. "CHICAGO PEACE" and "PINK PEACE"—two deeper-hued improvements over the original "PEACE" rose—are good examples of this group.

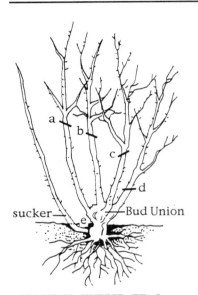

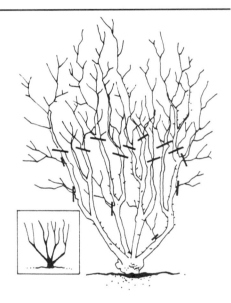

PRUNING HYBRID TEAS

Principles of pruning Hybrid Tea roses: (a) high pruning for more and earlier blooms; (b) pruning to remove twiggy and cross branches; (c) pruning 1 inch below a canker; (d) severe pruning for removal of winter damage; (e) removal of sucker from understock. "Bud Union" marks region at which plant was grafted.

USING HAND-PRUNERS

Proper application of the hand-pruner to the rose cane. The cutting blade must be on the lower side to ensure a clean cut.

PRINCIPLES OF PRUNING A FLORIBUNDA

The cutting back of this class of rose is usually not as severe as on a Hybrid Tea.

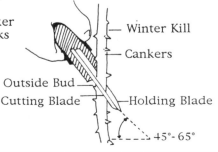

CUTTING GARDEN FOR ROSES

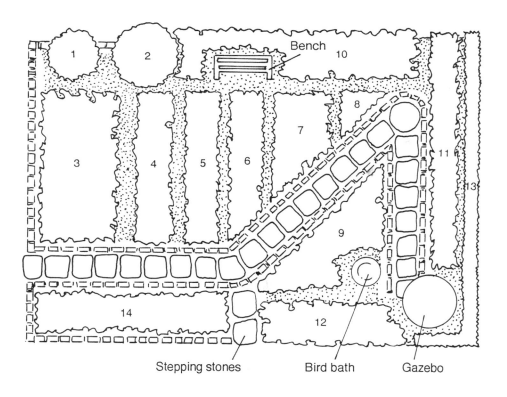

1-Grandiflora "Love"
2-Climbing Rose "Blaze"
3-Floribunda "Carefree Beauty"
4-Floribunda "Impatient"
5-Floribunda "French Lace"
6-Floribunda "Marina"
7-Grandiflora "Queen Elizabeth"

8-Hybrid Tea "Peace"
9-Hybrid Tea "Fragrant Cloud"
10-Floribunda "Simplicity"
11-Hybrid Tea "Dolly Parton"
12-"Climbing America" on trellis
13-Hybrid Tea "Tropicana"
14-Hybrid Tea "Tropicana"

Floribunda. Although smaller-flowered than hybrid teas, floribundas give a greater density of bloom over a longer period. They are generally hardier, lower-growing, and bushier than the hybrid teas, forming their flowers in clusters or "sprays." They are most effective where an impressive mass of color is desired, growing just 3 to 4 feet in most areas. Many outstanding single-flowered and semi-double types belong to this class, resembling wild roses in a vivid color range. "JOSEPH'S COAT" (tricolored red, orange and pink) and "FASHION" (rosy red) are outstanding examples of this class.

Climbers. In great demand to create rose arbors and hedges, climbers will grow to 20 feet. Trained along a fence or up a trellis, they produce incredible quantities of blooms. "AMERICAN PILLAR" (small carmine-red roses held in immense clusters), "BLAZE" (scarlet-red), and "DR. HUEY" (deep crimson-red) are superb.

Hedging. The best hedging effects with roses are when the roses are trained over wires strung between posts, but the variety "ROBIN HOOD" (rosy red) is self-supporting. "THE FAIRY" (pale pink) is an everblooming shrub rose good for hedging if supported, as are many of the new "MEIDILAND" landscape roses, such as "BONICA" (a clear pink). These all produce relatively small flowers, but with such an incredible density of bloom that they will outshine most larger-flowered roses.

Miniatures. Outdoors, miniatures are good for edging rose beds, and massing in rock gardens and containers. Indoors, they will make a delightful pot plant when given sufficient light. Growing barely 12 inches tall, each plant almost smothers itself in tiny, thimble-size blooms—perfect in form and far less demanding than any of the other rose classes. "STARINA" (an orange-red),

"ORANGE HONEY" (peach-colored), and "GREEN ICE" (lime-green fading to white) are three outstanding varieties for Pennsylvania.

Species Roses. The most common rose native to Pennsylvania is *R. virginiana*—the pasture rose. Growing lovely, shell-pink, 2 1/2-inch-wide flowers, it is low-growing and thus suitable for covering slopes. Because of its wide distribution throughout the state, many people think that the multiflora rose (*R. multiflora*) is also native, but actually it is an aggressive immigrant from China that has become such a serious agricultural pest that its planting is banned in many Pennsylvania rural communities.

Probably the most desirable species rose is the rugosa rose (*R. rugosa*), because it is virtually foolproof. Plants produce dense foliage cover and thick stems covered with sharp thorns. Pink, white, or rose-purple, highly fragrant flowers are produced all summer, followed by large, ornamental, orange-red fruits called "hips." It makes a good natural hedge, growing to 5 feet high without support. "ALBA" (a lovely single white), "FRAU DAGMAR HARTOP" (a free-flowering and single pink), "RUBRA" (a red), and "HANSA" (a huge double purple) are good variety selections for garden display and hedging. Plants grow to 5 feet high and 5 feet wide. They prefer well-drained, sandy, or humus-rich loam soil and full sun. Plants are highly pollution-tolerant, disease-resistant, and pest-resistant. A good selection of rugosa roses rings the herb garden at Longwood Gardens, Kennett Square.

Sassafras
(Sassafras albidum)

A small native tree (50 feet by 50 feet), popular among colonists for planting as hedgerows and groves for wildlife cover.

Often multi-stemmed with sinuous trunks that are deeply fissured, plants produce an umbrella-like canopy of mostly three-fingered leaves that turn orange, red, and purple in fall. Plants are attractive as a lawn highlight, especially when two or three are grouped together along a fence. The shredded roots have a pleasant fragrance and are used by herbalists to make a refreshing drink, sassafras tea, with a flavor reminiscent of sarsaparilla.

Shadblow, Sarvistree
(Amelanchier laevis)

This species and *A. canadensis*—both small trees native to Pennsylvania—are difficult to tell apart, except in April when the beautiful, white, hawthorn-like flowers appear against a background of unfurling leaves. At this time *A. laevis* has a bronze cast to its leaves, while *A. canadensis* is mint-green. A hybrid form of amelanchier—*A. x grandiflora*—won an award of merit from Britain's Royal Horticultural Society. All the amelanchiers are beautiful underplanted with drifts of daffodils, for they bloom together in a beautiful, yellow and white color harmony.

Among the first trees in spring to flower, plants grow to 30 feet high, and produce edible fruits in June, resembling blueberries. Though these trees have a tendency to produce smooth, dove-gray, multiple trunks, they can be pruned to a single trunk. The oval, pointed, serrated leaves turn beautiful russet colors in fall. Deserves to be in every Pennsylvania garden.

Silk Tree, Hardy Mimosa
(Albizzia julibrissin)

Though not reliably hardy in the northern and high-elevation parts of Pennsylvania, this beautiful, low-spreading tree is worth trying since it has a tropical-looking appearance, displaying layered, mimosa-like foliage reminiscent of mimosa trees on the plains of Africa and the streets of quaint Bahamian villages. Conspicuous clusters of bright, rosy pink, powderpuff flowers appear in midsummer. Plants grow to 30 feet, but spread to 40 feet, and withstand poor soils, drought and high wind. Flowers best in full sun. "CHARLOTTE" and "BRYON" are wilt-resistant clones. "ROSEA" is thought to be hardiest for Pennsylvania conditions. A beautiful shade tree with wide, spreading branches and an airy tree canopy that casts filtered shade, allowing grass to grow right up to the trunk.

Silverbell, Carolina
(Halesia carolina)

A stately tree reaching 30 to 40 feet in height and 20 to 30 feet wide, usually forming a broad, rounded leaf canopy. Leaves are oval, dark green, and 2 to 5 inches long. The best feature of this native Pennsylvania tree is its 1/2-inch-long, four-lobed, bell-shaped, gleaming white flowers that hang from the axils of the leaves in early June. Prefers well-drained, humus-rich acid soils. Beautiful as an understory tree in woodland and planted along streams. The spring floral display is more noticeable when trees are backed by deep green evergreen foliage.

Smoketree, Smokebush
(Cotinus coggyria)

Left unpruned, smoketrees will grow to 15 feet tall and equally wide. In late spring billowing flower panicles give the appearance of a plant covered with pink, purple, or gray smoke, depending on variety. Some red-leaved varieties are available, but these generally need to be heavily pruned each year to maintain the deep dark purple coloration. "VELVET CLOAK" is an especially good, purple-leaved variety. Smoketrees tolerate a wide range of soils. For the best "smoke" display give them good drainage in a sunny, sheltered position. The branches are brittle and susceptible to wind damage.

Sourwood
(Oxydendron arboreum)

Native to southwestern Pennsylvania, this handsome deciduous tree offers two ornamental benefits—first in summer from dense clusters of fragrant, white urn-shaped flowers, and then in fall with rich burgundy foliage. The flowers cover the tree in August with a beautiful lacy effect. Plant balled and burlapped trees in humus-rich, acid soils with good drainage in full sun or partial shade. Not a good city tree, but superb in the suburbs or country as a lawn specimen and at the edge of woodland.

Spirea, Vanhoute
(Spirea x vanhouttei)

Valued for its cascading fountain effect with branches arching to the ground, covered in snow-white flowers in late May. Oval foliage is dark green in summer. Best used as an informal hedge in full sun and allowed to reach its mature height of 6 to 8 feet and width of 10 to 12 feet without pruning. Prefers a fertile loam soil that drains well.

Spruce, Colorado
(Picea pungens)

These strong, dense, pyramid-shaped trees can attain 30 feet in 35 years. The wild species is highly variable in leaf color—ranging from dark green to light blue and even silvery white. Buy plants carefully in order to get matching colors for garden display. "HOOPSI" is an especially beautiful silver-blue form. "MOORHEIMII" is more compact with good blue foliage. "MONTGOMERY" is a slow-growing dwarf mounded plant reaching only 5 to 6 feet high, good for rock gardens and foundation plantings. All forms of Colorado spruce are desirable evergreens for Pennsylvania, with a preference for moist soil and full sun. Creates a good windbreak and screen for privacy.

Sweetgum, American
(Liquidamber styraciflua)

A stately, 60- to 75-foot, pyramid-shaped shade tree native to Pennsylvania. Foliage resembles a maple, 5 to 6 inches long and about as wide. Spiny, pendant, golfball-size fruits persist into winter. Twigs have corky wings. Though variable in its fall coloring, leaves can turn yellow, orange, and red to deep purple. For best fall coloring, earmark nursery-grown trees in the fall for spring planting. Trees prefer slightly acid soils and full sun. "OBTUSILOBA" is a sterile variety that does not drop fruit—a benefit when shading a driveway or patio.

Sweet Shrub
(Calycanthus floridus)

One of the best plants for fragrance in the garden, sweet shrub grows 6 to 9 feet high, with a mounded, spreading habit, covering itself with masses of dusky red, 1- to 2-inch flowers in May and June, with a fragrance reminiscent of cantaloupe. The dark green oval leaves turn brilliant yellow in fall. Grows in sun or light shade. A cream-colored form is also available.

Tree of Heaven
(*Ailanthus altissima*)

This species is native to China, but likes Pennsylvania so much it even grows in the impoverished soil of Center City, Philadelphia, where park superintendents call it the "tree of hell" because of its propensity to seed itself on every vacant lot. Plants grow fast—up to 6 feet a year. Leaves are composed of oval leaflets, forming a large, palm-like whorl. Flowers are yellowish, and borne in huge clusters, with males and females on separate trees.

Trumpet Creeper
(*Campsis radicans*)

Though the wild species is native to Pennsylvania, it is the hybrid form, "MADAME GALEN," that produces the best ornamental effect. The vining plants will grow up to 6 feet in a single season, with wisteria-like foliage. Orange trumpet-shaped flowers, up to 4 inches wide, contain nectar attractive to hummingbirds, hence a tendency among some nurserymen to call it the "hummingbird vine." Plants grow in sun or shade, tolerate poor soil, and are good to place along fence rails, up trellises, and over arbors.

Tulip Tree, Yellow Poplar
(*Liriodendron tulipifera*)

These trees grow a trunk as straight as a telephone pole, with a leafy oval canopy of almost square-shaped leaves. After 10 years the crown is covered with beautiful yellow flowers the size of teacups. Tulip trees are native to Pennsylvania, grow up to 5 feet a year, and light up the landscape in fall with brilliant golden yellow leaves. Good for creating a small grove and lining driveways. William Penn planted tulip poplars as an avenue lead-

ing from the boat dock to the entrance of his house, Pennsbury Manor. They are still thriving.

Tupelo, Black   Black Gum
(*Nyssa sylvatica*)

Just one of these beautiful trees can light up the horizon with intense red fall foliage color. Native to Pennsylvania, plants produce a billowing, mounded leaf canopy and a stout, charcoal-gray trunk. Grows to 75 feet high and 50 feet wide. Creates a magnificent lawn accent where it has room to spread.

Umbrella Pine
(*Sciadopitys verticillata*)

To see a branch of this evergreen tree in a Christmas decoration is enough to make you want it. Perhaps the most beautiful of all needle evergreens, the plant forms a dense pyramid with dark, glossy green leaves arranged in an "umbrella" effect. Trees are extremely slow-growing, and with age develop pendulous, spreading branches and a graceful effect. Cones are 2 to 4 inches long and 1 to 2 inches wide, green the first year and ripening to brown during the second year. Prefers fertile, humus-rich acid soils. Will grow in filtered bright light, but generally prefers full sun. A wonderful accent for rock gardens and planted in pairs at the entrance to a home. The species is the recipient of a Gold Medal Award from the Pennsylvania Horticultural Society.

Viburnum, European Snowball
(*Viburnum opulus*)

Though there are numerous good viburnum species suitable for Pennsylvania gardens, the European snowball bush is the most showy and the most widely planted. The sterile flowers of the variety

"STERILE" are up to 2 1/2 inches around and cover the plants for 3 to 4 weeks in mid-spring, starting off green, then turning white. Tolerates even poor soil if grown in full sun, with good drainage. Makes a good lawn highlight or massed in a shrub border. Susceptible to aphids which distort new foliage.

Virginia Creeper
(Parthenocissus quinquifolia)

A fast-growing vine, native to Pennsylvania. The ivy-like, deeply indented leaves are dark green in summer, turning brilliant red and purple shades in fall. Generally a better wall covering than English ivy because of its faster growth and fall color. Plants tolerate poor soil and light shade, provided drainage is good.

Weigelia, Old-fashioned
(Weigelia florida)

One of the most decorative flowering shrubs to follow the peak azalea season. Plants thrive on any well-drained soil in full sun. In late May the plant covers itself with tubular, funnel-like flowers ranging from white and pink to deep red, depending on variety. Plants reach 9 feet tall and spread to 12 feet wide. Leaves resemble azaleas but do not have good fall color. Plants frequently suffer some branch die-back, and need the dead wood removed. "MONT BLANC" is a good white; "NEWPORT RED" is one of the best red-flowered forms; "VARIEGATA" is a pale pink with beautiful variegated leaves edged pale yellow or cream.

Willow, White
(Salix alba)

A fast-growing tree reaching 75 to 100 feet with a spread of 50 to 100 feet, and eventually making a broad, round-topped crown. The bark is a yellowish-brown and the bright yellow branch tips create a distinctive landscape feature in winter. Trees are either male or female. The flowers are upright catkins on the males—popularly called "pussy-willows." Easy to transplant because of its spreading fibrous root system. A branch cut from the tree in spring will generally root in moist soil to form a new tree. Especially beautiful along streams or overhanging ponds in full sun. Limbs are brittle and break in ice storms.

Several other willows are worth consideration in the home landscape, including the corkscrew willow (*S. matsudana*), producing contorted stems valued by floral arrangers, and the pussy willow (*S. caprea*), a multi-stemmed type whose main appeal is its silky white male flowers produced in early spring.

Winterberry
(Ilex verticillata)

Native to moist waysides and stream banks of Pennsylvania, this deciduous holly loses its leaves as masses of red berries ripen, presenting an unusually dramatic berry display that persists until the New Year. "CHRISTMAS CHEER" is a particularly fine selection, and a hybrid, "SPARKLEBERRY" (a cross between *I. serrata* and *I. verticillata*), won a Gold Medal Award from the Pennsylvania Horticultural Society for its vigor and bright scarlet-red berries. Plants grow in sun or light shade, creating an attractive lawn highlight or informal hedge. The berries appear only on female plants, but pollination from a male American holly or wild male winterberry can substitute for a male cultivated variety.

Wintercreeper Euonymus
(Euonymus fortunei var. coloratus)

Deep green, glossy oval leaves turn purple in late fall. Plants creep to form a 12-

inch-dense carpet effect. Wintercreeper euonymus benefits from shearing every 3 or 4 years. Tolerates many different soil types in sun or shade, provided drainage is adequate. The variety "LONGWOOD" is especially good for ground cover effect.

Winterhazel
(Carylopsis spicata)

Hardy deciduous flowering shrub valued for its bright yellow pendant flowers that bloom even ahead of forsythia in early spring. Plants grow to 10 feet high, with an equal spread, and look good planted at the edge of woodland in a fertile, humus-rich soil. Good companion to *Rhododendron mucronulatum*, which flowers at the same time with rosy pink flowers.

Wisteria, Japanese
(Wisteria floribunda)

Aggressive flowering vine capable of climbing to 30 feet and more, covering itself in May with pendant flower clusters up to 2 feet long, mostly in blue, but also in pink and white. Some years the flowering display can be sparse—caused by a late spring frost that can blast the unopened flower buds, thus killing them. But most years the display is magnificent. Plants are suitable for training along fence rails and arbors as well as up the side of buildings by means of trellises. They prefer full sun and fertile loam soil.

Witch Hazel
(Hamamelis x intermedia)

The witch hazels are the earliest flowering shrubs, usually blooming at the first sign of a warming trend in February and March (depending on the variety). Whenever the sun is shining and the temperature rises above 45° F, the four-petalled, spidery, fragrant yellow or orange-red flowers unfold and decorate the leafless dark gray branches. If planted near a walk and backed by dark evergreens, a witch hazel in full bloom is sensational. Some of the best varieties are hybrids of Asian species, botanically identified as *Hamamelis x intermedia*. "ARNOLD'S PROMISE" grows to 20 feet high with bright yellow flowers. "DIANA" won a Gold Medal Award from the Pennsylvania Horticultural Society for its reddish flowers.

Don't overlook the native Pennsylvania witch hazel *H. virginiana*. Its spidery yellow flowers are the last from any flowering tree to bloom—usually appearing in November. Witch hazels prefer moist, but well-drained, humus-rich acid soils. They are difficult to transplant, except from containers, and prefer a sheltered location.

Yellow-wood
(Cladrastis lutea)

A fine, deciduous, flowering shade tree native to Kentucky and other southern states, but happy in most Pennsylvania landscapes. Plants grow large, oval serrated leaves that turn yellow in fall. Fragrant white flower clusters resembling locust blossoms occur every other year in June. A beautiful lawn highlight, it prefers fertile, humus-rich loam soil in full sun. Branches are brittle and break easily unless the tree is located in a sheltered position, or is shaped by pruning excessively long branches.

Yew
(Taxus species)

The best long-lived needle evergreens are within this family. Three species— *T.baccata* (English yew), *T. cuspidata* (Japanese yew) and the hybrid *T. x me-*

dia—are good to use for hedges. They have shiny, dark green, short, flat needles. Newer growth is an attractive light green. Plants are slow-growing but can reach tree-like proportions. They tolerate heavy pruning and can be sheared to create topiary. Red, flesh-like berries appear on female plants in fall and persist into winter. These are poisonous. Transplant, balled and burlapped, into loam soil with good drainage. Plants prefer a sunny position.

CHAPTER 9

Vegetables and Herbs

In 1976, when the Arab oil boycott created horrendous gas lines across North America, and Pennsylvanians saw the possibility of food shortages and spending most of their time bored at home, more vegetable gardens were planted than at any time in the nation's history, except during World War II's "Victory Garden" campaign. President Ford delivered a speech (called his "Win" speech) in which he called for more Americans to plant vegetable gardens as one of 10 ways to fight inflation.

At the time, I was employed as director of the National Garden Bureau, an information office sponsored by the American garden seed industry. My principal duty was to write and mail a series of news releases to the media, encouraging the planting of garden seeds. Ford handed us a heaven-sent gift. Realizing that a model vegetable garden was needed to help beginner gardeners get started, I dashed off a small space plan just 10 feet wide by 15 feet long, capable of producing $300 worth of fresh vegetables. It was then offered as an exclusive to the *Washington Post*, which ran it in their Sunday gardening section. By 10:00 a.m. Monday morning, I received a call from the White House, saying that President Ford had seen the model vegetable garden and wanted to plant it in the White House grounds. I still have a formal letter from the White House confirming their wishes, and during the following four months I made several trips to Washington. Following meetings with White House officials and groups with a vested interest in a White House vegetable garden, I wrote several position papers satisfying various concerns, such as who would tend the garden (the White House gardener), who would harvest the crops (the White House cook), and whether millions of backyard gardeners would hurt the American farmer (a concern voiced by the U.S. Department of Agriculture). One by one the obstacles were overcome, the enthusiasm gained momentum, and a site was selected in a sunny south-facing position on the White House lawn. Everything was set to go when suddenly the war in Vietnam de-escalated, and the President had to focus all his attention on bringing it to an end. His advisers decided that planting a vegetable garden would be seen as too frivolous, and so the vegetable garden was never planted.

In the years that followed, vegetable gardens dwindled, while ornamental gardening flourished. The price of fresh vegetables has stayed relatively low, and Americans are planting perennials, roses, and annuals for cutting in unprecedented numbers. Personally, if I ever missed a season without my plot of spring peas, snap beans, and luscious tomatoes, I'd feel I'd lost a year of my life. I don't plant vegetables to save money— I do it to enjoy freshness and flavor I can't buy at the supermarket and for the peace of mind that comes with knowing that what I eat has been grown without chemicals.

Of course, vegetable gardening in Pennsylvania is not without problems, not the least of which is the nuisance of deer, groundhogs, raccoons, and rabbits. In my experience, there is no better control than fencing out these foraging animals. The fence can be as simple as an enclosure made from inexpensive birdnetting stapled to posts, or several strands of electric wire, producing a nasty shock that doesn't harm the animals.

I find the worst insect pests to be *cut worms* (grubs that stay curled up in the soil during the day and venture out at night, cutting young seedlings at the soil line); *slugs* (in wet weather, they are most troublesome, eating anything young and tender, especially lettuce); *bean beetles* (they skeletonize bean plants and have a special liking for pole beans); *flea beetles* (their favorite food is eggplant); *Japanese beetles* (grape vines are their preference); and *cucumber beetles* (if they sting a melon plant or cucumber vine, it's almost certain to introduce wilt disease). The caterpillar larva of the *cabbage white butterfly* can skeletonize cabbages, and *squash vine borers* are apt to attack your zucchini. Some years the *corn ear worm* devastates sweet corn by ravaging the tenderest part of the cob.

I've found that an organic insecticide combining pyrethrum (a powder made from the petals of an African daisy) and rotenone (a powder made from the roots of a tropical tree) is a good all-purpose control for most garden insects. Insecticidal soap is also an effective and safe control, though its effect is short-lived—especially after rainfall. Dipel—a bacterial control containing BT (*Bacillus thuringensis*)—is a good natural insecticide effective against caterpillar-type pests, such as the *cabbage white butterfly*. Those pesky slugs I control mostly by hand-picking populations in the early morning. A good way to protect compact crops such as cabbage, lettuce, cauliflower, and broccoli is to encase them in "floating row covers"—an inexpensive, lightweight white fabric which covers plants and does not hinder their growth. That way you not only ensure protection against most insects, but also most wild animals such as deer. Floating row covers are becoming such an economical and accepted way of guarding rows of vegetables that they are readily available from local garden supply centers.

Pennsylvania is a wonderful state for cultivating a vast assortment of tasty vegetables—from fast-growing, cool-weather crops such as lettuce and spinach, to warm-weather kinds that require a longer growing season such as cantaloupes, watermelons, and tomatoes. Pennsylvania soils are naturally acid, favoring the growth of most vegetables. (A soil test submitted to the Soil Testing Laboratory at Penn State University will tell you if the soil is, in fact, too acid and in need of liming.) Also, many famous varieties of vegetables were developed in Pennsylvania—such as the "SUPERSTEAK VFN" hybrid tomato, "GREEN ICE" looseleaf lettuce and "SUMMER SWEET" hybrid sweet corn—either at Burpee's Fordhook Farm in Doylestown, or at Abbott & Cobb's research farm in Trevose. There are many places to see model vegetable gardens, including Longwood Gardens, at Kennett Square, and the Peter Wentz Farmstead, a restored colonial farm with a wonderful, old-fashioned vegetable and herb garden, at Worcester, Pennsylvania. Twilley Seeds, in Trevose, and Penn State University both conduct extensive vegetable trials to evaluate old established and new varieties of vegetables, and the Rodale Research Farm, in Maxatawny, is an All-America Vegetable Trial Garden.

Another often overlooked advantage to gardening in Pennsylvania is the wealth of manure available from poultry farms, horse farms and dairy farms. Truckloads of well-decomposed animal manure can be delivered to your site at modest cost, and many farmers are willing to let you take it away free, if you do the hauling. Connoisseurs of manure, like wine connoisseurs, have their individual preferences, but the general consensus is that cow manure has the edge over horse manure for the very best results, probably because the cow has a more complicated digestive system than the horse, and its manure is the richest in nutrients. Just look in the classified section of your local newspaper at planting time for sources of manure under Farm and Garden Supplies.

Another overlooked natural resource is the wealth of leaves that Pennsylvania's trees produce. Collected onto a tarp, shredded with a lawn mower to hasten their decomposition, and piled into wire-enclosed "bins," they turn into a precious, nutrient-rich soil conditioner called "leaf mold," which can be spread over the garden in spring to create both a wonderful, fluffy planting bed and a clean, weed-suffocating mulch.

Perhaps the wisest investment for a Pennsylvania vegetable gardener, after good soil, is irrigation, and the very best to consider is drip-irrigation—especially the kind that delivers moisture to plant roots, oozing drops of moisture through micro-pores in the hose walls at the turn of a faucet. Parts of Pennsylvania in summer can experience low rainfall and long periods of drought, and it doesn't pay to rely on natural rainfall to supply sufficient water. The Amish favor inexpensive drip systems that simply snake up and down rows of plants for as little as $40 to cover 500 square feet of vegetable garden, dripping moisture along the hose length. Some are made of a lightweight plastic material that can be thrown away at the end of the season; others are more durable (and more costly), made from recycled automobile tires (see list of sources, page 224).

PLANNING, PLANTING, AND HARVESTING

Planning

Planning for the new season's vegetable garden can begin as soon as the old garden has been killed off by frost in fall, and the dead leaves and roots added to a compost pile. Although it's important to study seed catalogs as soon as they arrive (usually the week after Christmas), study also some of the catalogs that offer organic remedies to fertilizing and insect control. The *Nitron* and *Gardens Alive* catalogs are especially valuable for learning how to maintain a chemical-free garden (see list of sources). Fertilizing and insect control for vegetables are much more important than they are for flowers.

Although you will want to stay with vegetable varieties that are tried and true, always test some new varieties—especially any that have won All-America Awards. When deciding what to plant where, avoid planting the same crop in the same part of the garden. This is particularly important for disease-susceptible crops such as peas, beans, and cabbage.

If you have no experience with garden layouts, use the sample garden featured here as a guide, adding or deleting varieties to your own preference. Make it *your* garden, featuring the kinds of vegetables you and your family will want most. Make

VEGETABLE GARDEN PLAN

This sample planting plan shows how many kinds of vegetables can be grown in an "automatic garden," some as double rows. The same system can be used to grow flowers. This plot is 500 square feet and can be planted from a kit.

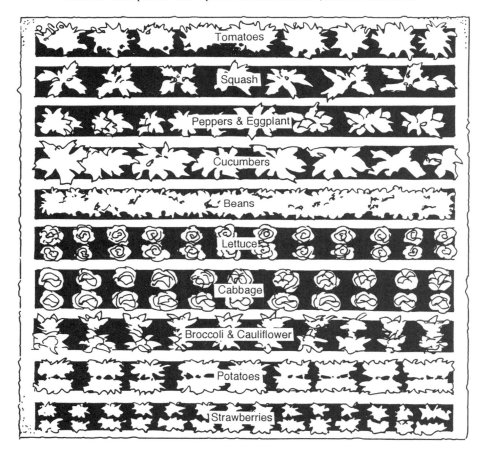

Tomatoes - one row

Squash - one row

Peppers & Eggplant - one row

Cucumbers - one row

Beans - two rows

Lettuce - two rows

Cabbage - two rows

Broccoli & Cauliflower - two rows

Potatoes - two rows

Strawberries - two rows

it fun, ask the children what they want to grow, and turn the project into a family affair. Actual site preparation—digging the ground and soil-conditioning—can begin as soon as the frost is out of the soil.

Sunlight and Moisture

The more sun the better, but if your garden receives 6 hours of direct sunlight each day, that is sufficient to gain worthwhile yields of vegetables.

If shade falls on your vegetable garden during the midday, it will reduce yields and slow plant growth. Shaded sites can be improved by judicious pruning of overhanging branches or by mulching between rows with strips of shiny aluminum foil, which helps to improve the available light through reflection.

Good drainage is also essential. Although all vegetable plants need adequate amounts of water during their entire growth cycle, their roots must never be waterlogged. The easiest way to improve a poorly drained site is to create raised beds.

Digging

Most sites for a vegetable garden need digging to a depth of at least 1 foot, but the more soil depth you provide, the better. For a completely new site where nothing but turf has been growing, hire a person with a roto-tiller to come in and roto-till the soil thoroughly. Spading a new site can be backbreaking work. Better to save your energy for applying soil conditioners and screened topsoil over the roto-tilled site to increase soil depth. If your site is unusually poor—hard Pennsylvania shale, for example—then don't even try to dig down a foot. Simply build a raised bed and bring in a good dump-truck load of screened topsoil (check the classified section of your local newspaper for a convenient supplier).

If, after digging the site, the soil needs lime to correct acidity or an organic soil conditioner to improve aeration, or fertilizer to improve its nutrient content (a soil test will let you know), then apply all these additives at the same time and rake level. This will create a fine, pulverized, crumbly surface in which to plant seeds.

A good system of growing vegetables is to create raised rows that are simply 2-foot-wide strips of soil raked from the pathways into a mound and then flattened on top with the back of the rake to create a level planting area. For large vegetables—such as tomatoes, it's room for one row of plants; for smaller vegetables—such as lettuce, two rows can be accommodated along the row, which should be raised above the walkway about 4 inches. This then allows a 3-foot width of black plastic to be rolled out along the raised row with 2 inches on either side anchored with soil along the pathway. The black plastic warms the soil, conserves moisture, acts as a weed barrier, and if you are using drip irrigation hose, it acts as a protective cover.

Raking

A rake and a spade are the two most important tools in any vegetable garden. Most small-space vegetable gardens can be planted and cared for using only these tools. In addition to using the prongs of the rake for leveling and collecting to one side any large stones, weed roots and trash, get into the habit of using the flat back of the rake. This helps level the soil and creates a fine, crumbly soil surface.

Soil Conditioner

All vegetable gardens benefit from a compost pile. This can be as simple as a tidy pile of garden refuse contained in a chicken-wire enclosure, or it can be an attractive type of enclosed commercial compost bin into which all kinds of garden and kitchen wastes are placed for decomposition, and used the following season as a soil conditioner. A well-made compost pile will not only act as a soil conditioner—adding valuable humus to aerate compacted soil particles—it can be a complete natural fertilizer. In addition to green plant waste, such as grass clippings and hedge trimmings (which provide nitrogen), use large amounts of shredded leaves and kitchen waste such as banana skins, potato peelings, grapefruit rinds (for phosphorus), and wood ashes (for potash).

Fertilizer

If you rely on horticultural peat as a soil conditioner you will most certainly need to use fertilizer to provide sufficient nutrients for worthwhile yields, since peat is sterile. Other forms of soil conditioner—such as garden compost, decomposed animal manure, and leaf mold—will provide plenty of nutrients, but even with these natural organic products you may need to use a booster application of commercial fertilizer, applied in granular or liquid form.

Unless a soil test tells of some serious imbalance requiring correction by a heavy dose of one particular nutrient, use a general purpose fertilizer, such as 5-10-5 or 10-10-10. This can be applied by hand, sprinkled on the ground in granular form, and mixed into the upper soil surface before planting. One of the finest fertilizer brands—Peters Plant Foods—is manufactured near Allentown, and it has built a reputation for making fertilizers that contain valuable trace elements.

Read fertilizer directions carefully to determine the proper method and rate of application over a growing season, since fertilizers are not all alike. Some are fast-acting, drain from the soil quickly and need booster applications at regular intervals. Others are slow-acting or timed-release, and one application may be enough. Also, there are fertilizers you can dilute with water for application to the plants. The famous Miracle-Gro plant food—formulated by a New Jersey soil scientist from Rutgers University—is popular with many gardeners because it is mixed with water and applied to the soil as a liquid feed, either by using a simple spray gun attached to your garden hose, or by using a watering can.

Planting

When sowing seeds directly into the garden, it is easiest to use the straight row method of stretching out a ball of string and making a furrow into which to plant the seeds. Read the seed packet directions carefully to determine the depth at which to plant. You can make a furrow with the handle of your rake very easily by simply drawing it along the edge of the string and making a depression in the soil. Buying ready-grown transplants from a garden center saves time, but remember there are some vegetables you should not transplant, like all root crops, snap beans, garden peas, and corn.

V e g e t a b l e   P l a n t i n g   C h a r t

VEGETABLE		Seed per 100 feet	Plants per 100 feet	Space between row (feet)	Space between plants plants (inches)	Depth of planting (inches)	Approximate field planting dates	Time to maturity (days)
Asparagus		.5 oz.	50-75	4	18-24	6-8	April	2-3 yr.
Beans,	dwarf snap	8 oz.	0	1.5-3	3-4	1-1.5	May 15-Aug. 1	50-65
	pole snap	4 oz.	0	4	4-8	1-1.5	May 15-June 1	50-75
	green shell	8 oz.	0	2-3	2-4	1-1.5	May 15-June 1	90-100
	dry shell	8 oz.	0	2-3	2-4	1-1.5	May 15-June 1	90-100
	dwarf lima	1 lb.	0	1.5-3	4-8	1-1.5	May 20-June 10	75-80
	pole lima	8 oz.	0	4	6-8	1-1.5	May 20-June 1	80-100
Beets		1 oz.	0	1-1.5	1-3	.5-1	April 1-July 10	50-70
Broccoli,	early	.25 oz.	60	3	12-24	plants	April 1-15	75-100
	late	.25 oz.	60	3	18-24	plants	June 15-July 10	90-100
Brussels sprouts		.25 oz.	60	3	18-24	plants	May 15-June 15	90-130
Cabbage,	early	.25 oz.	70	2-3	9-18	plants	April 15-May 20	60-90
	late	.25 oz.	60	2-3	9-24	.5	June 15-July 1	90-120
Cabbage,	Chinese	.25 oz.	0	1.5-3	10-18	.5	July 15	75-100
Carrots		.5 oz.	0	1-2	1-3	.25-.5	April 1-July 10	55-90
Cauliflower,	early	.25 oz.	60	2-3	12-18	plants	April1-15	75-100
Sweet	late	.25 oz.	60	2-3	12-18	.5	June15-July 10	90-120
Celery,	early	.25 oz.	200	2-3	4-6	plants	April 20-May 15	75-100
	late	.25 oz.	200	2-3	6	1/8	July 1-15	100-200
Chives		0	100	2-3	1-1.5	plants	April	0
Corn, sweet,	early	.25 oz.	0	2.5-3	8-10	1.5	May 1-July 1	70-80
	late	.25 oz.	0	2.5-3	10-12	1.5	May 1-July 1	85-100
Cucumber		.5 oz.	0	3-6	12	1-1.5	May 10-June 15	60-80
Eggplant		.25 oz.	60	3-4	18-24	plants	May 20-June 1	90-100
Endive		.25 oz.	0	1.5-2	8-12	.25-.5	May 1-July 15	60-90
Horseradish		0	100	3-4	12-15	6	April 1-15	180
Kale		.25 oz.	0	1.5-2	12-24	.5	July 15-Aug. 1	50-200
Kohlrabi		.25 oz.	0	1.5-2	4-6	.5	April 1-Aug. 1	60-75
Leek		.5 oz.	0	1.5-2	3-4	.5	April 1-15	130-180
Lettuce		.25 oz.	0	1-2	9-15	1-1.5	April 1-Aug. 1	45-75
Onion,	plants	.5 oz.	600	1.5-2	3-4	plants	April 1-15	110
	sets	2 oz.	0	1-2	1-3	.5	April 1-15	100-120
	for sets	2 oz.	0	1-1.25	crowded	.25-.5	April 1-15	90-100
Parsley		.5 oz.	0	1-1.5	4-12	.25-.5	April 1-Aug. 1	60-90
Parsnip		.5 oz.	0	1.5-2	3-4	.25-.5	April 15-30	95-110
Peas		1 lb.	0	2-3	2-3	1-1.5	April	50-80
Pepper		.25 oz.	80	1.5-3	12-24	plants	May 20-June 1	70-90
Potato,	sweet	1 pk.	80	3-3.5	12-18	plants	May 20	115-125
Pumpkin,	vine	.5 oz.	0	6-10	36-60	1	May 20-June 1	90-110
Radish		1 oz.	0	1	1	.5	April-August	25-35
Rhubarb		1 oz.	25	3-4	2-3	plants	April 1	2 yrs.
Rutabega		.25 oz	0	1.5-2	5-8	.5	July 1	90-120
Spinach		1 oz.	0	1-1.5	2-4	.5	April & Aug.	40-60
Squash,	winter	1 oz.	0	6-10	36-60	1	May 15-June 1	90-110
	summer	1 oz.	0	3-5	36-60	1	May 15-June1	50-80
Swiss chard		1 oz.	0	1.5-3	6-12	.5-1	April 15	50-60
Tomatoes		.25 oz.	40	3-5	36-60	plants	May 20-June 1	75-100
Tomatoes,	staked	.25 oz.	75	3-4	15-24	plants	May 20-June1	75-100
Turnip		.5 oz.	0	1-2	2-6	.25-.5	April 25-July 1	50-80
Watermelon		.5 oz.	0	6-10	24-36	1	May 20-June 1	70-95

Avoid stepping onto newly dug soil. Place a board along planting rows to step on so your feet don't compact the soil. After covering seed with soil, firm the surface gently with your foot.

Consider dusting peas and beans with ''inoculant''—a black powder that helps promote populations of nitrogen-fixing soil bacteria. Yields of peas in particular are greatly increased.

When choosing transplants—such as cabbage, broccoli, cauliflower, tomatoes, peppers, and eggplant—look for compact plants; small, stocky plants generally will survive transplant shock better than plants that are stretched, and produce better yields. Use a hand trowel to make holes for transplanting, and firm the soil so there is good soil contact around roots. Be sure that transplants are properly ''hardened-off'' before transplanting. Good growers place transplants in a cold frame for several days to ''acclimatize'' them, since jumping directly from a protected greenhouse environment to an exposed garden environment can seriously weaken plants. If you are growing transplants yourself and don't have a cold frame to hold them in, simply set them out in a sheltered area covered at night with clear plastic sheets, for at least 3 nights.

Water

Moisture is especially important at time of fruit formation. Deprived of moisture at time of tasseling, sweet corn yields will be affected; poor flavor in radishes is a sign of moisture stress. Even 5 or 6 days without a good soaking, heavy rain will stop most plants from growing and reduce yields. Long-handled watering wands are extremely useful. They allow you to poke the nozzle through bushy leaves and drench the soil immediately at the root zone. Soaking leaves too frequently can lead to fungus diseases.

During dry spells the easiest way to get water into a garden in the absence of drip irrigation is by hooking up a garden hose and fixing a lawn sprinkler to the end. Then set the lawn sprinkler in the garden to saturate the soil overnight. Don't just stand there playing the hose onto the garden once over lightly. The water has to penetrate, drench the soil, and get deep down to roots.

If your vegetable garden is located in a remote area, far from any convenient water supply, consider installing a rain barrel under a roof overhang. To conserve water in the soil during dry spells, lay down a thick layer of mulch at the beginning of the season soon after your plants are up. Grass clippings, shredded leaves, hay, and pine needles are examples of efficient mulch material that will decompose and add valuable fiber (or humus) to the soil. Wait until the soil is thoroughly warmed before applying an organic mulch, as it will tend to keep soil cool and inhibit growth of plants that enjoy warm soil temperatures—such as tomatoes and melons. For these plants it's better to use black plastic for mulching, as this tends to warm the soil.

Thinning

Once your seeds are up, they may need thinning out. When plants are crowded, thinning is essential, and it is best started in the very early stages, just when the plants emerge. Very fine seedlings, like carrots, may need thinning several times in stages before you have your plants the correct distance apart for full maturity. Seedlings can be thinned by snipping off the tops of the undesirable sprouts. This eliminates root damage to the remaining seedlings.

16 EASY STEPS TO SUCCESS

1. PLAN
Plan on paper the garden size and selection of varieties using the "WIN" garden as a model. Delete or substitute varieties according to personal preference and local conditions.

2. TEST
Test soil to determine acidity and need for lime.

3. PROVIDE SUN
Select site in a sunny, well-drained location. Start work on a dry day when soil is not wet or sticky.

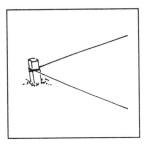

4. STAKE
Stake out the area using string and pegs.

5. CONDITION SOIL
Apply soil conditioner such as peat moss or garden compost to the site if needed.

6. LIME
Sprinkle lime on acid soils at rate of 5 lbs. per 100 square feet every 3 years.

7. DIG
Dig over site to depth of 1 foot. Remove large stones and weed roots. Break up clods, and mix in soil conditioner thoroughly.

8. FERTILIZE
Apply fertilizer at recommended rate.

16 EASY STEPS TO SUCCESS

9. RAKE.
Rake level. Remove small stones and weed roots.

13. WEED
Mulching helps control weeds. A few minutes a day is time better spent than trying to catch up on 2 weeks of neglect.

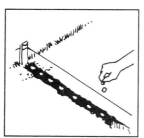

10. PLANT
Plant seeds or transplants, saving tender varieties until after last frost date.

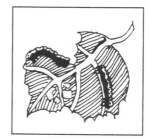

14. CONTROL PESTS
Keep watch for pests and disease so early treatment can be administered. Check with local experienced gardeners to find out the main pest problems in your area and safe, effective controls.

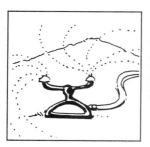

11. WATER
Water thoroughly at time of planting, also during dry spells. Even a week without drenching rain will reduce yields and slow down growth.

15. HARVEST
Pick fruit crops regularly. The more you pick the more will come.

12. THIN
Thin seedlings, leaving room for strongest plants to develop fully.

16. SUCCESSION-PLANT
Make succession plantings to gain maximum return from minimum space.

KITCHEN GARDEN DESIGN
BASED ON QUADRANT GARDEN AT PETER WENTZ FARMSTEAD

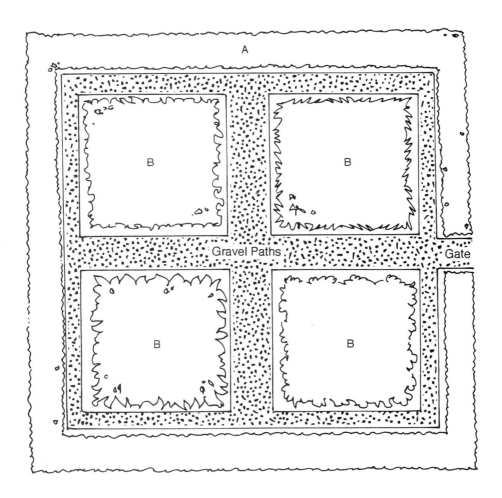

A: Border featuring perennial herbs (mint, chives); perennial vegetables (rhubarb, asparagus, horseradish) and berry bushes (strawberries, raspberries, red currants, blackberries)

B: Annual vegetables, rotated each year - one block devoted to bean crops, one to cabbage, one to squash, one to root crops

Succession Planting

To keep a vegetable garden productive (and attractive) practice succession planting. When one crop is harvested, plant another crop either of the same or a different vegetable in its place, so there is always something coming along, providing a plentiful supply. For example, most planting plans can accommodate two plantings of cabbage—one started in spring for summer harvesting and the other planted in summer for fall harvesting. The same is true for beets, carrots, spinach, snap beans, lettuce, and radishes. A row of garden peas for harvesting in June can be replanted with Brussels sprouts for harvesting in fall and winter months. This type of intensive planting is the key to continuous production.

There is one special problem to guard against with succession plantings. Over most of Pennsylvania spring rains are common, and the garden gets adequate moisture to get the plants off to a good start. In midsummer and fall, however, we often experience prolonged dry spells. Keep a special eye on the water situation with succession plantings if you want the best results.

Harvesting

To gain maximum productivity from your garden, harvest from it regularly, especially crops like tomatoes, zucchini squash, peppers, and eggplant. The more you keep these picked, the more new flowers and fruit will form to replace them.

Special harvesting tips are given in the individual sections about each vegetable. For advice on the best time to pick beets, how to tell when a watermelon is ripe, and the proper procedure for picking zucchini squash, turn to the appropriate vegetable section.

To get the greatest nutritional value from your garden vegetables, always try to reduce the time between picking and eating to as little as possible. The longer you keep any vegetable, the greater the vitamin loss. Cooking a vegetable too long also will reduce its nutritional content.

Sweet corn is particularly susceptible to flavor and nutritional loss soon after harvesting. Within 12 hours after picking, most sweet corn varieties start to convert their sugar into starch and lose that sweet, milky flavor.

After picking vegetables, don't leave them in the sun to wilt. Put them in a basket and cover with a cloth, or place them in the shade until you can get them to the kitchen.

Swap varieties with neighbors and friends. Decide if the variety you grew is as flavorful as the one your neighbor tried. That will help you decide whether to stick to your variety or make a switch the following season.

Starting Vegetable Seeds Indoors

Some varieties of vegetables need starting indoors to get good, strong transplants for setting out into the garden when warm weather arrives. In most cases they are varieties that require a longer than usual growing season in which to mature, so the early start helps you to gain an earlier crop.

Broccoli, cauliflower, cabbage, eggplant, parsley, peppers, and tomatoes are examples of vegetables that will benefit from being started indoors 6 to 8 weeks ahead of transplanting.

Many kinds of household containers can be used as seedling trays to start these seeds, such as empty milk cartons and produce trays. Alternatively, you can use regular seedling trays or seed starting kits purchased through a local garden supply center. These may be ready-filled with a sterile planter soil, or you can purchase a bag of potting soil separately.

If you use garden topsoil for starting seedlings, bake it in a 300° F oven for 2 hours to destroy harmful fungus and bacteria. Otherwise your seedlings may perish from a common soil disease called "damping-off," which is identifiable when the tiny seedlings keel over at the soil line and die.

Set your seedling trays where they will receive an even distribution of bright light—but not direct sunlight. If all you have is a windowsill, raise the tray to the level of the pane with a book so the seedlings won't have to stretch their necks to get above the pane.

Consider buying or building a cold frame to harden-off your seedlings before transferring them to the garden, otherwise they can suffer transplant shock.

Frost Dates

Although there are zone maps showing approximate last frost dates for different sections of the state, it is far better for you to check this out locally by asking more experienced gardeners in the neighborhood or finding out from local garden supply centers and local county agents.

It's also useful to know the first expected frost date in fall and to listen to weather forecasts so that before frost hits and kills off tender plants, you can gather any immature fruit for ripening indoors. Tomatoes, for example, can be gathered in the green stage, and they will ripen indoors over several weeks even without light. A map showing first and last frost dates for Pennsylvania can be found in Chapter 1.

Container Gardening

If you want to enjoy growing fresh vegetables but don't have any garden space, you might want to consider the benefits of container gardening. It's possible to grow a wide range of vegetables in containers on patios and balconies, provided you have a sunny spot.

The larger the container, the more successful your efforts are likely to be. Small containers dry out rather quickly, so try to use something with at least a gallon capacity. Redwood tubs, metal buckets, plastic bins, and concrete planters are suitable, provided they have good drainage in the bottom. Even with large containers, you will probably need to water your plants every day and provide a fertilizer feed at least once a week when the flowers and fruit start to form.

Tomatoes are the most worthwhile vegetable for container gardening, followed by peppers, eggplant, chard, and zucchini squash, although virtually any kind of vegetable can be grown that way, even stalks of corn.

Many kinds of fragrant herbs will grow in a kitchen window, particularly parsley, mint, chives, and thyme, but again you must remember to water them daily.

A suitable soil mix for container-grown vegetables is equal parts of garden topsoil, peat moss, and sand.

RECOMMENDED VEGETABLES FOR PENNSYLVANIA GARDENS

The following vegetables are most suitable for Pennsylvania's climate, though some of them—like the artichoke—are a little challenging.

Artichoke

This perennial crop is excluded from many Pennsylvania vegetable gardens because it requires too long a growing season, normally does not bear well until the second season after planting, and takes up too much room in a small garden. Many people prefer to grow artichokes in their flower borders and foundation plantings, since its silvery green, toothed foliage is a decorative contrast with dark evergreens, accepting fruit as a bonus if the season is favorable.

Artichokes do reasonably well in southerly areas such as the Delaware/Pennsylvania borderlands where winters are mild, but the roots will not survive a severe winter freeze. Chances of success are enhanced if roots are stored indoors over winter in 3-gallon containers and transferred to the garden after frost-danger. To grow from seed, start indoors 8 to 10 weeks before the last frost date and then transplant to stand 4 feet apart. The edible portion is a cluster of bud scales, which must be picked before the flower petals develop. The buds are picked with 2 inches of stem attached, and then immersed in boiling water until the base feels tender to the touch of a fork (usually 20 minutes). The bud scales are removed one at a time and the base is sufficiently tender to be eaten. The closer to the heart, the more that can be eaten. A vigorous plant can produce as many as 50 edible buds in a season, but three or four is an accomplishment in any part of Pennsylvania. If left to open, the edible flower buds develop a mass of purple petals resembling a thistle. These will dry to make beautiful centerpieces in dried flower arrangements.

Each year the artichoke produces a mass of shoots, or suckers, from its underground root system. The secret of a productive plant is to prune back all but four of the strongest shoots. (The variety "GREEN GLOBE," if started early from seed and transplanted after danger of frost, will usually produce artichokes the first season, given plenty of moisture during dry spells.)

Both slugs and rodents can be serious pests.

Artichoke, Jerusalem

The so-called Jerusalem artichoke is the biggest misnomer in the plant kingdom. It isn't an artichoke but a native American sunflower. It forms bushy, tall clumps of stems and leaves with masses of yellow flowers above ground and fleshy, edible tubers underground.

This is not a plant to grow in small-space gardens. It reaches heights of 6 feet and spreads aggressively. You should find a special place where it can grow almost wild. Plants are grown from tuberous roots covered with 2 inches of soil in spring and spaced 2 to 3 feet apart.

Harvesting can begin in late summer and fall, 100 days after planting. Tubers can be dug from the ground among established clumps at any time of year. To cook, boil in water like potatoes, but do not eat more than two tubers at a time, twice a week. They contain insulin highly beneficial to people prone to diabetes, but too much at a meal can cause stomach upset.

Plants are generally pest-free in Pennsylvania, though wireworms can scar the tubers.

Asparagus

Asparagus used to need a lot of space to yield a good supply, but with the introduction of all-male hybrid varieties—such as "BEN FRANKLIN" (developed in Holland) and "JERSEY GIANT" (developed at Rutgers University)—25 plants can yield as much as 75 plants of old non-hybrids like "MARY WASHINGTON." Asparagus spears grow from thick, fleshy root systems that need a fertile sandy or loam soil free of weeds.

Planting asparagus from seed is very easy and inexpensive. With old varieties growing from seed would require an extra year to gain a worthwhile harvest, compared to roots, but with the new all-male hybrids growing from seed means that a light harvest is possible the next season. The trick is to transplant 8- to 10-week-old seedlings. In hybrid varieties these suffer less transplant shock than roots.

Asparagus is one of the earliest spring crops, since the edible "spear" is actually a young stem that is tender and succulent when it strikes through the soil in early May.

To grow good asparagus dig a trench 1 foot deep, and mix into the bottom plenty of decomposed garden compost, well-rotted leaf mold, animal manure, or peat moss. Set the roots in the bottom on mounds of earth 1 foot apart, and splay out the roots like the arms of an octopus. Cover with 4 inches of topsoil cleared of stones and weed roots and add a phosphorus-rich fertilizer. As the asparagus spears start to grow, fill in the trench around them. Asparagus may benefit from a sprinkling of lime every other season. The trenched area in which you plant asparagus must be kept free of weeds. This is best done by laying down a thick layer of mulch—such as hay, shredded leaves, or similar organic material.

The best time to plant asparagus roots is in spring about 4 weeks before your last frost date. Delay planting seedlings until after the last spring frost date. When the spears are thick enough to harvest, cut them at soil level on a diagonal using a sharp knife. Let the thinner asparagus shoots grow on, and do not cut back the mature foliage until fall when the feathery leaves turn brown and brittle.

Some asparagus plants will produce bright red berries and seeds. These are females, and the seeds will often germinate so readily they create overcrowded conditions like weeds. It is much better to avoid the old asparagus varieties and grow only the new all-male hybrids. Although all-male hybrids may produce a small percentage of females, they produce thicker spears, and up to three-times heavier yields.

Beans, Lima

The famous Fordhook Lima Bean was named for Fordhook Farm, the seed testing and breeding facility for Burpee Seeds, near Doylestown. It was the world's first large-seeded bush lima bean, as opposed to a pole bean. The tall, climbing types need hefty, long poles for support; the dwarf, compact bush lima beans need no support.

Lima beans are extra-sensitive to cold conditions, and any prolonged cold, wet spell will normally rot the seed in the ground before it has a chance to emerge. For this reason, it's best to wait well after your last frost date (at least 10 to 14 days) before attempting a planting of lima beans. Sow the seed directly into the garden, covering the seed with 1 inch of soil. The seedlings may need thinning so that each plant is spaced 5 inches apart in rows 30 inches apart. When planting pole types, use either a trellis or poles in teepee fashion to support the heavy vines.

The variety "FORDHOOK 242" is considered an improvement over the original Fordhook because it has disease resistance. To protect the crop from foraging animals, cover plantings with floating row covers or a "varmint cage."

Beans, Snap

Some people still call this vegetable by its old-fashioned name, string bean, but today that term is completely outdated. Plant breeders bred the strings out of beans more than 50 years ago, and the only way to get a true string bean is to grow a "heritage" variety.

After tomatoes, most people consider snap beans to be the most important vegetable in any Pennsylvania vegetable garden. They are easy to grow throughout the state, and take up relatively little room in comparison to their potential yields.

Perhaps the biggest problem about snap beans is deciding which to choose. There are green-podded, yellow-podded, and even purple-podded varieties; there are bush types, pole types, and other variations.

The green-podded, bush-type snap bean is always a good choice because home gardeners tend to prefer green beans over the yellow wax beans, probably because green beans look better when they are canned and frozen.

Putting up poles to support the tall, towering vines of pole beans is too much trouble for most people; the bush varieties are earlier by as much as 2 weeks. Bush snap beans are simple to grow. The seeds are large and easy to handle, and once you have them up and growing they tend to take good care of themselves.

The danger period is right at the moment of germination when they can fall prey to slugs.

Plant the seeds about 1 inch deep after frost-danger. Space seeds close together at first (2 inches apart) because cutworms, pheasants, and chewing pests sometimes take a heavy toll of the young seedlings. If you get a good stand, thin the plants to about 6 inches apart. Watch the foliage for any signs of Japanese beetles or similar insect pests.

Plants are susceptible to damage by bean beetles which are most destructive in the larva stage when they are yellow, soft-bodied, and covered in soft spines. Control with a rotenone-pyrethrum spray or insecticidal soap. To resist damage by rabbits, woodchucks, and deer place a wire cage over plantings or use floating row covers. Many types of snap beans do well in Pennsylvania, notably "BLUE LAKE," among the green-podded varieties, and "GOLD CROP," an award-winning yellow-podded bean.

There is a special tender-flavored class of snap bean called Italian, or Romano, beans. These have flat pods and a melt-in-the-mouth flavor when boiled in water for just a few minutes. Try "ROMA II" and "JUMBO" for a distinctly gourmet experience, sprinkling a few bacon bits on them for a touch of finesse.

Beets

There are red beets, white beets, and yellow beets, but the red variety is the most popular. In addition to edible round roots that become soft and sweet when cooked, they have tender, leafy tops that can be served as cooked greens.

Beet seeds are generally grouped together in clusters that give the appearance of being one seed, so no matter how you space your seeds you will still have thinning-out problems as each seed cluster sprouts three or four seedlings. Although beets are hardy and will tolerate light frosts, germination is hindered by cold, so wait until your last frost date before sowing the seed 1/4 inch deep. Direct-sow beets since they resent transplanting. As soon as the seed has sprouted, start thinning at once by snipping unwanted seedlings at their soil line with scissors. Thin to stand 3 inches apart in rows 12 inches apart. A second thinning-out operation may be necessary before beets are properly thinned for good root development. Water daily in the absence of rain, as a dry spell will stop their growing.

Start harvesting beets after about 50 days—or when the beets are the size of a golfball.

Although all beet tops are good to eat as cooked greens, some red beet varieties have a rather unappetizing deep purple coloring. Others—such as "LUTZ GREEN LEAF"—are a dark, glossy green—as appealing as a spinach leaf. "BURPEE'S GOLDEN" also has delicious tops.

Consider planting hybrid beets such as "RED ACE" and "PACEMAKER." Hybrids are extra-fast-growing and the tenderest of all.

Broccoli and Cauliflower

Consider a planting of broccoli in spring, followed by a planting of cauliflower in summer to mature in fall.

Over much of Pennsylvania people have difficulty growing cauliflower from a spring planting. It is extra-sensitive to hot weather, and often the hot, humid days of summer set in before the heads have properly matured. Hybrid varieties—such as "SNOW CROWN"—offer the best chance of success from a spring planting. If you plant cauliflower in midsummer as 6-week-old seedlings, the young plants will take the heat as long as you keep them watered. The cooler days of September will arrive by the time the cauliflower head starts to develop. This provides perfect conditions for maturity and harvesting.

In fall, it is best to fold the outside jacket leaves over the head to protect it from any frost and to keep the head snow white. Of course, there is a purple cauliflower that doesn't need its head blanched, but as the first frost date of fall closes in, it still benefits from having the jacket leaves covered over for frost protection.

You can grow broccoli the same way to mature as a spring or fall crop. Broccoli grows easily as a spring crop if you start seed indoors 6 weeks before outdoor planting, and set out transplants about 4 weeks before the last expected frost date. Set the plants to stand 2 feet apart in rows spaced 3 feet apart.

A further point about broccoli: it will normally grow one huge terminal head, which is composed of tight flower bud clusters. Cut the head before you see any yellow flower petals peaking through the buds, and leave the plant to develop smaller heads on side shoots that grow out as soon as the main head is cut.

"COMET" is the earliest broccoli—maturing in 55 days, but "PREMIUM CROP" grows a larger head and matures only a few days later. Both won All-America Awards.

Devastating damage can be caused to cauliflower by larvae of cabbage white butterflies—a small, ravenous, green caterpillar. The most popular control is a bacterial insecticide called BT (short for *Bacillus thuringensis*) which destroys only caterpillar-like pests. The cabbage maggot can be controlled by applying rotenone to the soil or a similar insecticide that lists the cabbage maggot on the label.

Brussels Sprouts

Brussels sprouts mature in October from a midsummer planting and actually improve in flavor after frost. They are so hardy the tight little green buds stay firm and edible until Christmas over most of Pennsylvania, providing fresh greens at a time when store prices are high.

It is difficult for Brussels sprouts to succeed as a summer crop over most of Pennsylvania. Summers are too hot for them, except in isolated, high-altitude areas like the Pocono Mountains, where micro-climates create cooler summer conditions. Grow them as a succession crop to follow a planting of garden peas that can be all picked and eaten by the end of June. Pull up the pea plants and substitute Brussels sprouts to get double value from the same space. Hybrid varieties, such as "JADE CROSS," are recommended. The hybrids give two or even three times the yield per plant of older kinds. However, "LONG IS-LAND IMPROVED"—a standard variety—performs well over most of Pennsylvania, but for something really different, try "ICARUS," one of a new race of sprouts with low bitterness and a distinctly sweet flavor.

Seeds of Brussels sprouts are best started indoors, 6 weeks before outdoor planting. Space these plants 2 feet apart in rows 3 feet apart.

Aphids can destroy Brussels sprouts, colonizing the upper stem sections. Spray with insecticidal soap or dust with rotenone.

Cabbage

Though regular green cabbage is the most widely grown, red cabbage is popular for shredding into salads or pickling, and savoy cabbage has beautiful textured leaves and a buttery yellow heart with the sweetest flavor.

Some excellent cabbage varieties for Pennsylvania include "STONEHEAD" hybrid (which is disease-resistant), "OS CROSS" hybrid (with mammoth heads), "RUBY BALL" hybrid (a red), and "SAVOY ACE" hybrid (a savoy type).

Start seed indoors 6 weeks before outdoor planting. Transplants will tolerate mild frosts, provided they are hardened-off. Start another batch of seeds in mid-August for a crop to mature during cool fall weather.

When choosing cabbage, always check the catalog or seed packet description to see how many days are needed for maturity. Some take as little as 60 days from transplanting; giant varieties can take more than 100!

Space plants 1 1/2 to 2 feet apart in the row (depending on variety), and keep watered during dry spells. Since chewing pests can be troublesome, keep careful watch so you can deal with colonies while they are small and before they reach plague proportions. To control damage by caterpillars, especially the larvae of the cabbage white butterfly, spray plants with BT (*Bacillus thuringensis*), a safe, effective, organic pest control. Alternatively, cover cabbage rows with floating row covers. This also prevents damage from rabbits, ground-hogs, and deer. To control cabbage maggots, rake rotenone into the upper soil surface around plants.

Cabbage, Chinese

There are heading and non-heading varieties. The non-heading are faster-maturing and easier to grow. Time plantings so that plants mature during cool nights of late spring and early summer, and also during fall. Seed may be direct-sown, covered with 1/4 inch of soil. Keep soil moist, and thin seedlings to stand at least 12 inches apart in rows spaced 2 feet apart.

Heading varieties grow upright, with thick midribs and elongated, tightly packed heads. Milder in flavor than regular green cabbage, the leaves are cooked as a vegetable green, or the head can be grated to use as coleslaw. An excellent heading variety is the hybrid "JADE PAGODA" (65 days to maturity), forming large upright heads. Early-maturing, loose-leaf types—such as "JOI CHOY" (maturing in 45 days)—are eaten braised, like celery and Swiss chard. The crispy, white midrib can be chopped into soup.

Slugs can be a major pest problem, controlled by using slug bait or hand-picking populations in the early morning.

Cantaloupes

A wide-open space, free of any shade, is necessary to develop the full flavor of cantaloupes. Fertile, sandy, humus-rich loam soil suits them best. Also, growers have found that a layer of black plastic mulch will vastly improve yields and earliness. The plastic maintains a warm soil temperature and conserves moisture that is so essential to growing full-sized fruit. Clear plastic works even better, but it also encourages weed growth in the row, while black plastic suffocates weeds.

Use strips of black plastic about 3 feet wide, and lay them on top of the cultivated soil. Cover the edges so that the wind won't blow them away. Then punch holes in the center at 3-foot intervals through which to plant seeds. Direct-sow seeds 1/2 inch deep after frost danger, or start indoors in individual peat pots 4 weeks before outdoor planting. Space plants 3 feet apart in rows 6 feet apart, allowing the vines to knit together along the rows.

An old-fashioned favorite among Amish farmers is "JENNY LIND"— shaped like a turban, small, and sweet. Two outstanding modern varieties developed in Pennsylvania are "BURPEE HYBRID" and "AMBROSIA" hybrid. For a Crenshaw-type melon, grow Burpee's "EARLY CRENSHAW" hybrid. The fruits weigh up to 20 pounds each, and the flavor is superior to any other melon. Where space is limited, you can train cantaloupes up a trellis, supporting the fruit with slings, or plant a short-vine type like "HONEYBUSH."

Poor flavor in cantaloupes is caused by a number of shortcomings, but most often it is a combination of poor soil fertility and excessive rain at the time the fruit is ripening. You can tell when a cantaloupe is ripe by pressing lightly on one end to feel if it is slightly soft. The finest specimens have golden netting, but the ribs are still green. When you see a cantaloupe with yellow ribs, it is generally overripe.

Melon plants are highly susceptible to wilt disease introduced by the cucumber beetle, which chews the stems and infects the vine. Spray transplants immediately with a safe insecticidal soap or organic insecticide that lists effectiveness against the beetle.

Carrots

Although long, tapering carrots are the most desirable, it's not everyone who can provide the deep, fine soil they demand, so stump-rooted kinds generally succeed best in Pennsylvania gardens.

Carrot seed is fine and needs to be direct-sown about 3 weeks before the last frost date, since seedlings will tolerate mild frost. Cover seed with a shallow layer of soil—just enough to anchor the seeds (1/16 inch is ideal). The row must be kept moist constantly, since any drying out, once the seed has started to germinate, will kill it. Any crusting of the soil will impair germination because carrot seedlings are too weak to penetrate any kind of soil crust.

Immediately after you see the carrots are up, thin them lightly by snipping crowded seedlings with scissors. Do this again a week later until you have the strongest seedlings standing 1 1/2 inches apart in rows spaced 1 foot apart. One way to avoid this rigorous thinning is to pre-germinate carrot seed in a moist paper towel, then use a moist pencil point to transfer the germinated seeds into their growing positions.

Generally, the smaller the core of a carrot, the sweeter the flavor. A variety with consistently small cores is Burpee's "SHORT 'N SWEET," developed in Pennsylvania.

Malformed carrots, cracking, and forking are normally caused by obstructions in the soil, such as stones and weed roots, or by insects or dryness. Though maggots can be pests, tunneling into carrot roots, they are hard to control. Covering rows with floating row covers will prevent the adult fly from making soil contact to lay eggs.

Celeriac

This slow-growing vegetable develops a swollen edible root like a turnip, with a celery-like flavor.

Direct-sow seed in spring a week before the last expected frost date; for a fall crop sow in mid-August, covering with 1/4 inch of soil in rows spaced 2 feet apart. Just like celery, it requires excessive amounts of water during dry spells and a humus-rich, fertile loam soil. Thin plants in the row to 4 inches apart. Celeriac roots take at least 110 days to mature. They must be washed and peeled, and the crisp interior diced before boiling or added to soups and stews.

Celery

Celery is challenging to grow since it needs a fertile, humus-rich soil and regular watering, plus protection from pests such as slugs.

Start seed indoors 8 weeks before planting outside. Although celery tolerates cold conditions, cool nights will cause it to go to seed, so delay transplanting outdoors until after the last expected frost date.

Celery tastes best when the edible stems are blanched (light excluded). This results in a crisp, clean, gourmet flavor, though it reduces the nutritional value. However, celery has high edible fiber content that makes it valuable as a health food. The blanching is done by heaping up soil around the stalks several weeks before picking or eliminating the light by using a mulch of leaves or a paper collar.

Celery seed is tiny, should be covered with less than 1/4 inch of fine soil, and can be direct-sown. Space plants 6 to 8 inches apart in rows 24 to 30 inches apart. Plants are susceptible to slug damage, controlled by slug bait, or hand-picking slug infestations in the morning. Powdery organic insecticides raked into the upper soil surface will control the carrot fly, which can spoil celery plants.

Chard

Planted at the same time as beets, around the last frost date, chard starts to mature within 60 days, growing fleshy, crinkled green leaves with succulent midribs. The more you pick the leaves and the edible leaf stalks, the more new leaves will grow from the inside to replace them. Once the plant is established and cropping, it is so hardy that it will remain productive until a hard winter freeze. Furthermore, it is rarely troubled by pests or disease.

Leaves of chard are an excellent substitute for spinach, and unlike spinach, hot summer heat will not affect them.

The midribs can be cut into stalks and braised like spears of asparagus with melted butter and breadcrumbs to make a delicious, nutritious side dish. There are two kinds of chard: a white-ribbed type and an ornamental red-ribbed variety referred to as "RUBY" chard, or "RHUBARB" chard. The red-ribbed kind is highly decorative and adds an interesting color highlight to the garden—even to mixed flower borders. There is also a mixture called "RAINBOW" which includes a golden ribbed variety. Direct-sow seeds several weeks before the last expected spring frost date, thinning to stand at least 12 inches apart in rows 2 feet apart.

Collards

Collards are closely related to cabbage but easier to grow since they tolerate summer heat and mature earlier. They are really a non-heading cabbage with sweetly flavored leaves.

Direct-sow seed 1/4 inch deep, thinning plants to stand 1 1/2 feet apart in rows spaced 3 feet apart. Three sowings a year can be made—one in spring to mature in late spring; another in late spring to mature in summer; and a final sowing in late summer to mature in fall, when frost can improve the flavor of the leaves.

Corn Salad

Also called lamb's lettuce and fetticus, the main value of corn salad is its earliness and hardiness as a winter and spring green. People who are used to spinach and lettuce may find the flavor rather bland. Corn salad doesn't make much of an impression by itself. However, it blends well with other vegetables, especially root crops and more flavorful greens.

Direct-sow seed 6 weeks before the last frost date, covering with 1/4 inch of soil. Thin plants to stand 5 to 6 inches apart in rows 12 inches apart. Corn salad grows quickly, a first picking possible within 40 days.

Cress

There's not much point in finding space for cress in a vegetable garden. It will grow just as well in a kitchen window with nothing more than a damp kitchen paper towel to grow on. Once you add water and place it in a shaded window at room temperature, the seed will swell up and split, producing tasty white stalks topped with tangy green leaves that add a spicy flavor to sandwiches, salads, and egg dishes. Harvest the edible green leaves and white stalks by cutting with scissors.

Cucumbers

These very popular vegetables take up a lot of space when left to trail along the ground, so some gardeners like to train them up a trellis where they grow up and not out. Also, some good, space-saving bush cucumber varieties are available—such as Burpee's "BUSH CHAMPION," a slicing-type cucumber. There are slicing cucumbers for salads and pickling varieties for canning and preserves.

Cucumbers thrive in hot weather and are susceptible to frost damage, so seed is best direct-sown after frost-danger, covered with about 1/2 inch of soil. Growth is fast, and the plants will climb by themselves up a trellis, hanging on with their tendrils.

Cucumber plants have male and female flowers. Only the female flowers bear fruit, and the males generally appear first. You'll be able to recognize the females when they do arrive, because they will have a baby cucumber already formed underneath the flower.

When this female flower is pollinated by insects transferring pollen from a male, it will swell up and mature very quickly. If pollination doesn't take place, the cucumber embryo will shrivel up and die. The problem of pollination is especially important when planting all-female cucumbers, which produce a larger percentage of female blossoms than males. These are mostly grown by commercial growers seeking extraordinarily high yields. If you want to grow one of these all-females, be sure you plant a regular cucumber variety so enough male flowers are available for pollination.

Disease takes a heavy toll on cucumbers, so read the catalog description or packet label carefully to make sure you are buying a hybrid variety that is disease resistant, such as "MARKET-MORE."

Direct-sow seeds in groups of four to six seeds, spaced 3 feet apart in rows at least 4 feet apart, and allow the vines to knit together. When grown up a trellis, space plants closer together—2 feet apart.

Cucumbers are susceptible to damage by cucumber beetles, which are yellow with black stripes or black spots. When the beetle chews a vine, it infects the plant with wilt disease. Organic insecticides—such as rotenone-pyrethrum sprays—are effective.

Eggplant

Because they are slow-growing warm-season plants, eggplants are best started indoors 6 to 8 weeks before outdoor planting after frost-danger. Space 2 feet apart in rows 3 feet apart.

Eggplants are used extensively in Italian and Greek cooking, though eggplant fritters are such a popular side dish they are sold frozen at the supermarket. The large, pear-shaped fruits are quite deco-rative and are fully mature when they have a handsome black gloss to them.

Another appealing quality about eggplants is their ability to succeed in containers. If you have little more than a sunny patio or a balcony you can grow them, using pots with a gallon capacity. Before the fruits form they produce large, purple-pink flowers that are quite decorative.

In choosing your own varieties, decide which shape you want: round, oval or cylindrical. The all-around favorite is "DUSKY" hybrid, growing lots of medium-size, oval-shaped fruits.

Plants are highly susceptible to damage by flea beetles (leaves look like they have been damaged by gunshot). Frequent spraying with an insecticidal soap, a rotenone-pyrethrum spray, or other insecticide is essential to control this pest.

Endive

Resembling lettuce, endive has growing conditions identical to loose-leaf lettuce. The rich, green leaves have curly, ragged edges, while the heart of the plant is buttery yellow, crunchy, and delicious to eat in salads or as a cooked side dish.

Since plants will tolerate crowding and light frost, direct-sow seed, 1/4 inch deep, 3 weeks before the last expected frost date, thinning so that plants are 9 inches apart. For a fall crop, plant after August 15. Plants mature in 65 days.

The loose rosette of leaves may need to be tied together in a bunch to blanch the inside and promote a sweet flavor. Outer edges of leaves are slightly bitter, but this combination of bitter sweetness is appreciated by salad connoisseurs.

Plants are susceptible to slug damage. Control with slug bait or hand-pick infestations in the early morning.

Kale

A nutritious green-leaf crop, so hardy

that plants will remain in the garden until Christmas. Direct-seed early in spring, 3 weeks before the last expected frost, and again after August 15 for fall and winter harvests. Cover seeds with 1/2 inch of soil, and thin plants to stand 12 inches apart in rows 2 feet apart. Start to harvest the young, deep-green leaves after 50 days and use as cooked greens. A light frost helps to improve the flavor. The variety ''BLUE SCOTCH CURLED'' is popular.

Plants are generally pest-free when grown as a fall crop. To control the cabbage worm in spring and summer, spray with BT (*Bacillus thuringensis*).

Kohlrabi

This curious-looking member of the cabbage family forms a swollen, round stem just above the soil line. The skin is peeled, and the interior has a clean, crisp, turnip-like flavor that is delicious raw in salads or diced and cooked as a side dish.

Kohlrabi needs to grow fast during cool weather. When given adequate moisture, it will mature within 55 days of direct-sowing, 3 weeks before the last frost date. Sow seeds 1/2 inch deep, and thin the seedlings to stand 6 inches apart in rows 2 feet apart. Basically, there are two kinds—white-stemmed and purple-stemmed. ''GRAND DUKE'' hybrid—an All-America Winner—grows the biggest crop. Plants are generally pest-free.

Leeks

These relatives of the onion can stay in the garden until freezing weather. Though they require a long growing season to fully mature (100 days or more), young leeks can be harvested earlier to flavor soups and salads, much like scallions.

Either direct-seed in early spring (seedlings will tolerate mild frosts) or start indoors 6 weeks before outdoor planting. Cover the seed with about 1/4 inch of soil. Thin the plants to 1 inch apart and maintain at least 1 foot between rows. Blanching—or whitening the stalks—improves their flavor. Wrap a collar of newspaper around the stalk and hold in place with a rubber band.

Lettuce

In any seed display or catalog listing, the number of lettuce varieties may even exceed tomatoes. They are indeed high on the list of most-favored vegetables. Basically, there are two kinds: the loose-leaf type and the heading varieties. Loose-leaf is much easier to grow and requires only 45 days to harvest from seed direct-sown several weeks before the last frost date. It even tolerates crowding. If the outside leaves are harvested first, more leaves will replace them from the inside. That way you always have a row of lettuce growing, until hot weather induces them to go to seed. Cover seed with no more than 1/4 inch of soil—just enough to anchor it. Good loose-leaf varieties include Burpee's ''GREEN ICE'' and ''RED SAILS,'' an All-America Winner with ornamental ruffled red outer leaves.

Head lettuce needs proper spacing (1 foot apart), and usually 75 days to harvest. For earliest yields start seed indoors 2 weeks before outdoor planting and transplant. Top-rated head lettuce varieties include ''BUTTERCRUNCH'' and ''BOSTON BIBB'' (sometimes sold in gourmet restaurants as ''KENTUCKY LIMESTONE'').

For maximum productivity make two succession plantings of lettuce: one in spring and the other after August 15, to mature in fall. Extra-early crops are possible by sowing lettuce under floating row covers in February, and extended harvesting is possible by covering plants in October with floating row covers.

The most serious lettuce pest is the slug, which can crawl down to the heart and cause bitter, brown discolorations. Control with slug bait or floating row covers (which also protect from rabbits, woodchucks, and deer).

Mustard

This nutritious vegetable green is related to cabbage. The plants mature unusually fast from seed direct-sown. The tender, green leaves will be ready for harvesting within 40 days. Plant seed 1/4 inch deep in rows spaced 1 1/2 feet apart, and thin to at least 12 inches apart in the row. Although mustard is heat-tolerant, it turns bitter during hot weather. Burpee's "FORDHOOK FANCY" has dark green, frilly leaves.

Okra

Relishing hot, humid weather, this member of the hibiscus family produces long, pointed, green seed pods that are tender and succulent when very young. They take on a tough, fibrous texture when the least bit overmature, so regular picking is important to keep new flowers and pods forming. The pods are cooked as a vegetable side dish and also used extensively in soups, meat curries, and stews.

Direct-sow 10 to 14 days after the last spring frost date, soaking the hard seeds overnight in a moist paper towel to encourage germination. Cover the seed with 1/2 inch of soil, and thin plants to 12 inches apart in rows 3 feet wide.

Pods are generally ready for picking within 55 days of sowing seeds, and any overmature pods can be left to dry for use in dried flower arrangements.

"ANNIE OAKLEY" hybrid is a heavy-yielding variety. Plants are generally pest-free in Pennsylvania.

Onions

Onions from sets planted around March will not grow such big bulbs as onions from 6- to 8-week-old transplants started from seed, but they are easier to plant. Onions are biennials (flowering and setting seed the second year). Since sets are already year-old bulbs, they grow a seed stalk that weakens the plant, while seedlings will direct all their energy into growing a big bulb. Onions are extremely hardy and make good growth during cool weather.

Sets cost more than seeds, but they serve a double purpose. Within 2 or 3 weeks of planting sets, you'll most likely see them produce healthy, long leaves. When several of these are about 12 inches long, you can use them as scallions in salads and cooking.

For this reason, many gardeners prefer to buy onion sets in 1-pound bags and plant them close together, even touching. As they develop their lance-like leaves, thin the row by pulling every other onion to use as a scallion, leaving room for the remaining onions to swell up to full-sized table onions. They will store through winter. There are yellow-, red-, and white-skinned onions.

Direct-sow seed 3 weeks before the last expected frost date, or start indoors 4 weeks before outdoor planting. Cover seed with 1/4 inch of soil, spacing plants to at least 4 inches apart in rows spaced 6 inches apart. Biggest bulbs need a fertile, humus-rich soil high in phosphorus. Well-decomposed stable manure is especially beneficial.

For really big onions, try "WALLA WALLA." A yellow-skinned onion, the crisp, white flesh is sweet and mild. If you want a long-storage onion, try "SPARTAN BANNER," a USDA introduction that will stay hard for 6 months, even stored at room temperature.

Onion flies lay eggs at the base of bulbs, and the maggot larvae will tunnel inside. Rake an organic insect dust into the upper soil surface to deter the adult.

Parsley

A favorite garnish for soups, salads, and egg dishes, parsley will remain productive into December. Bushy plants of parsley can be potted up and placed in a sunny kitchen window. Seed can be direct-sown or started indoors 8 weeks before planting outside, soaking the seeds in a moist paper towel overnight to encourage quick germination. Young transplants will tolerate mild frost. Cover seed with 1/4 inch of soil, thin seedlings to 6 inches apart, and maintain at least 1 foot of space between rows. Both curly and plain-leaf varieties are available.

Parsley can be damaged by a caterpillar called the parsley worm, but generally the damage is slight and the plant recovers. Woodchucks, however, will eat parsley down to the roots. Caging with a wire tunnel—or covering with a floating row cover—will generally guard the parsley against a woodchuck.

Parsnips

Because parsnips require a long growing season (130 days), and because carrots are a much better known root vegetable, the popularity of parsnips is not what it used to be. They are a tasty side dish served boiled and mashed, and they can be harvested until the ground freezes.

Direct-sow seed in early spring, or after August 15 for a fall harvest, covering seed with 1/2 inch of soil. Thin seedlings to stand 2 inches apart in rows spaced 12 inches apart.

Peanuts

Peanuts are not nuts at all but closely related to peas and beans. They have a very strange way of growing—the plants are low and spreading like clumps of clover, and start to produce yellow, pea-shaped flowers. After pollination these send out aerial shoots, or probes, which dig into the soil and form the peanuts underground. At least 110 days are needed to produce worthwhile harvests, but tasty peanuts can be grown successfully throughout Pennsylvania.

Seed packets offer seeds still in the shells. Since there are normally two or three seeds inside each shell, it is best to break open the shell and then plant the seeds individually, though you can plant the whole shell. Direct-sow a week after the last expected frost date, covering with 1 inch of soil and thinning plants to stand at least 2 feet apart in rows 3 feet apart.

Peas, Garden

Most people used to consider garden peas a poor crop for small gardens because a lot of plants are needed for any worthwhile yield. However, new varieties of garden peas have been developed with more peas to the pod ("GREEN ARROW" produces 10 or 11 peas per pod) and greater productivity. Also, there is a whole new race of snap peas (such as "SUGAR SNAP," for example) growing plump, sweet peas and edible pods, greatly increasing the yield of a row of peas. There are also Chinese snow peas that are best harvested while the pods are flat and before the peas swell the pod. A big advantage of peas is that they are fast-growing, finished by the Fourth of July, and that's plenty of time to clear the pea patch for a planting of something else, such as snap beans or zucchini squash, gaining two crops from one space.

For a fall crop, sow seeds August 15, choosing a variety like "MAESTRO," resistant to mildew disease, otherwise fall harvests are likely to be unsuccessful.

Peas are hardy and tolerate frosts, allowing them to be planted several weeks before the last frost. They need constant moisture and fertile soil to grow quickly.

Direct-sow seed 4 weeks before the last expected frost date, covering with 1 inch of soil. To aid germination you may want to sandwich the seeds between a moist paper towel overnight. You may also want to sprinkle "inoculant" over the seeds before planting outdoors. This black powder encourages nitrogen-fixing bacteria that greatly improve yields. Tall varieties (such as "SUGAR SNAP") will need staking, but other varieties (such as "GREEN ARROW") will grow erect unaided.

The most serious pest problem is foraging animals such as deer and woodchucks. These may need to be fenced out of pea rows. To avoid wilt diseases, change the planting location every year.

Peppers

Although there are two kinds of peppers planted in home gardens—sweet bell peppers and hot chili peppers—it is the sweet bell peppers that most people grow.

Pepper seed needs handling very much like tomato seed. Start indoors about 8 weeks before transplanting outside after all danger of frost. The plants are extremely brittle, and care should be taken both while transplanting and when picking fruit not to break branches.

Some bell peppers turn yellow, orange and black when ripe, but most gardeners prefer the kind that turn from green to red. They are edible at the green or red stage, but once they have turned red they soon go soft and rot. Bell peppers are good sliced in salads, eaten raw like apples, or stuffed with chopped meat and tomatoes. Hybrid varieties are not only earliest, but also more productive and more disease-resistant than standard varieties. The All-America Winner "GYPSY" is a sweet yellow pepper changing to red. It is so cold-tolerant that it will produce generous yields early,

even during cold weather when other peppers are sulking. "BIG BERTHA" bears gigantic fruit up to 10 inches long.

Space pepper plants at least 2 feet apart in rows spaced 3 feet apart. They grow well in gallon-capacity containers. A common pepper ailment, blossom end rot, can be controlled by ensuring adequate lime content to the soil so the roots are supplied with calcium, and by frequent watering. Symptoms of the disease are a black discoloration at the blossom end of the pepper fruit, which spreads over almost the entire fruit. Peppers are also susceptible to sunscald, a physiological disease caused by too much exposure of the fruit to sun. Plenty of leafy growth to shade the fruit will deter the disease.

Potatoes

Pennsylvania has an ideal climate for two kinds of potatoes: the true Irish potato and the sweet potato, or yam. It is the Irish potato that is most widely planted, since the tubers develop quickly even during cool weather.

The sweet potato is a member of the morning glory family. It prefers a sandy, humus-rich loam soil. Both Irish and sweet potatoes are susceptible to frost damage and should not be planted into the garden until frost-danger is past.

Irish potatoes are planted from small tubers that are best bought from a local garden supply center. Alternatively, you can use ordinary supermarket potatoes that have started to sprout. Set these into the garden, and cover them with soil. In a loose, crumbly soil, the seedling potatoes can be pressed into the soil surface and covered over with a layer of mulch, such as straw or shredded leaves. Then, later in the summer when you want to have some tender young "new" potatoes, you can pull back the mulch and pick them without digging. Good varieties for Pennsylvania include red-skinned "RED PONTIAC" and white "KATAHDIN." Cover with 1 inch of soil and plant 2 feet apart in rows spaced 3 feet apart. Potatoes can be lifted from the soil after the top growth has turned brown.

Sweet potato tubers also sprout green shoots that can be used for planting, though most gardeners buy young rooted transplants from specialist mail-order suppliers. Popular varieties include "PORTO RICO," growing a compact vine and yellow tubers, and "CENTENNIAL." Although "CENTENNIAL" grows sprawling vines, it bears the largest tubers—red on the outside and deep orange within. For heaviest yields, mound the soil along the rows, giving the roots room to set large quantities of tubers.

The Colorado potato beetle (yellow with dark stripes) is a menace to Irish potatoes. Control it with an organic spray labelled effective against the pest, such as a rotenone-pyrethrum spray.

Pumpkin

Normally, plants require 10 feet of row width for the enormous vines to stretch out. Although there are bush varieties with compacted vines, they still will need 6 feet of width.

A fun way to grow pumpkins is in the form of a children's den. Construct a frame with wire mesh sides and a roof, then plant pumpkins around the sides. The vines will take over the whole construction, completely covering the den and making it a perfect hide-away for the kids. The vines will flower and form fruits for the children to pick in the fall.

It's easy to carve your name on a pumpkin. Just take a sharp point when the pumpkin is small—about the size of a melon—and scratch the skin with your letters. The scratches will form a scab, and your name will grow with the pumpkin.

Most people grow pie pumpkins because they are excellent for desserts and Jack o'lanterns. However, there are special varieties capable of growing to more than 100 pounds. The secret to growing a giant is plenty of nitrogen-rich fertilizer and moisture. It's the moisture that increases a pumpkin's weight. Using the variety "ATLANTIC GIANT," a New Jersey farmer living near Trenton grew a monster of more than 700 pounds. The Churchville Nature Center, in Churchville, Pennsylvania, organizes a giant pumpkin contest each year, attracting contestants not only from Pennsylvania and New Jersey, but from as far away as Texas and Canada.

Direct-sow seeds after frost-danger, covering with 1 inch of soil. To grow a giant, use black plastic as a mulch, and allow the vine to set several fruit. Examine these when they are grapefruit-size and remove all but the one that seems to be perfectly formed and with a thick stem section. Then, all the energy is directed into one enormous fruit.

Infestations by borers can kill pumpkin vines. Borers are worms that burrow into the stems, causing wilt. Once the borer enters the vine it is almost impossible to eradicate. Dusting plants with rotenone will discourage borers and other potential insect pests.

Radish

This highly popular root vegetable matures early when little else has started to produce. Direct-sow seeds 4 weeks before the last expected frost date, covering with 1/4 inch of soil. Plants relish cool weather and abundant moisture. Less than 25 days from sowing the seed to harvesting is not unusual for radishes. Usually, two plantings are possible in spring and a third in September for fall harvest. When radish seedlings are up, moderate thinning is normally necessary to space them 3/4 inch apart in double rows with 1 foot of space between each double row. "CHERRY BELLE" is the earliest. However, there are many others from which to select, including white, red and white bicolored, icicle-shaped, and even a variety with black skin.

Rhubarb

Though normally grown from year-old roots planted in spring, rhubarb is easily grown from seeds direct-sown several weeks before the last expected frost date. In a humus-rich, fertile loam soil, watered during dry spells, a harvest from seedlings is possible the following season. Space plants 3 feet apart.

A common problem with rhubarb is root rot. The roots do need planting about 3 inches deep, but the hole should not be covered over all at one time. Position the root so that the crown is just peeking through the surface; then, as the rhubarb shoots develop, fill in the hole around them.

When harvesting the stalks be sure to discard all the green leaf area, since this contains a toxin. There's not much chance of a person eating the leaf accidentally since it is highly distasteful.

Rhubarb is a perennial, coming up year after year. It can be harvested early when little else in the garden is ready. It stays productive over a long period right through summer. The variety called "VALENTINE" has thick stalks that are red all along the stems.

Rutabaga

Similar in appearance to turnips, but with a stronger flavor, rutabagas require a longer growing season. They are valued as a root crop because of their excellent winter keeping qualities.

Since rutabagas prefer a cool growing season, they are best planted to mature as a fall crop with the seed direct-sown in July. Cover seed with 1/4 inch of soil, and thin seedlings to stand 6 inches apart in rows 2 feet apart. The mature roots should be dug from the ground before the ground freezes and stored over winter in moist sand or peat in a cool basement.

Dusting plants with rotenone will discourage the cabbage maggot and flea beetles.

Salsify

Although this uncommon root vegetable requires a lengthy growing season (120 days) compared to other root crops, it has a strong following among French cooks and gourmet vegetable gardeners as a side dish. The delicate flavor is slightly suggestive of oysters.

Salsify is hardy and is valuable as a fall crop, remaining edible in the garden until Christmas over much of Pennsylvania. Roots lifted in fall will store over winter in a box of moist sand in a cool basement.

Sow seed 1/2 inch deep after the last spring frost date. Thin the seedlings to 3 inches apart in rows spaced 2 feet apart. Since the roots will grow to 1 foot in length, the soil should be deeply cultivated and not lumpy. For a fall crop sow seed in July.

Soybeans, Edible

A good deal has been written about the wonders of soybeans. They offer one rare quality among vegetables: rich protein, equivalent in nutritional value to meat.

Although the edible soybean has a growth habit similar to agricultural soybeans, it does not have such an oily flavor and is much more pleasant to eat when cooked. Unfortunately, the tiny pods are difficult to shell, yielding just two or three small beans each, and it takes a long time to gather enough for a decent meal.

In fact, the only efficient way for the average person to enjoy them is to cook the beans in the pods, using salted water; then serve them in bowls as hot snacks. Simply pick up a pod, pinch it between your fingers and the beans will squirt into your mouth. The beans can also be dried for storage over winter in a dry cupboard, and they freeze well for later use, such as in soups.

The varieties "BUTTERBEAN" and "FISKBY V" crop heavily in Pennsylvania. Plant the seed 1 inch deep, 6 inches apart, in rows spaced 3 feet apart.

Deer and woodchucks can be extremely destructive to edible soybeans, but floating row covers or a wire tunnel placed along the row will afford protection.

Spinach

The earliest spring crop; direct-sow seed 6 weeks before the last expected frost date. Germination will take place even in a cool soil as low as 40° F. The plants themselves are extremely hardy and make rapid growth during cool, rainy weather, producing fresh greens rich in vitamins and minerals.

Cover seed with 1/4 inch of soil and thin plants to stand 6 inches apart. The seed is susceptible to "damping-off" disease. Germination is aided by placing seed in a damp paper towel overnight. Hybrid varieties such as "MELODY" (an All-America Winner) will mature in just 45 days.

Spinach cannot tolerate hot weather. As soon as the days turn hot and humid the plants will go to seed. When this occurs, pull up the plants and replant the space with a warm-season crop such as summer squash. A second planting of spinach by September 1 will mature in fall, and any plants not harvested will usually remain edible in the garden until spring.

Although spinach is widely used as a cooked vegetable, one of its favored uses is in a salad, instead of lettuce. Spinach-based salads command premium prices in many gourmet restaurants.

Because spinach is susceptible to heat, seedsmen offer several heat-tolerant spinach substitutes—particularly New Zealand spinach and Malabar spinach. Both should be direct-seeded after frost-danger. Though both are vining plants, New Zealand spinach is best left to cover the ground, spreading 3 feet wide, while Malabar spinach is best trained up posts or along a fence. Its lustrous, heart-shaped leaves are highly ornamental.

Squash

Like potatoes, pumpkins, and sweet corn, the great family of squash originated on the North American continent. They were in an advanced, cultivated state among the Indian tribes when William Penn reached Pennsylvania. Squash can be broadly classified as "summer squash" (best for eating fresh) and "winter squash" (best for storage).

America's most popular squash is the zucchini, a summer squash. Growing on upright, bushy plants, it takes up far less space than the rambling vines of most winter squash. It is both easy to grow and productive. The hybrid variety "RICHGREEN" is predominantly female. Though it sets a small number of male flowers sufficient for pollination, most are female. First fruits can be harvested within 50 days of direct-sowing after frost-danger. The long, slender, glossy green fruits form only on female flowers, but once they are pollinated by insects they soon swell up, ultimately producing enormous fruits weighing several pounds. Never allow your zucchini squash plants to grow fruit to this size. Pick them when they are young—about 6 inches long. The more you pick, the more new flowers and fruit will form; once you allow a few fruits to swell up like balloons, the plant's energy is quickly depleted.

Individual plants need 3 feet of space, and so the seeds are best planted in groups of three or four, and then thinned to one sturdy healthy plant. When plants start to flower, examine them carefully for male and female flowers (the females have a small, immature baby zucchini underneath the flower). To ensure an early fruit set, pick a male flower and peel away the petals to expose its powdery yellow "nose." Rub this on the shiny nose of as many females as possible. This form of hand-pollination is more reliable than insects.

Other popular kinds of summer squash include crookneck squash and pattypan squash. Vegetable spaghetti is classified as a summer squash, but its oval fruits are best harvested after the fruit has reached the size of a melon and turned a creamy yellow color. When cooked, the interior unravels in strands like spaghetti.

Winter squash include the popular acorn types and butternuts. Breeders have developed bush forms of acorn squash, and these take up not much more room than a zucchini plant. They are much later-maturing and not so productive.

Seeds of all squash are large and easy to handle. Just cover them over with 1 inch of soil, sown directly into the garden after frost-danger. For pest control, see Pumpkins.

Sweet Corn

Sweet corn is a highly developed type of grass that originated in Mexico, though its wild ancestors are all extinct. Ears of corn with sweet, milky kernels are formed when pollen from the tassel on top of the plant falls on the silks, which project from leaf joints midway down the stalk. Wind blows and shakes the pollen about, and to ensure successful cross-pollination corn is best planted in a broad bed containing three rows. Space the rows at least 2 1/2 feet apart, with 8 inches between plants. Corn needs highly fertile, nitrogen-rich soil. When the tassel and silks are forming, they require generous amounts of moisture. If these conditions are lacking, yields may be cut in half.

Choose among yellow, white, and bicolored varieties of corn. There are many new, "extra sweet" corns that have superior flavor, but many of them produce this superb flavor only if they are isolated from other corns. Any cross-pollination can cause them to become starchy.

Probably the most widely planted sweet corn in Pennsylvania is "SILVER QUEEN," a white variety that requires no isolation to produce its sweet flavor. An earlier variety is "HOW SWEET IT IS," an All-America Winner developed by Abbott & Cobb, of Trevose, Pennsylvania, with super-sweetness that persists for up to 10 days if stored in the vegetable bin of your refrigerator. Abbott & Cobb is also responsible for a family of white, yellow, and bicolored corns called "SUMMER SWEET" hybrids—all with the same long storage quality, if isolated from other corns.

An ear of corn is ripe when the silk has turned brown and the ends are shrivelled. After picking, always eat—or freeze—corn immediately. It quickly deteriorates in flavor once it has left the corn stalk.

Seed can be sprouted in a moist paper towel before planting to ensure highest germination, or direct-sow seed after frost danger. Cover with 1 inch of soil. Flashing disks strung from poles may be necessary to scare away birds, especially pheasants and crows. A pest called the corn ear worm can enter the developing cobs through the silk. Normally, damage is superficial, though commercial growers take precautions by spraying plants at the silk stage to deter entry of the worm. Organic insecticides are effective.

Tomatoes

An Ohio seedsman is credited with developing the first commercially successful tomato—a variety called "PARAGON." It was round and smooth and had a pleasant, juicy flavor. Since then hundreds of good varieties have been introduced, and the tomato is now the most popular home garden vegetable in Pennsylvania. Though many types exist, it is the large-fruited red varieties that home gardeners prefer. Other sought-after qualities are good flavor and earliness.

There is a lot of tomato disease in Pennsylvania, so it is important to choose disease-resistant strains. The varieties listed below perform exceptionally well in the state. Those marked with an asterisk (*) were developed in Pennsylvania.

Disease-resistant varieties have the initials *VF* after a variety name, indicating resistance to verticillium and fusarium wilt, the two most destructive tomato diseases.

Start tomato seed indoors 8 weeks before the last expected frost date. Harden

VARIETY	COMMENTS
*"BIG BOY" hybrid	First hybrid large-fruited tomato, though it lacks disease resistance.
*"SUPERSTEAK" hybrid	Grapefruit-size tomatoes; good flavor, smooth, round shape. Excellent disease resistance.
*"PIXIE" hybrid	Earliest to ripen (55 days). Medium-size fruit. Dwarf vine suitable for pots and indoor culture.
*"EARLY PICK" hybrid	Earliest large-fruited variety (66 days). An improvement over "Big Early" hybrid.
"EARLY CASCADE" hybrid	Medium-size fruits are early, and the "everbearing" vines will continue cropping until fall frost, long after other tomatoes have exhausted themselves. Just two plants are capable of yielding 1000 fruits!
"SUPERSONIC" hybrid	Crack-resistant and disease-resistant. Heavy-yielding and large-fruited. Smooth, round, red, flavorful tomatoes.
"SWEET 100" hybrid	Flower stems uncoil like a watch spring, each flower cluster capable of setting 100 extra-sweet cherry-size tomatoes—up to 1000 fruits on a single vine.
"ROMA" hybrid	Best Italian pear tomato; exceptionally heavy yields.

off seedlings in a cold frame before setting them into the garden. Be prepared to cover them over with "hot caps" or floating row covers if frost threatens. Set the plants 3 feet apart in rows spaced 3 feet apart. A mulch of black plastic over the soil will ensure earliest and heaviest yields. The soil should be well-drained, with a high humus content, and a high phosphorus content to ensure early fruit ripening. Too much nitrogen (often caused by relying heavily on animal manure) can delay ripening.

Stake plants to save space. The easiest way to do this is to make tomato towers from circles of builder's wire. The tomato plants grow up the center of the towers. As the plants grow tall they push side branches through the wire mesh and become self-supporting. Tomato flowers are self-pollinating. The slightest breeze will mix up the pollen and ensure pollination, though low night-time temperatures can inhibit fruit-set.

If you have the space, you might be tempted to try some of the other interesting kinds of tomatoes, such as the cherry type, so popular in summer salads, and the yellow pear tomatoes that make tasty cocktail snacks.

If you don't have garden space, grow some compact vine types in gallon containers, especially Burpee's "PIXIE" hybrid.

Though larvae of the Colorado potato beetle and the tomato hornworm will attack tomatoes, damage is generally not sufficiently severe to warrant control. Tomato fruits are susceptible to sunscald, a pale blemish that appears on the side of fruit (when insufficient foliage cover shades the fruits); and also to blossom end rot, a black discoloration at the blossom end of fruit. Blossom end rot is generally a sign of lack of calcium (lime) or irregular watering that prevents the roots from taking up sufficient calcium.

Turnips

These fast-growing root vegetables are an underrated food, probably because the older varieties had a sharp, pungent flavor. New hybrids—such as "TOKYO CROSS"—are so sweet and moist it is difficult to believe you are eating turnip. The flavor of this variety is best when roots are the size of a golfball.

Turnips like cool weather and frequent watering. Direct-sow seed 4 weeks before the last expected frost date, covering seed with 1/4 inch of soil. The seedlings will need thinning to about 3 inches apart. Plant turnips after August 15 for a fall crop.

Plants are generally pest-free except for deer damage. Caging rows—or using floating row covers—will deter deer. The cabbage maggot and flea beetle, which sometimes inflict damage, can be controlled by dusting with rotenone.

Watercress

If you have a clear, running stream near your home, you may already have watercress growing in great abundance. It is wild throughout most parts of Pennsylvania. Watercress is so hardy that bunches can be gathered during the winter months to eat as fresh greens in salads. Watercress spends most of its life as a compact rosette of dark green leaves, but in summer watercress grows tall and bitter, and goes to seed.

Seed can be direct-sown into regular garden soil and plants transferred to a shallow pond or running stream. A simpler method of propagation is to find a bed of watercress and pull up roots to transplant.

Watermelon

One of the delights of a Pennsylvania

summer is biting into a luscious slice of local watermelon. They are easy to grow if you have the space, since the best watermelons are produced on sprawling vines. An open, sunny location with no shade during any part of the peak daylight hours is necessary for maximum flavor and yields.

A sandy, fertile, humus-rich soil is essential, and the vines seem to resent any kind of disturbance. After all danger of frost, direct-sow seed in groups spaced 8 feet apart. Cover the seeds with 1/2 inch of soil. They must have regular amounts of moisture at all stages of development. Covering the soil with black plastic improves yields.

The Stover Farm, near Doylestown, Pennsylvania, has a tradition of growing watermelons, and their favorite is a yellow-fleshed "icebox" variety, "YELLOW BABY." It is not only the earliest-ripening watermelon in their trials, it is cold-tolerant, ripening over a longer season. Also, the fruits have only half the seeds of other icebox varieties such as "SUGAR BABY." The flesh is yellow, like a pineapple, and deliciously sweet.

If your preference is for a large, oblong watermelon—to feed the family at a barbecue—then try the All-America Winner, "SWEET FAVORITE" hybrid. Individual fruits weigh up to 20 pounds.

Much publicity has been given to "seedless" watermelons, such as "JACK OF HEARTS," but they need a lot of space since the seedless watermelon will not set fruit unless a regular variety is planted nearby to ensure pollination. Best to leave these to professional growers, such as the Amish.

About the most difficult part of growing watermelons is telling when the fruit is ripe. One way to test for ripeness consists of rapping the watermelon with a knuckle and listening to the sound that it makes. If it sounds like tapping your forehead (a dull sound), the watermelon is underripe; if it sounds like tapping your chest (a hollow sound), it is ripe; and if it sounds like tapping your stomach (a soft sound), the watermelon is overripe.

HERBS

Early colonists relied on herbs for many reasons. Herbs were used for flavoring meals, to eliminate household odors, as medicine for the treatment or relief of numerous ailments, and as dyes and insect repellents, among other useful purposes. Some fine examples of kitchen herb gardens can be seen at Pennsbury Manor, near Morrisville (Bucks County), and the Peter Wentz Farmstead, near Worcester (Montgomery County), a restored colonial farm where George Washington spent the night during his Philadelphia campaign. The design for the Peter Wentz herb garden is a particularly good one to follow, since it features four square beds (or quadrants) laid out inside a rectangle. Perennial herbs are laid out around the inside of the rectangle, while annual herbs and vegetables are concentrated in the quadrants.

Medicinal gardens were known as *Physick Gardens*, and a good example of such an herb garden can be seen on the grounds of the Pennsylvania Hospital, in the historic district of Philadelphia, at 8th and Pine Streets.

Today, there are many specialist herb gardens in Pennsylvania, not only supplying herb plants, but also making herb products for sale, particularly herbal wreaths and potpourris. One of the best herb gardens in North America operates from Port Murray, New Jersey, which is close to the Pennsylvania border, within sight of the Delaware Water Gap (see sources in the Appendix). They exhibit annually at the Philadelphia Flower Show in the trade section.

Herb gardens can be highly decorative as well as being functional. The most popular design features pie-shaped beds laid out like a cartwheel, with paths forming the spokes, and a beehive or birdbath at the center as a focal point.

Following is a list of the most useful herbs and a guide to their culture and use.

Popular Pennsylvania Herbs

Angelica
(Angelica archangelica)

Hardy perennial, up to 8 feet tall, with an erect habit. Licorice-flavored leaves and stems are most often used to flavor onions and pork. Also for flavoring cookies and candies. Large, flat flower clusters are borne in midsummer.

Mostly propagated from seed direct-sown, since plants grow fast.

Anise Hyssop
(Agastache foeniculum)

Hardy perennial, up to 3 feet tall, with an erect habit. Related to mint, plants produce beautiful, lavender-blue flower spikes in summer, so ornamental they are often grown in mixed perennial borders. The leaves are used to brew a refreshing tea, while the seeds are used in potpourris. Easily grown from division and from seed direct-sown after frost-danger in spring.

Basil, Sweet
(Ocimum basilicum)

Tender annual, 6 inches to 2 feet tall depending on variety, with a bushy habit. Prefers sun and moist soil. Pinch flower heads to keep plants compact. Add to pesto, pasta, and salads; garnish soups, vegetables, and side dishes (especially beans and tomato dishes). Direct-sow

seed after frost or start seed indoors 4 weeks before outdoor planting.

Several highly ornamental varieties include: "GREEN RUFFLES" (with large, pointed, ruffled green leaves); "DARK OPAL" (with bronze foliage suitable for growing as a background to dwarf annuals); and "GREEN BOUQUET" (a cushion-type, compact plant with small leaves suitable for edging beds and borders).

Borage
(Borago officinalis)

Hardy annual, 2 to 3 feet tall. Prefers sun and good drainage. Blue, star-shaped flowers are ornamental, attractive to butterflies and bees. A decorative garnish imparting a cucumber-like flavor. Direct-sow seed after frost-danger or start seed 4 weeks before outdoor planting.

Burnet
(Sanguisorba minor)

Hardy perennial, 18 inches tall, with a low, spreading habit. Prefers sun. Leaves used for salads and flavoring cold drinks. Direct-sow seed after frost-danger, or start indoors 6 weeks before outdoor planting.

Catnip
(Nepeta cataria)

Hardy perennial, 3 to 4 feet tall, growing

DECORATIVE HERB GARDEN

This garden plan also works well planted with
annuals, roses, perennials or a combination of everything.
*Asterisk denotes variety for culinary use.

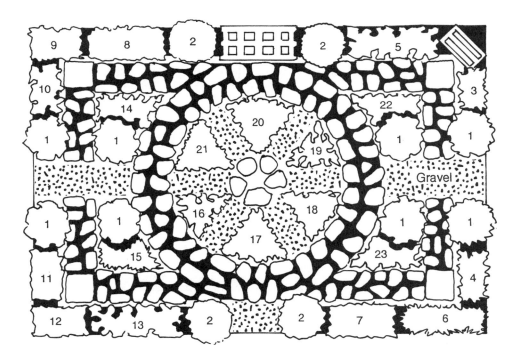

1-Hardy Orange (Poncirus trifoliata)
2-Sweet Bay (Laurus nobilis)*
3-Yarrow (Achillea filipendulina)
4-English Lavender (Lavandula angustifolia)
5-Chili Pepper (Capsicum annuum)*
6-Chive (Allium schoenoprasum)*
7-Garlic Chive (Allium tuberosum)*
8-English Thyme (Thymus vulgaris)*
9-Pyrethrum (Chrysanthemum coccineum)
10-Cheddar Pink (Dianthus gratianopolitanus)
11-Basil (Ocimum Basilicum)*
12-Teasel (Dipsacus sylvestris)

13-Butterfly Milkweed (Asclepias tuberosa)
14-Golden Marguerite (Anthemis tinctoria)
15-Pineapple Sage (Salvia elegans)*
16-Rosemary (Rosmarinus officinalis)*
17-American Marigold (Tagetes erecta)*
18-Garden Valerian (Valeriana officinalis)
19-Scarlet Bee-balm (Monarda didyma)*
20-Sweet Heliotrope (Heliotropum
  arborescens)
21-Dill (Anthem graveolens)*
22-Nasturtium (Tropaeolum majus)*
23-Lamb's-ears (Stachys byzantina)

in sun or shade. Cats like its fragrance. Gray-green leaves used mostly to brew a refreshing tea. Propagated from seed direct-sown after frost-danger, and by division.

Chamomile, German
(Matricaria recutita)

Hardy annual that reseeds, up to 3 feet tall, with a spreading habit. Finely cut foliage, masses of white, daisy-like flowers and weak stems cause the plants to flop over into pathways. Prefers sun and good drainage. Use flowers to brew tea, and for potpourris. Direct-sow seed after frost-danger in spring.

Chamomile, Roman
(Anthemis nobilis)

Hardy perennial, 9 inches high, with a mounded habit. Finely cut foliage and small, white, daisy-like flowers, which dry to a button-like, fragrant seed head used in making a refreshing tea and scenting bath water.

Chives
(Allium schoenoprasum)

Hardy perennial, 10 inches tall, with a clump-forming habit. Grows in sun or light shade. Pungent, onion-like flavor, used to garnish salads and to flavor spreads and omelettes. Plants produce masses of globular, pink flower heads in June, decorative even in mixed perennial borders. Easily grown from seed direct sown, and also by division. Reseeds itself readily.

Coriander, Cilantro
(Coriandrum sativum)

Tender annual, 2 feet tall, with an erect habit. Prefers sun, producing pungent, parsley-like leaves and flat, white flower clusters in early summer, resembling

wild carrot. Use the leaves to season Chinese, Indian and Mexican foods; the aromatic seeds are used in confections.

Dill
(Anethum graveolens)

Hardy annual, 3 feet tall, with an erect habit. Prefers full sun, and reseeds itself aggressively. Leaves are used in flavoring salad dressings, fish sauces, dips, potato salads, and pickles. Seed heads are dried and added to potpourris. Flat, yellow flower heads are highly decorative, produced in midsummer, and valued for cutting.

Fennel, Florence
(Foeniculum vulgare azoricum)

Hardy annual, 3 feet tall, resembling dill with its erect, branching stems and wide flat yellow flower clusters. Forms a bulbous lower stem portion that is delicious sliced into soups and salads for adding a licorice-like flavor. Propagated by seed direct sown after frost-danger, though seedlings will tolerate mild frosts.

Lavender, English

See Perennial section.

Lavender Cotton
(Santolina chamaecyparissus)

Hardy perennial, marginally hardy in Pennsylvania, 15 to 24 inches tall, with a mounded, spreading habit. Useful for ground cover and edging in sheltered positions. An effective moth repellent. Choice of gray-leaved or green; finely indented, with button-like, yellow flowers in summer. Propagated by seed started indoors 6 to 8 weeks before outdoor planting, and by division.

Lemon Balm
(Melissa officinalis)

Hardy perennial, 24 inches tall, with an

erect habit. Adds a lemony flavor to cold drinks. Leaves make a refreshing tea. Produces small, inconspicuous white flowers. Propagate by seed direct-sown in spring or late summer, or by division of year-old plants.

Marjoram
(Origanum majorana)

Tender annual, 8 to 12 inches high, with a low, spreading habit. Popular grown as a pot plant; mostly used to season stews, meats, and salads. Direct-sow seeds after frost-danger. Small, pale pink flower clusters appear in midsummer.

Mint
(Mentha species)

Hardy perennial, 24 inches tall, with an erect, clump-forming habit. Prefers sun and moist soil. Pick flower spikes to keep compact. Leaves used in teas, salads, and cold drinks; also as a flavoring for lamb and roasted potatoes. Many kinds are available, including spearmint, peppermint, and applemint, as well as orange, pineapple, and chocolate mint. Mostly propagated by division.

Oregano
(Origanum vulgare)

Hardy perennial, 1 to 2 feet tall, with a low, spreading habit. Prefers full sun. Leaves used as a seasoning for tomato dishes and pizza. Small light pale pink flower clusters appear in midsummer. Propagate by seed direct-sown in spring or late summer, and by division. Popular for growing in pots.

Parsley

See Vegetable section.

Rosemary
(Rosmarinus officinalis)

Tender perennial, 3 to 4 feet tall, with an erect habit. Prefers sun and well-drained soil. Needle-like leaves are used to flavor sauces, soups and stews, tomato purees, pork, and roast beef. Propagated by seed started indoors 8 weeks before outdoor planting after frost-danger, and by division. Popular for growing in containers. Plants produce a woody stem if wintered-over under glass; they can be pruned to create a beautiful, straight trunk with a ball-shaped crown of leaves on top.

Sage
(Salvia officinalis)

Hardy perennial, 2 to 3 feet tall, with a bushy spreading habit. Prefers sun and good drainage. Spear-shaped leaves are used as seasoning for meats and in stuffing for poultry. Choice of gray-leaved, golden variegated, purple variegated, and tricolor. Propagated by seed direct-sown and by division of year-old clumps. Attractive, tubular flowers in blue, white or pale pink are produced in early summer.

Savory, Winter
(Satureja montana)

Hardy perennial, 2 feet tall, with a high, mounded, spreading habit. Prefers full sun and sandy soil. A strong flavor accent for meats and stews. Propagated by seed and by division of year-old plants. Masses of decorative white, tubular flowers occur in late summer. Generally a more useful plant than summer savory.

Sweet Woodruff
(Asperula tinctorium)

Hardy perennial, 6 to 12 inches high. Tolerates shade and moist areas. Used for flavoring May wine and potpourris, and as a natural insect repellent. Propagated by seed direct-sown, and by division. The leaves are finely cut, forming a star shape, and decorative as a shade-loving ground cover. Masses of small, white flowers appear in May.

Tarragon, French
(*Artemisia dracunculus*)

Hardy perennial, 24 inches tall, with an erect habit. Prefers sun or semi-shade. An aromatic seasoning for vinegar and salad dressings, and for meat and fish sauces. Use sparingly because of its strong flavor. True French tarragon is propagated only from division. Avoid the inferior ''Russian'' tarragon.

Thyme, English
(*Thymus vulgaris*)

Hardy perennial, 1 to 2 feet tall, with mounded, spreading habit. Prefers sun and good drainage. An aromatic seasoning for meats, soups, sauces, and stuffing. Creeping thyme is low-growing, suitable for planting in dry walls and between flagstone. There is also a lemon-scented thyme and ornamental varieties with no fragrance, but excellent for creating a ''flowering lawn'' effect. Propagated by seed direct-sown after frost-danger and by division.

Watercress

See Vegetable section.

Wormwood, Southern
(*Artemisia absinthum*)

Hardy perennial, 3 to 4 feet tall, with an erect habit. Prefers full sun and good drainage. Aromatic, silvery, willow-like leaves are used for insect repellent and potpourri. Direct-sow seed after frost-danger, or propagate by division.

CHAPTER 10

Fruits and Berries

Pennsylvania grows excellent crops of apples, pears, peaches, nectarines, plums, and cherries—classified as orchard fruits—and also excellent grapes, blueberries, raspberries, blackberries, and strawberries—classified as berry crops. Apricots, though hardy in Pennsylvania, are risky because the flowers open earlier than on other fruit trees and are prone to frost.

Generally speaking, berry fruits in home gardens can be grown without sprays, but orchard fruits usually need protection from insects and fungus diseases—preferably by choosing disease-resistant plants, and also by using a spray schedule involving organic formulations for both insect and disease control.

When choosing fruit trees, always check to see whether the variety you are buying is ''self-pollinating'' or whether it needs another variety for successful fruiting. The two varieties must flower at the same time and should be located no more than 100 feet apart. Of course, a neighbor's trees can pollinate yours. Also, the presence of a beehive greatly increases fruiting.

All fruit trees need full sun and good air circulation. Soil must have good drainage. Pruning is usually necessary after every harvest, mostly for shaping the tree, opening out the interior for increased light penetration and air circulation, and the removal of ''constrictors''—branches and twigs that can cross, rubbing against each other.

Keep a 3-foot radius around the trunk of fruit trees free of turf, and mulch the area with shredded leaves, straw or similar organic mulch. This conserves soil moisture, suffocates weeds, reduces risk of mower damage, and facilitates fertilizing and irrigation.

EXAMPLES OF GRAFTING

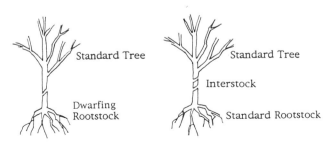

Standard Tree

Dwarfing Rootstock

Standard Tree

Interstock

Standard Rootstock

One of the finest fruit gardens in North America can be seen at Eleutherian Mills, part of the Hagley Foundation, north of Wilmington, along the Brandywine River. Situated close to the Pennsylvania border, Eleutherian Mills is where Eleuthère Irénée duPont—founder of the duPont chemical dynasty—established his house and garden in the French style, with an emphasis on espaliered fruit trees. Apple trees, for example, are trained over an arbor to form a tunnel, and as "cordons" (ropes) along low fence rails to form an edging to pathways. Pear trees are trained into compact cone shapes; peaches have their branches splayed out like a fan and woven into each other to create a living fence.

ESPALIER TRAINING OF DWARF FRUIT TREES

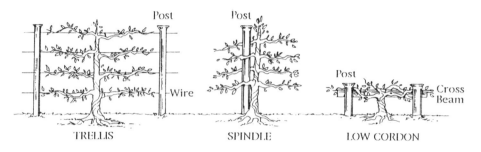

Peter Lindtner, who supervises the fruit orchard at Eleutherian Mills, gained his experience first at a fruit tree experiment station in Czechoslovakia, and then in Canada. He was also responsible for supervising the planting of a model dwarf fruit tree demonstration garden at Longwood Gardens. The Longwood display garden features dwarf fruit trees that have brought about a revolution in fruit tree cultivation. Some dwarf fruit trees are genetic dwarfs (they grow naturally that way)—such as "NORTH STAR" pie cherry and "GARDEN SUN" peach. However, most dwarf fruit trees are the result of grafting a popular fruit tree variety (such as "GRANNY SMITH") onto a special dwarfing rootstock. Sometimes more than one graft is involved either because an intermediate graft must be inserted to make the dwarfing rootstock compatible with the selected variety, or to create a stronger root system than is possible with one graft. Where there is a choice always choose "inter-stem" grafted fruit trees, as they live longer and produce highest yields.

The advantages of dwarfing are numerous: each tree requires no more than 10 square feet of growing space, and since they grow to no more than 10 feet in height, they are easier to prune, easier to inspect for pests and diseases, easier to protect from pests and diseases, and easier to harvest. They are easy to train, and they pro-duce fruit sooner after planting—sometimes the same year. They bear normal-size fruit and are long-lived. Peter Lindtner's favorite training techniques involve the horizontal cordon (especially good for plums and apples), the spindle or cone (popular with pears), and the trellis (especially effective with peaches and nectarines). See diagrams.

The Delaware Valley College of Science and Agriculture, in Doylestown, maintains an extensive collection of fruit trees—particularly apples, including old varieties (such as "NEWTOWN PIPPIN," "GRANNY SMITH," and "GRIMM'S GOLDEN") and newer disease-resistant kinds (such as "LIBERTY," "JONAFREE," "MAC-FREE," and "FREEDOM"). Many of these are grown as semi-dwarf trees that don't need a stepladder to pick the fruit. The college also has an extensive collection of peaches and nectarines.

At Penn State University, fruit tree trials concentrate on growing apples as "hedges," since the hedge system ensures the largest cropping per acre.

Following are some specific tips for growing the main fruit crops. One tip that applies to all these crops is to control deer. The only reliable way to keep deer away from orchard fruits is to fence them out. The fencing doesn't need to be substantial. Commercial fruit orchards fence deer out mostly by using electrified wire. I have found that inexpensive bird-netting—strung from 6-foot-high poles—is sufficient to keep them out of a small home orchard. But, of course, a more substantial fence may be aesthetically more attractive.

It is also important to realize that all orchard fruits demand excellent drainage. If a site drains poorly, create raised planter boxes and drain the area with drainage pipes.

ORCHARD FRUITS

Apples

Pennsylvania has exactly the right conditions for quality apples—particularly sharp winters to provide the right number of "cold days" needed for prolific spring flowering, and a moderately long, frost-free growing season so that even the famous "GRANNY SMITH" apple (which needs 150 frost-free days to ripen) can bear good yields of tasty fruit.

There are three kinds of apple trees—dwarf, semi-dwarf, and standard, referring to the mature height. The dwarfs can be grown in tubs and wherever space is limited, staying below 10 feet in height, with light pruning. They are good choices for espalier training. Semi-dwarf trees generally stay below 15 feet in height, with light pruning to keep the plants shapely. Semi-dwarf trees are also suitable for espalier training, and growing as a hedge. Standard apple trees grow to 20 feet high. Unless you have a neighbor with apple trees, grow more than one variety, since apples like to be cross-pol-linated. Crabapples will also pollinate regular apples.

Apple trees bloom in spring—usually in early May. Several diseases prevalent in Pennsylvania can affect yields—especially *cedar-apple rust* (a fungus that creates ugly orange spots on apple foliage, transmitted to apples from native juniper trees); *apple scab* (a fungus that overwinters in leaf litter), and *fireblight* (a fungus disease that browns leaves, making them appear as though scorched). The disease-resistant apple "FREEDOM," developed by the New York Fruit Experiment Station, in Geneva, New York, is resistant to all three diseases. Alternatively, there are organic sprays formulated with both an insecticide and a fungus control. These combine rotenone and pyrethum to control aphids, fruit flies, leafhoppers, and other insects, plus copper and sulphur to fight scab, fireblight, and other diseases.

Apple trees can produce a large number of branches, and rigorous thinning is needed every fall, after the leaves have dropped, not only to keep the tree in tidy shape, but also to thin out constricting

TYPES OF SUPPORT FOR FRUIT TREES AND GRAPEVINES

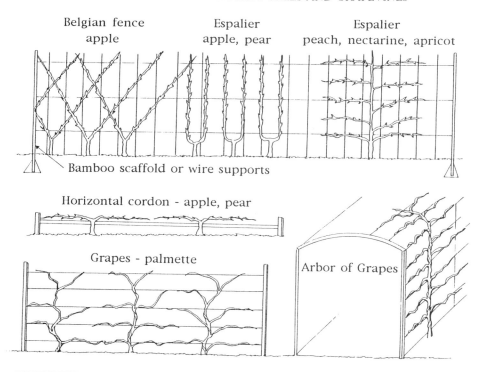

Belgian fence
apple

Espalier
apple, pear

Espalier
peach, nectarine, apricot

Bamboo scaffold or wire supports

Horizontal cordon - apple, pear

Grapes - palmette

Arbor of Grapes

branches and ensure good air circulation throughout the tree canopy.

Apricots

Though flavored like peaches, apricots can be treated like plums. There may be several seasons when frost nips the blossoms and prevents a crop, unless espaliered against a protective wall or fence. "DWARF MOORPARK" as well as "MOONGOLD" are two good dwarf-size apricot varieties. Growing no more than 8 feet high, these varieties can be easily covered with a horticultural fabric to protect flowers from a late frost.

Cherries

Ripening in early July, there are sour cherries (called pie cherries) and sweet cherries, preferred for fresh eating. The best dwarf sour cherry is "NORTH STAR," while the best dwarf sweet cherry is "STAR STELLA." Actually, "STAR STELLA" will grow into a standard-size tree, but it bears at a young age, and can be kept compact by pruning. There is a true dwarf form of "STAR STELLA," called "COMPACT-STELLA."

The biggest problem is birds eating the fruit. Protect by covering the tree with birdnetting at time of ripening.

Peaches and Nectarines

Since nectarines are a mutation of peaches (originally called "fuzzless peaches"), their cultural needs are the same. They bloom earlier than apples by 2 weeks, and the blossoms are more susceptible to frost damage in exposed sites. They are harder to grow than apples in other ways—the fruit is highly susceptible to leaf curl, causing leaf drop and premature fruit drop, and also to rotting unless sprayed with an organic fruit tree spray just before the buds open, again before the fruit ripens, and also after the leaves have fallen from the trees. This protects against the leaf curl and the fruit rot diseases. Calcium deficiency in the soil can induce fruit rot, which can be corrected by liming if a soil test shows any deficiency.

Borers are also a problem of peaches and nectarines. The worms hatch from eggs laid at the base of the trunk by a night-flying moth, and burrow into the trunk. Their presence is detected by a gummy sap oozing from holes. The best protection is to encircle the trunk of young trees with a protective commercial tree wrap.

The Pennsylvania Amish community is famous for growing a peach the size of a small grapefruit. Called "J.H. HALE," it has white flesh and is called the champagne of peaches for its delicious, chin-dripping flavor. Unlike many other newer peach varieties, it needs another peach tree as a pollinator. A favorite old-fashioned variety among Bucks County farmers is "IRON MOUNTAIN." Extremely late-ripening, it is the ugly duckling of peaches. Greenish-yellow when ripe, and the size of a large plum, the white flesh is incredibly delicious—even juicier and more sweetly flavored than a "J. H. HALE."

Pears

Closely related to apples, pears can tolerate a little shade. Their biggest problem is fireblight disease, spread by sucking insects such as aphids and leafhoppers. This can be prevented with three applications of Bordeaux mixture (1 tablespoon per quart of water). Apply when 20% of blossoms are open, again when 65% are open, and again when all blossoms are open. Already infected branches can be cut away with a sharp pruning tool, dipping the blade into a solution of 10% liquid bleach between each cut to sterilize the tool. The variety "HARROW DELIGHT" (an early-ripening pear that resembles the famous "BARTLETT") is fireblight-resistant.

Asian pears differ from standard pears in many ways. They are shaped like an apple, but they are exceedingly sweet and juicy, flavored like a pear. At the supermarket produce counter they often sell for $1.00 apiece. They have shiny, heart-shaped leaves—more decorative than the standard pear's dull, lance-like leaf—and in fall the leaves of Asian pears turn beautiful russet colors, including red and yellow, while standard pears have no fall coloration. Also, Asian pears are naturally resistant to fireblight disease.

Plums

There are two kinds—European and Japanese—with the European generally more reliably hardy than the Japanese. Most home garden plantings require no special sprays—particularly the variety "STANLEY" (a blue-skinned, oval-shaped European plum that ripens in late August and early September) and "SHIRO" (a yellow, round-shaped Japanese plum that ripens in mid-August). However, all trees should be protected from borers with a commercial tree wrap.

BERRY FRUITS

Blueberries

Wild types of blueberries are native to Pennsylvania, and so the climate is perfect for many cultivated varieties. They like an acid soil, and apart from protection from birds, they are carefree plants, cropping continuously for most of July and August. Plants grow to 4 feet high. "BLUERAY" is not only self-pollinating, it grows the largest berries—some as big as a quarter.

Grapes

When colonists started settling Pennsylvania they found many wild grape varieties—this encouraged them to plant many vineyards. Throughout Pennsylvania there are many commercial vineyards producing table wines, including Concord Vineyards, at Chadds Ford, Chester County; Susan's Vineyard, near Doylestown, Bucks County, and Sandcastle Winery, in Erwinna, Bucks County.

The growing of grapes commercially is not an easy enterprise, and anyone considering a commercial venture should obtain a series of booklets produced by Penn State University about grape management. These are available through any local county agent's office and they are updated annually.

For the home gardener, grapes are best grown over an arbor or along a section of split-rail fence, with several varieties allowed to intermingle their vines. Space plants at least 5 feet apart for growing up over an arbor and 8 feet apart for growing along fence posts. Different colors—for example, a red, a black, and a white variety—will help to make the planting ornamental and more appealing.

Though grape varieties are generally classified as wine grapes and dessert grapes, many serve both purposes. For strictly dessert quality, there are also "slipskins" (which have tough skins but sweet, juicy interiors) and "seedless" (which have tender skins and an interior free of seeds). "CONCORD"—a black dessert-quality grape—is a popular "slipskin" variety for Pennsylvania, while "LAKEMONT SEEDLESS" (a white seedless) and "SUFFOLK RED" (a red seedless with a larger berry) are good seedless varieties for Pennsylvania. Don't be tempted to grow "CONCORD SEEDLESS"—the grapes are pathetically small and disappointing.

Susan Gross, owner of Susan's Vineyard, near Doylestown, has done considerable testing of grape varieties, and her favorite for both dessert quality and wine-making is "CAYUGA," a white variety introduced by the New York Experiment Station at Geneva. It has to be seen to be believed. The grape clusters are so huge and prolific they hang from the vines like a curtain. You will need both hands to hold one bunch. The grapes themselves are the size of a marble, have a golden glow, and are so tightly packed on the vine you cannot pass a piece of paper between the berries. In fact, the vines are so eager to bear that "cluster thinning" (removing every other fruit cluster 7 to 10 days after flowering) is often necessary so the vines don't break from the sheer weight of fruit.

"CAYUGA" has better disease resistance than "CONCORD"—especially against powdery mildew and black rot, the two most common Pennsylvania grape diseases. For a disease-free black grape grow "STEUBEN." It ripens a few days earlier than "CONCORD," has larger grape clusters, and the same sweet flavor.

To fatten up berries of *seedless* grapes some growers treat them with gibberellic acid, a growth hormone available from garden centers. This is done by dipping the grape clusters into the acid 7 to 10 days after flowering. But don't give the treatment to *seeded* grapes. Grapes with seeds produce the hormone naturally, and an overdose may have adverse effects.

Black-rot—a fungus disease—can destroy an entire crop, rendering the fruit black, shrivelled, and almost mummified. The disease is prolific during hot, wet weather. Control by planting resistant grape varieties and by fungicidal sprays that should begin as soon as the leaves start to unfurl.

To prevent heavy losses of grapes to birds, yellowjackets, raccoons, and Japanese beetles, consider covering the vines with a fine netting or a horticultural fabric.

Proper pruning is essential to control grape vines. The "four-arm" system is the most common method of training vines in a home garden (see diagram). It consists of pruning the vine so four main branches are trained along wires or fence rails, the lower rail 3 1/2 feet from the ground and the upper rail 5 feet from the ground.

Pruning is done after the grapes have been harvested and the leaves have fallen. If trained along wires, sturdy posts are needed to bear the weight of heavily laden vines.

Raspberries and Blackberries

Called "bramble fruits" because the canes are usually thorny, raspberries grow erect canes ideal for planting in 4-foot-wide rows, while blackberries tend to grow arching canes that need more width—or training against a trellis or fence. They are relatively care-free, although Japanese beetles will eat the leaves and fruit, and deer relish blackberry canes.

The raspberry variety "HERITAGE" is everbearing. It will bear a modest crop of fruit on old canes, starting in July, and a bumper crop starting in late August. For maximum yields it is best to cut most of the canes to the ground after fruiting, leaving every fourth clump of canes to bear the summer crop. "TITAN" (a giant "purple" fruiting raspberry) and "ROYALTY" (a giant red) grow fruit as large as small strawberries—both fruiting for several weeks in July. The black-fruited raspberry called "BLACK HAWK" bears summer crops, while the yellow-fruited variety "FALL GOLD" bears moderate crops, but more sweetly flavored than any other raspberry. Space 2 feet apart.

Blackberries ripen a month later than most raspberries. "DARROW" is heavy-bearing with fruit an inch or more

FOUR-ARM TRAINING OF GRAPEVINE

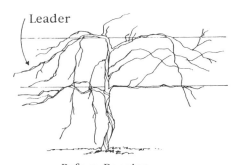

Before Pruning

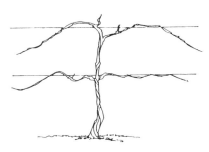

After Pruning

long; "CHESTER" is similar in size, but thorn-free, and hardier than older thorn-free varieties. Space 6 feet apart.

Strawberries

The whole of June is strawberry-picking time in Pennsylvania, and "U-Pick" strawberry farms can be found throughout the state. Many of the best varieties have been developed by the USDA fruit experiment station in Beltsville, Maryland.

There are four kinds of strawberries. The first is the wild "Alpine" strawberry called "Fraises des Bois." These have small conical fruits and compact, bushy plants that produce masses of star-shaped white flowers ideal for edging beds and borders. The second kind is the "June-bearer" that produces a bumper crop just once a year—during the month of June. The variety "EARLIGLO" is a favorite because of its large-size fruits, sweet flavor and disease resistance. The third kind is the "everbearer" that produces a bumper crop in June and a moderate crop in September. "SUPERFECTION" is a good example. The fourth kind is the "day neutral" strawberry that produces a bumper crop in June, then several flushes of fruit in summer and fall. Developed from a wild strawberry found in Brighton Canyon, Utah, the fruiting of day-neutral strawberries is not controlled by day-length like others, and they will continue cropping through the summer months provided they are watered regularly. "TRISTAR" produces medium-size berries that are sweet and juicy.

Strawberries prefer a fertile, sandy, well-drained soil in full sun. They grow best in mounded rows and raised beds, particularly in soil that is enriched with well-decomposed stable manure and a general purpose granular fertilizer raked into the upper soil surface. They fruit best if the runners and flowers are removed the first season. This directs the plant's energy into producing a vigorous root system capable of extra-large berries and yields the following season. They require mulching to prevent competition from weeds, and though straw is the preferred soil covering, some growers prefer to grow strawberries in raised rows that are covered with black plastic.

Set plants 12 inches apart in rows spaced at least 2 feet apart. Since strawberry plants are almost always sold in bundles with bare roots, inspect the roots for any sign of rotting before planting. Separate the plants carefully and splay out the roots in the planting hole so they are not tangled. If necessary, trim the roots with scissors to help splay them out. Make sure the crown of the plant sits snuggly at ground level—not too low or it will rot, not too high or it will dehydrate.

To save garden space, strawberries can be grown in containers—especially wooden half-barrels and also special "strawberry urns." These are usually terra-cotta pots that have pockets around the sides and a wide top so strawberry plants can be grown on the top and around the sides, the flowers and fruit hanging down the sides like a curtain.

APPENDIX

Places of Interest

The following are mostly historic places and public gardens, many of them referred to in the text. Since times of opening can vary from year to year, it is best to telephone ahead for current information. Some of the gardens are free; others charge admission.

The gardens are divided into five geographical areas, with the area around Philadelphia containing the greatest number of attractions.

SOUTHEASTERN PENNSYLVANIA

Allentown's Malcolm W. Gross Memorial Rose Garden

Large collection of modern and old garden roses maintained by the Allentown Chamber of Commerce. Peak flowering occurs in late June and late September. Open daily dawn to dusk. Admission is free.

Located on Cedaridge Parkway, Allentown, PA 18105. Phone: (215) 437-9661.

Ambler Campus, Temple University

Visual interest all year with more than 800 species and cultivars of mostly woody plants and herbaceous perennials. Special attractions include a greenhouse display, dwarf shrub garden, woodland garden, a 3-acre orchard, small-space herb gardens, and a formal perennial garden. The gardens are open daily, dawn to dusk. Admission is free.

Located at Butler Pike and Meetinghouse Road, Ambler, PA 19002. Phone: (215) 643-1200.

Appleford

A 22-acre site with both formal and informal garden spaces, owned by the citizens of Lower Merion Township. One of the most interesting formal areas is a parterre garden featuring geometric-shaped beds, edged in boxwood, for displaying a superb collection of tree-form roses. The gardens are open daily, dawn to dusk. Admission is free. The house is open for group tours by special arrangement.

Located at 770 Mount Moro Road, Villanova, PA 19085. Phone: (215) 525-9430.

Awbury Arboretum

A 57-acre arboretum which began as the private estate of shipping magnate Henry Cope. Today it resembles an English park, featuring many long vistas and woodland trails. Of special interest are a 250-year-old black oak and a 110-year-old river birch. Open daily, dawn to dusk. Admission is free.

Located at Chew Avenue and Washington Lane (Germantown), Philadelphia, PA 19138. Phone: (215) 843-5592.

Barnes Foundation Arboretum

This superb 12-acre garden surrounds the Barnes Museum, North America's most important collection of Impressionist art, including works by Van Gogh, Renoir, Cezanne and Monet. The arboretum is laid out like an English park, with beautiful lawn vistas and a diversity of unusual ornamental tree cultivars, selected for their aesthetic value, form, texture, and seasonal interest (including a Chilean monkey-puzzle tree at the extreme limit of its hardiness range). There is also a beautiful, secluded woodland garden surrounding a free-form pond, a rock garden, a greenhouse collection, and an area devoted to displaying unusual shrubs. The garden is open September through June from 9:30 am to 4:30 pm, Monday through Saturday, and on Sundays from 1:00 pm to 4:30 pm; the rest of the year, Monday through Friday only. Admission is free.

Located at 57 Lapsley Lane, Merion, PA 19066. Phone: (215) 664-8880.

Bartram's Garden

A 27-acre estate once part of a large farm owned by botanist John Bartram (1699-1777), a friend of Benjamin Franklin and Carolus Linnaeus, the Swedish botanist. Bartram introduced many native American trees into cultivation, including the Franklin tree (*Franklinia alatamaha*) which became extinct in the wild soon after Bartram discovered a small grove of trees near Savannah, Georgia. The ''Common Garden''—a simple layout of herbaceous plants in rectangular beds arranged in a square—features a succession of color from annuals and perennials that were popular in Colonial times. Open May to October, Wednesday to Sunday, and the rest of the year, Wednesday to Friday, noon to 4:00 pm. There is a small admission charge.

Located at 54th and Lindbergh Blvd., Philadelphia, PA 19143. Phone: (215) 729-5281.

Bethlehem Public Rose Garden

Collection of modern and old garden roses. Peak flowering time is late June and September. Open daily, year round. Admission is free.

Located at 8th Avenue and Union Blvd., Bethlehem, PA 18067. Phone: (215) 865-7079.

Bowman's Hill Wildflower Preserve

A 100-acre preserve on the River Road south of New Hope, Bucks County, containing numerous walking trails and observation areas in a wilderness setting. Scenic Pidcock Creek and other rocky tributaries of the Delaware River meander through the preserve, creating microclimates for a diverse range of native plants, including bog plants and ferns, and over 1000 species of trees, shrubs, vines, and wildflowers. The preserve has two plant sales a year when many difficult-to-find wildflowers can be purchased. Open Monday through Saturday, 9:00 am to 5:00 pm and Sunday, noon to 5:00 pm. Admission is free.

Located on Route 32, Washington Crossing Historic Park, New Hope, PA 18938. Phone: (215) 862-2924.

Brandywine River Museum and Conservancy

A blend of art and nature in a unique setting. The museum garden features mostly native American species that are readily available to the gardener, such as black-eyed Susans, cardinal flowers, purple loosestrife, butterfly weed, and swamp hibiscus. A particularly beautiful nature trail follows the Brandywine

River, parts of it along a boardwalk that allows visitors to cross sections of wetlands in comfort. Open daily dawn to dusk. There is an admission charge for the museum only.

Located on Route 1 near Route 100, Chadds Ford, PA 19317. Phone: (215) 459-1900 or 388-7601.

Cedaridge Farm

A photography garden designed by gardening writer and photographer Derek Fell. Theme areas include a walled vegetable garden, a cutting garden with Victorian-style gazebo, a cottage garden with old-fashioned roses and perennials, a waterlily pond, a stream garden, naturalized bulb plantings, several perennial borders, a shade garden, an orchard, and a moss garden. Color harmonies and many structures are inspired by paintings of the great French Impressionist painters. Property dates to 1790. Open to groups by appointment only.

Located in Tinicum Township. Mailing address: Box 1, Gardenville, PA 18926. Phone: (215) 766-0699.

Chanticleer

A beautiful country estate of two combined properties, each with its own garden and character. Magnificent tree specimens abound, with expansive lawns sweeping down to the edges of woodland. Around the house are formal gardens featuring superb examples of evergreen ground covers. These include a swimming pool garden and a formal rose garden. Groups of 20 or less may tour the property by appointment. Admission is free.

Located in St. David's, PA (mailing address: Box 347, Wayne, PA 19087). Phone: (215) 688-5020.

Curtis Arboretum

Former estate of the famous Philadelphia publisher, Cyrus H. Curtis, founder of the *Saturday Evening Post, Farm Journal,* and the *Ladies Home Journal.* Sweeping lawn vistas and magnificent old trees create a park-like atmosphere. Open 8:00 am to dusk, year round. Admission is free.

Located at Church Road and Greenwood Ave., Wyncote, PA 19095. Phone: (215) 884-7675.

Delaware Valley College of Science and Agriculture

The beautiful college campus incorporates the Henry Schmeider Arboretum, with an emphasis on woody plants and herbaceous perennials. The 800-acre site also includes fruit orchards with an extensive apple tree collection, a woodland garden, an herb garden, hedge trials and 16,000 square feet of greenhouses featuring an extensive orchid collection. Open daily from 8:30 am to 4:30 pm. Admission is free.

Located at Route 202 and New Britain Road, Doylestown, PA 18901. Phone: (215) 345-1500.

Ebenezer Maxwell Mansion

The house reflects the Victorian architecture of the mid-19th century. Gardens include the original period iron fence, along with formal and natural garden designs. A well-planted combination annual/perennial garden and a small water garden are good examples of small-space design. Open April to December, Thursday to Saturday, 1:00 to 4:00 pm. Admission to the garden is free. There is an admission charge for the tour of the mansion.

Located at 200 West Tulpehocken Street, Philadelphia, PA 19144. Phone: (215) 438-1861.

Fairmount Park Horticulture Center

Fairmount Park is the largest city park in North America, totalling 8000 acres. It contains the Philadelphia Zoo, ten 18th-century mansions, over 200 sculptures, as well as a conservatory, Japanese garden (see next listing), azalea garden, rock garden, and outstanding tree collections. The park itself is open daily without restriction. The Horticulture Center is surrounded by beautiful gardens and contains a conservatory display. The center is open daily, 10:00 am to 4:00 pm. A highlight of the year is the Harvest Show, staged by the Pennsylvania Horticultural Society.

Located at Horticulture Drive near Belmont Avenue, Philadelphia, PA 19131. Phone: (215) 686-1776, ext. 81287.

Fairmount Park Japanese House and Garden

A beautiful reconstruction of a traditional Japanese tea house and gardens. The garden represents a small-scale reproduction of the landscape of Japan. Superb use of ground covers and evergreens as accents. Open daily, 10:00 am to 4:00 pm, April through September. There is a small admission charge.

Located on Horticulture Drive near Belmont Park. Phone: (215) 686-1776, ext. 81220.

Fordhook Farm

Former test gardens and breeding station for America's largest mail-order seed house, W. Atlee Burpee Co. Now maintained by Burpee family members as a bed-and-breakfast inn. The property includes the David Burpee Memorial Garden, featuring popular varieties of flowering annuals and vegetables. Open

daily, May through October, 8:00 am to 4:30 pm. Admission is free.

Located on New Britain Road, Doylestown, PA 18901. Phone: (215) 345-1766.

Hagley Museum and Eleutherian Mills

This restored industrial complex occupies 200 acres along the banks of the beautiful Brandywine River. Here, among steeply wooded banks, Eleuthère Irénée duPont, a French immigrant, established water-powered grinding mills for the manufacture of gunpowder. He sited his house and formal, French-style "potager" garden on a hill overlooking the mills and the Brandywine. Riverside trails lead along wildflower areas and groves of native trees, including redbuds, dogwoods, and American beech. Ruined buildings and rusting machinery are garlanded with vines such as wisteria, climbing roses and trumpet creeper. Open Tuesdays, Saturdays, and holidays, 9:30 am to 4:30 pm, and Sundays, 1:00 to 5.00 pm. Closed Mondays except major holidays. There is an admission charge which includes a tour of the mansion.

Located at Routes 100 and 14, Greenville, Wilmington, DE 19807. Phone: (302) 658-2401.

Haverford College Arboretum

A campus arboretum consisting of 216 acres with 400 species of trees and shrubs. Haverford is home to two direct descendants of the original Penn Treaty Elm (the tree under which William Penn signed his treaty with the Indians when he first arrived in Pennsylvania) and includes a pinetum containing a fine selection of conifers. Open daily, dawn to dusk. Admission is free.

Located at Lancaster Avenue (Route

30) and College Lane, Haverford, PA 19041. Phone: (215) 896-1101.

Henry Foundation for Botanical Research

A 50-acre woodland and meadow garden mostly featuring native North American plants collected from the wild. This is a connoisseur's garden where rare and unusual wild plants of ornamental value are given precedence. Open Monday through Friday, 10:00 am to 4:00 pm. Admission is free.

Located at 801 Stony Lane (off Henry Lane), Gladwyne, PA 19035. Phone: (215) 525-2037.

Highlands

A 190-year-old country estate that was once a model farm. Today the grounds feature a fine stone house, walled English-style pleasure garden, mature trees, and beautiful old outbuildings. Open Monday through Friday, 9:00 am to 4:00 pm. Admission is free.

Located at 7001 Sheaff Lane, Ft. Washington, PA 19034. Phone: (215) 646-9355.

Hill-Physick-Keith House

A famous Colonial doctor, Philip Syng Physick, occupied the property for 20 years. Built in 1786, the house features a small but well-designed 19th-century walled city garden. There is an admission charge.

Located at 321 South 4th Street, Philadelphia, PA 19106. Phone: (215) 925-7866.

Independence National Historical Park

Early Philadelphia was the center of American horticulture. The Independence National Historical Park and its gardens are reminders of the horticultural history that was made in Philadelphia. Use the brochure, "The Gardens of Independence"—available at the visitors center—to locate individual gardens such as Franklin Court, Independence Square, and the Rose and Magnolia Tribute Gardens. Open daily, 9:00 am to 5:00 pm. Admission is free.

The Visitors Center is located at 3rd and Chestnut Streets, Philadelphia, PA 19106. Phone: (215) 597-8974.

Jenkins Arboretum

Mostly native flora growing along woodland paths and stream banks that run through sunny meadows. Contains a good collection of azaleas, rhododendrons, and ferns. Open daily, 8:00 am to dusk. Admission is free.

Located at 631 Berwyn-Baptist Road, Devon, PA 19333. Phone: (215) 647-8870.

Longwood Gardens

Largest display garden in the world with almost 5 acres under glass, founded by Pierre S. duPont as a weekend retreat. Admission charged.

Located at Routes 1 and 52, Kennett Square, PA 19348. Phone: (610) 388-1000.

Meadowbrook Farm

A beautiful, highly formal, private garden created by Mr. and Mrs. J. Liddon Pennock, Jr. The gardens are designed as outdoor rooms along a series of terraces surrounding a large stone house. Creative use is made of potted topiaries and unusual evergreen ground covers. Also features decorative antique structures, such as a temple of love imported from England and a Victorian-style bath house. Reservations are necessary, and visitors must be in groups of 12 to 35.

Pennock's commercial greenhouses are adjacent to the estate and are open to the public during normal business hours without restriction.

Located at 1633 Washington Lane, Meadowbrook, PA 19046. Phone: (215) 887-5900.

Morris Arboretum

A 175-acre arboretum containing some of Philadelphia's rarest and largest trees, including a magnificent oak allée. Today the Victorian-style landscape garden comprises 3500 different trees and shrubs, and beautiful woodland trails along the Wissahickon Creek. In early May the azaleas are an especially impressive feature, followed in June by roses—both antique garden roses and modern kinds. An indoor fern garden, planted in a Victorian-style hothouse located next to a colorful rose garden, is a unique attraction. A visit to the Morris Arboretum is worthwhile at any time of year. Open daily, April to October, 9:00 am to 5:00 pm; the rest of year to 4:00 pm. There is a small admission charge.

Located on Hillcrest Avenue, between Germantown and Stenton Avenues (Chestnut Hill), Philadelphia, PA 19118. Phone: (215) 242-3399.

Nemours Foundation

Founded by Alfred I. duPont, this 300-acre estate is one of the finest examples of French-style gardens in America and includes a Louis XVI-style French chateau. Though the formal gardens recall the Palace of Versailles, with expansive vistas, baroque statuary and magnificent fountains, there are also informal areas where 12 man-made, free-form lakes flow into one another. The garden also features a beautiful Victorian-style conservatory and a large cutting garden. Alfred I. duPont built Nemours while head of the duPont Company, but following a reorganization that deposed him, he surrounded Nemours with a high stone wall, the top embedded with broken glass. Open Tuesday through Sunday, by appointment only. Admission includes a tour of the mansion and a glass of wine on the terrace.

Located on Rockland Road, near Route 202, north of Wilmington, DE 19899. Phone: (302) 573-3333.

Pennsbury Manor

This historic, 43-acre site is a superb reconstruction of the country home of William Penn, founder of Pennsylvania. In addition to the comfortable brick manor house, the site has 23 structures in stone and wood, including a formal fenced-in flower garden, a kitchen garden with a Colonial-style outhouse and well-head, orchards with beehives, a vineyard with rail-fence supports, a smokehouse, an icehouse, and a boathouse containing a replica of the barge used by William Penn to gain access to the site, which required a 5-hour journey by oarsmen rowing upstream from Philadelphia. Closed Mondays and holidays. Open Tuesday to Saturday, 9:00 am to 5:00 pm, and Sunday, 1:00 to 4:00 pm. There is a small admission charge.

Located on the banks of the Delaware River, east of Bordentown Road and north of Exit 29 of the Pennsylvania Turnpike. Follow the signs from Morristown. Phone: (215) 946-0400.

Pennsylvania Horticultural Society

The society's offices feature an 18th-century style garden maintained by members. The formal garden displays topiary accents in square-shaped beds against a decorative gazebo. The beds change with the seasons—mostly bulbs in spring, annuals in summer, chrysanthemums in autumn, and varieties of pansies into the winter months. Adjacent to the main display garden is an herb garden. Open daily, 9:00 am to 5:00 pm. Admission is free.

Located at 325 Walnut Street, Philadelphia, PA 19106. Phone: (215) 625-8250.

Peter Wentz Farmstead

Entering this 18th-century Colonial-style farm is like stepping back 300 years in time. Established by a "privateer," the stone house—in a distinctive black-and-white design—has a Colonial herb garden next to the kitchen, laid out in a "quadrant" design. The property also features several animal shelters, a beautiful stone barn and other outbuildings. During his Valley Forge campaign, George Washington stayed in the house, occupying one of its bedrooms. Open Tuesday through Saturday, 10:00 am to 4:00 pm, and Sundays from 1:00 to 4:00 pm. Admission to the garden is free. There is a small charge to tour the house.

Located at Schultz and Shear Roads, Worcester, PA 19490. Phone: (215) 584-5104.

Philadelphia Zoological Garden

This is the oldest zoological garden in America. Animals are seen in a natural setting, with the carefully selected plantings—such as ornamental grasses—simulating natural habitats. The Solitude, a manor house owned by William Penn's grandson, John Penn, was originally built in 1785 and was the first site of the zoological garden. The house itself was restored in 1976 and can be seen as a part of the zoo tour. Open daily, 9:30 am to 5:00 pm, except some holidays. There is an admission charge.

Located at 34th Street and Girard Av-

enue, Philadelphia, PA 19104. Phone: (215) 243-1100.

Physick Garden

A small, 1/8-acre garden of plants that were grown in the 18th century for medicinal purposes. The garden was originally requested in 1774 by the physicians of Pennsylvania Hospital as a ready source of botanicals for hospital use, but was actually planted two centuries later in 1976 in celebration of the nation's Bicentennial. Open Tuesday to Saturday, 10:00 am to 4:00 pm, Sunday, 1:00 to 4:00 pm. There is no admission charge.

Located at 8th and Pine Streets, Philadelphia, PA 19107. Phone: (215) 829-3971.

Ridley Creek State Park

The main feature of this 2000-acre park is the Colonial Pennsylvania Plantation—a farm museum maintained as an 18th-century, self-sufficient working farm, complete with enclosed vegetable gardens and animal pens. The property is made to look even more authentic by a resident family that dresses in period costume, staging cookery and craft demonstrations. Open weekends from mid-April to mid-November, weekends 10:00 am to 4:00 pm. There is a small admission charge.

Located on Sycamore Mills Road, Media, PA 19063. Phone: (215) 566-4800.

Rockwood Museum

This magnificent manor house, a fine example of rural Gothic architecture, was constructed for merchant banker Joseph Shipley. It features a Victorian-style conservatory and a number of beautiful outbuildings in a 70-acre, park-like landscape that emulates the English "garden-esque" style of landscape design. The grounds integrate manicured lawns and long vistas with trees in contrasting shapes, hues, and textures to create a "tapestry" of sophisticated color. Woodland walks lead to rocky streams and secluded glades. Open Tuesday through Saturday, 11:00 am to 3:00 pm; closed on major holidays. Admission to the gardens is free.

Located at 610 Shipley Road, Wilmington, DE 19809. Phone: (302) 571-7776.

Scott Arboretum

Located on the campus of Swarthmore College, the arboretum features an up-to-date diversified collection exceeding 5000 kinds of highly rated ornamental woody plants and herbaceous perennials. These include 300 varieties of azaleas, 2000 types of rhododendron, 200 hollies, plus extensive collections of magnolias, lilacs, flowering cherries, cotoneasters, and flowering bulbs. A special planting feature is the Wister Garden, a secluded woodland garden that has some of the finest rhododendron specimens in Pennsylvania. Rustic trails criss-cross a slope leading down to a stream, the edges of the path planted with thousands of naturalized spring-flowering bulbs and shade-loving perennials such as hostas and ferns. Open dawn to dusk. Admission is free.

Located on Route 320 (Chester Road), Swarthmore, PA 19081. Phone: (215) 447-7025.

Star Roses Display Gardens

Maintained by the Conard-Pyle Company, leading rose growers, these gardens occupy a site where a condition of the deed requires payment of one red rose each year to a descendant of Wil-

liam Penn. The display garden is surrounded by fields of roses and experimental plantings. Open during daylight hours from May to October, with peak flowering in June and September. Admission is free.

Located on US Route 1 (opposite the Red Rose Inn), West Grove, PA 19390. Phone: (215) 869-2426.

Tinicum National Environmental Center

Within sight of Philadelphia International Airport and the skyscrapers of Center City, this sanctuary is the biggest freshwater tidal marsh in Pennsylvania, a unique wetlands area that is little changed from the time when William Penn sailed up the Delaware River estuary seeking firm, high ground to establish his "greene country towne"—the City of Philadelphia. Natural stands of beautiful, mostly indigenous freshwater plants—such as wild rice, swamp hibiscus, pickerel weed, waterlilies, and common reed—help in maintaining the appearance of an untouched wilderness. The area is also a sanctuary for water birds—especially white egrets, blue herons and many species of ducks and geese.

Located at Lindbergh Boulevard and 86th Street, Philadelphia, PA. Phone: (215) 365-3118.

Tyler Arboretum

Also called the Painter Arboretum, the 700-acre wooded site includes 20 miles of hiking trails that lead along meandering creeks, through bogs, and across wildflower meadows. Some of the trees are spectacular, including a giant sequoia planted between 1856 and 1860, a grove of towering bald cypress, and a cedar of Lebanon with massive, outstretched branches. Though the arboretum is noted for its wild beauty, cultivated gardens are displayed around a visitors center. A fragrance garden is laid out along terraces that feature stone retaining walls. A rhododendron glade contains many fine native Pennsylvania species and hybrids. Open daily, 8:00 am to dusk. There is a small admission fee.

Located at 515 Painter Road, Lima, PA 19037. Phone: (215) 566-5431.

Wallingford Rose Gardens

This vast collection of roses, plus prime specimens of hollies and rare trees was begun in the early 1900's on the site of a peach orchard. The rose garden includes 80 varieties of climbing roses in addition to displays of old garden roses and new varieties, such as hybrid teas. A greenhouse and nursery are also open to visitors. Visitation is by appointment only.

Located on Route 252 (Providence Road) at Brookhaven Road, Wallingford, PA 19086. Phone: (215) 566-2110.

Winterthur Museum and Gardens

Founded by the late Henry F. duPont, this English-style landscape garden has more than 200 acres under cultivation, mostly using flowering bulbs, Pennsylvania wildflowers, hybrid rhododendrons, azaleas, and ferns for a naturalistic, ornamental effect. Though mostly a woodland garden, there is a small formal area behind the museum featuring a beautiful sunken garden with reflecting pool, and meadows planted with drifts of daffodils. A unique feature in the woodland garden is "The March Walk"—a trail planted with trees, flowering shrubs, and spring-flowering bulbs that bloom in March. Some of the tulip poplar trees are the tallest specimens to be found in the state. A tree peony garden is a colorful feature in May. The museum itself contains one of the world's most valuable collections of antiques. Open Tuesday through Saturday, 10:00 am to 4:00 pm, and Sunday, noon to 4:00 pm. Closed on major holidays. There is a small admission charge for the gardens, and a separate charge for the museum. In addition to a self-guided walking tour, visitors can ride a tram through the gardens.

Located on Route 52, Winterthur, DE 19735. Phone: (302) 654-1548.

Wyck House

The oldest house in Philadelphia, dating from the 17th century, the Wyck House was the home of nine generations of the same Quaker family until the grounds were opened to the public in 1973. The well-documented gardens are not only important as a botanical collection (many of the old garden roses date to 1750 and still bloom today), but also as an artifact of early American life. A beautiful boxwood garden with a gazebo as a focal point, and a productive kitchen garden are little changed from the original garden design. Open Tuesday, Thursday, and Saturday from May to October, 1:00 to 4:00 pm. There is an admission charge.

Located at 6026 Germantown Avenue, Philadelphia, PA 19144. Phone: (215) 848-1690.

SOUTH CENTRAL PENNSYLVANIA

Amish Farm and House

An operating farm with gardens and animals preserved to show the life of an Amish family. Open daily. Admission is charged.

Located at 2395 Route 30 East, Lancaster, PA 17602. Phone: (717) 394-6185.

Amish Homestead

An educational exhibit of an Amish dairy farm, occupied by an Amish family who use horses for ploughing and hauling. Guided tours of farmhouse, outbuildings, and gardens. Open daily. Admission is charged.

Located at 2034 Lincoln Highway East, Lancaster, PA 17602. Phone: (717) 392-0832.

Botanical Gardens of the Reading Museum

An interesting collection of trees, shrubs, perennials, and roses. Garden is open during daylight hours. No admission is charged.

Located at Museum Road, Wyomissing, PA 19610. Phone: (215) 373-1525.

Conestoga House and Garden

The estate of the late James H. Steinman includes a beautiful example of Colonial Revival architecture, while the expansive gardens reflect various European styles, particularly English and French. Annuals, perennials, and tropical plants are used extensively to decorate beds and borders, terraces and courtyards. Most of the plants displayed at Conestoga House are grown in greenhouses on the property. During the year some 60 hanging baskets are produced, plus 1500 bedding plants, 600 geraniums, and 1000 poinsettias. The gardens are open June 15 through September 30. There is no admission charge, but reservations to tour the property must be made in advance.

Located at 8 West King Street, Lancaster, PA 17603. Phone: (717) 291-8793.

Coover Arboretum

Specializing in trees and shrubs of or-namental value. Open daily, by appointment only.

Located on Route 3, at Dillsburg, PA 17019. Phone: (717) 766-6681.

Hershey Rose Gardens

Not only roses, but also theme gardens using annuals, flowering bulbs, perennials, ornamental grasses, trees and shrubs. The original 3 1/2-acre rose garden was established by Milton Hershey in 1937, featuring 3500 roses. Situated on a hill overlooking the Hershey chocolate factory, the expanded gardens now cover 23 acres. Open daily, April to October, 9:00 am to 5:00 pm. There is a small admission charge.

Located opposite the Hershey Hotel, Hershey, PA 17033 (the gardens at the rear of the Hershey Hotel are also spectacular). Phone: (717) 534-3493.

Landis Valley Museum

This is the largest museum devoted to Pennsylvania German rural life. Outdoor displays include beautiful herb gardens. Open Tuesday through Saturday, 9:00 am to 5:00 pm, and Sundays, 12 noon to 5:00 pm, year round. Admission is charged.

Located at 2451 Kissel Hill Road, Lancaster PA 17602. Phone: (717) 569-0401.

Masonic Homes Arboretum

A historic garden featuring a valuable collection of trees and shrubs. Open daily during daylight hours. Admission is free.

Located in Elizabethtown, PA 17033. Phone: (717) 367-1121.

Mont Alto Arboretum

Valuable collection of ornamental

woody plants. Open daily, during daylight hours. Admission is free.

Located on the Mont Alto Campus of Pennsylvania State University, Mont Alto, PA 17237. Phone: (717) 749-3111.

Reading Public Museum and Gallery

A diverse collection of flowering trees, shrubs, perennials, and sculpture. Open Monday through Friday, 9:00 am to 5:00 pm, Saturday, 1:00 to 5:00 pm, and Sunday, 1:00 to 5:00 pm. There is a small admission charge.

Located at 500 Museum Road, Reading, PA 19611. Phone: (610) 371-5850.

Reading Rehabilitation Hospital

This beautiful garden provides horticultural therapy to its patients. Planted with trees, shrubs, perennials and flowering annuals, the site is an official All-America Display Garden. Open daily during daylight hours. Admission is free.

Located on Morgantown Road, Reading, PA 19607. Phone: (610) 777-7615.

Rodale Research Center

An experimental farm established by *Organic Gardening & Farming* magazine in 1972, in addition to the original Rodale Farm in nearby Emmaus. Occupying 330 acres, the new farm grows agricultural and garden crops by organic methods, without the need for chemical fertilizers or pesticides. Includes an All-America Selection vegetable garden, plus flower gardens and fish farming fa-

cilities. Guided and self-guided tours are offered daily, May through October, though summer and autumn are the best times. The center conducts gardening and cookery workshops showing how to use culinary herbs, make dried flower arrangements, and other skills. An annual GardenFest, held in early August, includes wagon rides, gardening seminars, bluegrass music, and craft demonstrations. Admission is free.

Located at 611 Siegfriedale Road, Kutztown, PA 19530. Phone: (215) 683-6383.

Sunken Garden of Riverfront Park

A beautifully landscaped public garden that is open daily, 6:00 am to 10:00 pm. Admission is free.

Located at Front and Verbeke Streets, Harrisburg, PA 17101. Phone: (717) 255-3020.

Wildwood Arboretum and Botanical Garden

This 200-acre campus includes wetlands, meadows and woodland providing sanctuary and habitat for many species of plants and animals. The beautiful display gardens are designed with an emphasis on using native plants in combination with garden cultivars. Open daily all year during daylight hours. Peak color is April through November. Admission is free.

Located at 3300 North Cameron Street Road, Harrisburg, PA 17110. Phone: (717) 780-2300.

SOUTHWESTERN PENNSYLVANIA

Eisenhower Farm

President Dwight Eisenhower once said

that he considered his greatest accomplishment to be the stewardship of this property and his leaving it to the world in better condition than he found it. Landscaped gardens with many mature trees surround the Pennsylvania farmhouse.

Located adjacent to the Gettysburg Battlefield; all visitors must board shuttle buses at the National Park Visitor Center. Tickets are available on a first-come basis.

National Park Visitor Center phone: (717) 334-1124.

Fallingwater

Frank Lloyd Wright is considered one of America's finest architects. In the Laurel Highlands, south of Pittsburgh, Wright created what many consider to be America's most beautiful architectural work. Designed in 1936 for Pittsburgh department store owner Edgar J. Kaufmann, Wright built a weekend retreat among steeply sloping, boulder-strewn woodland above a waterfall on Bear Run Creek. Fallingwater is not only an architectural marvel with its original furnishings and artwork intact, it is one of the most spectacular natural settings ever conceived for a house anywhere in the world. Rather than build the house on the bank opposite to the falls in order to give the occupants a splendid view, Wright chose to build the house directly above the falls, integrating the work of man and nature in a powerful harmony that contrasts a dramatic modernistic architectural structure with the wild informality of nature.

The house itself is beautifully landscaped with rhododendrons, azaleas and mountain laurel. Nature trails wander out into the surrounding woodland of mostly deciduous hardwoods. There is a rocky overlook that provides a magnificent overall view of the house and waterfall combined. Open for guided tours from April through November, every day except Monday, from 10:00 am to 4:00 pm.

The rest of the year Fallingwater is open for weekend tours only, weather permitting. Reservations are required to guarantee admission, for which there is a charge. The best time to view Fallingwater is in autumn when the surrounding deciduous trees turn to brilliant shades of red, yellow, and orange, and the waterfall is in full flow.

Located at Mill Run, PA 15464, about a 2-hour drive south of Pittsburgh. Phone: (412) 329-8501.

Hartwood

Historic mansion and garden. Open daily, dawn to dusk. Garden admission is free.

Located at 215 Saxonburg Road, Pittsburgh, PA 15238. Phone: (412) 767-9200.

National Apple Museum

The area around Biglerville, north of Gettysburg, specializes in the growing of apples. In April 1990, the Biglerville Historical and Preservation Society opened the museum to honor the founders of Pennsylvania's important apple industry with displays and artifacts in a restored 1857 barn. Open April through October, Saturdays and holidays, 10:00 am to 5:00 pm, and Sundays, noon to 5:00 pm. Admission is charged.

Located at 154 West Hanover Street, Biglerville, PA 17307. Phone: (717) 677-4556.

Old Economy Kitchen and Gardens

An intensively planted kitchen garden featuring herbs, fruits, and vegetables. Open Tuesday to Saturday, 9:00 am to 4:00 pm, and Sunday, noon to 4:00 pm. Closed on holidays except Memorial Day, July 4, and Labor Day. Admission is charged.

Located at 148 Church Street, Ambridge, PA 15003.

Pittsburgh Civic Gardens Center

A beautiful display garden, open Monday through Friday, 8:30 am to 4:30 pm. Admission is free. Located at 1059 Shady Avenue, Pittsburgh, PA 15232. Phone: (412) 441-4442.

Pittsburgh Zoo

Carefully landscaped micro-environments present a garden-like atmosphere and recreate the impression of a natural habitat for the zoo animals. Open daily, 9:00 am to 5:00 pm. Admission is charged.

Located on Hill Road, Pittsburgh, PA 15206.

Phipps Conservatory

"The Longwood Gardens of Western Pennsylvania." Set in a beautiful downtown park, the main feature is a spectacular Victorian conservatory with 2 1/2 acres of plantings under glass, including theme gardens. Open daily, 9:00 am to 5:00 pm. Admission is charged.

Located in historic Shenley Park, Pittsburgh, PA 15213. Phone: (412) 622-6915.

Pittsburgh Conservatory and Aviary

A tropical garden featuring exotic birds. Open Wednesday to Sunday, 9:00 am to 8:00 pm, closed on major holidays. Admission is charged.

Located at Allegheny Commons West, Ridge Avenue and Arch Street, Pittsburgh, PA 15212. Phone: (412) 323-7235.

NORTH CENTRAL PENNSYLVANIA

Pennsylvania State University Test Gardens

An extensive trial garden is planted each year to evaluate the performance of hundreds of varieties of flowering annuals, home garden vegetables, and roses. Plant breeders from all over the world pay the university to have their best varieties placed on display. Many are submitted for judging by All-America Selections.

At the flowering peak, the first week of August, the university hosts a gathering of seedsmen from all over the world for The International Seed Conference. Open daily, July to September, 8:00 am to 8:00 pm. Admission is free.

Located at the intersection of Bigler Road and East Park Avenue, near the football stadium, University Park, PA 16802. Phone: (814) 865-2571.

NORTHWESTERN PENNSYLVANIA

Mums by Paschke

A community garden claimed to present the world's largest autumn display of cushion chrysanthemums. Open September 1 to November 10, Monday to Saturday, 9:00 am to 8:00 pm, and Sunday, noon to 8:00 pm. Admission is free.

Located at 12286 Main Road, North East, PA 16428. Phone: (814) 725-9860.

USEFUL SOURCES

The following list of mail-order suppliers is by no means complete. It represents reliable companies who provide horticultural products, with a large number of customers in Pennsylvania.

For a more complete list of sources, obtain a copy of *Gardening by Mail—A Sourcebook*, by Barbara Barton. Containing 390 pages, it lists 2500 plant and product sources, completely indexed by plant, product, and location. The catalogs offered are free unless stated otherwise.

Seeds

W. Atlee Burpee Co.
300 Park Avenue, Warminster, PA 18974

The world's largest mail-order seed house, offering mostly flowering annuals, vegetables, herbs, and easy-to-grow perennials. Their full-color catalog also features bedding plants, nursery stock, shrubs, and flowering bulbs.

Gurney's Seed & Nursery Co.
110 Capitol
Yankton, SD 57079

Large selection of unusual and hard-to-find flowers and vegetables grown from seed. Also a large selection of trees, shrubs, and flowering bulbs.

Harris Seeds
3670 Buffalo Road
Rochester, NY 14624

Specialists in vegetables grown from seed, their full-color catalog also offers a choice selection of flowering annuals and easy-to-grow perennials.

Johnny's Selected Seeds
Foss Hill Road
Albion, ME 04910-9731

Specialists in vegetable seeds, Johnny's recently expanded their annual catalog to include flowers. All their offerings are tested for good cold-hardiness and maturity during a short growing season.

Orol Ledden & Sons
P.O. Box 7
Sewell, NJ 08080

Good source for vegetables grown from seed; also lawn grass mixtures, flower seeds, supplies, and tools.

Earl May Seed & Nursery Co.
208 North Elm Street
Shenandoah, IA 51603

Earl May has one of the best trial gardens in North America, almost on a par with Penn State University. His full-color catalog offers a fine selection of vegetables grown from seed; also garden flowers, herbs, bulbs and nursery stock.

Mellinger's
2310 West South Range Road
North Lima, OH 44452

Dependable, family-owned business with a comprehensive catalog offering seeds and nursery stock, tools, and supplies.

George W. Park Seed Co.
Highway 254 North
Greenwood, SC 29647

This family-owned business started in Pennsylvania, printing its first catalog by water power. The company is best known for its comprehensive listing of flowers, though it does have an extensive vegetable section, and each year invites customers to its test gardens which cover several acres. Park also issues one of the finest fall-planting catalogs, with excellent offerings of bulbs.

Pinetree Garden Seeds
New Gloucester, ME 04260

Compared to all other companies, their prices for vegetable and flower seeds are consistently the lowest. They also offer bulbs, tools, and books.

Stokes Seeds
39 James Street
St. Catherine's, Ontario
L2R 6R6 Canada

There used to be a Stokes seed company operating out of Philadelphia. Then one branch of the family emigrated to Canada and set up a seed business. The Philadelphia connection fell on hard times, but the Canadian company has thrived, doing considerable business with gardeners throughout North America. Stokes offerings in flower and vegetable seeds are exceptional, and their prices are reasonable. Many Pennsylvania professional growers, including quite a few Amish farmers, rely on Stokes.

Thompson & Morgan
P.O. Box 1308
Jackson, NJ 08527

Reputed to offer the widest range of seed in the world, founders of the company sold seeds to Charles Darwin and Claude Monet. Many unusual new offerings appear in the catalog each year, but the company is best known for rare, hard-to-find varieties.

Twilley Seed Co.
P.O. Box 65
Trevose, PA 19047

Owned by wholesale seed growers Abbott & Cobb, Twilley's many varieties of cantaloupes, watermelons, tomatoes, and sweet corn are exceptional. Their cantaloupe "STAR HEADLINER" is grown by more Amish farmers than any other melon, and their "SUMMER SWEET" extra-sweet hybrid corns are noted for retaining their sweetness longer than other varieties. The company has a comprehensive test garden at their headquarters in Trevose for both flowers and vegetables grown from seed.

Perennial Plants

Some perennial plant growers also produce bulb catalogs. Also, some perennial classes (such as garden lilies and bearded iris) are listed under bulbs.

Kurt Bluemel
2740 Greene Lane
Baldwin, MD 21013

Specialists in ornamental grasses, but with a comprehensive listing of up-to-date perennials, particularly perennials that blend well with grasses, such as astilbes. The descriptive two-color catalog costs $3.00.

Bluestone Perennials
7211 Middle Ridge Road
Madison, OH 44057

A comprehensive selection of popular perennials at competitive prices, shipped in small sizes, but carefully packaged for safe delivery.

Klehm Nursery
197 Penny Road
South Barrington, IL 60010

Specialists in tree peonies, herbaceous peonies, and hybrids. Klehm's quality is unequalled. Their catalog also features many top-quality perennials, particularly hybrid daylilies and hostas.

Limerock Ornamental Grasses
RD 1
Port Matilda, PA 16870

An extensive collection of hardy ornamental grasses, all Pennsylvania-grown on the company's farm near Penn State University. Their catalog has good descriptions and presents suggested landscape uses.

Spring Hill Nurseries
6523 North Galena Road
Peoria, IL 61632

The largest perennial plant growers in North America, Spring Hill maintains a comprehensive test garden in Tipp City, near Dayton, Ohio. Spring Hill has a main spring catalog featuring a good cross section of popular varieties, and they also conduct specialty mailings offering economical collections, such as garden lilies, daylilies, hostas, asters, and poppies. Spring Hill is also associated with Breck's Bulbs (see bulb listings).

Wayside Gardens
P.O. Box 1
Hodges, SC 29695

The leading mail-order nursery, associated with Park Seeds, specializing in ornamental trees and shrubs, though Wayside also offers good selections of perennial plants and bulbs. They are often the "first" to make introductions of new hybrid woody plants, such as the David Austin "Heritage" series of hybrid English roses. Wayside has special relations with leading European breeders, such as the Bloom family, perennial specialists in England.

White Flower Farm
Route 63
Litchfield, CT 06759

Try to visit White Flower Farm's trial gardens in early summer when their perennial plant displays are at their peak. The farm itself is a paradise with retail plant outlet and gift store. White Flower Farm maintains excellent stocks of leading perennial varieties, and they offer a comprehensive bulb catalog in the fall.

Bulbs

B & D Lilies
330 P Street
Port Townsend, WA 98368

The initials stand for the owners, Bob and Diana, who produce America's most comprehensive color catalog devoted to lilies, including many of de Graaf's most famous hybrids, plus the scarce Madonna lily (*L. candidum*) and hard-to-find species.

Breck's Bulbs
6523 North Galena Road
Peoria, IL 61632

Largest suppliers of bulbs for fall planting, Breck's started in Boston, and today maintains an office in Holland to supervise the growing and shipment of top-quality Dutch bulbs, particularly daffodils and tulips.

Cooley's Gardens
P.O. Box 126
Silverton, OR 97381

Specialists in tall bearded iris. Beautiful color catalog available for $2.00.

Daffodil Mart
Route 3
Gloucester, VA 23061

Probably the most comprehensive list of hybrid daffodils in North America, many developed by owner Brent Heath. Their black-and-white catalog costs $1.00. In March, it's worth making a special trip to see their growing fields, crowded with thousands of daffodils in full bloom.

Dutch Gardens
P.O. Box 200
Adelphia, NJ 07710

Claiming to ship bulbs direct from Holland at wholesale prices, the Dutch Gardens catalog is perhaps the most colorful of all of those featuring fall-planting varieties. The strength of the catalog is its listings of tulips and daffodils, but hyacinths and amaryllis are also well represented.

Charles H. Mueller
Lenteboden
River Road
New Hope, PA 18936

In addition to a mail-order business mostly in daffodils, tulips and other spring-flowering bulbs, the company maintains display gardens which they describe as their "living bulbs catalog."

In spring, between April 15 and May 15, visitors are invited to tour the gardens and make out their orders for fulfillment at the proper planting time in the autumn. The company sells only top-quality bulbs—the kind that win show awards.

Rex Lilies
P.O. Box 774
Port Townsend, WA 98368

A comprehensive selection of garden lilies, including hybrids and species, many grown in the fields surrounding this beautiful port city. Their full-color catalog costs $1.00.

Swan Island Dahlias
P.O. Box 800
Canby, OR 97013

A family-owned business with possibly the largest selection of tuberous dahlias in North America, many from their own breeding program. Though many show-quality "dinnerplate-size" varieties are included, their most popular variety is "JAPANESE BISHOP"—a bronze-leaf, single-flowered, scarlet red dahlia similar to "THE BISHOP OF LLANDAFF." The full-color catalog costs $2.00.

Van Bourgondien
245 Farmingdale Road
Babylon, NY 11702

Specialists in spring-flowering and summer-flowering bulbs. Also suppliers of perennial plants.

Trees and Shrubs

Carlson's Gardens
P.O. Box 305
South Salem, NY 10590

Excellent source of top-quality azaleas and rhododendrons, including mature specimens. In May and June their display garden is well worth visiting. The owner, Bob Carlson, has hybridized numerous outstanding plants.

Girard Nursery
P.O. Box 428
Geneva, OH 44041

Specialists in hardy azaleas, rhododendrons, and other ornamental woody plants.

Jackson & Perkins
1 Rose Lane
Medford, OR 97501

Once located in New York state, the company still specializes in roses, with many of their own hybrids winning All-America awards for excellence. In recent years the company has expanded into offering perennial plants and flowering bulbs.

Forrest Keeling
Highway 79
Elsberry, MO 63343

Pioneers of the "milk carton" method of propagating trees and shrubs. Healthy cuttings are rooted in extra-deep "bottomless" pots, elevated on wire-screen benches so that when the taproot penetrates the bottom of the pot it is "air pruned," shriveling up and dropping off below the bottom, allowing vigorous side roots to fill the pot. The extra-large root system lessens transplant shock. This system increases the success of planting native American trees, especially oaks. The company deals primarily in large quantity orders.

Musser Forests
Route 119
Indiana, PA 15701

Specialists in hardy conifers, the company also offers azaleas, rhododendrons, and other ornamental trees and shrubs for home landscapes.

Roses of Yesterday & Today
802 Brown's Valley Road
Watsonville, CA 95076

An especially good source of old garden roses. Their catalog has excellent descriptions and costs $1.00.

Fruits, Berries, Herbs, and Vegetable Plants

Hartmann's Plantations
310 60th Street
Grand Junction, MI 49056

Specialists in blueberries, but also growers of unusual fruits—such as hardy paw paws. Also features good selections of strawberries, blackberries, and raspberries, plus fruiting ground covers such as American cranberry, partridgeberry, and winterberry. Hartmann's is an especially good source for "interstem" dwarf apple trees.

J.E. Miller Nursery
Canandaigua, NY 14424

An excellent source of hardy fruit trees and berry bushes. Specialists in supplying apples, pears, peaches, nectarines, apricots, cherries, plums, strawberries, raspberries, blueberries, asparagus, and other perennial edible plants.

Piedmont Plant Company
P.O. Box 424
Albany, GA 31703-8501

Specialists in supplying vegetable plants by mail, including tomatoes, peppers, eggplant, onions, sweet potatoes, cabbage and other popular vegetables suitable for transplanting.

Rayners
P.O. Box 1617
Salisbury, MD 21801

A reliable source of virus-free strawberry plants; also has a good selection of raspberries and blueberries.

Stark Bros. Nursery
Louisiana, MO 63353

America's largest mail-order supplier of fruit trees, particularly apple, pear and peach, presenting a fine selection of disease-resistant trees. Stark's colorful catalog also features shade trees and ornamental shrubs.

Well Sweep Herb Farm
317 Mt. Bethel Road
Port Murray, NJ 07865

A complete source of popular and hard-to-find herbs and herbal products.

Water Plants

Lilypons Water Gardens
6800 Lilypons Road
Lilypons, MD 21717

A long-established mail-order source for waterlilies and other aquatic plants. Also sells ornamental fish suitable for ponds.

Perry's Water Gardens
191 Leatherman Gap Road
Franklin NC 28734

Renowned international breeder of waterlilies. Specialists in tropical and hardy kinds, as well as other useful water plants.

Slocum Water Gardens
1101 Cypress Gardens Blvd.
Winter Haven, FL 33880

Leading supplier of waterlilies, lotus, and other aquatic plants for ornamental pools, ponds, and lakes.

Wildflowers

In addition to the following, call or visit Bowman's Hill Wildflower Preserve, near New Hope, and the Henry Foundation, Gladwyne, for information on plant sales involving wildflowers propagated on the premises.

Gardens of the Blue Ridge
Route 221
Pineola NC 28662

Probably the most popular source of native North American wildflowers.

Putney Nursery
Putney, VT 05346

An excellent source for wildflowers.

Tools and Supplies

Capability Books
Highway 46
Deer Park, WI 54007

The best mail-order source for garden books, covering a wide variety of subjects.

Gardener's Supply
128 Intervale Road
Burlington, VT 05401

Issues a colorful catalog featuring many useful garden aids, such as frost extenders and propagating materials.

Gardens Alive
5100 Schenley Place
Lawrenceburg, IN 47025

A more specialized catalog that features mostly organic insect and pest controls.

International Irrigation Systems
1555 Third Avenue
Niagara Falls, NY 14304

Manufacturers of an inexpensive, disposable system of drip irrigation, originally developed by duPont. The system sweats beads of moisture along a flexible hose, one version of which can be buried permanently beneath the soil. Also, it is the only system that will work from a gravity-fed water source, and other low-pressure sources.

Kinsman Company
River Road
Point Pleasant, PA 18950

Suppliers of quality garden tools, including English-made spades and garden forks, German-made shredders, plus compost bins, cold frames, rubber boots, arbors and plant supports. In addition to a colorful catalog issued twice a year, the company has a retail store in the picturesque community of Point Pleasant on the Delaware River.

Nitron Formula
4605 Johnson Road
Fayetteville, AK 72702

Publishes a full-color catalog that features organic fertilizers, both liquid and granular, to feed lawns, vegetable gardens, and flower gardens, as well as non-toxic pest-control products.

Ringer Research
6860 Flying Cloud Drive
Eden Prairie, MN 55344

Offers an extensive range of organic fertilizers and pest controls for vegetables, fruit trees, lawns, and flower gardens.

Smith & Hawken
25 Corte Madera
Mill Valley, CA 94941

Sells a complete line of tools and furnishings for the garden.

COUNTY AGENTS

Pennsylvania has 67 County Agents Offices, each with an Extension Service Agent, responsible to the United States Department of Agriculture. These specially trained agents are dedicated to providing help to farmers and gardeners. They supply answers to questions about every aspect of horticulture and agriculture, ranging from the first and last frost dates for your area, to recommended spraying schedules for various orchard fruits. By contacting the County Agent in your area you can also obtain a kit for conducting a reliable soil test, and receive helpful brochures with advice on specific subjects, such as lawn care, house plant care, container gardening, vegetable gardening, canning, and storage.

To locate the office nearest to you, look in the Blue Pages of your telephone directory under Cooperative Extension Service, usually in the section headed Government Offices, County.

In addition to using the County Agents as a resource, you should consider joining the Pennsylvania Horticultural Society. Membership includes the use of their Gardening Hot Line and admission to the Philadelphia Flower Show members preview. For membership information contact:

The Pennsylvania Horticultural Society
325 Walnut Street
Philadelphia, PA 19106

General Index

A

Abbott & Cobb, 160
Acid soil, 13, 112
Aden, Paul, 73
Africa, 105
Air pruning, 127
Alatamaha River (GA), 1
Alkaline soil, 13
All-America Selections, 6, 30, 31, 33, 34, 35, 36, 37, 38, 44, 61, 67, 68, 160, 161, 181, 184, 215
Allegheny Mountains, 8, 10
Allegheny Plateau, 8
Allentown, PA, 5, 164, 205
Allentown's Malcolm W. Gross Rose Garden, 205
Ambler, PA, 8, 55
Ambler Campus, Temple University, 205
American Gardener's Calendar, 145
Amish, 3, 4, 5, 9, 161, 200, 213, 214, 219
Ammann, Jacob, 4
Amsterdam, 88
Animal pests, 22
Annuals, 27-50
Anthracnose, 22
Aphids, 24, 130, 141, 199
Apple scab, 199
Appleford Garden, 205
Apps, Darrell, 69
Arab oil embargo, 6, 159
Arbustum Americanum, 124
Arctic, 10
Arnold Arboretum, 124
Asexual reproduction, 58

Austin, David, 149
Awbury Arboretum, 205

B

B & D Lilies, 220
Backfill, 128
Bacterial wilt, 21
Balled trees, 126
Baltimore gneiss, 9
Barnes Foundation, 8, 206
Barton, Barbara, 218
Bartram, John, 1, 24, 206
Bartram, William, 1
Bartram's Gardens, 206
Bear Meadows, PA, 111
Beetles
    bean, 24
    Colorado, 24, 185, 189
    cucumber, 24, 160
    flea, 160
    Japanese, 24, 121, 149, 160, 203
    Mexican bean, 25, 160
Beltsville, MD, 203
Benary, Ernst, 6
Bergman Rariflora Nursery, 124
Berkshire Mountains, 79
Berries, 197, 200, 222
Bethlehem Public Rose Garden, 208
Biennials, 30, 51
Biglerville, PA, 216
Birds, 22, 23, 200, 203
Black rot, 22, 203
Black plastic, in drip irrigation, 20, 25, 163
Blights, 22
Blossom end rot, 18
Bluemel, Kurt, 70, 219

Bluestone Perennials, 219
Bone meal, 73, 88, 106
Bordeaux mixture, 22, 200
Borders, 60
Borers, 130, 185, 200
Boron, 16, 25
Botanical Gardens of Reading
    Museum, 214
Bowman's Hill Wildflower Pre-
    serve, 7, 8, 111, 112, 117,
    125, 140, 206, 232
Brandywine Conservancy, 8, 111,
    206
Breck's Bulbs, 220
Britain, climate of, 55
Brooks, Martin, 124
Brown rot, 22
Bryn Mawr College, 220
BT *(Bacillus thuringensis)*, 2, 175,
    176, 181, 208
Bucks County, 1, 9, 111, 124, 191,
    202
Bulb planting charts, 89-92
Bulbs
    fall-flowering, 94, 100-104
    forcing, 104
    general, 56, 87, 220
    spring-flowering, 87-94, 95-100
    summer-flowering, 94, 100-104
Burbank, Luther, 3
Burpee, David, 3
Burpee, W. Atlee, 3
Burpee Seeds, 3, 36, 38, 41, 43,
    44, 45, 67, 68, 75, 218

C

Cabbage white butterfly, 160
Cabbage worms, 24-25
Calcium, 14, 16, 18, 200
California, climate of, 11
Campbell Soup Company, 124
Canada, climate of, 10, 219
Capability Brown, 123
Capability's Books, 224
Captan, 5
Carlson's Gardens, 221
Carrot fly, 178

Cation exchange capacity, 16
Cedar apple rust, 22, 199
Cedaridge Farm, 48, 207
Chadds Ford, PA, 111, 202
Chanticleer, 207
Chelsea Flower Show, 7
Chemical controls, 25
ChemLawn, 121
Chester County, 1, 2, 85, 111
Chicago, 69, 78
Church, Thomas, 85
Churchville Nature Center, 185
Clause (French breeder), 6
Climate, influence of, 10-12
Cold frame, 105, 166, 171
Collegeville, PA, 66
Colonial Plantation, 1
Compost, 14, 22, 25, 95, 164
Conard-Pyle Company, 7, 141,
    149, 212
Concord Vineyards, 202
Conestoga House, 54, 214
Container gardening, 171
Cooley's Gardens, 220
Cooperative Extension Service, 18,
    225
Coover Arboretum, 207
Cope, Henry, 205
Copper, 22
Corn ear worm, 160, 189
County Agents, 17, 18, 171, 225
Courtyard garden, 49, 151
Craig, Dick, 35
Craton, 8
Curtis, Cyrus H., 207
Cutting gardens, 48
Cutworms, 25, 160

D

Daffodil Mart, 220
Damping-off disease, 29, 171
Daylilies—The Perfect Perennial,
    69
De-thatching, 122
Deer, 22-24, 94, 126, 160, 199
Deer repellent, 23
Deerfield Garden, 28, 134

Dehydration, 126
Delaware, 172
Delaware River, 10, 12, 81, 206
Delaware Valley, 7
Delaware Valley College, 7, 124,
    199, 207
Delaware Water Gap, 10, 192
Dexter, Charles O., 131
Digging, 163
Dipel, 24, 160
Diseases, plant, 21, 121, 126, 130
Doe Run Farm, 54, 55, 57, 112
Dogwood decline, 124, 130
Dormancy, 12
Doylestown, PA, 3, 45, 191, 202
Drainage, 21, 163
Drip irrigation, 20, 22, 161, 166
duPont, Alfred I., 3, 210
duPont, Eleuthère I., 2, 198
duPont, Henry F., 3, 55, 87, 123,
    213
duPont, Pierre S., 2
Dutch Gardens, 220

E

Earl May Seed & Nursery Com-
    pany, 218
Ebenezer Maxwell Mansion, 207
Eisenhower Farm, 215
Eleutherian Mills, 2, 198
Emmaus, PA, 5
Ephrata, PA, 148
Erwinna, PA, 225
Espaliers, 198

F

Fairmount Park, 7, 8, 146, 208
Fall planting, 127
Fallingwater, 216
Farm Journal, 207
Feasterville, PA, 124
Fencing, 3, 160
Fertilizing, 15, 16, 60, 88, 120,
    126, 128, 164, 167
Fireblight, 199, 200
Floating row covers, 23, 160

Florida, climate of, 10
Foliar feeding, 16
Ford, President Gerald, 159
Fordhook Farm, 3, 160, 173, 208
Formal gardens, 50
Forrest-Keeling Nursery, 126, 222
Fort Washington, PA, 123
Foster, Link, 79
Franklin, Benjamin, 2, 206
Frost, 11, 28, 171
Fruit
    berry, 202-204
    orchard, 199-201
Fruit flies, 199
Fruit trees, 197-199
Fry, Miles, 148
Fungus control, 11, 28, 171
Fusarium wilt, 189

G

Gable, Joseph B., 131
Gardeners Supply Company, 224
Gardening by Mail, 218
Gardens Alive, 161, 224
Gardens of the Blue Ridge, 223
Germantown, 29, 149
Germany, settlers from, 9
Gettysburg, PA, 9, 216
Gibson, Mary H., 7
Girard Nursery, 222
Gladwyne, PA, 7, 111
Grafting, 197
Grapevine training, 203
Grenville Collision, 8
Gross, Susan, 202
Groundhogs, 160
Grow light, 29
Gulf of Mexico, 10, 12
Gurney Seed & Nursery Company,
    218
Gypsum, 14
Gypsy moth, 130

H

Hagley Foundation, 191, 208
Hallowell, Thomas H., Jr., 112

Hampton Court Palace, 134
Hardening-off, 30, 166
Harper, Pamela, 55
Harris Seeds, 5
Harrisburg, PA, 9
Harvest Show, 7
Hastings, W. Ray, 6
Haverford College, 8
Heating cable, 168
Hedge trimmers, 129
Henry, Josephine, 7
Henry Foundation, 7, 75, 111, 209,
    223
Herbicides, 25
Herbs, 159, 191-196
Hershey, Milton, 7
Hershey, PA, 132
Hershey Gardens, 7, 27, 149, 214
Highlands, The, 123, 209
Hill, Lewis and Nancy, 69
Himalaya Mountains, 8
Hoop house, 51
Hosta Book, The, 73
Hummingbirds, 65, 155
Humus, 14, 15, 22, 119, 166
Hutton, Dick, 149
Hydrology, 18

I

Ice, 12
Impressionism, 206
Independence National Historical
    Park, 8, 209
Inoculant, 44, 166
Insecticidal soap, 160
Insects, 22, 121, 130, 161
    beneficial, 24
International Irrigation Systems,
    224
Irrigation, 28, 120, 161, 166

J

Jackson & Perkins, 221
Jacob's Ladder Wild Gardens, 111
Jan de Graaff, 75
Japan, daylilies from, 69
Jaynes, Richard, 146

Jefferson, Thomas, 2
Jiffy-7 peat pots, 29, 44
Johnny's Selected Seeds, 218

K

Kennett Square, 15, 27, 54, 124
Keukenhof, Holland, 88
Kinsman Company, 224
Kitchen garden design, 169
Klehm Nurseries, 69, 78, 220
Krauskopf, Joseph, 7
Kroll, Arthur, 69
Kutztown, PA, 5

L

Lacewings, 24, 198
Ladew Topiary Garden, 140, 143
Ladies Home Journal, 207
Ladybugs, 24
Lancaster, PA, 3, 9, 54
Landis Valley Museum, 214
Landisville, PA, 5
Landreth, David, 2
Lawn care chart, 122
Lawn Doctor, 121
Lawn mower, 126
Lawn spreader, 121
Lawn sprinkler, 18, 19, 20, 29, 120
Leaf hoppers, 22, 199
Leaf mold, 14, 15, 22, 95, 161
Leaf spot, 22
Leaming's Run Garden, 41, 94
Lenni-Lenape Indians, 1
Lenteboden Bulb Garden, 88, 97,
    99, 221
Lewis & Clark expedition, 144
Light, 11
Lilypons Water Gardens, 107, 223
Lima, PA, 8, 124
Lime, 15, 120
Limerock Ornamental Grasses, 70,
    220
Lindtner, Peter, 198
Linnaeus, Carolus, 206
Liverpool, 123
Loam, 13, 104
Logan, James, 1

Long Island, 73
Longwood Gardens, 2, 27, 29, 33,
    40, 54, 55, 70, 73, 85, 101,
    111, 123, 137, 146, 149, 152,
    160, 209
Lowe, Jeannette, 45
Lyme disease, 23

M

Maggots, 24
Malathion, 5
March Walk, 87
Marliac, Latour, 107
Marshall, Humphrey, 124
Maryland, climate of, 10
Maxatawny, PA, 6
McGourty, Frederick, 55
McMahon, Bernard, 144
Meadow Garden, 111
Meadowbrook Farm, 56, 210
Meilland (rose breeders), 149
Mennonites, 5, 8
Mice, 23, 105, 127
Mildew, 45
Milky spore, 24, 121
Miller Nursery, 222
Miracid, 15
Miracle Gro, 164
Missouri, 126
Mites, 21,24, 130
Montclair, NJ, 73
Montgomery County, 1, 111, 112, 191
Morris Arboretum, 7, 55, 123, 136,
    139, 149, 210
Mothballs, 105
Mowing, 121, 126
Mueller, Charles H., 88, 221
Mulches, 20, 25, 60, 120, 126,
    128, 149, 166, 197, 222
Mushroom soil, 15, 95
Musser Forests, 222

N

Narberth, PA, 8
National Apple Museum, 216
National Arboretum, 124, 138,
    144, 148

National Garden Bureau, 159
Nearing, Guy, 131
Nematodes, 25
Nemours Garden, 3, 210
New Haven, CT, 146
New Hope, PA, 100, 111, 125, 206
New Jersey Pine Barrens, 117
New York Central Park, 124
New York Fruit Experiment
    Station, 199, 202
Nitrogen, 14, 16, 164
Nitrogen-fixing bacteria, 16
Nitron Formula, 161, 224
NPK, 16
Nursery bed, 58

O

Ohio, 67, 189
Ohio River, 10, 12
Old Economy Kitchen and
    Gardens, 216
Onion flies, 182
Oregon, 75
Organic Gardening & Farming
    magazine, 6, 215
Orol Ledden & Sons, 218
Ott's Greenhouses, 66

P

Pacific Northwest, 11, 144
Painter Arboretum, 212
Painter Brothers, 124
Park Seeds, 6, 51, 218
Parsley worms, 25
Parterre garden, 56
Peat, 15, 95, 104, 120
Penn, John, 211
Penn, William, 1, 4, 123, 125, 149,
    187, 208, 210, 119, 130, 199,
    202, 212, 225
Penn State University, 5, 6, 16, 17,
    21, 27, 35, 40
Penn's Woods, 125
Pennock, J. Liddon, 209
Pennsbury Manor, 1, 8, 191, 210
Pennsylvania Horticultural Society,
    27, 48, 49, 55, 125, 210, 225

Pennsylvania Hospital, 8, 191, 211
Per-annuals, 51
Perennials, 51, 219
Perlite, 15
Perry's Water Gardens, 223
Pests, 21, 22, 168
Peters Plant Foods, 164
pH, 14, 15, 16
Philadelphia, 1, 2, 3, 7, 8, 13, 123,
    135, 155, 208, 219
Philadelphia Flower Show, 7
Philadelphia Zoo, 208, 211, 222
Phipps Conservatory, 7, 217
Phosphorus, 16, 88, 164
Physick Garden, 8, 191, 211
Piedmont Crystalline Belt, 9
Piedmont Plant Company, 211
Pierce Brothers, 2, 124
Pinetree Garden Seeds, 219
Pittsburgh, 7, 10, 13, 217
Pittsburgh Civic Gardens Center,
    217
Pittsburgh Conservatory, 217
Pittsburgh Zoo, 217
Plant pathology laboratories, 21
Planting, steps in, 164, 166, 168
Planting chart for vegetables, 165
Plugging lawns, 119
Pocono Mountains, 10, 11
Pollination, 188, 197
Polypropyline, 11, 23, 120
Pools, garden, 109
Port Matilda, PA, 70
Port Murray, NJ, 16, 223
Portland, OR, 7
Potash, 16, 164
Pots, clay, 104
Potting soil, 104, 105
Powdery mildew, 21
Praying mantis, 25
Precipitation, 12
Presby Memorial Iris Gardens, 73
Pruning, 129, 150, 203
Putney Nursery, 223
Pyrethrum, 24, 160, 199

Q

Quakers, 1, 2, 7, 9, 213

R

Rabbits, 160
Raccoons, 160
Rain gauge, 19
Rainfall, 12, 19
Raking, 163
Rayners, 223
Reading Public Museum and
    Gallery, 215
Reading Rehabilitation Center, 215
Rex Lilies, 221
Ridge and Valley region, 8
Ridley Creek State Park, 1, 211
Ringer Research, 224
Rochester, NY, 112
Rock, Joseph, 78
Rockwood Garden, 123, 210
Rodale, J.I., 5
Rodale Press, 5, 160
Rodale Research Center, 215
Rodent repellent flakes, 94
Rodents, 23, 94, 126
Root division, 58
Root feeding, 129
Rooting hormone, 60
Roses, 56, 149-152
Roses of Yesterday & Today, 222
Rotenone, 22, 24, 160, 180, 186,
    199
Roundup, 25
Royal Botanical Gardens, Kew, 3
Royal Horticultural Society, 153
Royal Sluis (breeders), 6
Rust disease, 22
Rutgers University, 141, 164, 173
Rydal, PA, 112

S

Sakata Seeds, 6
Sandcastle Winery, 202
Saturday Evening Post magazine,
    131, 207
Saunders, A.P., 78
Savannah, GA, 1
Scott Arboretum, 7, 212
Seeding lawns, 119
Seeds, 27, 28, 58, 170, 218

Shipley, Joseph, 123, 124, 211
Shrubs, 123, 221
Six-packs, plant, 27
Slocum Water Gardens, 223
Slug bait, 24
Slugs, 22, 24, 28, 160
Smith & Hawken, 224
Snow, effects of, 12
Soaker hose, 20, 21
Sodding lawns, 119
Soil, 13, 14, 119
    acid, 13
    alkaline, 13, 16
    clay, 13, 104
    loam, 13, 104
    sandy, 13, 104
Soil conditioner, 164, 167
Soil pH, 15
Soil test, 15, 16, 18, 119, 160, 162
Soil test kit, 17
Soldier bugs, 25
Sources, 218
Spring Hill Nurseries, 220
Sprinkler system, 18
Squash vine borers, 160
Staking, 126, 128, 200
Star Roses, 7, 149, 212
Stark Bros. Nursery, 223
State College, PA, 5, 6
Steinman, James H., 214
Stewartstown, PA, 131
Stock
    grafting, 127
    seedling, 127
Stokes Seeds, 5, 219
Stover Farm, 191
Stover Mill Gardens, 69
Styer, J. Franklin, 125
Succession planting, 168, 170
Suckers, 127
Sulphur, 14, 22
Sunken Garden Riverfront Park,
    215
Sunlight, 163, 167
Sunscald, 21
Super phosphate, 88
Susan's Vineyard, 202
Susquehanna River, 10, 12
Swainton, NJ, 42, 94

Swarthmore College, 7, 8, 131,
    143, 144, 149

T

Temperature, 11
Temple University, 8, 55
Thinning, 166, 168
Thompson & Morgan, 219
Thouron, Sir John, 54
Ticks, 23
Timber Press, 73
Tomato hornworm, 27, 190
Tools, 224
Transplants, 27, 28, 126, 127
Tree planting diagram, 128
Tree wraps, 23, 126, 128, 129
Trenton, NJ, 185
Trichogramma wasp, 25
Twilley Seeds, 5, 160, 219
Tyler Arboretum, 7, 124, 136, 137,
    143, 212

U

Unionville, PA, 54
United States Department of Agri-
    culture, 18, 159, 182, 204, 225
United States Forest Service, 128
Upper Black Eddy, PA, 81

V

Valley Forge State Park, 111
Van Bourgondien, 221
Vegetable garden plan, 162
Vegetable planting chart, 165
Vegetables, 159-191, 222
Vermiculite, 15
Versailles, gardens of, 210
Verticillium wilt, 189
Vick, Albert, 112
Vick's, James, 112
Victory Gardens, 159

W

Walker Gladiolus Farm, 103
Washington, George, 2, 191, 211

Washington Crossing, PA, 117
Washington Post, 159
Water, 18, 19, 60, 166
Water garden, 59
Water garden planting diagram,
    109
Water plants, 87, 106
Watering cans, 20
Watering wands, 19, 20
Wayne, PA, 8
Ways with Wildflowers, 117
Webworms, 25
Weeds, 21, 25, 26, 121, 168
Weevils, 25
Wentz Farmstead, 8, 160, 169,
    191, 211
West Grove, PA, 7
White House vegetable garden,
    159
Wildflowers, 111-117, 223
Wilmington, DE, 2, 11, 198

Wilt diseases, 21
Winds, 11, 12
Winterthur, 55, 62, 87, 111, 123,
    213
Wissahickon Creek, 210
Wissahickon schist, 9
Wister, John C., 131
Woodchucks, 24
Wyke House, 149, 213

Y

Yellowjackets, 203
Yellows disease, 22
Yoder Bros., 67
York, PA, 132

Z

Zones of hardiness, 10, 11

Plant Index

Page numbers refer to main listings in the text. Botanical names are given in italics. Common names are in standard type.

A

Abies concolor, 139
Acanthus mollis, 60
Acanthus spinosus, 60
Acer ginnala, 145
Acer nigra, 145
Acer, palmatum, 145
Acer platanoides, 145
Acer rubrum, 145
Acer saccharinum, 145
Acer saccharum, 145
Achillea fillipendulina, 53, 61
Achillea millefolium, 52, 61
Achillea ptarmica, 61
Achillea taygetea, 61
Acidanthera bicolor, 103
Aconite, winter, 95
Acorus calamus, 109
Adiantum pedatum, 114
Aesculus hippocastanum, 136
Aesculus pavia, 136
Aesculus x carnea, 136
African daisy, 46
Agapanthus africanus, 100
Agastache foeniculum, 192
Ageratum houstonianum, 30
Ailanthus altissima, 155
Ajuga reptans, 52, 65
Albizzia julibrissin, 153
Alcea rosea, 37
Alchemilla mollis, 74
Allium christophii, 95
Allium giganteum, 95
Allium moly, 95
Allium schoenoprasum, 95

Allium schoenoprasum, 194
Allium species, 95
Alyssum, 30
Alyssum, yellow, 52, 61
Amaranthus tricolor, 30
Amaryllis, 95, 105
Amelanchier canadensis, 153
Amelanchier laevis, 153
Amelanchier x grandiflora, 153
American sycamore, 134
Anchusa italica, 61
Andromeda, Japanese, 130
Anemone blanda, 62, 96
Anemone coronaria, 96
Anemone, French, 96
Anemone pulsatilla, 62
Anemone x hybrida, 61
Anethum graveolens, 194
Angelica, 192
Angelica archangelica, 192
Anise hyssop, 192
Anthemis nobilis, 194
Anthemis tinctoria, 52, 72
Antirrhinum majus, 42
Apples, 199
Apricots, 200
Aquilegia candensis, 114
Aquilegia x hybrida, 52, 67
Arabis alpina, 62
Arborvitae, American, 130
Armeria maritima, 82
Arrow head plant, 108
Artemesia absinthum, 196
Artemisia dracunculus, 196
Artemisia schmidtiana, 62
Artichoke, 172

Artichoke, Jerusalem, 172
Aruncus dioicus, 71
Asclepias tuberosa, 65
Ash
    green, 130
    mountain, 130
Asparagus, 165, 173
Asperula tinctorium, 195
Aster alpinus, 62
Aster, China, 31
Aster novae-anglae, 52, 62
Aster novae belgii, 52, 62
Aster x frikartii, 62
Astilbe x arendsii, 52, 63
Aubretia deltoidea, 52, 63
Aucuba japonica, 131
Aurinia saxatile, 61
Autumn crocus, 102
Azaleas, 72, 131

B

Baby's breath
    annual, 31
    perennial, 63
Bachelor's buttons, 31
Balloon flower, 63
Balsam, 31
Bamboo, 71
Barberry, Japanese, 132
Basil, 192
Beans
    lima, 165, 173
    snap, 165, 174
Bear's breech, 60
Beauty berry, 132
Beautybush, 132
Bee balm, 64
Beech, European, 132
Beets, 165, 174
Begonia
    hardy, 64
    tuberous, 32, 100
    wax, 32
Begonia grandis, 64
Begonia x semperflorens, 32
Begonia x tuberhybrida, 32, 100
Belamcanda chinensis, 101
Bellflower

    globe, 64
    willow-leaf, 64
Bellis perennis, 68
Bells of Ireland, 32
Berberis thunbergii, 132
Bergamot, 64
Betula nigra, 133
Betula papyrifera, 133
Birch
    paper, 133
    river, 133
    white, 133
Black-eyed Susans, 53, 64, 113
Blackberries, 203
Blackberry lily, 101
Blanket flower, 70
Blazing star, 75
Bleeding heart, 52, 65
Bloodroot, 113
Blue mist shrub, 133
Blue-eyed grass, 113
Bluebell
    English, 96
    Spanish, 96
    Virginia, 117
Blueberries, 202
Bluegrass, Kentucky, 119
Bluets, 113
Borage, 192
Borago officinalis, 192
Boxwood, 133
Brassica oleracea, 37
Broccoli, 165, 175
Broom, Scotch, 134
Browallia, 46
Brussels sprouts, 165, 176
Buddlea davidii, 134
Burnet, 192
Burning bush, 134
Butterbur, Japanese, 71
Butterfly bush, 134
Butterfly weed, 65
Buttonwood, 134
Buxus sempervirens, 133

C

Cabbage, 165, 176
    Chinese, 165, 176

Caladium x hortulanum, 101
Calendula officinalis, 32
Calla lily, 101
Callery pear, 135
Callicarpa dichotoma, 132
Calliopsis, 33
Callistephus chinensis, 31
Caltha palustris, 77
Calycanthus floridus, 154
Camassia scilloides, 96
Camellia japonica, 135
Campanula carpatica, 52
Campanula glomerata, 64
Campanula media, 64
Campanula percisifolia, 64
Campsis radicans, 155
Candytuft, 46
    perennial, 52, 65
Canna x generalis, 101
Cantaloupes, 177
Canterbury bells, 46, 64
Cardinal climber, 46
Cardinal flower, 65
Carnation, 46
    perennial, 80
Carpet bugle, 52, 65
Carpinus caroliniana, 142
Carrots, 165, 177
Carya ovata, 141
Carylopsis spicata, 157
Caryopteris incarna, 133
Caryopteris x clandonensis, 133
Cat-tail, 108
Catalpa, northern, 135
Catalpa speciosa, 135
Catharanthus roseus, 44
Catnip, 52, 192
Cauliflower, 165, 175
Cedar
    atlas, 135
    deodora, 136
    Japanese, 137
Cedar of Lebanon, 135, 136
Cedrus atlantica, 135
Cedrus deodora, 136
Cedrus libani, 136
Celeriac, 178
Celery, 165, 178
Celosia cristata, 33

Celosia plumosa, 33
Centaurea cyanus, 31
Centaurea montana, 77
Cerastium tomentosum, 52, 83
Cercis canadensis, 148
Chaenomeles speciosa, 148
Chamaecyparis pisifera, 138
Chamomile
    German, 194
    Roman, 194
Chard, Swiss, 165, 178
Checkered lily, 96
Cheiranthus allionii, 84
Cherries, 200
    Japanese, 136
Chestnut, European, 136
Chinese lanterns, 52, 66
Chionanthus virginicus, 140
Chionodoxa luciliae, 97
Chives, 95, 194
Christmas rose, 72
Chrysanthemum, 52, 46
Chrysanthemum leucanthemum, 69
Chrysanthemum x moriflolium, 66
Chrysanthemum x superbum, 68
Cilantro, 194
Cimicifuga racemosa, 82
Cimicifuga simplex, 82
Cladastris lutea, 157
Clematis maximowitziana, 136
Clematis montana, 136
Clematis paniculata, 136
Clematis viticella, 136
Cleome hasslerana, 33
Clivia miniata, 101
Cockscomb, 33
Colchicum autumnale, 102
Coleus x hybridus, 33
Collards, 179
Colocasia esculenta, 102
Columbine, 52, 67
    wild, 114
Cone flower, 52, 67
Consolida ambigua, 37
Convallaria majalis, 98
Coral bells, 52, 67
Coreopsis grandiflora, 34, 52, 68
Coreopsis tinctoria, 33
Coreopsis verticillata, 52, 84

Coriander, 194
Coriandrum sativum, 194
Corn salad, 179
Cornflower, 31
Cornus alba, 138
Cornus florida, 138
Cornus kousa, 138
Cosmos bipinnatus, 34
Cotinus coggyria, 153
Crabapple, Japanese, 137
Cranesbill, 117
Crape myrtle, 137
Crataegus phaenopyrum, 140
Crataegus viridis, 140
Creeping Jenny, 114
Cress, 179
Crocosmia x crocosmiiflora, 103
Crocus chrysanthus, 96
Crocus tomasinianus, 96
Crocus vernus, 96
Crown imperial, 97
Cryptomeria japonica, 137
Cucumbers, 165, 179
Cucurbita pepo, 42
Cushion mum, 66
Cyclamen neopolitanum, 102
Cyclamen persicum, 102
Cypress
    bald, 137
    false, 138
Cypripedium acaule, 115
*Cypripedium calceolus
        parviflorum,* 115
Cytisus scoparius, 134
Cytisus x praecox, 134

D

Daffodils, 97
    autumn, 103
Dahlia hybrids, 34, 102
Daisy
    English, 68
    painted, 52, 68
    Shasta, 52, 68
Dames rocket, 114
Daylilies, 52, 69
Delphinium elatum, 52, 69

Dianthus barbatus, 84
Dianthus caryopteris, 80
Dianthus chinensis, 34
Dianthus deltoides, 80
Dianthus gratianopolitanus, 80
Dianthus plumarius, 80
Dianthus species, 52, 80
Dicentra cucullaria, 114
Dicentra eximia, 65
Dicentra spectabilis, 52, 65
Digitalis grandiflora, 82
Digitalis purpurea, 35
Dill, 194
Dogtooth violet, 97, 114
Dogwood
    flowering, 138
    kousa, 138
    red-twig, 138
Douglas fir, 139
Dusty miller, 46
Dutchman's breeches, 114

E

Echinacea purpurea, 52, 67
Echinops ritro, 71
Eggplant, 165, 180
Eleagnus angustifolia, 146
Elephant's ear, 102
Endive, 165, 180
Eranthis hyemalis, 95
Erythronium americanum, 97, 114
Erythronium hybrids, 97
Eschscholzia californica, 40
Eulalia grass, 70
Euonymus alatus, 134
*Euonymus fortunei,*156
Eupatorium purpureum, 74
Euphorbia marginata, 42

F

Fagus grandiflora, 133
Fagus sylvatica, 132
Fennel, Florence, 194
Ferns, 52, 114
    maidenhair, 114
    ostrich, 114

Fescue, 119
Festuca ovina glauca, 52
Filipendulina rubra, 77, 116
Fir
    concolor, 139
    white, 139
Firethorn, 139
Floss flower, 30
Flowering tobacco, 39
Foam flower, 114
Foeniculum vulgare azorica, 194
Forget-me-not, 46
    water, 108
Forsythia suspensa, 139
Forsythia viridissima, 139
Forsythia x intermedia, 139
Four o'clocks, 35
Foxgloves, 35
Fraxinus pennsylvanica, 130
Freesia x hybrida, 97
Fringe tree, 140
Fritillaria imperialis, 97
Fritillaria meleagris, 96

G

Gaillardia pulchella, 35
Gaillardia x grandiflora, 70
Galanthus elwesii, 98
Gay flower, 35
Gazania, 46
Geraniums, 35
    Armenian, 71
    blue, 71
    wild, 117
Geranium maculatum, 117
Geranium psilostemon, 71
Geranium x grandiflorum, 71
Gerbera jamesonii, 52
Geum chiloense, 52, 71
Giant allium, 95
Ginkgo biloba, 140
Gladiolus x hortulanus, 102
Gleditsia triacanthos inermis, 141
Globe amaranth, 36
Globe thistle, 71
Gloriosa daisies, 52, 36
Glory-of-the-snow, 97

Goatsbeard, 71
Gold dust plant, 131
Golden chain tree, 143
Golden Marguerite, 72
Golden rain tree, 140
Gomphrena globosa, 36
Gourds, 42
Granny's bonnets, 67
Grapes, 202
Grecian windflower, 62
Gypsophila elegans, 31
Gypsophila paniculata, 52, 63

H

Halesia carolina, 153
Hamamelis virginiana, 157
Hamamelis x intermedia, 157
Harlequin flower, 99
Hawthorn, Washington, 140
Hedyotis caerulea, 113
Helenium autumnale, 82
Helianthemum nummularium, 52, 81
Helianthus annuus, 43
Helianthus x multiflorus, 52, 83
Helichrysum bracteatum, 43
Heliopsis helianthoides scabra, 83
Heliotrope arborescens, 36
Helleborus niger, 72
Helleborus orientalis, 72
Hemerocallis citrina, 69
Hemerocallis fulga, 69
Hemerocallis hybrids, 69
Hemlock, Canadian, 140
Herbs, 191-196
Hesperis matronalis, 114
Heuchera sanguinea, 67
Heucherella, 68
Hibiscus, perennial, 52
Hibiscus moscheutos, 36
Hibiscus syriacus, 148
Hickory, shagbark, 141
Hippeastrum hybrids, 95
Holly
    American, 141
    blue, 141
    English, 141
    Japanese, 141

Hollyhock
  annual, 37
  perennial, 53
Hollywood juniper, 143
Honesty, 47, 72
Honeysuckle
  Japanese, 142
  scarlet, 142
Hornbeam, American, 142
Hosta seiboldiana, 53, 72
Hyacinth
  Dutch, 97
  grape, 98
  wild, 96
Hyacinthoides hispanicus, 96
Hyacinthoides non-scriptus, 96
Hyacinthus orientalis, 97
Hydrangea arborescens, 142
*Hydrangea ortensis,*142
Hydrangea macrophylla, 142
Hydrangea paniculata, 142
Hydrangea quercifolia, 142

I

Ilex aquifolium, 141
Ilex cornuta, 141
Ilex crenata, 141
Ilex opaca, 141
Ilex rugosa, 141
Ilex serrata, 156
Ilex verticillata, 156
Ilex x meserveae, 141
Impatiens balsamina, 31
Impatiens wallerana, 37
Ipomoea tricolor, 39
Iris
  bearded, 53, 73
  blue flag, 108
  crista, 115
  Dutch, 98
  dwarf crested, 115
  ensata, 74
  Japanese, 74
  Siberian, 74
  snow, 98
  yellow flag, 108
Iris pseudacorus, 108

Iris reticulata, 98
Iris sempervirens, 65
Iris versicolor, 108
Iris x germanica, 53, 73
Italian bugloss, 61

J

Jack-in-the-pulpit, 111
Job's tears, 47
Joe-pye weed, 74
Johnny jump-up, 74
Joseph's coat, 3
Juniper
  Chinese, 142
  spreading, 143
Juniperus chinesis, 142
Juniperus horizontalis, 143

K

Kaffir lily, 101
Kale, 165, 180
  ornamental, 37
Kalmia latifolia, 111, 145
Kerria japonica, 143
Kniphofia uvaria, 81
Kochia, 47
Koelreuteria paniculata, 140
Kohlrabi, 165, 181
Kolkwitzia amabilis, 132

L

Laburnum vossii, 143
Lady's mantle, 74
Lady-slipper
  pink, 115
  yellow, 115
Lagenaria vulgaris, 42
Lagerstroemia indica, 137
Larkspur, 37
Lathyrus latifolius, 53, 84
Lathyrus odoratus, 43
Laurel, mountain, 111, 145
Lavender
  cotton, 194
  English, 52, 75

Lavendula angustifolia, 75
Leadwort, 53
Leeks, 165, 181
Lemon balm, 194
Lenten rose, 72
Lettuce, 165, 181
Leucojum aestivum, 99
Leucojum vernum, 99
Liatris pycnostachya, 75
Liatris spicata, 75
Ligustrum japonica, 148
Lilac
    common, 143
    summer, 134
Lilium auratum, 76
Lilium canadense, 113
Lilium lanceolatum, 76
Lilium philadelphicum, 117
Lilium species, 75
Lily
    Canada, 113
    garden, 52, 75
    wood, 117
Lily leek, 95
Lily-of-the-Nile, 100
Lily-of-the-valley, 98
Limonium sinuatum, 42
Liquidamber syraciflua, 154
Liriodendron tulipifera, 155
Lobelia, 47
Lobelia cardinalis, 65
Lobularia maritima, 30
Locust
    black, 133
    thornless honey, 141
London plane tree, 134
Lonicera japonica, 142
Lonicera sempervirens, 142
Loosestrife
    purple, 76
    yellow, 64
Lotus, 107, 109
Lunaria biennis, 72
Lupines, 76
Lupinus polyphyllus, 76
Lychnis chalcedonica, 53, 76
Lycoris squamigera, 103
Lysimachia nummularia, 114

Lysimachia punctata, 64
Lythrum salicaria, 76

M

Madagascar periwinkle, 44
Magnolia
    saucer, 144
    southern, 144
    sweetbay, 144
    star, 144
Magnolia grandiflora, 144
Magnolia soulangiana, 144
Magnolia stellata, 144
Magnolia virginiana, 144
Mahonia aquifolium, 145
Mahonia bealei, 144
Maltese Cross, 76
Malus floribunda, 137
Maple
    amur, 145
    black, 145
    Japanese, 145
    Norway, 145
    red, 145
    silver, 145
    sugar, 145
Marigold
    African, 38
    French, 38
    pot, 32
Marjorum, 195
Marsh marigold, 77
Marsilia mutica, 109
Matricaria recutita, 194
Matteuccia pennsylvanica, 114
Matthiola bicornis, 43
May apple, 115
Meadowfoam, 77
Melissa officinalis, 194
Melons, 177
Mentha species, 195
Mertensia virginica, 117
Mimosa, hardy, 153
Mint, 195
Mirabilis jalapa, 35
Miscanthus sinensis, 70
Molucella laevis, 32

Monarda didyma, 64
Money plant, 72
Montbretia, 103
Moonflower, 47
Morning glory, 39
Moss rose, 41
Mountain bluet, 77
Mountain laurel, 111
Mullein, giant, 77
Muscari armeniaca, 98
Muscari botryoides, 98
Mustard, 182
Myosotis palustris, 108
Myriophylum aquaticum, 109

N

Naked ladies, 103
Narcissus hybrids, 97
Nasturtiums, 39
Nectarines, 201
Nelumbo hybrids, 107
Nelumbo lutea, 108
Nepeta cataria, 192
Nicotiana alata, 39
Nymphaea hybrids, 107
Nymphaea odorata, 117
Nyssa sylvatica, 155

O

Oak
    English, 146
    pin, 146
    red, 146
    white, 146
    willow, 146
Obedient plant, 77
Ocimum basilicum, 192
Oenothera fruticosa, 77, 116
Okra, 182
Olive, Russian, 146
Onions, 165, 182
    ornamental, 95
Opuntia humifusa, 81
Orange, hardy, 146
Oregano, 195
Origanum majorana, 195
Origanum vulgare, 195

Ornithogalum umbellatum, 99
Oxydendron arboreum, 154

P

Pachysandra terminalis, 147
Paeonia officinalis, 78
Paeonia suffruticosa, 78
Pansies, 39
Papaver nudicaule, 53, 41
Papaver orientale, 81
Papaver rhoeas, 41
Paperwhites, 105
Parrot's feather, 109
Parsley, 165, 183
Parsnips, 165, 183
Parthenocissus quinquifolia, 156
Pasque flower, 62
Patience plant, 37
Peaches, 201
Peacock flower, 103
Peanuts, 183
Pears, 201
Peas, 165, 183
Pelargonium x hortorum, 35
Penstemon, 53
Peony
    herbaceous, 53, 78
    tree, 78
Peppers, 165, 184
Periwinkle, 147
Perovskia atriplicifolia, 82
Persian buttercup, 98
Petunia x hybrida, 40
Phlox
    blue, 79
    creeping, 53, 79
    creeping blue, 79
    early border, 80
    summer, 53, 80
Phlox divaricata, 79
Phlox drummondii, 40
Phlox maculata, 80
Phlox paniculata, 80
Phlox stolonifera, 79
Phlox subulata, 79
Physalis alkegengi, 66
Physostegia virginiana, 77
Picea pungens, 154

Pickerel rush, 109
Pieris japonica, 130
Pincushion flower, 44, 80
Pine
    eastern white, 147
    Japanese black, 147
    mugo, 147
Pinks
    annual, 34
    perennial, 52, 80
Pinus mugo, 147
Pinus strobus, 147
Pinus thunbergiana, 147
Plantain lily, 72
Platanus occidentalis, 134
Platycodon grandiflorus, 63
Plums, 201
Podophyllum peltatum, 115
*Polianthus x tuberosa,*104
Poncirus trifoliata, 146
Pontederia cordata, 109
Poplar hybrids, 147
Poppy
    California, 40
    Iceland, 41
    Oriental, 53, 81
    Shirley, 41
Populus hybrids, 147
Portulaca grandiflora, 41
Potatoes
    hybrid, 184-185
    sweet, 165, 185
Prickly pear cactus, 81
Primula, 53
Privet, Japanese, 148
Prunus campanulata, 136
Prunus serrulata, 136
Prunus species, 136
Pseudotsuga menziesii, 139
Pumpkins, 165, 185
Pyracantha coccinea, 139
Pyrethrum roseum, 68
Pyrus calleryana, 135

Q

Quaker ladies, 113
Queen-of-the-prairie, 116

Quercus alba, 146
Quercus coccinea, 146
Quercus palustris, 146
Quercus phellos, 146
Quince, flowering, 148

R

Radish, 165, 185
Rainbow plant, 101
Ranunculus asiaticus, 98
Raspberries, 203
Red hot poker, 81
Redbud, 148
Rhododendron maximum, 111
Rhododendron mucronulatum, 157
Rhododendron species, 131
Rhubarb, 165, 186
Robinia pseudoacacia, 133
Rock cress, 62
    false, 63
Rock rose, 81
Rosa multiflora, 152
Rosa rugosa, 149, 152
Rosa virginiana, 152
Rose(s), 149-152
    floribunda, 152
    hybrid tea, 151
Rose of Sharon, 148
Rosemarinus officinalis, 195
Rosemary, 195
Rudbeckia hirta, 53, 64, 113
Rudbeckia hirta burpeeii, 36
Rutabaga, 165, 186
Ryegrass, perennial, 119

S

Sage, 195
    Russian, 82
    violet, 82
Sagitarria latifolia, 108
Salix alba, 156
Salix caprea, 156
Salix matsudana, 156
Salsify, 186
Salvia officinalis, 195
Salvia splendens, 41
Salvia x superba, 53, 77, 82

Sanguinaria canadensis, 113
Sanguisorbia minor, 192
Santolina chamaecyparissus, 194
Saponaria ocymoides, 83
Sarvistree, 153
Sassafras albidum, 152
Satureja montana, 195
Savory, winter, 195
Scabiosa atropurpurea, 44
Scabiosa caucasica, 80
Scarlet sage, 41
Sciadopitys vertillata, 155
Scilla sibirica, 99
Sea pinks, 82
Sedum spectabile, 52, 83
Shadblow, 153
Silk tree, 153
Silver mound, 62
Silverbell, Carolina, 153
Sisyrinchium angustifolium, 113
Smokebush, 153
Smoketree, 153
Snakeroot, 82
Snapdragon, 42
Sneezeweed, 82
Snow-in-Summer, 42, 52, 83
Snowdrop, 98
Snowflake
    spring, 99
    summer, 99
Soapwort, 83
Sorbus aucuparia, 130
Sourwood, 154
Soybeans, edible, 186
Spanish dagger, 85
Sparaxis tricolor, 99
Speedwell, 84
Spider flower, 33
Spinach, 165, 187
    Malabar, 187
    New Zealand, 187
Spirea, 63
    Vanhoute, 154
Spirea x vanhouttei, 154
Spruce, Colorado, 154
Spurge, Japanese, 147
Squash, 165, 187
Squill, Siberian, 99

Star flower, 99
Star-of-Bethlehem, 99
Star-of-Persia, 95
Statice
    annual, 42
    perennial, 53
Sternbergia lutea, 103
Stock, 43
Stokes aster, 62
Stokesia laevis, 62
Stonecrop, 83
Strawberries, 204
Strawflower, 43
Sundrops, 116
Sunflower
    hybrids, 43
    false, 83
    perennial, 83
Sweet corn, 165, 188
Sweet flag, 109
Sweet heliotrope, 36
Sweet pea, 43
    perennial, 53, 84
Sweet scabious, 44
Sweet shrub, 154
Sweet William, 47, 84
Sweet woodruff, 195
Sweetgum, 154
Syringa vulgaris, 143

T

Tagetes erecta, 38
Tagetes patula, 38
Tarragon, French, 196
Taxodium distichum, 137
Taxus baccata, 157
Taxus cuspidata, 157
Taxus media, 157
Thrift, 82
Thuja occidentalis, 130
Thunbergia, 47
Thyme, English, 196
Tiarella cordiolia, 114
Tickseed, 84
Tiger lily, 76
Tomatoes, 165, 189
Tree of Heaven, 155

Trillium, large-flowered, 116
Trillium grandiflorum, 116
Tritelia uniflora, 99
Tropaeolum majus, 39
Trumpet creeper, 155
Tsuga canadensis, 140
Tuberose, 104
Tulip species, 99-100
Tulip tree, 155
Tulipa fosteriana, 100
Tulipa kaufmanniana, 100
Tupelo, black, 155
Turnips, 165, 190
Typha latifolia, 108

U

Umbrella pine, 155

V

Venidium, 47
Verbascum bombycifera, 77
Verbascum olympicum, 77
Verbena x hybrida, 44
Veronica spicata, 53, 84
Viburnum dilatatum, 144
Viburnum
    linden, 144
    snowball, 155
Viburnum opulus, 155
Vinca, annual, 44
Vinca minor, 147
Viola blanda, 117
Viola cornuta, 74
Viola papilionacea, 116
Viola pennsylvanica, 117
Viola tricolor, 52, 74
Viola x wittrockiana, 39
Violet, common, 116
Virginia creeper, 156

W

Wallflower, Siberian, 84
Water clover, 109
Watercress, 165, 190
Waterlilies, 107, 109
Watermelon, 165, 190
Weigelia florida, 156
Willow
    corkscrew, 156
    pussy, 156
    white, 156
Windflower, 96
Winterberry, 156
Wintercreeper euonymus, 156
Winterhazel, 157
Wisteria, Japanese, 157
Wisteria floribunda, 157
Witch hazel, 157
Wormwood, southern, 196

X

Xeranthemum, 47

Y

Yarrow, 53, 61
Yellow poplar, 155
Yellow-wood, 157
Yew, 157
Yucca filamentosa, 53, 85

Z

Zantedeschia aethiopica, 101
Zinnia elegans, 45
Zoysia, 119